SharePoint 2013 User's Guide

Learning Microsoft's Business Collaboration Platform
Fourth Edition

Tony Smith

Apress·

SharePoint 2013 User's Guide

ISBN-13 (pbk): 978-1-4302-4833-0

ISBN-13 (electronic): 978-1-4302-4834-7

President and Publisher: Paul Manning
Lead Editor: Jonathan Hassell
Technical Reviewer: Ralph Mercurio
Editorial Board: Steve Anglin, Mark Beckner, Ewan Buckingham, Gary Cornell, Louise Corrigan, Morgan Ertel,
    Jonathan Gennick, Jonathan Hassell, Robert Hutchinson, Michelle Lowman, James Markham,
    Matthew Moodie, Jeff Olson, Jeffrey Pepper, Douglas Pundick, Ben Renow-Clarke, Dominic Shakeshaft,
    Gwenan Spearing, Matt Wade, Tom Welsh
Coordinating Editor: Mark Powers
Copy Editor: Thomas McCarthy
Compositor: SPi Global
Indexer: SPi Global
Artist: SPi Global
Cover Designer: Anna Ishchenko

Distributed to the book trade worldwide by Springer Science+Business Media New York, 233 Spring Street, 6th Floor, New York, NY 10013. Phone 1-800-SPRINGER, fax (201) 348-4505, e-mail orders-ny@springer-sbm.com, or visit www.springeronline.com. Apress Media, LLC is a California LLC and the sole member (owner) is Springer Science + Business Media Finance Inc (SSBM Finance Inc). SSBM Finance Inc is a Delaware corporation.

For information on translations, please e-mail rights@apress.com, or visit www.apress.com.

Apress and friends of ED books may be purchased in bulk for academic, corporate, or promotional use. eBook versions and licenses are also available for most titles. For more information, reference our Special Bulk Sales–eBook Licensing web page at www.apress.com/bulk-sales.

Any source code or other supplementary material referenced by the author in this text is available to readers at www.apress.com/9781430248330. For detailed information about how to locate your book's source code, go to www.apress.com/source-code/.

Contents at a Glance

Contents

About the Author

Tony Smith is the Director of Practice Development for DataLan Corporation, a Microsoft Gold Certified partner located in White Plains, New York. Tony coauthored *SharePoint 2010 User's Guide: Learning Microsoft's Business Collaboration Platform, SharePoint 2007 User's Guide: Learning Microsoft's Collaboration and Productivity Platform, and SharePoint 2003 User's Guide.* He has worked with SharePoint technologies since they were originally introduced in 2001 and with SharePoint 2013 since its initial beta release. He also has experience designing and deploying SharePoint solutions in a wide range of organizations across many industries. With a background that includes business analysis, network engineering, and application development, Tony has 20 years' experience engineering business solutions. He regularly makes presentations to engineers, analysts, and business decision makers. You can find additional information about Tony and about topics discussed in this book at www.sharepointextras.com.

About the Technical Reviewer

Ralph Mercurio is a SharePoint engineer with DataLan Corporation, located in White Plains, NY. Ralph, who has been involved with SharePoint since 2007, is focused on delivering high-quality solutions to a wide customer base.

Acknowledgments

I have worked with Apress for many years writing books that provide people with the knowledge they need to take advantage of SharePoint, and I am always impressed with the dedication of its staff to providing quality publications. Creating a book like this is a team effort, and everyone at Apress has been great to work with. I would like to specifically thank several people that have been instrumental in helping to bring this book together. I want to thank Mark Powers for coordinating all of the activities that went into creating this book. I would also like to thank Tom McCarthy for copyediting, and the lead editor, Jonathan Hassell.

I would also like to thank the technical editor, Ralph Mercurio, for his hard work reviewing the book to help ensure its accuracy and for providing valuable insight and feedback.

Finally, this book would not be possible without the support and understanding of my wife, Lynn. She encouraged me through this process and helped in any way she could as I disappeared into the world of SharePoint 2013 while writing this book.

Introduction

SharePoint 2013 is Microsoft's business collaboration platform. It offers web management, content management, reporting, search, and social capabilities that can be brought together to yield comprehensive business solutions. The solutions this platform allows can be created more quickly and are more cost effective than custom-developed solutions, and what is more, the platform provides a far greater degree of flexibility than packaged solutions can.

That said, in many situations where SharePoint is introduced, people struggle to understand and use the platform. In other situations people have difficulty expanding their use of SharePoint from a basic intranet or document management environment to a business solution platform. This book addresses these struggles and needs. It is meant to serve as a complete reference to all the capabilities available in SharePoint to help you understand how to configure and use them.

This book was created for SharePoint users at all levels. Beginners are introduced to information to help them make effective use of the capabilities the platform offers. Intermediate users are provided the details they need to manage SharePoint resources. Advanced users are offered a foundation upon which to understand all of the capabilities the platform contains and are shown how to create solutions that take advantage of these capabilities.

A deep knowledge of the capabilities available in SharePoint, experience working with a variety of organizations, and an understanding of how to successfully combine them to reach effective business solutions: all these have been brought between the covers of this book. I hope this information will enable you to gain an in-depth understanding of SharePoint 2013 and more effectively manage and use the platform.

Whom This Book Is For

The goal of the book is to provide the knowledge anyone needs to use the Microsoft SharePoint 2013 platform. Whether you are new to SharePoint, are moving from a previous version, or are a longtime user, this book will give you the information you need to take effective advantage of the capabilities of SharePoint Foundation 2013 and SharePoint Server 2013.

If you are looking for a resource that offers you an easy-to-follow and detailed understanding of SharePoint, this book is for you. As a user guide, it does not require you to have any programming knowledge. It does, however, assume you have a basic understanding of web sites and how to navigate them. Some topics also require a working knowledge of Microsoft Office applications, such as Word and Excel.

How This Book Is Structured

This book organizes the capabilities of the SharePoint platform into a format that serves as an end-to-end reference guide, a guide you can read through to learn about all SharePoint has to offer or to look up specific topics. It includes step-by-step instructions, figures, tables, and examples. Its chapters describe all of the SharePoint capabilities so that you can used them as building blocks for solutions.

Chapter 1: Introduction to SharePoint Technologies

This chapter introduces you to what SharePoint is and the capabilities it offers. It describes what's new in this 2013 version and its uses and benefits.

Chapter 2: Understanding Sites

This chapter provides an overview of site collections and sites and describes their structures and components. Included is a review of the various site templates available in SharePoint Foundation and SharePoint Server, along with details of their purposes, layouts, and features.

Chapter 3: Working with Sites

In this chapter you are given an understanding of how to manage sites. You learn how to create sites, navigate them, and manage their security, layouts, structures, and features.

Chapter 4: Pages, Apps, and Web Parts

Pages, apps, and web parts are used to organize and present information to site users and to incorporate business solutions into a SharePoint environment. This chapter shows you how to create and configure the various types of pages available through SharePoint and how to configure web parts and app parts within them.

Chapter 5: Managing Lists and Libraries

Lists and libraries store the content managed in the SharePoint environment. In this chapter you learn how to create and manage lists and libraries, including how to configure columns and work with views.

Chapter 6: Working with Lists

This chapter details the different types of lists SharePoint offers and describes their structures and views. You also learn how to create and manage items in these lists.

Chapter 7: Working with Libraries

In this chapter the different types of libraries available in SharePoint are discussed, as well as how to add and manage their content. You also learn about the various advanced features different types of libraries make available.

Chapter 8: Working with Site Columns, Content Types, and Term Sets

Site columns, content types, and term sets enable you to standardize and centralize the management of list and library metadata. In this chapter you learn how to create and manage these elements to enhance list and library management.

Chapter 9: Workflows and Information Management Processes

This chapter presents you with the capabilities that introduce process automation into SharePoint. You learn how to create and manage workflows, use content organizers to automate the routing of content, and create information management policies to govern document development.

Chapter 10: Records Management

When documents require structured retention, records management is used to support both internally defined and externally mandated regulatory requirements. In this chapter you learn how to configure and use the platform's records management capabilities to govern content.

Chapter 11: Search

A search platform can be used to locate information in SharePoint and throughout the rest of your enterprise. This chapter shows you how to configure the SharePoint search features, such as query rules and result sources, and how to use these features to support enterprise searches.

Chapter 12: Personalization and Social Features

SharePoint includes a comprehensive set of personalization and social features, which enhance personal productivity and facilitate communication and collaboration. In this chapter you learn how to configure and use personalization features (such as the profile, My Tasks, and Alerts) and social features (including newsfeeds, community sites, blogs, and wikis).

Chapter 13: Metrics and Reporting

This chapter introduces you to the reporting capabilities available in SharePoint. The storage, audit, usage, and search reports SharePoint provides are explained in detail, and you discover how to create and share these reports.

Chapter 14: Enterprise Office Services

SharePoint includes capabilities that extend the reach of Microsoft Office personal productivity tools to introduce team productivity functionality. In this chapter you learn about several enterprise office services available in SharePoint, including Office Web Apps, Excel Services, Form Services, and Visio Services.

CHAPTER 1

■ ■ ■

Introduction to SharePoint Technologies

SharePoint 2013 is Microsoft's business collaboration platform. It provides tools people need to effectively manage and share information, automate business processes, collaborate, and interact with others. SharePoint works with Microsoft Office technologies to enable individuals to better organize content, share work, and take information with them wherever they go.

SharePoint is designed to help in achieving the following goals:

- Provide business users with faster, more comprehensive access to actionable information. The goal is not only to provide access to more information but to make it possible to locate the most relevant information to allow people to rapidly respond to business needs.

- Enable individuals to find the most relevant people to work with, to connect with them, and to allow them to work together effectively. Teams can easily share information regardless of location, and communities of people sharing common interests can be formed.

- Improve individual and team productivity by making it easy to create and manage information and allowing this information to be made available as part of related business processes.

- Reduce the cost and time of providing enterprise-wide business solutions by providing a set of application services that work together and can be combined into business solutions.

Whether you are new to SharePoint, experienced with SharePoint 2013, or moving from a previous version to SharePoint 2013, this SharePoint 2013 User's Guide is designed to provide the information you need to be successful with SharePoint. The author provides a real-world look at how to effectively use all the capabilities the platform offers. He includes numerous examples showing how to take advantage of these capabilities and suggesting points to consider as you create and work with your SharePoint solutions.

The guide discusses the basic and advanced capabilities of both SharePoint Foundation 2013 and SharePoint Server 2013. It provides step-by-step instructions to explain how to use these capabilities to create solutions.

What Is Microsoft SharePoint 2013

SharePoint 2013 is available as on-premise-installed software that can be tailored to your organization's needs or as a hosted, cloud-based service. Whether you host SharePoint internally or via the cloud, capabilities and features available depend on the edition and level of the product in place.

Locally Hosted SharePoint

When SharePoint is hosted internally in your organization or through a general third party as a dedicated solution, the Microsoft SharePoint platform is available in three different editions: SharePoint Foundation 2013, SharePoint Server 2013 Standard Edition, and SharePoint Server 2013 Enterprise Edition.

SharePoint Foundation was called Windows SharePoint Services prior to SharePoint 2010. It was renamed to better represent its purpose and to align it with other Microsoft Windows Server foundation services. SharePoint Foundation offers fundamental collaboration services in the SharePoint platform, upon which all other capabilities are provided. These include:

- A web-centric information management and presentation platform

- Lists for storing and managing structured information, including contacts, links, and announcements

- Libraries for storing and managing documents

- Security services enabling granular management of environment security across sites, lists, libraries, and content and including security trimming of materials so that only individuals with access to an item will see references to it

- Authentication services providing native Active Directory integrated access management as well as the ability to extend the environment to use alternate security access providers

- Environment and information management structures that allow easy resource configuration and management

- Integrated workflow services providing the core for creation of process-centric solutions

Microsoft SharePoint Server 2013 Standard Edition extends the capabilities provided by SharePoint Foundation by adding services that extend the platform and add rich enterprise content management and workflow capabilities. These include:

- Managed web content development

- Enterprise-level document management

- Full-featured records retention and management

- Enterprise-wise search services

- People integration and social networking services

- Personalized content and alerts

- User profile management services

- Enterprise taxonomy and folksonomy management

- Web analytics

- Extended workflow configuration capabilities

Microsoft SharePoint Server 2013 Enterprise Edition extends the SharePoint platform even further by adding services that enable data integration and business intelligence services. These include:

- External system data and application integration
- Reporting and analysis services
- Data visualization and consolidation
- Calculation services
- Web-based form management and automation

The capabilities provided by the platform are used to create solutions that bring together people, information, systems, and business processes. Microsoft summarizes the wide range of capabilities provided by SharePoint 2013 within the following categories:

- *Share*: SharePoint provides enterprise collaboration and social capabilities designed to support teamwork and idea and knowledge sharing with others.
- *Organize*: Features are provided that allow you to organize all of your project materials, such as documents and tasks, as well as team communication and project status.
- *Discover*: Comprehensive search tools are available to help you find information that you need and allow you to locate people based on their background, expertise, and interests.
- *Build*: Intranet, extranet, and internet solutions that host the information and applications people need can be easily created.
- *Manage*: SharePoint provides comprehensive tools that allow delegation of management responsibilities to the owners of the processes and related information, and it provides tools to automate the management and governance of processes and information.

The capabilities of SharePoint let you create solutions to support your organization's business needs in a cost-effective, easily managed way, where the SharePoint environment becomes your central system for managing and accessing enterprise systems and information.

As the version of SharePoint your organization implements determines the features made available, the version decision is often made by weighing the organization's business needs over time. When your organization hosts SharePoint, you control and manage the environment structure and accessibility and have full flexibility to create custom solutions or introduce third-party solutions, if needed, to extend the available capabilities to meet business needs.

Office 365, Cloud-Hosted SharePoint

For organizations that do not want to manage their own SharePoint environment but want to take advantage of what SharePoint provides, Microsoft offers SharePoint Online. SharePoint Online is part of Microsoft's Office 365 solution, which includes hosted versions of SharePoint, Exchange Server, Lync, and the Office client programs maintained and managed by Microsoft. SharePoint Online is available on a subscription model, in progressive subscription levels that allow selection of the service level that best maps to the needs of the organization.

An organization using Office 365's SharePoint Online can work with and manage its SharePoint solutions without the responsibility of managing a SharePoint infrastructure. This service, however, comes with some functionality limitations concerning the types and depth of custom solutions that can be created on the platform and the types of third-party solutions that can be leveraged.

As with locally hosted SharePoint, these capabilities are used to create solutions that bring people, information, systems, and business processes together, and SharePoint Online offers the same wide range of capabilities listed in the last section.

The capabilities of SharePoint allow you to create solutions to support your organization's business needs in a way that is cost effective, can be easily managed, and allows the SharePoint environment to become your central system for managing and accessing enterprise systems and information.

The Evolution of SharePoint

Microsoft's SharePoint technology was first introduced in 2001, with the release of SharePoint Portal Server 2001. This product provided some basic tools designed to let users publish and find documents. It allowed creation and management of document taxonomies and represented the first step in providing a way to catalog and search for documents across an enterprise.

Microsoft next released SharePoint Team Services, which extended the document and publishing capabilities of SharePoint Portal Server 2001 by offering information collaboration. It allowed groups of individuals to work together to manage documents and lists of information, including contact lists, event lists, and link lists.

In 2003, Microsoft completely re-architected SharePoint and released Windows SharePoint Services 2.0 and SharePoint Portal Server 2003 as part of the introduction of the first Microsoft Office system. The focus of these technologies was to provide a foundation for the collection of applications, servers, and services that work together to improve user and team productivity. These products allowed organizations to introduce a variety of collaborative business solutions that were previously very difficult and costly to create and maintain.

In 2007, Microsoft released Windows SharePoint Services 3.0 and Microsoft Office SharePoint Server 2007. With the release of these technologies. Microsoft extended its Office vision to include capabilities that supported the creation of business solutions. These capabilities include content management; collaboration; business information management; workflow; intranet, extranet, and internet support; and business integration services. With this release, SharePoint became a business productivity platform with which full-featured business applications could be created and information from other applications, data sources, and systems could be aggregated.

In 2010, the SharePoint platform was enhanced to make it easier to create full-featured business solutions and allow it to be leveraged as your organization's main platform for document management, reporting, and web content management. This version also introduced new capabilities, including full-featured records management, new Microsoft Office integration services, global metadata, taxonomy management, and basic social networking services. With this release Windows SharePoint Services was renamed SharePoint Foundation. Microsoft also introduced the services architecture to permit more flexible scaling and sharing of services. The SharePoint 2010 platform provides a foundation for quickly creating productive business solutions in a cost-effective manner.

With the release of SharePoint 2013, Microsoft has again extended the SharePoint platform. To help you organize and share information and interact with others, it includes new capabilities, such as a new set of social features, content synchronization and sharing tools, application publishing and sharing, mobile integration, and layout management. SharePoint 2013 also enhances previously existing functionality in the areas of document and records management, business intelligence, search, web content management, and workflow.

Exploring What's New in SharePoint 2013

SharePoint 2013 has several new capabilities and updates previously existing SharePoint capabilities. Among the most noteworthy new and enhanced capabilities are the following:

- *User Interface Enhancements*

    - Drag and drop documents into libraries

    - Introduction of Design Manager, which provides a step-by-step approach for creating designs, master pages, and layouts

    - The ability to create designs for the SharePoint environment using Dreamweaver and other standard design tools

    - Cross-platform support through the use of HTML5

- *Web Content Management Enhancements*
  - iFrame dynamic content embedding
  - Better video support, including thumbnail previews
  - Dynamic content, such as JavaScript and JQuery, insertion support
  - Image renditions for displaying different-sized versions of an image on different pages
  - Language translation services, supporting both human and machine translations
  - Cross-site content publishing, allowing content managed in one location to be made visible in multiple site collections
  - Designating lists and libraries as catalogs for reuse of content across publishing site collections
  - Navigation definitions through term sets
  - Category pages for aggregating content meeting–defined criteria or parameters
- *Records Management Additions*
  - In-place holds that preserve content at the time of the hold but allow users to continue working with the content
  - eDiscovery center to facilitate the management of discovery cases
  - Site-based retention, allowing retention policies to be created in a site and applied to all items in the site
- *Search Architecture*
  - Federated searching across SharePoint and Internet search engines
  - Native PDF indexing
  - Document previews, allowing review of the document content within the search results page
  - Search results groupings combining related results
  - Personalized results ranking
  - Result type styles that can be defined by type of content returned
  - Query rules management where conditions and correlation actions can be specified
  - Visual refiners with counts
- *SharePoint 2013 Workflow Platform*
  - New workflow platform providing a rich set of workflow features to SharePoint
  - No-code declarative authoring environment, using XAML files to define workflows and manage their execution
  - A set of new workflow actions and features, including declarative authoring, rest, and service bus messaging

- *New Social Computing Features*
    - The ability to follow content and people
    - Community sites designed to manage information exchange between people
    - Activity feeds showing information about people, documents, sites, and tags being followed
    - The ability to connect to people based on experience and skills
    - Like functionality
    - Reputation builder, allowing the collection of reputation points toward badges that can be earned
    - Aggregated task management views
- *Business Intelligence Enhancements*
    - Power View, enabling the creation of interactive visual representations of data
    - In-memory BI engine, allowing quick analysis of millions of rows of data
    - Excel services enhancements in data exploration, calculated members, and timeline controls
    - PerformancePoint service enhancements in filtering, filter search, and iPad support
    - The ability to comment on Visio diagrams within Visio Services
- *Mobile Access Enhancements*
    - HTML5 rendering to support Windows Phone 7 & 8, iPhone iOS5, and Android 4.0 and later
    - Device-specific targeting through channels defined to render a site in multiple ways to target specific browsers
    - Geolocation field-type support
- *New App Architecture*
    - Functionality added to sites in a safe way that isolates the application's functionality
    - SharePoint App Store. allowing on-premise and hosted SharePoint environments to download apps

In the chapters that follow, we discuss the new and updated capabilities of SharePoint 2013 and describe how they can be used to create business solutions.

Understanding the Value of SharePoint 2013

SharePoint 2013 provides an information management and sharing platform, a document and record management platform, a workflow platform, a business process management framework, a social platform, and a development platform on which Information Worker solutions can be created. The building blocks needed to create comprehensive business solutions are available and can be easily assembled into scalable enterprise solutions.

In today's work environment, information management and business processes often rely on individuals' knowledge of available information and manual business processes to address many needs. As organizations grow dependent on specific individuals to complete activities, it becomes very difficult to allow others to participate in them.

In these situations finding information is also a challenge. Individuals spend a large amount of time locating needed materials and information, frequently perform duplicative work, and re-create information when it cannot be located. Building custom solutions to attempt to automate these processes and the information management environment can be a costly and difficult exercise.

SharePoint 2013 can provide organizations with a solid foundation of information management, collaboration, workflow, social, and data integration capabilities that combine to create solutions simplifying automation of business processes and information management environments. With it, solutions are created more rapidly and provide broader business value.

SharePoint Building Blocks

SharePoint 2013 includes many capabilities that can be combined to create enterprise business solutions. The core capabilities that these solutions are built on include the following:

- Sites provide a structure for securing, storing, and organizing information and solutions.

- Lists are containers for storing structured information,

- Libraries are containers for storing and managing documents.

- Workflows automate business processes.

- Records management extends document management capabilities to manage documents through their full life cycle.

- Alerts can notify users when information is added, changed, or removed.

- Web Parts allow existing information to be organized and presented and provide additional business logic and functionality to be incorporated into the environment.

- Search provides the ability to locate information.

- Personalization and social capabilities allow users to create and manage their own information, communicate with others, and find others based on their skill and experience.

- Data integration capabilities allow information outside SharePoint to be incorporated into SharePoint solutions,

In this book we explore these tools in detail and describe how they are configured and used. We discuss the components that make up a SharePoint 2013 environment and provide the information you need to effectively use these components to build business solutions.

CHAPTER 2

■ ■ ■

Understanding Sites

Sites are the main constructs in SharePoint for organizing and storing all content and resources. They provide locations for people to work together and interact with content and processes. Sites can contain lists, libraries, pages, workflow, web parts and apps.

Those familiar with previous versions of SharePoint are already aware of lists and libraries, which are used to store information within SharePoint. In SharePoint 2013 lists and libraries are part of the new SharePoint app architecture. They still perform the same functions but are now classified as apps. An app is a distinct piece of functionality that is used to provide capabilities within a SharePoint site. By default the only apps initially available within SharePoint Foundation and SharePoint Server are the default list and library templates. The default lists and libraries will be discussed in detail in Chapter 5.

- *Lists*: SharePoint includes a variety of standard lists and the ability to create custom lists. Lists are available to facilitate communications and track information. Several of the available standard list types also have extended capabilities that help them support their primary functions. For example, contact lists have Outlook integration features that allow the contained contact details to be made available within the Outlook Contacts area. The standard lists can be tailored and custom lists created to meet specific information management needs. Lists are discussed in detail in Chapters 5 and 6.

- *Libraries*: Libraries are used to manage all media to be stored in SharePoint, including documents, forms, web pages, images, and videos. Different types of libraries are available to store and manage the different types of media. Libraries are discussed in detail in Chapters 5 and 7.

Along with list and library apps used to store information, workflows and web parts are core features used to introduce and manage business solutions within SharePoint. Additional capabilities can also be introduced through apps.

- *Workflows*: Workflows are used to incorporate information and people into business processes. SharePoint provides a variety of standard workflows based on the version of SharePoint you are using. Customized workflows can also be created using tools such as SharePoint Designer and Visual Studio. Workflows are discussed in more detail in Chapter 9.

- *Web Parts*: A web part is an application component available within a page in a SharePoint site. Web parts are used to display information and introduce application functionality. They are discussed in more detail in Chapter 4.

- *Apps*: An app is a solution made available within SharePoint pages through an app part. Like web parts, apps introduce business functionality into the SharePoint sites. Apps, however, leverage a different architecture, allowing them to be hosted from environments other than the SharePoint farm. Apps are made available through the online SharePoint app store or through locally managed corporate app repositories. Apps are discussed in detail in Chapter 4.

In this chapter we will familiarize you with the general layout and structure of SharePoint sites. We will discuss the default site templates available across SharePoint Foundation and SharePoint Server, including their layouts and functions, and identify the different site templates.

Understanding Site Collections and Sites

Before we talk about sites, you need to understand how sites are organized. As we mentioned earlier, sites are the fundamental storage and organization tool within SharePoint used to host and manage all SharePoint materials and functionality. Sites themselves are grouped and organized within site collections. Site collections are created by SharePoint IT administrators as the main containers for storing and managing related sites. A site collection defines the storage location (database) where sites and site resources are stored and maintained. A site collection also defines the overall features to be made available within the contained sites, determines overall security configurations, determines overall navigation hierarchies, and defines general policies for content and resource management. As part of creating a new site collection, your IT administrator defines the database in which the resources will be stored and managed and can identify storage limits to restrict the volume of content stored in the collection. The IT administrator will also identify site collection administrators. Site collection administrators are individuals that have complete administrative control over the site collection and all contained sites.

The overall capabilities available within a site collection are determined by the site collection features active within it. Site collection administrators determine the features to be made available within their sites. There is a default set of active features available within a created site collection that is based on the template selected when the collection was created. A set of default site collection features is available as part of SharePoint Foundation, and additional features are available when SharePoint Server is in place. The default site collection features available in both SharePoint Foundation and SharePoint Server include the following:

- *Custom Site Collection Help*: This feature, when active, creates a library used to store custom help materials for use within the site collection.

- *Open Documents in Client Applications by Default*: When this feature is active, documents that have both client applications and web applications available to open them will default to opening in the client application. Documents of this type include Microsoft Office files. For example, a Word document will open in Microsoft Word—assuming Word is installed on the computer. When this feature is active, Office documents will open in the Office client by default. When this feature is deactivated, a Word document will open in Office Web Applications within the web browser—assuming Office Web Applications have been installed in the environment.

- *Search Server Web Parts and Templates*: Activating this feature will add the Search Server Web Parts and Display templates to the sites within the site collection. These web parts and templates allow search functionality to be added to sites within the collection.

- *Three-State Workflow*: This feature, when activated, will make the three-state workflow available within the site, allowing workflows to be created against lists and libraries that can promote documents through three status levels. You could, for example, create a workflow that promotes a document status from Draft to In Progress to Final.

When SharePoint Server is in place, there are several additional features beyond those just described that are available within the site collection. These additional features provide a variety of business solution capabilities and include the following:

- *Content Deployment Source Feature*: This feature provides functionality that will allow the site collection to be a source for content deployment. Content deployment features allow content in a source site collection to be made available within other site collections in the environment.

- *Content Type Syndication Hub*: Activating this feature introduces capabilities allowing the site collection to be a source, or hub, for globally managed metadata and for content types that can be used in other site collections in your environment.

- *Cross-Farm Site Permissions*: This feature allows applications deployed within the site collection to be made accessible to other locations within the farm.

- *Cross-Site Collection Publishing*: Activating this feature allows lists and libraries within the collection to be designated as catalogs for cross-site collection content publishing. Defining catalogs allows catalog content to be used within other site collections in the environment.

- *Disposition Approval Workflow*: This feature makes the disposition workflow available for use within the site. This workflow helps facilitate the expiring of content in the environment.

- *Document ID Service*: When this feature is active, all documents within the site collection are assigned IDs that can be used to identify and locate documents regardless of where they are moved within the environment.

- *Document Sets*: Enabling this feature makes the document sets content type available for use within the site collection. This content type allows document sets to be created and managed, which are used to group documents within special folders where they can share metadata, be passed through workflows, and managed as if they were a single item. Document sets are discussed in more detail in Chapter 7.

- *In Place Records Management*: When active, this feature allows documents to be declared as records in their source libraries within the collection. Declaring a document a record prevents it from being changed. Records management is discussed in detail in Chapter 10.

- *Library and Folder Based Retention*: This feature gives administrators the ability to override any retention schedules set against content types within lists and libraries. This in turn allows documents or list items that leverage these content types to be governed by policies against the list or library they are located within instead of against the item's content type.

- *Limited-Access User Permission Lockdown Mode*: When this feature is enabled, users assigned to the Limited Access permission level will not have the ability to access pages within the environment. Users are assigned to the Limited Access permission level automatically within the environment when the account has access only to resources contained within the site, not directly to the site itself. They must be given rights within the site that allows them to access the resources to which they have been granted rights.

- *PerformancePoint Services Site Collection Features*: Enabling this feature makes the PerformancePoint Services available to the site collection and allows for the creation of dashboards and scorecards for analytical data.

- *Publishing Approval Workflow*: This feature, which makes the web content publishing approval workflow available within the collection, allow approval processes to be defined for publishing pages within the environment.

- *Reporting*: When enabled, this feature creates site collection management reports.

- *Reports and Data Search Support*: This feature, when active, allows the enterprise search centers to support report searching. The feature includes a set of content types, site columns, and library templates that can be used to define materials to be made available within report searches.

- *Search Engine Sitemap*: Enabling this feature generates a site map on a recurring basis; when generated, it is used by the search engine to optimize search results. This feature, used only when the environment is configured to allow anonymous access, provides a consistent site map for all anonymous users.

- *SharePoint 2007 Workflows*: This feature makes the standard workflows that were part of SharePoint 2007 available within the current SharePoint 2013 environment site collection.

- *SharePoint Server Enterprise Site Collection Features*: Enabling this feature makes the SharePoint Server Enterprise edition features available for use within the site collection. This includes features such as Form Services, Visio Services, Access Services, and Excel Services.

- *SharePoint Server Publishing Infrastructure*: This feature creates a set of central libraries, content types, and page layouts needed to support the SharePoint site publishing features. These features enable the ability to create publishing pages within sites in the environment and the management of master pages. Publishing pages are discussed in more detail in Chapter 4.

- *SharePoint Server Standard Site Collection Features*: Enabling these features makes the capabilities that are part of SharePoint Server Standard edition available within the site collection. Included are such capabilities as my site, user profiles, and SharePoint enterprise search.

- *Site Policy*: When enabled, this feature allows information retention schedules to be created for standard site resources.

- *Video and Rich Media*: Enabling this feature makes a set of library templates, content types, and web parts available for storing and viewing rich media, including images and videos.

- *Workflows*: This feature makes the set of SharePoint 2013 out-of-the-box workflows available within the SharePoint lists and libraries. Workflow is discussed in detail in Chapter 9

■ **Note**   Some of the site collection features described here are available only in SharePoint Server Enterprise edition, not in SharePoint Server Standard edition.

Sites organize and house the information, workflows, services, and applications that make up the core of the SharePoint environment. These core elements are used to create business solutions within the environment. There are different types of sites available in SharePoint, each having different combinations of features enabled to support the purposes of the specific site type.

Not all SharePoint site templates are available in all versions of SharePoint. SharePoint Foundation includes a subset of the sites available in SharePoint Server. There are four categories of site templates available in SharePoint 2013. Each category includes multiple templates that can be used to create sites to address different needs. The following are the categories of site templates available by default in SharePoint 2013.

- *Collaboration*: The collaboration site templates are used to create sites supporting different ways for people to work together.

- *Enterprise*: Enterprise site templates are used to create sites for managing enterprise content or data sharing and management needs.

- *Publishing*: Publishing site templates create sites designed to support web content management needs. This category is available only when SharePoint Server is being used, not SharePoint Foundation.

- *Custom*: The custom category is displayed when custom site templates are created within SharePoint. This category includes all templates created by site administrators. Creating site templates is discussed in Chapter 3.

A template is a saved site structure and configuration designed to meet a specific need. When a site is created from a template, the newly created site will contain all of the resources saved in the template; it thus becomes a copy that can then be used and modified as needed. SharePoint also allows saving an existing site as a new site template and so provides the ability to extend the list of available site templates as needed.

The site templates available within the discussed categories are dependent on the version of SharePoint 2013 in use. SharePoint Foundation contains a subset of templates available within SharePoint Server. The following are the standard site templates available within SharePoint Foundation and SharePoint Server.

- **Collaboration Templates**

  - *Team Site*: This site template provides the most common set of resources needed for sites being used to facilitate general team collaboration and information sharing. This site template is available in both SharePoint Foundation and SharePoint Server. However, the capabilities available within the created sites differ slightly between SharePoint Foundation and SharePoint Server. The various features and structures are reviewed later in this chapter.

  - *Blog*: The blog template creates a site to manage information postings and comments, enabling social interactions on important topics. This template is available in both SharePoint Foundation and SharePoint Server.

  - *Project Site*: This template is used to create sites to manage projects and initiatives and includes resources to manage project content, status, and communications. It is available only in SharePoint Server.

  - *Community Site*: The community site template is used to create sites where groups of people come together to discuss, track, and manage important topics and common interests. It too is available only in SharePoint Server.

- **Enterprise Templates**

  - *Basic Search Center*: This site template is used to create a site containing pages where searches can be executed to find relevant content. This template is available in both SharePoint Foundation and SharePoint Server.

  - *Document Center*: The document center site template is used to develop sites for creating and managing enterprise documents. This template is available only in SharePoint Server.

  - *Records Center*: This site template is used to create sites to manage corporate records. The template allows for the upload and automated routing of documents and the creation and management of retention policies for these materials. It is available only in SharePoint Server.

  - *Business Intelligence Center*: This site template is used to create sites for viewing and analyzing business intelligence data, including KPIs, reports, and analytics. It too is available only in SharePoint Server.

  - *Enterprise Search Center*: This site template is used to create a site containing pages where searches for content, people, conversations, and videos can be executed. It is available only in SharePoint Server.

  - *Visio Process Repository*: This template is used to create sites that store and manage Visio process diagrams and related tasks, discussions, and communications. It is available only in SharePoint Server.

- ***Publishing Templates***
  - *Publishing Site*: The publishing site template is used to create sites for managing and presenting web content. This template is available only in SharePoint Server.
  - *Publishing Site with Workflow*: This template includes the same layout and structure as the publishing site but also has features enabled to support the approval of content as part of the publishing process. It is available only in SharePoint Server.
  - *Enterprise Wiki*: The enterprise wiki site template is used to create sites for capturing, managing, and storing knowledge. It is available only in SharePoint Server.

Structures and features of all of these site types are reviewed later in this chapter.

Site Structures and Layouts

All SharePoint sites have the same basic overall layout and structure and contain specific elements needed to navigate through the environment and manage site resources. The actual organization and layout of a SharePoint site's interface is configurable by environment managers. In this section the structural components and standard elements contained within a SharePoint site and their locations in the standard SharePoint site layout are described.

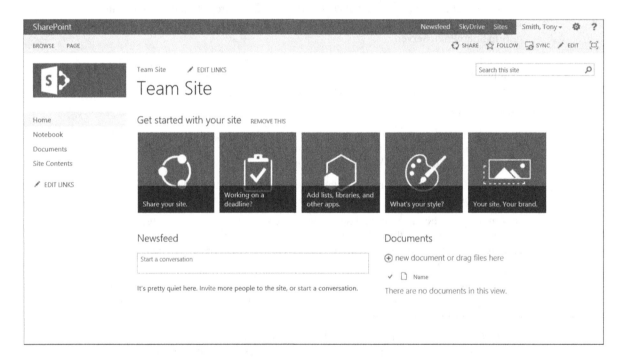

Figure 2-1. *Team site home page*

In this section each of the components making up the SharePoint 2013 environment are discussed.

My Site Menu

The My Site menu is located to the right in the banner area. These options are available only when SharePoint Server is in place.

Newsfeed   SkyDrive   Sites

Figure 2-2. *My Site menu*

The My Site menu options are listed in the banner and include the following elements:

- *Newsfeed*: The Newsfeed option, when clicked, will navigate to the My Site Newsfeed page.

- *Skydrive*: The Skydrive option navigates to the Documents library of the user's My Site.

- *Sites*: The Sites option navigates to the Sites page of the My Site showing sites the user is currently following and sites suggested for following.

The My Site capabilities of SharePoint 2013 are discussed in detail in Chapter 12.

User Menu

The User menu is located in the right-hand banner area in the default layout of the SharePoint 2013 environment. This menu is available in all versions of SharePoint 2013, with options depending on the version of SharePoint being used. The User menu provides access to the user details, as well as the ability to sign out of SharePoint, as seen in Figure 2-3.

Figure 2-3. *User menu*

The User menu options are accessed by clicking the user name. When SharePoint Foundation is being used, the User menu includes the following options:

- *My Settings*: My Settings allows you to navigate to the User Information page. This page permits you to view and manage your user profile details. The following information can be managed within the User Information page:

  - Personal Settings: These are details about the user, including name, e-mail address, mobile number, "about me" details, profile picture, department, job title, and SIP address. The information can be edited and saved.

  - Language and Region: The language and region option allows you to set your display language preferences for, if the user settings should be defined based on the server's settings, time zone and format, calendar format, and workweek.

  - My Alerts: The My Alerts on This Site allow you to manage the alerts you have configured within the SharePoint environment.

- *Sign Out*: The Sign Out option, when clicked, logs you out of SharePoint and prompts you to close the web browser window.

When SharePoint Server is in place, the User menu includes the following options:

- *About Me*: About Me navigates you to the My Site About Me page. This page allows you to manage your profile details and view your activities.

- *Sign Out*: The Sign Out option, when clicked, logs you out of SharePoint and prompts you to close the web browser window. This option is the same one used in SharePoint Foundation.

User settings, My Site, and profile information are discussed in more detail in Chapter 12.

Settings Menu

The Settings menu is located in the right-hand banner area next to the User menu. This menu includes site management options available to logged-on users based on their rights within the site. This menu, accessed by clicking on the Settings icon, includes a dynamic set of options based on a user's rights and available features within the site. The available options are discussed throughout this book in the context of how they are used while managing the various aspects of SharePoint.

Figure 2-4. *Settings menu*

Here are some of the more common options available through the Settings menu.

- *Shared With*: The Shared With option lists users with access to the current site or page. The Shared With window lists the users and provides the following options:

  - *Invite People*: This option allows you to identify users that should be granted Edit access to the resource.

  - *Email Everyone*: This option provides the ability to e-mail all users having access to the site.

  - *Advanced*: The Advanced option navigates to the site's permissions page.

- *Edit Page*: The Edit Page option is used to place the page in Edit mode. Page management is discussed in more detail in Chapter 4.

- *Add a Page*: Selecting this option opens the Add a Page window, which allows for the creation of a new SharePoint page.

- *Add an App*: This option is used to navigate to a page containing the apps that can be added to create new lists, libraries, and any other available app. Apps are discussed in more detail in Chapter 4.

- *Site Contents*: This option navigates you to the Site Contents page, where all of the lists, libraries, and other apps currently available within the site are listed.

- *Design Manager*: When SharePoint Server is in place, the Design Manager option is listed in the Settings menu. Selecting this option navigates you to the Design Manager Welcome page.

- *Change the Look*: When SharePoint Foundation is in place, the Change the Look option is listed in the Settings menu. Selecting this option navigates you to the Change the Look page.

- *Site Settings*: This option navigates you to the SharePoint Site Settings page.

- *Getting Started*: This option navigates you to the Getting Started page within the site.

Ribbon

The ribbon includes the contextual page management options available to you. Initially the ribbon displays the ribbon tabs, with the related options presented once a tab is selected. Figure 2-5 shows the page tab listing the options available for managing the currently displayed page.

Figure 2-5. Ribbon

Clicking on a ribbon tab shows the ribbon options for the selected tab. By default, these options overlay the navigation and title area. To remove the ribbon options from the display in order to see the navigation bar and title area, the Browse option can be selected. This option is always available as a ribbon tab.

Social Tools

The social tools are located to the right of the ribbon tabs. These options list the social capabilities available for the current page. Most of the social tools are available only in SharePoint Server and include the items listed in Figure 2-6.

Figure 2-6. Social tools

Availability of options in the social tools section is dependent on the version of SharePoint installed and includes the following:

- *Share*: The Share option is available in both SharePoint Foundation and SharePoint server. When Share is selected, the Share window is presented. This window allows identification of users to be granted edit rights to the site.

- *Follow*: Clicking on the Follow option adds the currently displayed item to your Follow list. Any changes to the item being followed are noted in your activity stream. This option is available only within SharePoint Server.

- *Sync*: The Sync option allows you to create a synchronized copy of the item currently being displayed on the local computer. Selecting this option will initiate the SharePoint Workspace synchronization process if Office 2010 is installed. With Office 2013 installed, the Sync window is presented and the information is synchronized directly to the local computer.

The social capabilities of SharePoint are discussed in detail in Chapter 12.

Page Management Tools

The page management tools allow management of the current page. Available next to the social tools, the listed options are dependent on the page being displayed.

Figure 2-7. *Page management tools*

The following options are available in the page management area.

- *Edit*: The Edit option is available within the SharePoint web part, wiki, and publishing pages. When clicked, the displayed page will enter Edit mode, where page content can be managed.

- *Focus on Content*: This option hides the title, navigation, and Quick Launch areas of the site; the content then fills the space these areas were using. This option allows the space for viewing site content to be maximized.

Navigation Bar

The navigation bar, which lists navigation options available to users within the site, allows users access to the resources hosted through the environment. Figure 2-8 shows the layout of the standard navigation bar.

Human Resources ▾   Information Technology ▾   Legal ▾   ✎ EDIT LINKS

Figure 2-8. *Navigation bar*

The navigation bar includes only those options that a user's security rights within the environment make available. How the navigation bar is managed depends on the version of SharePoint in use. When SharePoint Foundation is in use, the navigation bar can be configured either to allow options to be managed directly within the site or to inherit the navigation options of the parent site. When SharePoint Server is in place, navigation options can also be based on a term set. Within the term store a term set can be created that includes a set of options representing the desired navigation for the site. Referencing this term set causes the navigation bar option to be based on the information within the term set instead of on the site structure.

How to configure the navigation management approach and options is discussed in Chapter 3.

Search Bar

The Search bar allows you to enter text to perform a search. The search will initially be scoped against the current site. Performing a search navigates you to the search results page, where the items satisfying the search criteria are presented. When SharePoint Server is in place, a search center can be defined, allowing you to change the result source of the search by selecting a different option from the Result Source drop-down, as seen in Figure 2-9. SharePoint Search is discussed in detail in Chapter 11.

Figure 2-9. *Search bar*

Quick Launch Navigation

Located in the left-hand section of the site, the Quick Launch navigation area provides easy access to elements that are available within the site. The Quick Launch navigation options can be managed to include links to lists, libraries, subsites, and custom URLs. Any list or library in the site configured to be displayed in Quick Launch when added or edited within SharePoint is added to the Quick Launch navigation area for easy access. By default, the Quick Launch navigation includes links to the current site's home page and Site Contents page. Sites created from the various site templates include references to key site resources in the Quick Launch by default as well. Working with and managing SharePoint navigation, including Quick Launch, is discussed in Chapter 3.

Content Area

Located to the right of the Quick Launch navigation, the content area is the main body of the site page. This is the section that contains the elements that you want to make available through the site. This section may include documents, lists, web parts, apps, web content, and similar elements. The site's content area is divided into zones where content elements can be placed. The layout of this area and the configuration of the zones are dependent upon the page template in use. When a site is initially created, the home page will leverage the page template identified when the template was created. A user with appropriate rights can later change this layout. Two different types of zones are available on pages in SharePoint. The types available on a given page are dependent on the type of page being used. Standard SharePoint pages and SharePoint publishing pages contain web part zones where web parts can be placed and organized. Another type of page available in SharePoint is a wiki page. Wiki pages contain wiki zones. Wiki zones can contain web content, web parts, videos, and other types of content. Pages are discussed in detail in Chapter 4.

Standard Site Templates

Earlier in this chapter we listed the site templates available within SharePoint 2013. These templates are provided to create sites to meet a variety of needs. Selecting the best site template when creating sites is done by understanding the resources available and features enabled by default within a created site in order to determine how closely those resources map to your needs. In this section we will detail the layouts and configurations of each of the default templates available within SharePoint Foundation and SharePoint Server.

Collaboration

Collaboration site templates are those created to support collaboration efforts performed within SharePoint.

Team Site Template

The Team Site template is available in both SharePoint Foundation and SharePoint Server. This template is used to create sites that facilitate general team collaboration and information sharing. A team site contains resources needed to allow a team to bring together the resources needed to manage a variety of collaborative work efforts, including projects and other team initiatives. A team site has the Wiki Page Home Page feature enabled, which results in wiki pages being available within the site and having a wiki page being defined as the site's home page. Using a wiki page as the site's home page provides flexibility when configuring the layout and the resources available on the page, allowing a mix of web parts, web content, images, videos, and more.

The resources available in a team site and the home page layout vary slightly between SharePoint Foundation and SharePoint Server environments. When SharePoint Server is used, the SharePoint social capabilities are active within the team site by default. This includes the Newsfeed capabilities. Figure 2-1 shows the default team site home page layout for SharePoint Server environments. Since SharePoint Foundation does not include SharePoint social features, the Newsfeed functionality is not available for use and will not be included in the Team Site, as seen in Figure 2-10.

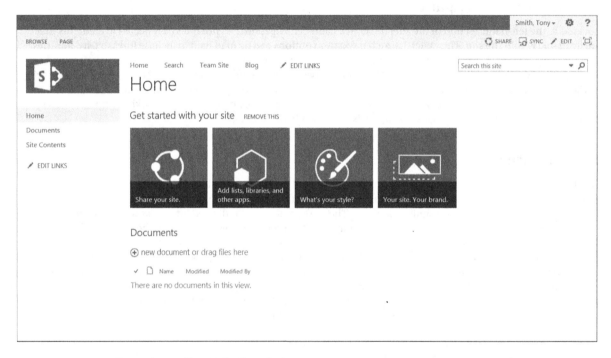

Figure 2-10. *Team Site option on SharePoint Foundation*

While the SharePoint Server and the SharePoint Foundation team sites both use a wiki page as the home page for the site, the layouts of the pages are different. In SharePoint Foundation the Team Site home page is configured with a single zone containing all of the presented resources. In SharePoint Server the Team Site home page is configured to include a three-zone layout. Wiki page layouts can be changed for existing pages, allowing you to update these initial layouts to meet your specific needs. Editing pages is discussed in Chapter 4.

A site created from the Team Site template includes components listed in Table 2-1.

Table 2-1. *Team Site Template Components*

Item	Type	In Quick Launch	In Content Area
Libraries and Lists			
Documents	Document library	Yes	Yes
MicroFeed (SharePoint Server only)	MicroFeed list	No	No
Site Assets	Document library	No	No
Site Pages	Wiki page library	No	No
Web Parts			
Get started with your site	Get started with your site web part	N/A	Yes
Site Feed (SharePoint Server only)	Site feed web part	N/A	Yes

The SharePoint services active within the team site by default also vary depending on whether SharePoint Foundation or SharePoint Server is used. The features active within a newly created site based on the Team Site template include the following:

- Access App (SharePoint Server only)

- Following Content (SharePoint Server only)

- Getting Started

- Minimal Download Strategy

- Mobile Browser View

- SharePoint Server Enterprise Site features (SharePoint Server only)

- SharePoint Server Standard Site features (SharePoint Server only)

- Site Feed (SharePoint Server only)

- Site Notebook (SharePoint Server only)

- Team Collaboration Lists

- Wiki Page Home Page

- Workflow Task Content Type (SharePoint Server only)

Available site features and their uses were discussed earlier in this chapter.

Blog Template

Like the Team Site template, the Blog template is available in both SharePoint Foundation and SharePoint Server. This template, which provides the structure necessary for managing blog resources, gives the ability to create and manage posts and comments and organize these communications into categories. Sites created from this template use a specialized web part page layout that includes a three-zone configuration, with one zone located in the Quick Launch area of the site. The site created from the Blog template is depicted in Figure 2-11.

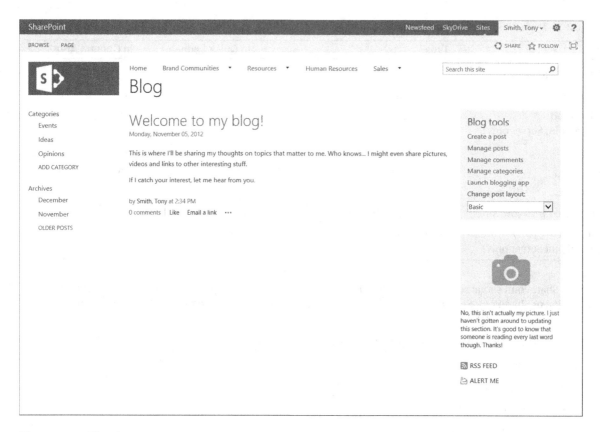

Figure 2-11. *Blog site*

A site created from the Blog template includes the components listed in Table 2-2.

Table 2-2. *Blog Template Components*

Item	Type	In Quick Launch*	In Content Area
Libraries and Lists			
Categories	Categories list	Yes	No
Comments	Comments list	No	No
Photos	Picture library	No	No
Posts	Posts list	No	Yes
Web Parts			
Archives	Archives web part	Yes	No
Blog Tools	Blog Tools web part	N/A	Yes
About This Blog	Content Editor web part	N/A	Yes
Blog Notifications	Blog Notifications web part	N/A	Yes

* The Quick Launch area in a Blog site includes a web part zone called Blog Navigator, where the items listed in the Quick Launch area are placed.

Blog sites allow you to track topics to discuss; they are often used as team communications tools to let people publish news, comment on posts, and respond to questions. Sites created from the Blog template include the following active site features:

- Access App (SharePoint Server only)

- Following Content (SharePoint Server only)

- Minimal Download Strategy

- Mobile Browser View

- SharePoint Server Enterprise Site features (SharePoint Server only)

- SharePoint Server Standard Site features (SharePoint Server only)

- Team Collaboration Lists

- Workflow Task Content Type (SharePoint Server only)

Project Site Template

The first of the collaboration site templates available in SharePoint Server but not SharePoint Foundation is the Project Site template. Sites created from this template are designed to support project management, including the management of tasks and resources for any type of project or initiative. A project site has a structure similar to a team site's, with added resources to track and manage project tasks. These sites use a web part page as the home page, including web parts to depict the project tasks, documents, and feed information. Figure 2-12 depicts the default layout of a project site.

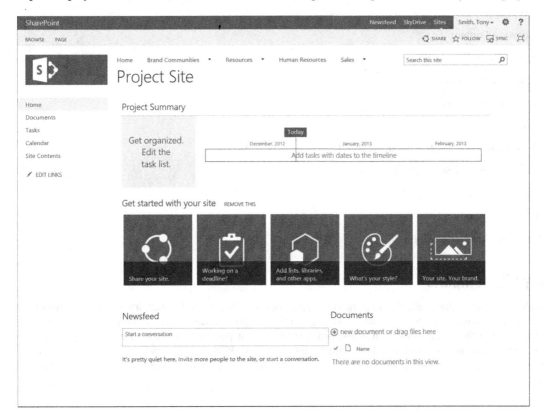

Figure 2-12. *Project Site*

A site created from the Project Site template includes components listed in Table 2-3.

Table 2-3. *Project Site Template Components*

Item	Type	In Quick Launch*	In Content Area
Libraries and Lists			
Calendar	Calendar list	Yes	No
Documents	Document library	Yes	Yes
MicroFeed	MicroFeed list	No	No
Site Assets	Document library	No	No
Tasks	Tasks list	Yes	No
Web Parts			
Project Summary	Project summary	N/A	Yes
Get started with your site	Get started with your site web part	N/A	Yes
Site feed	Site Feed web part	N/A	Yes

Sites created from the Project Site template have the following features active by default:

- Access App
- Following Content
- Getting Started
- Minimal Download Strategy
- Mobile Browser View
- Project Functionality
- SharePoint Server Enterprise Site features
- SharePoint Server Standard Site features
- Site Feed
- Team Collaboration Lists
- Workflow Task Content Type

Community Site Template

A second collaboration template available in SharePoint Server but not SharePoint Foundation is the Community Site template. This template is used to create sites where groups of people can discuss related topics. Community templates bring together the social features of SharePoint 2013 and allow people to join a community, participate in discussions, share experiences, and find others with similar interests, skills, and experiences. The Community Site uses a wiki page as the site's home page, with zones organized by default into a two-column layout, as seen in Figure 2-13.

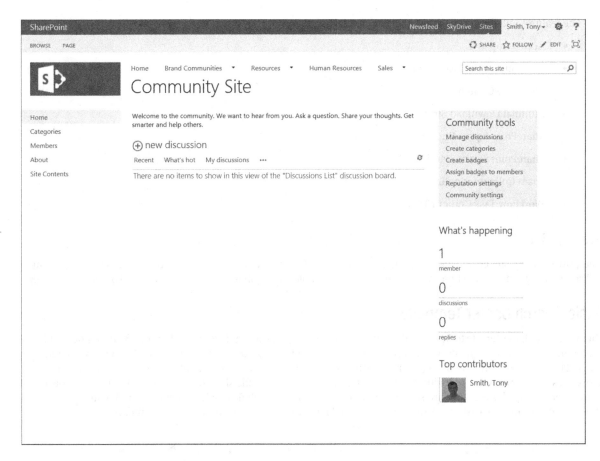

Figure 2-13. *Community Site home page*

A site created from the Community Site template includes components listed in Table 2-4.

Table 2-4. *Community Site Template Components*

Item	Type	In Quick Launch*	In Content Area
Libraries and Lists			
Categories	Categories list	Yes	No
Community Members	Community Members list	Yes	Yes
Discussion List	Discussion board	No	No
Site Assets	Document library	No	No
Site Pages	Wiki Page library	No	No
Web Parts			
Tools	Content Editor web part	N/A	Yes
Join	Join web part	N/A	Yes
What's Happening	What's Happening web part	N/A	Yes

The features initially active within a site created from the Community Site template include the following:

- Access App
- Community Site List Feature
- Following Content
- Minimal Download Strategy
- SharePoint Server Enterprise Site features
- SharePoint Server Standard Site features
- Team Collaboration Lists
- Workflow Task Content Type

Enterprise

Enterprise site templates create sites to support such business solution needs as business intelligence, records management, and searching. The following Enterprise templates are available within SharePoint Foundation and SharePoint Server.

Basic Search Center Template

The Basic Search Center site template is the only Enterprise template available in both SharePoint Foundation and SharePoint Server. This template, used to create sites configured to allow users to perform searches against content crawled by the SharePoint search engine, initially includes content stored in SharePoint. When SharePoint Server is in use, this can be expanded to include content in other sources such as file shares, web sites, and e-mail. The Basic Search Center provides the standard search elements, including a Search field, where text is entered to initiate a search, and a Results area, where results are displayed. Figure 2-14 shows the initial Search Center page.

Figure 2-14. *Basic Search Center site*

Once a search is executed, the Results page presents the items matching the search criteria and a refinement panel that can be used to filter the results. The search results page can be seen in Figure 2-15. Searches are discussed in detail in Chapter 11.

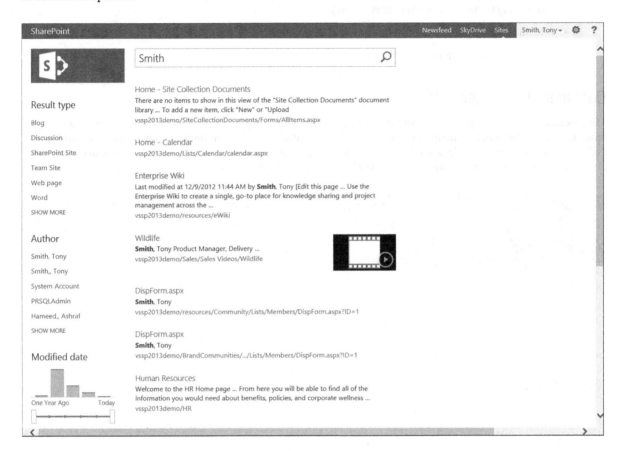

Figure 2-15. *Basic Search Center Results page*

The Basic Search Center site includes the resources detailed in Table 2-5.

Table 2-5. *Basic Search Center Template Components*

Item	Type	In Quick Launch	In Content Area
Libraries and Lists			
Tabs in Search Page	Search Tabs list	No	No
Tabs in Search Results	Search Tabs list	No	No
Web Parts			
Search Box	Search Box web part	N/A	Yes

The SharePoint services active within the basic search site include the following:

- Access App (SharePoint Server only)

- Following Content (SharePoint Server only)

- Team Collaboration Lists

- Workflow Task Content Type (SharePoint Server only)

Document Center Template

The Document Center template is a SharePoint Server template that is used to create sites designed to support enterprise document storage and management. Document centers include components needed to manage and collaborate with documents. These sites include a document library configured to support the creation of documents and their ongoing management and access. Figure 2-16 depicts the default layout of a document center.

Figure 2-16. *Document Center*

A Document Center site includes features and capabilities to support document management including versioning, document sets, and content types. This site uses a web part page as the home page of the site and includes the components listed in Table 2-6.

Table 2-6. *Document Center Template Components*

Item	Type	In Quick Launch	In Content Area
Libraries and Lists			
Documents	Document library	Yes	No
Tasks	Task list	Yes	No
Web Parts			
Content 1	Content Editor	N/A	Yes
Content 2	Content Editor	N/A	Yes
Newest Documents	Content Query	N/A	Yes
Modified By Me	Content Query	N/A	Yes

The Document Center has site features enabled to support the management of documents within the environment. These features include the following:

- Access App

- Following Content

- Metadata Navigation and Filtering

- Mobile Browser View

- SharePoint Server Enterprise Site features

- SharePoint Server Standard Site features

- Team Collaboration Lists

- Workflow Task Content Type

Records Center Template

The Records Center template is used to create sites designed to index and route files to libraries and folders for retention and archiving. Records can be deposited in the Drop Off Library by uploading them into the library or by configuring the library to receive e-mails and routing the documents to the library via e-mail. The Drop Off Library can be configured to route documents to the appropriate locations within SharePoint using content organizer, which allows for the creation of rules based on a document's properties. Content management is discussed in Chapter 7.

Figure 2-17 shows the default Record Center. This site is structured similarly to the Document Center in that it uses a web part page as the site's home page to organize content.

Figure 2-17. *Records Center home page*

Records Center sites include features and capabilities that support organizing content, locking content as corporate records, and retaining content based on document attributes. This site includes components listed in Table 2-7.

Table 2-7. *Records Center Template Components*

Item	Type	In Quick Launch	In Content Area
Libraries and Lists			
Drop Off Library	Document library	Yes	Yes
Web Parts			
Content [1]	Content Editor	N/A	Yes
Content [2]	Content Editor	N/A	Yes
Find by Document ID	Find by Document ID web part	N/A	Yes

Records Center sites have the features necessary to support the routing and retention of documents as corporate records. These features include the following:

- Access App
- Content Organizer
- Following Content
- Hold
- Metadata Navigation and Filtering
- SharePoint Server Enterprise Site features
- SharePoint Server Standard Site features
- Team Collaboration Lists
- Workflow Task Content Type

Business Intelligence Center Template

The Business Intelligence Center template is a SharePoint Server–only template used to create sites to host dashboards and analytics. BI Business Intelligence Center sites include a structure to manage various business intelligence–related resources such as dashboard pages, data connections, PerformancePoint scorecards, and Excel and Power View reports. Figure 2-18 depicts the default layout of a Business Intelligence Center.

Figure 2-18. *A Business Intelligence Center home page*

Sites created from this template include several lists and libraries used to manage the business intelligence resources. The lists and libraries available by default in a Business Intelligence Center include the elements listed in Table 2-8.

Table 2-8. Business Intelligence Center Template Components

Item	Type	In Quick Launch	In Content Area
Libraries and Lists			
Dashboards	Dashboards library	Yes	No
Data Connections	Data Connections Library for PerformancePoint	Yes	No
Documents	Document library	No	No
Images	Asset library	No	No
Pages	Document library	No	No
PerformancePoint Content	PerformancePoint Content list	Yes	No
Workflow Tasks	Task list	No	No
Web Parts			
Untitled	Content Editor	N/A	Yes

The Business Intelligence Center includes features to support the creation of dashboards and scorecards. These features include the following:

- Access App

- BI Center Data Connections Feature

- Following Content

- PerformancePoint Services Site Features

- SharePoint Server Standard Site features

- Workflow Task Content Type

Enterprise Search Center Template

The Enterprise Search Center template allows the creation of sites used to perform SharePoint searches. This template, available only in SharePoint Server, includes a set of links that can narrow searches to specific types or sets of results. The Enterprise Search Center allows the selection of the type of content to perform the search against. By default these options include the following:

- *Everything*: All content crawled by SharePoint

- *People*: SharePoint users

- *Conversations*: SharePoint social discussions

- *Videos*: Video files

- *Reports*: Report files (this option is not available by default but can be added by activating the necessary features)

An Enterprise Search Center includes a page to search for content and pages for displaying results, which vary based on the content searched. You can tailor these sites to meet your organization's searching needs. How to update the sites is discussed in Chapter 11. Figure 2-19 shows the default Enterprise Search Center site.

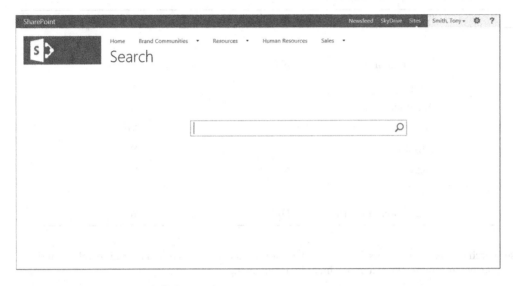

Figure 2-19. *Enterprise Search Center site*

Once a search has been performed, the search results page is presented. The results page allows you to access the resources located by the executed search and includes the options to search across the available areas, as seen in Figure 2-20.

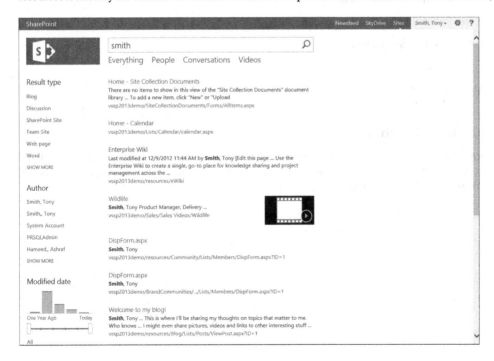

Figure 2-20. *Enterprise Search Center Results page*

Sites created from this template include the components listed in Table 2-9.

Table 2-9. *Enterprise Search Center Template Components*

Item	Type	In Quick Launch	In Content Area
Libraries and Lists			
Documents	Document library	No	No
Images	Asset library	No	No
Pages	Document library	No	No
Tabs in Search Pages	Tabs list	No	No
Tabs in Search Results	Tabs list	No	No
Workflow Tasks	Tasks list	No	No
Web Parts			
Search Box	Search Box web part	N/A	Yes

The Enterprise Search Center site contains the set of active features necessary to allow a user to search for and locate content within the environment. These features include the following:

- Access App
- Following Content
- SharePoint Server Enterprise Site features
- SharePoint Server Publishing
- SharePoint Server Standard Site features
- Team Collaboration Lists
- Workflow Task Content Type

Visio Process Repository Template

An additional site template available only in SharePoint Server is the Visio Process Repository template. It is provided to allow you to create sites structured to manage and share Visio process diagrams. This site has a web part page as the site's home page. The home page can be seen in Figure 2-21.

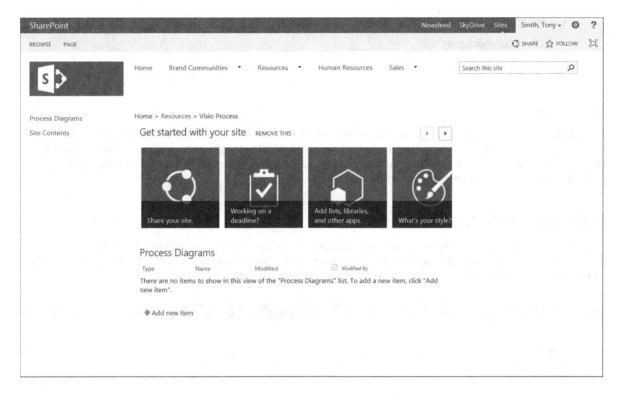

Figure 2-21. *Visio Process Repository site*

The Visio Process Repository site includes the features and components necessary to facilitate the management of Visio process diagrams. The materials available by default in a Visio Process Repository site are listed in Table 2-10.

Table 2-10. *Visio Process Repository Template Components*

Item	Type	In Quick Launch	In Content Area
Libraries and Lists			
Process Diagrams	Document library	Yes	Yes
Web Parts			
Getting Started with Your Site	Getting Started with Your Site web part	N/A	Yes

The Visio Process Repository site has the site features enabled to support the development and management of Visio process diagrams, including the following:

- Access App
- Following Content
- Getting Started
- Metadata Navigation and Filtering
- Minimal Download Strategy
- SharePoint Server Enterprise Site features

- SharePoint Server Standard Site features

- Team Collaboration Lists

- Workflow Task Content Type

Publishing

Publishing templates are used to create sites supporting the creation and sharing of web content for web sites. Publishing sites are not in SharePoint Foundation; they exist only within SharePoint Server. They allow you to create sites and site pages that use rich web content resources such as web text, videos, images, and web parts. The templates available in the Publishing template category include the following.

Publishing Site Template

The Publishing Site template is used to create sites that allow you to create web pages that contain web content including text, video, and images. They enable site owners to easily enter information to be presented as normal web pages within SharePoint. Figure 2-22 depicts a publishing site's default layout.

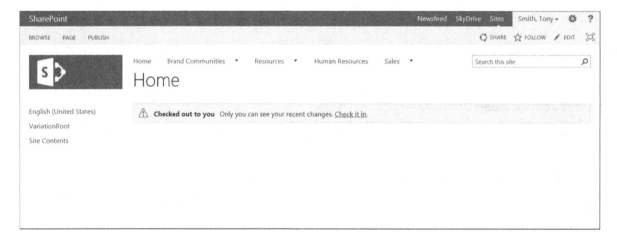

Figure 2-22. *Publishing site home page*

While a publishing site appears to have no content in the content area when it is initially created, the site uses a publishing page as its home page. This page includes several elements necessary to manage web content, including a location to enter web content, two summary link locations where links can be created to reference other information, and web part zones where web parts can be placed to add functionality to the site. The page layout can be updated by editing the page and selecting a different layout from the available publishing page layouts.

Publishing sites also contain several components that can be used to assist in the creation of web content pages. Table 2-11 lists the components making up a publishing site.

Table 2-11. *Publishing Site Template Components*

Item	Type	In Quick Launch	In Content Area
Libraries and Lists			
Documents	Document library	No	No
Images	Asset library	No	No
Pages	Document library	No	No
Workflow Tasks	Tasks list	No	No
Web Parts			
Page Image	Page Image Area	N/A	Yes
Page Content	Content Area	N/A	Yes
Summary Links	Summary Links Tool Part	N/A	Yes
Summary Links 2	Summary Links Tool Part	N/A	Yes

The items on the publishing home page are not in web part zones. They exist outside the zones, directly on the page itself. These items allow you to add images to the page, enter the content to be presented, and create links to other resources. Publishing sites also initially have the following features enabled to support web content publishing:

- Access App
- Following Content
- SharePoint Server Enterprise Site features
- SharePoint Server Publishing
- SharePoint Server Standard Site features
- Team Collaboration Lists
- Workflow Task Content Type

Publishing Site with Workflow Template

The Publishing Site with Workflow template is used to create sites similar to those created from the Publishing Site template. However, a site created from the Publishing Site with Workflow template extends the capabilities of the publishing site by providing the resources needed to allow web content approval as part of the content publishing process. Once a site is created from this template, you can configure the appropriate approval workflow to manage the content approval process. Workflow management is discussed in more detail in Chapter 9.

Sites created from the Publishing Site with Workflow template have the same layout and structure as Publishing Site template sites but a different set of default-activated features. They include the following:

- Access App
- Following Content
- Metadata Navigation and Filtering
- SharePoint Server Publishing
- Workflow Task Content Type

Enterprise Wiki Template

The Enterprise Wiki template is used to create enterprise wiki sites, which are designed to create interconnected web pages. These sites are used to create content-centric web pages that refer to each other to easily navigate between related pages. These sites provide an easy way to share information and promote collaboration. A site created from the Enterprise Wiki template can be seen in Figure 2-23.

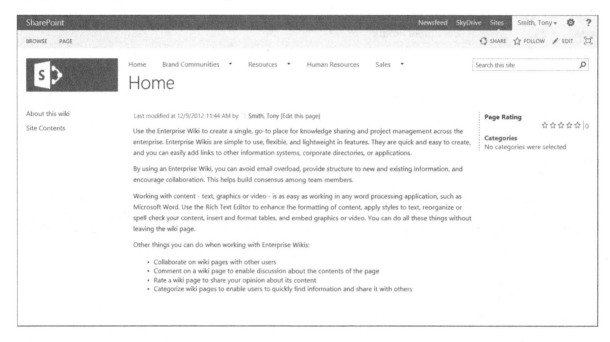

Figure 2-23. *An Enterprise Wiki site*

The home page of an enterprise wiki site describes how to use the wiki and includes page rating and page categorization capabilities. This page is a wiki page that can be edited to include the desired information. To support the management of the wiki, the enterprise wiki site includes the components listed in Table 2-12.

Table 2-12. *Enterprise Wiki Template Components*

Item	Type	In Quick Launch	In Content Area
Libraries and Lists			
Documents	Document library	No	No
Images	Asset library	No	No
Pages	Document library	No	No
Workflow Tasks	Tasks list	No	No
Web Parts			
Categories	Categories web part	N/A	Yes
Page Rating	Page Rating web part	N/A	Yes
Wiki Content zone	Wiki Content zone	N/A	Yes

Features active within a wiki site include the following, which support the creation and management of the wiki web content.

- Access App
- Following Content
- Team Collaboration Lists
- Workflow Task Content Type

SharePoint Portal Templates

SharePoint Server 2013 also has, along with the site templates described so far, a set of templates that are available only to technical administrators of SharePoint for creating new site collections. These templates are used to create new root sites within a SharePoint environment. However these templates are not available when you create new subsites within your portal.

The templates that are available only for the creation of new portals, or site collections, in SharePoint 2013 include the following:

Developer Site

The Developer Site template is designed to support the creation, testing, and publishing of Apps for Office and SharePoint. This site includes links to resources to help build Office and SharePoint apps and links to help publish these apps to the online store. You can use this site template as your starting point for creating and publishing your SharePoint 2013 Apps. Figure 2-24 depicts the layout of the site created from the Developer Site template located on the Collaboration tab of the Create Site Collection page. Site collections are created by SharePoint administrators through the SharePoint Central Administration site.

Figure 2-24. *Layout of a Developer site*

Developer sites contain the resources necessary to support the creation and publishing of Apps for both SharePoint and Office. These resources are defined in Table 2-13.

Table 2-13. *Developer Site Template Components*

Item	Type	In Quick Launch	In Content Area
Libraries and Lists			
App Packages	Document library	No	No
Apps in Testing	Custom list	Yes	Yes
Documents	Document library	Yes	No
Form Templates	Document library	No	No
MicroFeed	MicroFeed list	No	No
Site Assets	Document library	No	No
Site Pages	Wiki library	No	No
Style Library	Document library	No	No
Web Parts			
Get Started with Apps for Office and SharePoint	Get Started web part	N/A	Yes

Developer site collections have the following site collection and site features active by default to support app development:

- *Site Collection Features*
    - Disposition Approval Workflow
    - Document Sets
    - Library and Folder Based Retention
    - Reporting
    - SharePoint Server Enterprise Site Collection Features
    - SharePoint Server Standard Site Collection Features
    - Site Policy
    - Three-State Workflow
    - Video and Rich Media
- *Site Features*
    - Access App
    - Following Content
    - Getting Started
    - Minimal Download Strategy
    - Mobile Browser View

- SharePoint Server Enterprise Site Features

- SharePoint Server Standard Site Features

- Site Feed

- Team Collaboration Lists

- Wiki Page Home Page

- Workflow Task Content Type

eDiscovery Center

An eDiscovery Center portal allows you to manage content discovery and content holds to support legal investigations. This portal can be used to identify content from SharePoint, Exchange, and other sources and organize it into discovery cases for easy identification and access. The content can be placed on hold and can be exported or downloaded so that it can easily be shared with appropriate parties. Figure 2-25 shows the default layout of the eDiscovery Center portal home page.

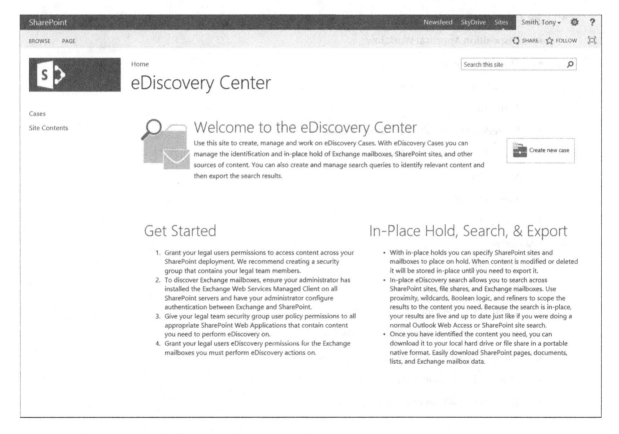

Figure 2-25. *eDiscovery Center home page*

Creation of cases and holds is discussed in detail in Chapter 10. To support content discovery and holds, eDiscovery Centers initially contain the resources detailed in Table 2-14.

Table 2-14. *eDiscovery Center Template Components*

Item	Type	In Quick Launch	In Content Area
Libraries and Lists			
Form Templates	Document library	No	No
Style Library	Document library	No	No
Web Parts			
Content [1]	Content Editor web part	N/A	Yes
Content [2]	Content Editor web part	N/A	Yes
Content [3]	Content Editor web part	N/A	Yes
Content [4]	Content Editor web part	N/A	Yes

To support the creation of discovery cases and holds, the eDiscovery Center portal has the following site collection and site features enabled by default:

- *Site Collection Features*
  - Disposition Approval Workflow
  - Document Sets
  - Library and Folder Based Retention
  - Reporting
  - SharePoint Server Enterprise Site Collection Features
  - SharePoint Server Standard Site Collection Features
  - Site Policy
  - Video and Rich Media
  - Workflows
- *Site Features*
  - Access App
  - Following Content
  - Metadata Navigation and Filtering
  - SharePoint Server Enterprise Site Features
  - SharePoint Server Standard Site Features
  - Team Collaboration Lists
  - Workflow Task Content Type

Community Portal

The Community Portal provides a way for you to identify community sites available across the SharePoint environment you have access to. You can search for communities you would be interested in joining and then follow and participate in community discussions and activities. Community sites allow you to connect with others who have similar interests or experience. The Community Portal also identifies the most popular of those available to you. Figure 2-26 depicts the default layout of the Community Portal home page.

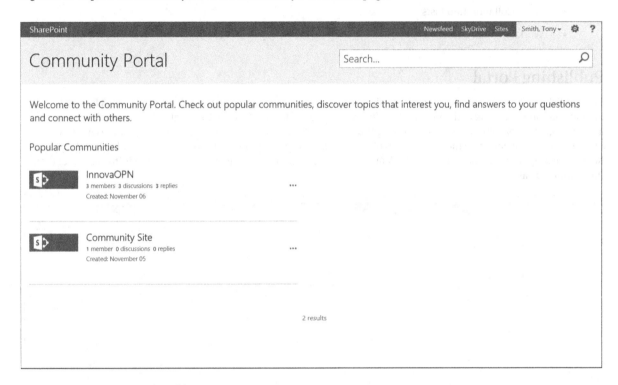

Figure 2-26. *Community Portal home page*

Working with community sites and the Community Portal is discussed in detail in Chapter 12. The Community Portal initially includes the elements identified in Table 2-15.

Table 2-15. *Community Portal Template Components*

Item	Type	In Quick Launch	In Content Area
Libraries and Lists			
Form Templates	Document library	No	No
Style Library	Document library	No	No
Web Parts			
Search Box	Search Box web part	N/A	Yes
Popular Communities	Popular Communities web part	N/A	Yes

The Community Portal, which allows individuals to locate and join desired communities, does not have any of the available site collection features enabled, but does have the following site features enabled by default.

- Access App

- Following Content

- Minimal Download Strategy

- Team Collaboration Lists

- Workflow Task Content Type

Publishing Portal

The Publishing Portal includes a structure designed to support the creation of intranet or Internet sites focused on information publishing and consumption. Its site and site collection features are enabled to support creation and management of web content for web sites. When created, a Publishing Portal's home page includes links and instructions to help facilitate the initial setup of a web site. Step-by-step instructions and links are displayed that help you configure navigation, the site's look and feel, security, and more. Figure 2-27 shows the initial layout of the Publishing Portal.

Figure 2-27. *Publishing Portal home page*

The Publishing Portal uses a publishing page as a home page that can be edited as needed to make it your intranet or Internet site's home page. (Working with a publishing page is discussed in detail in Chapter 4.) Table 2-16 shows the elements initially included in the publishing portal.

Table 2-16. *Publishing Portal Template Components*

Item	Type	In Quick Launch	In Content Area
Libraries and Lists			
Content and Structure	Content and Structure Reports list	No	No
Documents	Document library	No	No
Form Templates	Document library	No	No
Images	Asset library	No	No
Pages	Document library	No	No
Reusable Content	Reusable Content library	No	No
Site Collection Documents	Document library	No	No
Site collection images	Document library	No	No
Style Library	Document library	No	No
Workflow Tasks	Tasks list	No	No
Web Parts			
Page Content	Page Content area	N/A	Yes
Content [1]	Content Editor web part	N/A	Yes
Content [2]	Content Editor web part	N/A	Yes
Untitled [1]	Summary Links web part	N/A	Yes
Untitled [2]	Summary Links web part	N/A	Yes

The publishing portal has the following site collection and site features enabled by default to support intranet or Internet web development and publishing.

- *Site Collection Features*

    - Disposition Approval Workflow

    - Document Sets

    - Limited-Access User Permission Lockdown Mode

    - Publishing Approval Workflow

    - Reporting

    - SharePoint Server Publishing Infrastructure

    - Video and Rich Media

    - Workflows

- *Site Features*

  - Access App

  - Following Content

  - Metadata Navigation and Filtering

  - SharePoint Server Publishing

  - Workflow Task Content Type

Product Catalog

The Product Catalog portal is used to create and manage a searchable catalog of products or other items that can be published for use in other site collections in your SharePoint environment. The Product Catalog portal home page is a wiki page that includes a set of links providing guidance to walk you through creating a catalog of items and making the catalog searchable (see Figure 2-28).

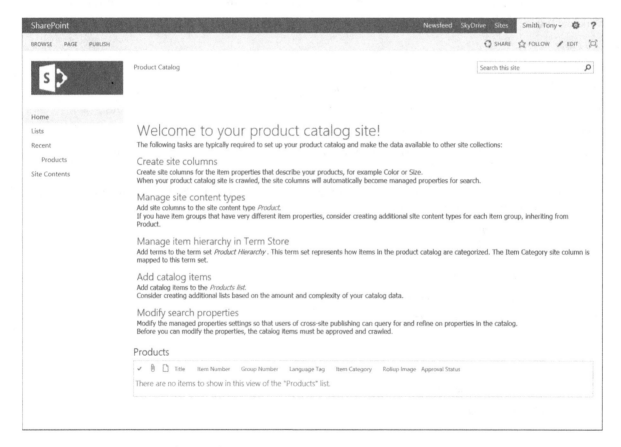

Figure 2-28. *The Product Catalog portal*

The Product Catalog portal initially contains the items listed in Table 2-17 to support the creation and management of a catalog.

Table 2-17. *Product Catalog Template Components*

Item	Type	In Quick Launch	In Content Area
Libraries and Lists			
Content and Structure	Content and Structure Reports list	No	No
Documents	Document library	No	No
Form Templates	Document library	No	No
Images	Asset library	No	No
Pages	Document library	No	No
Products	Products list	Yes	Yes
Reusable Content	Reusable Content library	No	No
Site Collection Documents	Document library	No	No
Site Collection Images	Document library	No	No
Style Library	Document library	No	No
Workflow Tasks	Tasks list	No	No
Web Parts			
Page Content	Page Content area	N/A	Yes

In this portal the site collection and site features enabled by default to support the creation and management of catalogs are as follows:

- *Site Collection Features*
    - Cross-Site Collection Publishing
    - Document Sets
    - Limited-Access User Permission Lockdown Mode
    - Reporting
    - SharePoint Server Publishing Infrastructure
    - SharePoint Server Standard Site Collection Features
    - Video and Rich Media
    - Workflows
- *Site Features*
    - Access App
    - Following Content
    - Metadata Navigation and Filtering
    - Workflow Task Content Type

CHAPTER 3

■ ■ ■

Working with Sites

Now that you have been familiarized with the layout and makeup of SharePoint sites across both SharePoint Foundation and SharePoint server, it is time to see how to work with and manage sites and site resources. There are many capabilities available within SharePoint site. This chapter will discuss how to use and manage SharePoint site features and review the capabilities of both SharePoint Foundation and SharePoint Server including the following:

- Navigating the environment
- Using the ribbon
- Managing security
- Managing navigation
- Updating look and feel
- Managing variations

Navigating the SharePoint Environment

Several methods can be used to navigate between sites within a SharePoint site collection hierarchy and among the elements within a single site. In this section the available navigation approaches are discussed.

Navigating Within a Site

As mentioned previously, sites created underneath other sites are called subsites. It is very common for sites of various types to contain such subsites. For example, a human resources site might have a subsite dedicated to providing HR benefit details. A client site containing individual project sites for the client would be another example. There are four main ways to navigate a site's subsites.

The first method leverages the navigation bar. This bar, seen in Figure 3-1, contains the list of navigation links created by site owners. They may include the following:

- Defining the navigation items within the site, which can be configured to include the subsites and pages within the current site, as well as custom links defined by a site manager.

- Configuring the navigation to inherit the navigation from the parent site, which provides navigation consistency between sites.

- Configuring the navigation to use a navigation term set to define the items presented.

Home   Brand Communities   ▾   Resources   ▾   Human Resources   Sales   ▾   ✎ EDIT LINKS

Figure 3-1. *Navigation bar*

The SharePoint navigation management options determine the approach used for navigation management. Navigation management is discussed later in this chapter.

The second method to navigate a site's subsites is to use the Site Contents page. This page is accessed by clicking the Site Contents link in the Quick Launch menu. Once on the Site Contents page, you can navigate to a subsite by clicking on its name in the Subsites section of the page (see Figure 3-2).

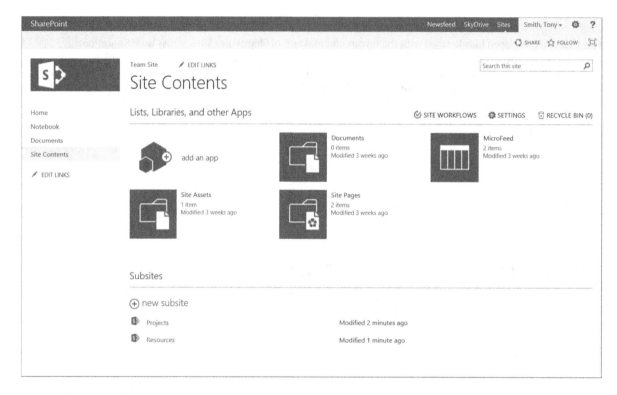

Figure 3-2. *Site Contents page*

You also use the Site Contents page to navigate to lists and libraries in the current site. These are found in the Lists, Libraries, and other Apps section of the page.

The third method is to navigate via the Settings menu. This menu can be used to access the Site Contents page just mentioned. This navigation option is available only to users having access to that menu. Accessing the Site Contents page using the Settings menu is done as follows:

1. Navigate to the site containing the subsite you wish to access.

2. Click the Settings icon to present the Settings menu, as shown in Figure 3-3.

Figure 3-3. *Settings menu*

3. On the Settings menu, click the Site Contents link.

4. On the Site Contents page, click the name of the subsite you wish to view. This will present the selected subsite's home page.

The fourth method used to navigate to a subsite is to use a web part that lists subsites on a site page. SharePoint Foundation, on its own, does not include a web part that lists sites under the current site. SharePoint Server has web parts that can be used to list subsites. Some of the most commonly used default web parts used to list sites include the following:

- *Site Aggregator*: This web part allows identification of a set of subsites to display.

- *Sites in Category*: This web part lists sites registered in the site directory associated with a selected category.

- *Table of Contents*: This web part lists the items displayed in the site's navigation, including any listed subsites.

Also available are many third-party web parts that provide site and content roll-up capabilities within SharePoint. These tools can be used in SharePoint Foundation and SharePoint Server. Adding web parts to pages and configuring them are discussed in Chapter 9.

Navigating Sites with Mobile Devices

SharePoint allows users with mobile devices, such as tablets and smart phones, to use the environment. There are four options for accessing SharePoint from mobile devices.

- *Contemporary view*: The contemporary view renders the SharePoint environment resources through an HTML5 mobile view. This view provides access to the SharePoint lists and libraries within the environment in a form compatible with mobile devices. Figure 3-4 shows the HTML5 mobile view.

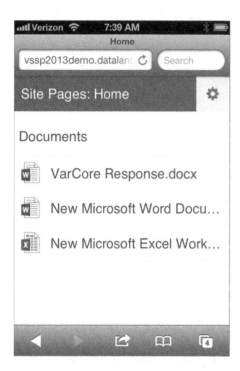

Figure 3-4. *Contemporary mobile view*

- *Classic view*: For mobile devices that cannot support HTML5, the classic view provides a standard HTML version of the mobile view. Like the contemporary view, the classic view provides access to the site's lists and libraries.

- *Full screen user interface*: The standard SharePoint interface can be configured for mobile devices. It provides the same layout and functionality on the mobile device as are available when the site is accessed from a standard web browser—assuming that the site's functionality is supported by the mobile browser.

- *Channels*: Alternative access interfaces can be defined for specific devices and web browser versions. These interfaces can be created for a mobile device or any other browser/device. When channels are used, an alternative master page is identified for use on the device, allowing a tailored display for that device. Channels are discussed in more detail later in this chapter.

The approach or approaches used to access the SharePoint environment from mobile devices are managed by a technical SharePoint Administrator.

■ **Note** Accessing sites using a mobile device requires configuring the SharePoint environment to make it available from the network the mobile device is connected to or connecting the mobile device to the network the SharePoint environment is connected to. Also, to open a document on a mobile or tablet device, there must be a program on it that can open the file.

Using the Ribbon

The ribbon is the main management interface for working with site resources. The ribbon provides context-centric options based on what is being viewed and whether you have permission to view the item. The available commands are organized under ribbon tabs. When a tab is selected, the associated commands are displayed on the ribbon. In the standard SharePoint layout, the ribbon commands appear over the navigation bar and title area. The ribbon always has a Browse tab that, when selected, hides the ribbon, making the navigation and title area visible again.

Ribbon tabs and options presented are context-sensitive based on the type of information displayed on the page. For example, if you select the Page tab while viewing a team site home page, the list of page management commands appears (see Figure 3-5). When you finish working with the ribbon commands, clicking the Browse tab will hide them, allowing the site title and navigation to be displayed.

Figure 3-5. *Page tab on the ribbon*

Creating Sites

Discussing the creation and management of sites in SharePoint 2013 needs to be broken down into two parts: creating root, or top-level, sites and creating subsites. A root site, the topmost site in a site collection, is created as part of the creation of the overall site collection. A subsite is a site created under an existing site. Sites can be nested to create any desired hierarchy. Subsites are created as needed by people with appropriate rights.

SharePoint root sites are typically created by a SharePoint technical administrator as part of creating a site collection. This discussion focuses on creating SharePoint subsites, which any individual having the Create Subsite right can do. By default, users with the Manage Hierarchy and Full Control permissions have this right.

Subsites can be created within any SharePoint root site or subsite. By default, Owners and Hierarchy Managers groups have the appropriate permission levels to create subsites. Managing permissions and groups is discussed later in this chapter.

To create a new subsite follow these steps:

1. Navigate to the site under which the new subsite is to be created.

2. Navigate to the Site Contents page, by selecting either the Site Content link from the Quick Launch area or the Site Contents option from the Settings menu, as seen in Figure 3-3.

3. On the Site Contents page, click the New Subsite option in the Subsites section.

4. On the New SharePoint Site page, execute the following steps:

    a. In the Title and Description section, enter the title to use for the site. This is the name that will be displayed in any reference to the site. You can also enter an optional description for the site.

    b. In the Web Site Address section, enter the URL for the site.

■ **Note**   It is considered a best practice to exclude spaces and special characters from the URL name of the site and for the URL and the site title to be similar. For example, if your site title is Human Resources, the URL name should be either HumanResources or HR.

---

    c.   In the Template Selection section, select the site template from which the new site should be created; the default site templates are grouped by type and have the features and layout detailed in Chapter 2.

    d.   In the Permissions section, specify whether the user access permissions for the site being created are to be the same as those of the parent site or whether unique permissions are to be used. If you choose to use the same permissions as the parent site, security will be inherited from the parent site (changing site permissions in the Managing Site Security section is discussed later in this chapter).

    e.   In the Navigation Inheritance section, select whether the new site's navigation bar is to inherit the options listed in the parent site's navigation bar or is to be managed within the subsite directly (managing the site navigation bar is discussed later in this chapter).

    f.   Once all of the necessary information has been entered or selected, click the Create button.

The subsite is created, and you are taken to the home page of the new subsite.

Deleting Sites

Anyone who has Hierarchy Manager or Full Control permissions within a site has the ability to delete the site. There are two ways to delete an existing SharePoint site. The first way is to delete it within that site's Site Settings page by performing the following steps:

1.   Navigate to the site you want to delete.

2.   From the Settings menu, select the Site Settings option.

3.   On the Site Settings page, in the Site Actions section, click the Delete This Site link.

4.   On the Delete This Site page, click the Delete button.

5.   On the deletion confirmation window, click the OK button.

The site is deleted, and you are taken to the Your Web Site Has Been Deleted page.

The second way to delete a site is found on the Sites and Workspaces page of the site's parent; that is, the site is deleted within its parent. This method can be used to delete only subsites, not the top-level site within a site collection. To delete a subsite within the Sites and Workspaces page, do the following:

1.   Navigate to the site containing the subsite you want to delete.

2.   From the Settings menu, select the Site Settings option.

3.   On the Site Settings page, in the Site Administration section, click the Sites and Workspaces link.

4.   On the Sites and Workspaces page, click the Delete icon for the subsite to be deleted.

5.   On the Delete This Site page, click the Delete button.

6.   In the deletion confirmation window, click the OK button.

The site is deleted, and you are returned to the Sites and Workspaces page. Sites can be deleted only when they do not contain subsites. If subsites are nested under the site being deleted, an error message will appear if you try to delete the site.

Managing Site Security

Management of security for a site is the responsibility of the site owner, who is responsible for assigning rights to users within their own sites. Rights are assigned either directly to a user or group (managed, by default, within an organization's Active Directory) or through SharePoint that users or groups are members of.

Security must be configured for every root site within SharePoint. By default, when a new root site is created, the user who created it will specify who the site collection administrators for the site will be, and these individuals will be the only people with access to the new site. These site collection administrators will then identify the users who are to be granted rights to the site and provide these users with the appropriate levels of access.

Subsites will either inherit their rights from the site in which they are contained or have unique permissions. The security approach used in a subsite is determined by the permission settings configured within the site. If security for a subsite is configured to be inherited from the parent site, security is not managed for the site directly; instead, security will be based on rights assigned in the parent site. If security for the subsite is configured to be unique, a site administrator will be required to assign the appropriate rights to individuals needing access to the site.

When you create your own site, it is important to understand the security needs of the individuals who will be using the site and to assign users the appropriate security to allow them to work with materials within the site.

Managing SharePoint Groups

SharePoint groups are used to combine user and group accounts to make security assignment easier. By default, user and group accounts are Active Directory users and Active Directory groups. User and group accounts will be assigned to SharePoint groups, and the SharePoint groups are then used to assign rights within sites. SharePoint groups can be used throughout a site collection hierarchy to assign rights within the various sites within the collection as well as to assign rights to contained lists and libraries. By default, when a new root site is created, a set of default SharePoint groups is also created. These groups are listed with their default permission levels in Table 3-1. Other SharePoint groups are created automatically when certain site collection or site features are enabled.

Table 3-1. *Default Security Groups*

Site Group	Default Permission Level	Purpose
Site Name Owners	Full Control	Contains users who can administer the site
Site Name Members	Edit, Contribute	Contains users who can create and edit content within the site's libraries and lists
Site Name Visitors	Read	Contains users who need the ability to view site content but not make changes
Approvers	Approve	Contains uses who have the ability to perform content approval for materials published within the site requiring approval
Designers	Design	Contains users who have the right to manage pages within the site, as well as the look and feel aspects of the site

(continued)

Table 3-1. (*continued*)

Site Group	Default Permission Level	Purpose
Hierarchy Managers	Manage Hierarchy	Contains users who can create subsites below the current site
Restricted Readers	Restricted Read	Contains users who can view site content but not look at previous versions or security information
Translation Managers	Restricted Interfaces for Translation	Contains users who can open lists and folders and use the remote interfaces
Excel Services Viewers	View Only	Contains users who can view the site but not interface with its contained content
Style Resource Readers	None in sit	Contains users who have read access to the Master Page Gallery and Style Library, which are required to browse the site

SharePoint groups can be created and customized to meet specific security needs within the SharePoint environment. In the next sections, how to manage SharePoint groups is discussed.

Creating SharePoint Groups

To create new SharePoint groups within SharePoint, do as follows:

1. Navigate to the site in which the group will be used.

2. On the site's home page, select the Site Settings option from the Settings menu.

3. On the Site Settings page, click the Site Permissions option from the Users and Permissions section.

4. On the Permissions page, select the Create Group command from the Permissions ribbon (see Figure 3-6).

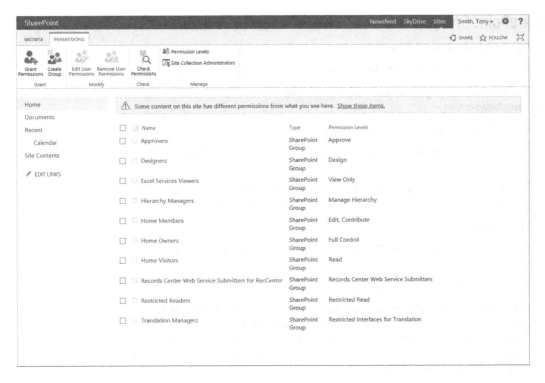

Figure 3-6. *Permissions page*

5. On the Create Group page, enter the following:

    a. In the Name and About Me Description section, enter the name for the new
        SharePoint group. You can also enter an optional About Me description. The About Me
        information is presented next to the name when the SharePoint Group is presented.

    b. If necessary, in the Owner section, update the SharePoint group owner information.
        The owner has the right to update the site's group information. By default, the owner
        is listed as the user creating the SharePoint group.

    c. In the Group Settings section, specify whether only group members or everyone has
        the ability to view group membership information. You can also define whether only
        the group owner or all group members can edit the group membership.

    d. In the Membership Requests section, specify whether users can request to join or
        leave the group and whether requests are to be automatically accepted. The e-mail
        address that requests should be sent to is also listed. This address can be changed
        when the Auto-accept Requests option is set to No. By default, the e-mail address will
        be set as the e-mail address of the user creating the group.

    e. If the current site does not inherit permissions from its parent, in the Give Group
        Permission to this Site section, select the permission level, if any, to grant the group
        within the current site.

    f. Once all of the necessary information has been entered, click the Create button.

The new SharePoint group is created, and you are taken to the new group's page, where you can add members.

Editing SharePoint Groups

To edit an existing SharePoint group, follow these steps:

1. On a site's home page, select the Site Settings option from the Settings menu.

2. On the Site Settings page, click the People and Groups option from the Users and Permissions section.

3. On the People and Groups page, do one of the following:

    a. Click the name of the group to edit in the Groups list located in the right-hand navigation area, click the Settings link, and select the Group Settings option.

    b. Alternatively, on this page, click the Groups header in the Groups list to present all groups, and click the Edit link next to the desired group name.

4. On the Change Group Settings page,

    a. In the Name and About Me Description section, you can update the group name or About Me details.

    b. In the Owner section, you can update the group owner.

    c. In the Group Settings section, you can update who can view the membership of the group, so that either only group members or everyone can view the group membership information; you can also update who can edit the membership of the group, so that either only the group owner or all group members are permitted to update the group membership.

    d. In the Membership Requests section, you can update whether people can request to join or leave the group and whether requests are to be automatically accepted; you can also update the e-mail address that requests are sent to.

    e. Once all information has been appropriately updated, click the OK button.

The SharePoint group is appropriately updated, and you are taken to the new group's page, where you can manage group members.

Deleting SharePoint Groups

Follow these steps to delete an existing SharePoint group:

1. On a site's home page, select the Site Settings option from the Settings menu.

2. On the Site Settings page, click the People and Groups option from the Users and Permissions section.

3. On the People and Groups page, do one of the following:

    a. Click the name of the group to delete in the Groups list located in the right-hand navigation area, click the Settings link, and select the Group Settings option.

    b. Alternatively, on this page, click the Groups header in the Groups list to present all groups, and click the Edit link next to the desired group name.

4. On the Change Group Settings page, click the Delete button.

5. On the deletion confirmation screen, click the OK button.

The SharePoint group is deleted, and you are taken to the Home Members group page.

Adding Users to SharePoint Groups

Add users to SharePoint groups as follows:

1.   Navigate to a site where the group is used .

2.   On the site's home page, select the Site Settings option from the Settings menu.

3.   On the Site Settings page, in the Users and Permissions section, click the People and Groups link.

4.   On the People and Groups page, do one of the following: click the name of the group from the Groups list, or click the Groups header and then the name of the group.

5.   On the People and Groups page, the membership will be displayed for the selected group. Click the arrow next to the New link to present the New menu.

6.   Select the Add Users option from the New menu.

7.   On the Grant Permissions screen,

   a.   In the Select Users section, enter the Active Directory users and groups to be added to the SharePoint group. As you type in the user or group information, matching entries, any of which can be selected, are listed below the entry box.

   b.   In the "Include a personal message…" section, enter text that would be included in a message to the added people.

   c.   The Show Options link can be clicked to show the "Send an email invitation" option, which identifies if an e-mail is to be sent to people added to the group.

   d.   once all users have been selected, click the Share button.

With users and groups added to the SharePoint group, you are returned to the group's page, where the members are managed.

Removing Users from a SharePoint Group

Use these steps to remove users from a SharePoint group.

1.   Navigate to a site where the group is used.

2.   On the site's home page, select the Site Settings option from the Settings menu.

3.   On the Site Settings page, in the Users and Permissions section, click the People and Groups link.

4.   On the People and Groups page, do one of the following: click the name of the group from the Groups list, or click the Groups header and then the name of the group.

5.   On the People and Groups page, the membership will be displayed for the selected group. Check the boxes in front of the users you wish to remove from the group, and click the Actions link to present the Actions menu.

6.   Select the Remove Users from Group option from the Actions menu.

7.   Confirm the removal of the users from the SharePoint group by clicking the OK button.

The selected users are removed from the SharePoint group, and the People and Groups page is updated to reflect the change.

Viewing SharePoint Group Permissions

Since SharePoint groups can be used across sites within a site collection, the ability to see all resources to which a group is assigned rights is very valuable. To view a group's permissions assignments, take the following steps:

1. On a site's home page, select the Site Settings option from the Settings menu.

2. On the Site Settings page, click the People and Groups option from the Users and Permissions section.

3. On the People and Groups page, click the name of the desired group in the Groups list located in the right-hand navigation.

4. On the People and Groups page, the membership will be displayed for the selected group. Select the Settings link to view the Settings menu options.

5. Select the View Group Permissions option from the Settings menu.

The View Site Collection Permissions window appears; it displays the sites, lists, and libraries where the group is assigned permissions and the permission levels assigned. Click any of the listed object names to go to the default page of an item.

Changing Permission Inheritance for a Site

As discussed, when you create a subsite, you have the ability to decide whether the subsite is to have unique permissions defined or whether it will inherit permissions from its parent site. After the site has been created, you can change this setting if security requirements for the subsite change. To change the permission inheritance settings for a subsite do the following:

1. Navigate to the site in which you need to change permission inheritance.

2. On the site's home page, select the Site Settings option from the Settings menu.

3. On the Site Settings page, click the Site Permissions option from the Users and Permissions section.

4. On the Permissions page, above the permission listings is a message identifying whether the site inherits permissions from its parent.

5. Update the permission inheritance as follows:

    a. If the site currently inherits permissions, the inheritance message will state "This web site inherits permissions from its parent." To stop inheriting permissions,

        i. Select the Stop Inheriting Permissions option from the Permissions ribbon.

        ii. Click the OK button on the confirmation message box.

        iii. On the Set Up Groups for this Site page, identify the default Visitor, Member, and Owner SharePoint groups for the site. For each, either select an existing SharePoint group or elect to create a new group. If you elect to create a new group, identify a name for the new group and the accounts to become members of the group.

        iv. Click the OK button to save.

b. If the site does not currently inherit permissions, the inheritance message will state "This web has unique permissions." To start inheriting permissions,

    i. Select the Delete Unique Permissions option from the Permissions ribbon.

    ii. Click the OK button on the confirmation message box.

The site permission inheritance settings are updated, and the Permissions page is refreshed to reflect the changes.

Managing Permission Levels

As discussed previously, SharePoint groups and individual users can be assigned permissions within SharePoint sites. When users are added, they are either assigned to a SharePoint group or granted rights through direct permission level assignments. How to manage permission level assignments to SharePoint groups was discussed in the "Managing SharePoint Groups" section.

Permission levels are sets of permissions grouped together to provide a specific level or class of rights within a site. There are six default permission levels in SharePoint Foundation and an additional six default levels when SharePoint Server is in place. The default permission levels in SharePoint include the following:

- SharePoint Foundation and SharePoint Server default permission levels:

  - *Full Control:* This permission level includes all available permissions and grants the assigned user administrative-level access to the site and all of the site's resources. This permission level cannot be changed or deleted from SharePoint.

  - *Design:* The Design permission level provides the ability to manage lists, libraries, and pages within a SharePoint site, as well as approve content and manage the site's look and feel.

  - *Edit:* This permission level allows the creation and management of libraries and listsand their contained content.

  - *Contribute:* This permission level provides the ability to manage content in a site's lists and libraries.

  - *Read:* The Read permission level provides read-only access to site resources.

  - *Limited Access:* This permission level is designed to be combined with list or library permissions to provide access only to specific lists and libraries within a site without granting rights to any of its other resources. This permission level cannot be changed or deleted from SharePoint. Nor can it be manually set. It is assigned by SharePoint only on the basis of other rights configurations.

- Default permission levels in SharePoint Server only:

  - *View Only:* As with the Read permission level, with this permission users can view pages, list items, and documents. However, with View Only permission, users can view these files only with an online viewer, such as viewing Microsoft Office documents through Office Web Applications. Files cannot be downloaded.

  - *Approve:* The Approve permission level grants the ability to edit and approve pages, list items, and documents when content is configured to require approval.

  - *Manage Hierarchy:* This permission level, which is similar to Contribute, allows the management of site content but adds the ability to create and manage subsites.

- *Restricted Read:* The Restricted Read permission level limits Read access in a site to viewing of pages, documents, and list items only—not viewing of item version history details or permissions information.

- *Restricted Interface for Translation:* This permission level is used when individuals or systems need only rights to translate content. It allows lists and folders to be opened and allows access by remote interfaces.

- *Record Center Web Service Submitters:* This permission level allows submittal of content to a site without providing higher levels of access, such as reading or editing, to the site.

Permission levels can be assigned to site users or groups as well as SharePoint Groups. To assign permission levels to a site user or group, do the following:

1. Navigate to the site where permissions need to be assigned. This should be a site where permissions are not inherited from the parent site.

2. On the site's home page, select Site Settings from the Settings menu.

3. On the Site Settings page, select the Site Permissions option from the Users and Permissions section.

4. On the Permissions page, click the Grant Permissions command on the Permissions tab of the ribbon.

5. In the Grant Permissions window, enter the following information:

    a. In the Invite People to Edit, Contribute section, select the users and groups to be assigned rights.

    b. If you do not want to add the entered users to the Contribute SharePoint group for the site, click the Show Options link to select a different group or permission level to which to assign rights.

    c. Once all the information has been selected, click the save button to save the rights.

The users and groups are assigned to the selected permission level or SharePoint group and you are returned to the Permissions page.

Adding Permission Levels

With SharePoint, permission levels can be created to meet specific security needs. To create a new permission level do the following:

1. Navigate to a site with unique permissions and where you are the administrator.

2. On the site's home page, select Site Settings from the Settings menu.

3. On the Site Settings page, select the Site Permissions option from the Users and Permissions section.

4. On the Permissions page, select the Permission Levels option from the Permissions ribbon tab.

5. On the Permission Levels page, click the Add a Permission Level link.

6. On the Add a Permission Level page, enter the following:

   a. In the Name and Description section, enter the name of the new permission level You can also enter an optional description. The description is presented next to the name when the permission level is listed for selection.

   b. In the Permissions section, check the boxes for all permissions that the new permission level should include. Choose the Select All option to add all the listed permissions.

   c. Once all of the necessary information has been entered, click the Create button.

The new permission level is created, and you are returned to the Permission Levels page.

Creating a New Permission Level As a Copy of an Existing Permission Level

When there is the need for a new permission level that closely mirrors an existing permission level, you can make a copy of the existing item to use as a starting point in creating the new permission level. Create a new permission level as a copy of an existing permission level as follows:

1. Navigate to a site with unique permissions and where you are the administrator.

2. On the site's home page, select Site Settings from the Settings menu.

3. On the Site Settings page, select the Site Permissions option from the Users and Permissions section.

4. On the Permissions page, select the Permission Levels option from the Permissions ribbon tab.

5. If the current site is not the root site in the site collection, a link will be available, under See Also in the left navigation area, called Manage Permission Levels on Parent Web Site. Click this link.

6. On the Permission Levels page, click the name of the permission level to copy.

7. On the Edit Permission Level page, click the Copy Permission Level button.

8. On the Copy Permission Level page, enter the following:

   a. In the Name and Description section, enter the name for the new permission level You can also enter an optional description.

   b. In the Permission section, update the permissions set for the permission level as appropriate.

   c. Once all of the necessary information has been entered and updated, click the Create button.

The new permission level is created, and you are returned to the Permission Level page.

Edit Existing Permission Levels

To edit an existing permission level, do as follows:

1. Navigate to a site with unique permissions and where you are the administrator.

2. On the site's home page, select Site Settings from the Settings menu.

3. On the Site Settings page select the Site Permissions option from the Users and Permissions section.

4. On the Permissions page, select the Permission Levels option from the Permissions ribbon tab.

5. If the current site is not the root site in the site collection, a link will be available, under See Also in the left navigation area, called Manage Permission Levels on Parent Web Site. Click this link.

6. On the Permission Levels page, click the name of the permission level to update.

7. On the Edit Permission Level page, update the following:

    a. In the Name and Description section, edit the permission level name and optional description text.

    b. In the Permissions section, update the permissions set for the permission level as appropriate.

    c. Once all of the necessary updates have been made, click the Submit button.

The permission level is updated, and you are returned to the Permission Level page.

Deleting Existing Permission Levels

To delete an existing permission level, take these steps:

1. Navigate to a site with unique permissions and where you are the administrator.

2. On the site's home page, select Site Settings from the Settings menu.

3. On the Site Settings page, select the Site Permissions option from the Users and Permissions section.

4. On the Permissions page, select the Permission Levels option from the Permissions ribbon tab.

5. If the current site is not the root site in the site collection, a link will be available, under See Also in the left navigation area, called Manage Permission Levels on Parent Web Site. Click this link.

6. On the Permission Levels page, check the boxes for all permission levels you want to delete, and click the Delete Selected Permission Levels link.

7. On the delete confirmation screen, click the OK button.

The permission level is deleted, and the Permission Level page is updated to reflect the change.

Managing Site Collection Administrators

The discussion so far has concerned how to manage SharePoint groups and permission levels to control the rights individuals have in the SharePoint environment. Defining site collection administrators extends security management by allowing identification of the individuals responsible for managing the overall environment. These individuals are automatically given administrative rights across the entire site collection hierarchy.

Follow these steps to manage site collection administrators:

1. Navigate to the top-level site.

2. On the site's home page, select Site Settings from the Settings menu.

3. On the Site Settings page, in the Users and Permissions section, click the Site Collection Administrators link.

4. On the Site Collection Administrators page, enter and remove users.

    a. To remove a user, click the x following the name of the account to remove.

    b. To add a user, type the name to be added and select the correct account from the type-ahead listing presented.

5. Once the list of users is correct, click the OK button to save the information.

The site collection administrators are updated, and you are returned to the Site Settings page.

Changing Site Details

There are several aspects of a SharePoint site that the site administrator can update as the need arises. For example, updatable information includes the title and description entered when the site was created. Being able to update site details is important as the site's needs change over time.

Updating the Site Title, Description, Logo, and URL

The site title, description, and URL entered when the site was created can be updated. Also, the site logo, the image that appears at the top of the created site, can be replaced. This allows the site to be properly branded for the organization or group it is created to support. To update the site title and description information entered when the site was created and the logo appearing at the top of the site, take these steps:

1. Navigate to the site to be updated.

2. On the site's home page, select Site Settings from the Settings menu.

3. On the Site Settings page, in the Look and Feel section, click the Title, Description, and Logo link.

4. On the Title, Description, and Logo page, update the following information:

    a. In the Title and Description section, update the site title and description information as needed.

    b. In the Logo and Description section, select a logo either from your computer or from SharePoint. Selecting the From Computer option allows you to upload a file to SharePoint for use as the site logo. Selecting a file in this way uploads the file to the site's Site Assets library and references it as the logo. Selecting the From SharePoint option opens the Select an Asset page, where a logo already in SharePoint can be chosen as the logo for the site. You can also enter a description to use as alternative text for the logo. The description is displayed when the mouse hovers over the logo.

    c. When you update information for a site other than the root site in the site collection, the Web Site Address section is listed. In this section the URL entered when the site was created can be updated.

    d. Once all updates have been made, click the OK button to save the changes.

The updates are applied to the site, and you are returned to the Site Settings page.

Configuring Regional Settings for a Site

SharePoint sites are designed for use throughout an organization. As a result, there are times when a site created within SharePoint is primarily used in time zones other than the one where the SharePoint server is located. For example, a team located in California might use a SharePoint site to manage a project's resources, but the SharePoint servers are located in the company's New York office. In such a case, site managers might wish to update the site's regional settings so that date and time displays are based on the users' locale instead of the server's location. To change a site's regional settings, do as follows:

1. Navigate to the site where the settings need to be changed.

2. From the site's home page, select the Site Settings option from the Settings menu.

3. On the Site Settings page, select the Regional Settings link from the Site Administration section.

4. On the Regional Settings page, update the following as appropriate:

   a. Time Zone: Select the standard time zone to use for determining date and time for activities performed.

   b. Locale: Specify the site's default location to determine how numbers and dates are presented.

   c. Sort Order: Identify sorting preferences to be used within the site.

   d. Calendar: Determine the calendar format for the site and whether week numbering is displayed in the date navigator.

   e. Enable an Alternate Calendar: Specify, if needed, a secondary calendar format to make this alternate information available in the site.

   f. Define Your Work Week: Specify the days of the workweek, the first day of the week, the first week of the year, and the start and ending time of the workday.

   g. Time Format: Specify the time format to be displayed (12- or 24-hour).

   h. Subsite settings: Identify whether the subsite (the site below the current site) should inherit the site settings.

   i. Once all other information has been appropriately updated, click the OK button to save the settings.

Updated settings will be saved, and you will be returned to the Site Settings page.

Defining the Welcome Page

The welcome page is the initial page displayed when you navigate to a site. SharePoint Server provides capabilities to the SharePoint environment that allow selection of the site's welcome page. The initial page does not have to be the site's default page. Any other page within the site can be the entry page. In fact, the welcome page for many SharePoint Server site templates is not the standard default.aspx page. It is often a page from the site's Pages library or SitePages library. Being able to change a site's welcome page to a page from a site's library lets you apply content approval and management rules to this page as you would to other site content.

To update the default welcome page for a site, follow these steps:

1. Navigate to the site where you wish to change the welcome page.

2. From the site's home page, select the Site Settings option from the Settings menu.

3.   On the Site Settings page, in the Look and Feel section, click the Welcome Page link.

4.   On the Site Welcome Page screen, enter the URL for the welcome page for the site, or click the Browse button to locate the appropriate page. Once the page is identified, click the OK button.

The site's welcome page is updated, and you are returned to the Site Settings page.

Managing Site Navigation

SharePoint sites contain two areas of navigation options, the Quick Launch and the navigation bar. The Quick Launch, located by default to the left of the site's content area, is typically used to list resources located in and under the current site: key lists, libraries, subsites, and so on. The navigation bar, by default, is located at the top of the content area. It is typically used to provide the site's global or standard navigation options, and it provides consistency in navigation within the site collection. In this section both these navigation resources are discussed, and how to manage the options contained within them is described.

Customizing Quick Launch Navigation for Sites

The Quick Launch menu, which typically includes navigation options within a site, can be managed by users with Design or Full Control rights. Management of Quick Launch navigation varies based on whether SharePoint Foundation or SharePoint Server is being used with the SharePoint Server Publishing Infrastructure site collection feature active within an environment.

Configuring the Quick Launch Display: Tree View and Standard View

The Quick Launch area has two displays that can be presented: standard view and tree view. Quick Launch view settings are managed through the Tree View options, which let you determine which of the views is included in the Quick Launch area. By default, the standard Quick Launch is enabled, displaying a set of links that access specified site lists, libraries, and subsites, as well as identified custom links. Standard Quick Launch can be seen in Figure 3-7. If this option is disabled, Quick Launch links are removed from the area, leaving only the Site Contents link.

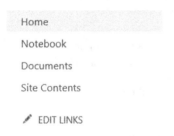

Figure 3-7. *Quick Launch standard view*

When tree view is enabled in the Quick Launch area, the Tree View Tool is placed in the area. The Tree View Tool lists all sites, libraries, and lists within the current site. The tool provides the ability to expand the listed subsites to view their contained lists, libraries, and subsites. Tree view is shown in Figure 3-8.

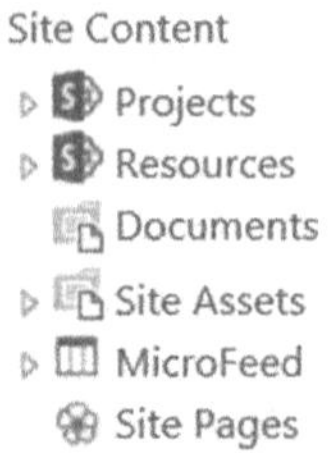

Site Content
 ▷ 🔷 Projects
 ▷ 🔷 Resources
    📑 Documents
 ▷ 📑 Site Assets
 ▷ ▭ MicroFeed
    ✿ Site Pages

Figure 3-8. *Quick Launch tree view*

Standard and Tree views for the Quick Launch menu can be managed as follows:

1. Navigate to the site to be updated.

2. On the site's home page, select Site Settings from the Settings menu.

3. On the Site Settings page, in the Look and Feel section, click the Tree View link.

4. On the Tree View page, update the following:

   a. In the Enable Quick Launch section, check or uncheck the Enable Quick Launch option to enable or disable the Quick Launch standard view.

   b. In the Enable Tree View section, check or uncheck the Enable Tree View option to enable or disable the Quick Launch tree view.

   c. Once all options are properly set, click the OK button.

The updates to the site are applied, and you are returned to the Site Settings page.

Configuring Quick Launch Options

While you can use the Tree View options discussed previously to determine which views are made available within Quick Launch, the available options can also be managed. Items can be reordered, and listed headings and links can be added, updated, or removed tailoring Quick Launch to help meet the navigation needs of your site.

Changing the Order of Quick Launch Items

Three options are available for managing Quick Launch menu items. The options differ based on whether the SharePoint Server Publishing Infrastructure feature is active. The first option, which is always available in SharePoint, allows navigation items to be managed directly in the Quick Launch menu.

To manage Quick Launch navigation items directly from the home page of the site, do the following:

1. Navigate to the site where you want to manage the Quick Launch menu.

2. On the site's home page, click the Edit Links option at the bottom of the Quick Launch area to place the links in Edit mode (see Figure 3-9).

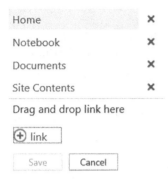

Figure 3-9. Quick Launch Edit mode

3. To reorder the listed items, drag and drop them into the appropriate order.

4. Once all items are in the appropriate order, click the Save option to save the changes made.

The changes to the Quick Launch menu are saved, and the Quick Launch menu returns to its standard view.

The second way to reorder Quick Launch options is through the Quick Launch management page, which is available in the Site Setting area when using SharePoint Foundation or using SharePoint Server without the SharePoint Server Publishing Infrastructure feature enabled. To edit the order of Quick Launch items through the Quick Launch management page, do as follows:

1. Navigate to the site where you want to manage the Quick Launch menu.

2. Select the Site Settings option from the Settings menu.

3. On the Site Settings page, select the Quick Launch option from the Look and Feel section.

4. On the Quick Launch page, select the Change Order option.

5. On the Quick Launch Change Order page, select the order numbers in front of the listed options to the desired order.

6. Once all items are set to the appropriate order, choose the OK button to save the changes.

The changes to the Quick Launch order are saved and you are returned to the Quick Launch page.

When SharePoint Server is used with the SharePoint Server Publishing Infrastructure feature enabled, the Quick Launch management option is not available in the Site Settings page. Instead, the Navigation option is available. This option is used to manage both the Quick Launch options and the navigation bar. To manage the order of Quick Launch through the Navigation option, do the following:

1. Navigate to the site where you want to manage the Quick Launch menu.

2. Select the Site Settings option from the Settings menu.

3. On the Site Settings page, select the Navigation option from the Look and Feel section.

4. On the Navigation Settings page, in the Structural Navigation Editing and Sorting section, highlight the options to be reordered and select the Move Down and Move Up options to reorder them.

5. Once the items are in the proper order, select the OK button to save the changes.

The changes will be saved, and you will be returned to the Site Settings page.

Adding New Headings and Links to the Quick Launch

As with reordering Quick Launch options, adding new headers and links can be done in three different ways. The first way to add new headers and links to Quick Launch is from within the Quick Launch area itself. To update the Quick Launch options in this way, do the following:

1. Navigate to the site where you want to manage the Quick Launch menu.

2. On the site's home page, click the Edit Links option at the bottom of the Quick Launch area to place the links in Edit mode (see Figure 3-9).

3. Click the + Link option at the bottom of the Quick Launch area.

4. In the Add a Link window, enter the following:

   a. In the Text to Display field, enter the text to appear in Quick Launch to represent the item.

   b. In the Address field, optionally enter the URL for the item to navigate to when clicked. When a URL is not entered, the item will be a header that cannot be clicked as a link.

   c. Click the OK button to save the information.

5. Click Save at the bottom of the Quick Launch to save the changes.

The changes to the Quick Launch menu are saved, and the Quick Launch menu is returned to standard view.

The second way to add new headings and links to Quick Launch is through the Quick Launch management page. As described earlier, this page is available through the Site Setting area when using SharePoint Foundation or using SharePoint Server without the SharePoint Server Publishing Infrastructure feature enabled. To edit the order of Quick Launch items through the Quick Launch management page, do as follows:

1. Navigate to the site where you want to manage the Quick Launch menu.

2. Select the Site Settings option from the Settings menu.

3. On the Site Settings page, select the Quick Launch option from the Look and Feel section.

4. On the Quick Launch page, do the following:

   a. To add a new link,

      i. Select the New Navigation Link option.

      ii. On the New Navigation Link page, enter the URL and description for the new link, select the header under which the link should be created, and click the OK button to save the new link.

   b. To add a new header,

      i. Select the New Heading option.

      ii. On the New Heading page, enter the optional URL and the description for the new header, and then click the OK button to save the new header.

   The new header or link is saved, and you are returned to the Quick Launch page.

When SharePoint Server is used with the SharePoint Server Publishing Infrastructure feature enabled, navigation options are managed through the Navigation Settings page. To add items to the Quick Launch through the Navigation Settings page, do the following:

1. Navigate to the site where you want to manage the Quick Launch menu.

2. Select the Site Settings option from the Settings menu.

3. On the Site Settings page, select the Navigation option from the Look and Feel section.

4. On the Navigation Settings page, in the Structural Navigation: Editing and Sorting section, do the following:

    a. To add a new link,

        i. Click the Add Link option.

        ii. On the Navigation Link menu, enter the Title and URL for the link, specify whether the link is to open in a new window, and enter an optional description for the link. You can also specify the audiences (users or groups) the link is targeted to. If you target a link to a user or group, the link is presented only to that user or group. Once all information has been entered, click the OK button to save the new link.

    b. To add a new header,

        i. Click the Add Heading link option.

        ii. On the Navigation Heading menu, enter the title for the heading, specify whether the link is to open in a new window, and enter an optional URL and description for the header. You can also specify the audiences (users or groups) the header is targeted to. If you target a header to a user or group, the header is presented only to that user or group. Once all information has been entered, click the OK button to save the new header.

5. On the Navigation Settings page, click the OK button to save the changes to the navigation.

The changes will be saved, and you will be returned to the Site Settings page.

Editing Headings and Links in Quick Launch

The first way to edit existing headers and links to the Quick Launch can be done from within the Quick Launch area itself. To update the Quick Launch options in this way do the following:

1. Navigate to the site where you want to manage the Quick Launch menu.

2. On the sire's home page, click the Edit Links option at the bottom of the Quick Launch area to place the links in Edit mode (see Figure 3-9).

3. Click the item to edit to highlight it. Then with the item highlighted, click the Edit Link icon displayed, as seen in Figure 3-10.

Figure 3-10. *Quick Launch with highlighted item*

4. In the Edit Link window, update the Text to Display and URL information as appropriate.

5. Once all information is updated, click the OK button to save the changes.

6. Click Save at the bottom of Quick Launch to save the changes.

The changes to the Quick Launch menu are saved, and the Quick Launch menu returns to standard view.

The second way to edit Quick Launch headings and links is through the Quick Launch management page. As described earlier, this page is accessible from the Site Setting page when using SharePoint Foundation or using SharePoint Server without the SharePoint Server Publishing Infrastructure feature enabled. To edit Quick Launch items, do the following:

1. Navigate to the site where you want to manage the Quick Launch menu.

2. Select the Site Settings option from the Settings menu.

3. On the Site Settings page, select the Quick Launch option from the Look and Feel section.

4. On the Quick Launch page, click the Edit icon in front of the item to edit (see Figure 3-11).

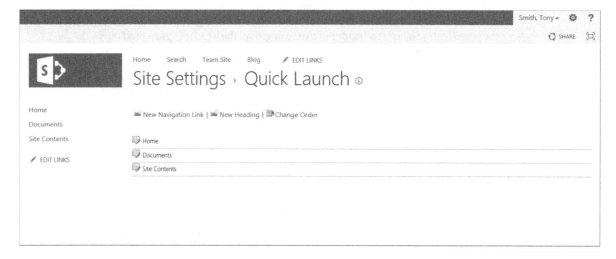

Figure 3-11. *Quick Launch management page*

5. In the Edit Navigation Link window, update the web address and description information as appropriate, and click OK to save the item.

6. Once all information is updated, click the OK button to save the changes.

The updated header or link is saved, and you are returned to the Quick Launch page.

When SharePoint Server is used with the SharePoint Server Publishing Infrastructure feature enabled, the navigation options are managed through the Navigation Settings page. To edit items in Quick Launch through the Navigation Settings page, do the following:

1. Navigate to the site where you want to manage the Quick Launch menu.

2. Select the Site Settings option from the Settings menu.

3. On the Site Settings page, select the Navigation option from the Look and Feel section.

4. On the Navigation Settings page, in the Structural Navigation: Editing and Sorting section, highlight the item to edit and click the Edit link.

5. In the opened Navigation Heading or Navigation Link window, update the details as appropriate, and click the OK button.

6. On the Navigation Settings page, click the OK button to save the changes to the navigation.

The changes will be save, and you will be returned to the Site Settings page.

Delete Headings and Links in Quick Launch

The first way to delete existing headers and links from Quick Launch is to do so within the Quick Launch area. To delete existing Quick Launch options in this way, do the following:

1. Navigate to the site where you want to manage the Quick Launch menu.

2. On the site's home page, click the Edit Links option at the bottom of the Quick Launch area to place the links in Edit mode (see Figure 3-9).

3. Click the x following the listed header or link.

4. Click Save at the bottom of the Quick Launch to save the changes.

The changes to the Quick Launch menu are saved, and the Quick Launch menu returns to standard view.

The second way to delete Quick Launch headings and links is through the Quick Launch management page when using SharePoint Foundation or SharePoint Server without the SharePoint Server Publishing Infrastructure feature enabled. To delete Quick Launch items, do the following:

1. Navigate to the site where you want to manage the Quick Launch menu.

2. Select the Site Settings option from the Settings menu.

3. On the Site Settings page, select the Quick Launch option from the Look and Feel section.

4. On the Quick Launch page, click the Edit icon in front of the item (see Figure 3-11).

5. In the Edit Navigation Link window, click the Delete button to delete the item.

6. In the confirmation window, click OK to confirm deletion of the item.

The selected header or link is deleted, and you are returned to the Quick Launch page.

When SharePoint Server is used with the SharePoint Server Publishing Infrastructure feature enabled, navigation options are managed through the Navigation Settings page. To delete items in Quick Launch from the Navigation Settings page, do the following:

1. Navigate to the site where you want to delete the Quick Launch item.

2. Select the Site Settings option from the Settings menu.

3. On the Site Settings page, select the Navigation option from the Look and Feel section.

4. On the Navigation Settings page, in the Structural Navigation: Editing and Sorting section, highlight the item to delete and click the Delete link.

5. On the Navigation Settings page, click the OK button to save the changes to the navigation.

The changes will be saved, and you will be returned to the Site Settings page.

■ **Caution** If you delete a Quick Launch heading that contains links, the links under the heading will also be removed from Quick Launch. If you wish to delete a header with links without removing the links under the header, first move the links out from under the heading.

Customizing the Navigation Bar

The SharePoint navigation bar is the main navigation tool for a SharePoint portal. Navigation can be based on either a site's structure or a customized set of metadata terms managed through a term set. In this section, how to configure and manage navigation within the site is discussed.

In talking about creating sites, we discussed how to choose whether the navigation bar should inherit its options from the parent site, list its own options based on the structure under the site, or based options on a term set. These settings can be updated and the navigation bar further customized through the site's navigation management tools.

Updating Navigation Bar Inheritance Settings

How you update the navigation bar within a SharePoint site depends on whether you are using SharePoint Foundation or SharePoint Server and, in SharePoint Server, whether the SharePoint Server Publishing Infrastructure site collection feature is enabled. The inheritance settings for the navigation bar determine the options presented in global navigation. To change the navigation bar inheritance settings in SharePoint Foundation or when SharePoint Server is in use with the SharePoint Server Publishing Infrastructure feature disabled, do the following:

1. Navigate to the subsite where you want to update the navigation bar's inheritance settings.

2. Select the Site Settings option from the Settings menu.

3. On the Site Setting page, select the Top Link Bar option from the Look and Feel section.

4. On the Top Link Bar page, update the inheritance settings as follows:

    a. If the site is currently inheriting its options from the parent site, click the Stop Inheriting Links option. The navigation bar will become manageable within the current site.

    b. If the site is currently managing its own navigation options, click the Use Links from Parent option, and then click OK on the confirmation screen. This will cause the navigation bar to inherit its options from the parent site.

The navigation inheritance settings will be updated. If SharePoint Server with the SharePoint Server Publishing Infrastructure feature enabled is in use, the navigation bar inheritance options are managed as follows:

1. Navigate to the subsite where you want to update the navigation bar's inheritance settings.

2. Select the Site Settings option from the Settings menu.

3. On the Site Settings Page, in the Look and Feel section, select the Navigation option.

4. On the Navigation Settings page, in the Global Navigation section, select the desired display option:

    a. If you wish the site to inherit navigation options from the parent site, select the "Display the same navigation items as the parent site" option. You can also specify whether subsites or pages are included in the navigation bar.

    b. If you wish the site to manage its own navigation options, select the "Structural Navigation: Display the navigation items below the current site" option. You can also specify whether subsites and whether pages are included in the navigation bar.

    c. If you wish the site to use a set of terms in a term store as the navigation options, select "Managed Navigation: The navigation items will be represented using a Managed Metadata term set," and then, in the Managed Navigation: Term Set section, select the term set to use.

5. Once the navigation inheritance options have been selected, click the OK button to save the settings and return to the Site Settings page.

The navigation inheritance settings will be updated, and you are returned to the Site Settings page.

Changing the Order of Navigation Bar Items

The order of navigation bar items can be managed directly on the site's navigation bar or through the navigation management tools, which include the Top Link Bar options in SharePoint Foundation or SharePoint Server with the SharePoint Server Publishing Infrastructure feature disabled or through the navigation settings in SharePoint Server with the SharePoint Server Publishing Infrastructure feature enabled.

To update navigation item order directly on the navigation bar, do the following:

1. Navigate to the site where you want to manage the navigation items.

2. On the site's home page, click the Edit Links option to the right of the navigation bar items to place the links in Edit mode (see Figure 3-12).

Figure 3-12. *Navigation bar management options*

3. To reorder the listed items, drag and drop them into the appropriate order.

4. Once all items are in the appropriate order, click Save to save the changes made.

The changes to the navigation menu are saved, and the menu returns to standard view.

The second way to reorder navigation bar options is through the Top Link Bar management page, which is available in the Site Setting area when using SharePoint Foundation or SharePoint Server with the SharePoint Server Publishing Infrastructure feature disabled. To edit the order of navigation bar items through the Top Link Bar management page, do the following:

1. Navigate to the site where you want to manage the navigation menu.

2. Select the Site Settings option from the Settings menu.

3. On the Site Settings page, select the Top Link Bar option from the Look and Feel section.

4. On the Top Link Bar page, select the Change Order option.

5. On the Top Link Bar Change Order page, select the order numbers by the listed options in the desired order.

6. Once all items are set to the appropriate order, choose the OK button to save the changes.

The changes to the navigation bar order are saved, and you are returned to the Top Link Bar page.

When SharePoint Server with the SharePoint Server Publishing Infrastructure feature enabled is in use, the Top Link Bar management option is not available in the Site Settings page. Instead, all navigation options are managed through the Navigation Settings page. To manage the order of navigation bar items when SharePoint Server is in place, do as follows:

1. Navigate to the site where you want to manage navigation menu options.

2. Select the Site Settings option from the Settings menu.

3. On the Site Settings page, select the Navigation option from the Look and Feel section.

4. On the Navigation Settings page, in the Structural Navigation: Editing and Sorting section, highlight the options you wish to reorder and select the Move Down and Move Up options to reorder the items.

5. Once the items are in the proper order, click the OK button to save the changes.

The changes will be saved, and you will be returned to the Site Settings page.

■ **Note**   When headers are available, moving items up and down will also allow moving links under available headers.

Adding New Headings and Links to the Navigation Bar

When the navigation bar is not inherited from the parent site and not based on a term set, you can customize options to meet your site's navigation requirements. There are three different ways to add new headings and links to the navigation bar. The options available depend on the version of SharePoint in use and whether SharePoint Server Publishing Infrastructure features are enabled on the site.

The first way to add options to the navigation bar is directly from the navigation bar itself. This method is available in all versions of SharePoint. To add new heading and links to the navigation bar using the navigation bar management tools, do the following:

1. Navigate to the site where you want to add navigation options.

2. Click the Edit Links option to show the editing options for the navigation bar (see Figure 3-12).

3. Click the +Link option to add a new link.

4. In the Add a Link window, enter the Text to Display as the option and the optional address information, and then click the OK button.

5. Click the Save button to save the navigation updates.

The new header or link will be added, and the navigation bar will return to standard view.

A second way to add options to the navigation bar is available when using SharePoint Foundation or when SharePoint Server with the SharePoint Server Publishing Infrastructure feature disabled is in use. This second method leverages the Top Link Bar management options as follows:

1. Navigate to the site where you want to add navigation options.

2. On the site's home page, choose the Site Settings option from the Settings menu.

3. On the Site Settings page, select the Top Link Bar option from the Look and Feel section.

4. On the Top Link Bar page, select the New Navigation Link option.

5. On the New Navigation Link page, enter the web address and description for the new option and click the OK button.

The new link will be added, and you will be returned to the Site Settings page.

A third approach to add options to the navigation bar is used in SharePoint Server with the SharePoint Server Publishing Infrastructure feature enabled. In this case the navigation bar is managed through the navigation management options. To add headers and links to the navigation bar in this way, do the following:

1. Navigate to the site where you want to add navigation options.

2. On the site's home page, choose the Site Settings option from the Settings menu.

3. On the Site Settings page, select the Navigation option from the Look and Feel section.

4. On the Navigation Settings page, in the Structural Navigation: Editing and Sorting section, do the following:

    a. To add a new link to the navigation bar,

        i.   Highlight the Global Navigation item.

        ii. Click the Add Link option.

        iii. On the Navigation Link menu, enter the title and URL for the link, specify whether the link is to open in a new window, and enter an optional description for the link. You can also specify the audiences (users or groups) the link is targeted to. If you target a link to a user or group, the link is presented only to that user or group. Once all information has been entered, click the OK button to save the new link.

    b. To add a new header to the navigation bar,

        i.   Highlight the Global Navigation item.

        ii. Click the Add Heading link option.

        iii. On the Navigation Heading menu, enter the title for the heading, specify whether the link is to open in a new window, and enter an optional URL and description for the header. You can also specify the audiences (users or groups) the header is targeted to. If you target a header to a user or group, the header is presented only to that user or group. Once all information has been entered, click the OK button to save the new header.

5. On the Navigation Settings page, click the OK button to save the changes to the navigation.

The changes will be saved, and you will be returned to the Site Settings page.

Edit Headings and Links to the Navigation Bar

As with adding items, editing items in the navigation bar is available when the navigation bar is not inherited from the parent site and not based on a term set. The three different options for editing headings and links in the navigation bar depend on the version of SharePoint in use and whether the SharePoint Server Publishing Infrastructure feature is enabled.

The first way to edit options in the navigation bar is directly from the bar itself. This method is available in all versions of SharePoint. Only custom links and headers can be edited directly from this view. Site and page references listed here cannot be edited. To edit the navigation bar's heading and links using navigation bar management tools, do the following:

1. Navigate to the site where you want to edit navigation options.

2. Click the Edit Links option to show the edit options for the navigation bar (see Figure 3-12).

3. Click the custom link or header to edit to show the Edit Link option, as seen in Figure 3-13.

Figure 3-13. *Navigation bar Edit Link option*

4. Click the Edit Link option for the navigation item to be edit.

5. In the Edit Link window, update the Text to Display and Address information as appropriate, and click the OK button.

6. Click the Save button to save the navigation updates.

The header or link is updated, and the navigation bar returns to standard view.

A second method for editing options in the navigation bar is available when SharePoint Foundation or SharePoint Server with the SharePoint Server Publishing Infrastructure feature disabled is in place. Edit through Top Link Bar management options by doing the following:

1. Navigate to the site where you want to edit navigation options.

2. On the site's home page, choose the Site Settings option from the Settings menu.

3. On the Site Settings page, select the Top Link Bar option from the Look and Feel section.

4. On the Top Link Bar page, select the Edit icon for the navigation item to be edited.

5. On the Edit Navigation Link page, update the item's web address and description as appropriate, and click the OK button.

The link will be edited, and you will be returned to the Site Settings page.

A third approach to edit options in the navigation bar is available only in SharePoint Server with the SharePoint Server Publishing Infrastructure feature enabled. In this case navigation management is handled through the Navigation Settings. The only editable options are custom headers and navigation elements, not those representing sites and pages within the current site. To edit navigation bar headers and links in this way, do as follows:

1. Navigate to the site where you want to edit navigation options.

2. On the site's home page, choose the Site Settings option from the Settings menu.

3. On the Site Settings page, select the Navigation option from the Look and Feel section.

4. On the Navigation Settings page, in the Structural Navigation: Editing and Sorting section, do the following:

   a. Highlight the custom link or header to be edited.

   b. Click the Edit option.

   c. In the Navigation Link or Navigation Heading window, update the information as appropriate, and click the OK button to save the changes.

5. On the Navigation Settings page, click the OK button to save the changes to the navigation.

The changes will be saved, and you will be returned to the Site Settings page.

Deleting and Hiding Headings and Links on the Navigation Bar

There are three approaches to deleting and hiding links in the navigation bar. Not all links can be deleted. Items representing sites and pages must be hidden to remove them from the navigation bar.

The first way to hide or delete navigation options is directly from the navigation bar itself. This method is available in all versions of SharePoint. To remove or hide headings and links in the navigation bar with navigation bar management tools, do the following:

1. Navigate to the site where you want to remove navigation options.

2. Click the Edit Links option to show the Edit options for the navigation bar (see Figure 3-12).

3. To the right of the navigation option is either the hide option (an eye) or the delete option (an x). To hide or delete the listed item, click the hide or delete option.

   a. If hiding the item, the hide option changes from an eye to a hyphen (-).

   b. If deleting an item, the item is removed completely from the navigation bar.

4. Click the Save button to save the navigation updates.

The navigation bar returns to standard view.

A second method for deleting or hiding options in the navigation bar is available with SharePoint Foundation or with SharePoint Server with the SharePoint Server Publishing Infrastructure feature disabled. To delete the options through Top Link Bar management options, doing the following:

1. Navigate to the site where you want to delete navigation options.

2. On the site's home page, choose the Site Settings option from the Settings menu.

3. On the Site Settings page, select the Top Link Bar option from the Look and Feel section.

4. On the Top Link Bar page, select the Edit icon for the navigation item to be edited.

5. On the Edit Navigation Link page, click the Delete button.

6. Click the OK button on the delete confirmation window.

The link will be deleted, and you will be returned to the Top Link Bar page.

A third approach to remove options in the navigation bar is available in SharePoint Server when the SharePoint Server Publishing Infrastructure feature is enabled. In this case the navigation bar is managed through the navigation management options. As with editing directly from the navigation bar, items representing sites and pages can be hidden but not deleted. Only custom links and headers can be deleted. To hide or delete headers and links from the navigation bar in this way, do the following:

1. Navigate to the site where you want to delete navigation options.

2. On the site's home page, choose the Site Settings option from the Settings menu.

3. On the Site Settings page, select the Navigation option from the Look and Feel section.

4. On the Navigation Settings page, in the Structural Navigation: Editing and Sorting section, do the following:

    a. Highlight the item to hide or delete.

    b. Click the Hide or Delete option.

    c. Click the OK button to save the changes made.

The changes will be saved, and you will be returned to the Site Settings page.

Configuring Managed Navigation for the Navigation Bar

The navigation bar can be configured to use a term set to govern navigation options. When the navigation is configured to use a term set, navigation is based on the items included in the term set. In order to support use of a term set to define the navigation optionsof a site, the term set must first be created, and then the navigation must be configured to leverage the term set.

Creating a Navigation Term Set

To create a term set to manage navigation, do the following:

1. Navigate to the root site in the site collection.

2. On the site's home page, choose the Site Settings option from the Settings menu.

3. On the Site Settings page, select the Term Store Management option from the Site Administration group.

4. On the Term Store Management Tool page, check the list of names in the Term Store Administrators section to verify you are an administrator. If you are not listed, do the following to add your account:

    a. Enter your account information in the Term Store Administrators box, and click the Check Names option to verify the account.

    b. Click the Save button to save the account.

5. Create a new term set for managing the navigation options.

    a. Select the desired term store group under which to create the new term set and select the New Term Set option from the drop-down menu.

    b. Enter the name for the new term set.

6. Configure the term set for managed navigation by doing the following:

    a. Click the Intended Use tab in the Term Store Management Tool (see Figure 3-14).

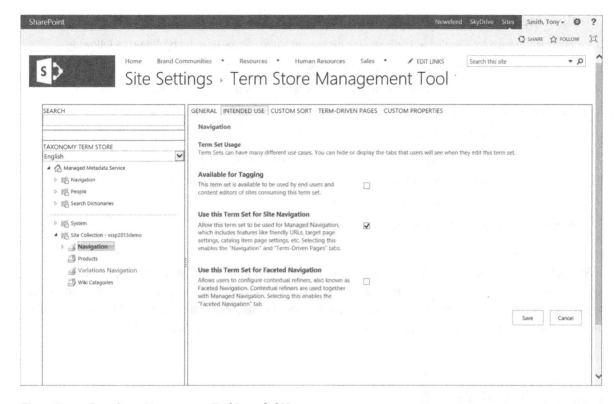

Figure 3-14. *Term Store Management Tool Intended Use page*

    b.   On the Intended Use page, select the Use This Term Set for Site Navigation option and click the Save button.

7.   Create terms for the term set. A term is created by doing the following:

    a.   Select the term set and select the Create Term option from the drop-down menu.

    b.   Enter the name for the new term.

    c.   Highlight the name of the new term and select the Navigation tab in the main area of the Term Store Management Tool.

    d.   In the Navigation Node Type section of the page, select Simple Link or Header to create a standard navigation link and enter the URL for the link or click the Browse button to browse to the desired URL. Then click the Save Button.

▨ **Note**   You can also use the term-driven page option to navigate to a page with options for defining content to be presented.

Configuring the Navigation Bar to Use the Term Set

Once a navigation term set is available, configure the navigation bar to use the term set by doing the following:

1. Navigate to the site where the term set will be used.

2. On the site's home page, choose the Site Settings option from the Settings menu.

3. On the Site Settings page, select the Navigation option from the Look and Feel section.

4. On the Navigation Settings page, do the following:

   a. In the Global Navigation section, select the Managed Navigation option.

   b. In the Managed Navigation Term Set section, select the created term set.

   c. Click the OK button to save the changes.

The navigation is updated to include the options listed in the term set.

■ **Note** This section described using a term set created within the site collection for managing navigation options. A SharePoint administrator can create a term set in SharePoint Central Administration for use across site collections. In this scenario the term set would be created in the Central Administration Managed Metadata Service, and the site configured to use the navigation options, just as described here in the "Configuring the Navigation Bar to Use the Term Set" section.

Using the Recycle Bin

SharePoint 2013 includes recycle bin capabilities that can be used to review and, if necessary, restore items previously deleted from SharePoint. Items that can be restored include documents, list entries, document libraries, lists, and sites. Deleted items are placed in the recycle bin for a set number of days, a period defined by the SharePoint technical administrator. Figure 3-15 depicts the recycle bin.

Figure 3-15. *The Recycle Bin*

The SharePoint recycle bin has two levels of functionality. The first is the site recycle bin. When items are deleted from the current site, they are listed in the site recycle bin until they are manually deleted or until the deletion date exceeds the purge period, defined as the number of days an item is retained before it is purged from the recycle bin. The second level of recycle bin functionality is the site collection recycle bin. This bin lists all items deleted across the site from the site recycle bins before the purge period ends. It gives site collection administrators a higher degree of control over managing deleted items and helps ensure information is properly protected from inappropriate deletion.

Viewing Items in the Recycle Bin

Users can view items placed in a site's recycle bin by doing the following:

1. Navigate to the site where you wish to access the recycle bin.

2. On the site's home page, click the Site Contents link in the Quick Launch area.

3. On the Site Contents page, click the Recycle Bin link, located to the right of the Lists, Libraries, and Other Apps header.

You will be navigated to the Recycle Bin page for the site. This page lists all items in the recycle bin.

Site collection administrators are also provided the ability to view just the items removed from the sites' recycle bins. This is also done through the site collection Recycle Bin page by selecting the Delete from End User Recycle Bin view. This is done as follows:

1. Navigate to the root site in the site collection.

2. On the site's home page, click the Site Settings option from the Settings menu.

3. On the Site Settings page, select the Recycle Bin option from the Site Collection Administration section.

Restoring Items from the Recycle Bin

To restore items from the site recycle bin or the site collection recycle bin, follow these steps:

1. Navigate to the Recycle Bin page or the site collection Recycle Bin page, as described previously.

2. On the site's home page, click the Site Content link in the Quick Launch area.

3. On the Site Contents page click the Recycle Bin link located to the right of the Lists, Libraries, and Other Apps header.

4. On the Recycle Bin or site collection Recycle Bin page, check the box for each item to restore and click the Restore Selection link.

The items are restored, and the Recycle Bin page is refreshed to reflect the change.

Deleting Items from the Recycle Bin

A site administrator has the ability to purge, or remove, items from the site's recycle bin so that other users will not have access to restore them. This is useful when a document was added to a library inappropriately and should be removed without letting library users access the item. Deleting the item from the library will remove it from general user access but does not protect against users with higher-level access rights to the library. Items can be removed from both the site recycle bins and the site collection recycle bin. To delete an item from the recycle bin do the following:

1. Navigate to the Recycle Bin page or the Site Collection Recycle Bin page, as described previously.

2. Delete items in either of the following ways:

    a. To delete select items from the recycle bin or site collection recycle bin, check the box for each item to delete and click the Delete Selection link.

    b. In the site collection recycle bin, all items in the recycle bin can be deleted by selecting the Empty Recycle Bin link.

3. On the deletion confirmation window, click the OK button.

The selected items are deleted from the recycle bin, and the Recycle Bin page is updated to reflect the changes.

Managing Site Design and Layout

The layout and look of the SharePoint environment can be tailored to meet an organization's design structure and layout. Several methods can be used to update the look of a SharePoint environment. They include the following:

- Selecting a theme for the environment that changes the colors and imagery of the existing layout.

- Creating new page layouts and master pages to create new layouts for the SharePoint environment.

- Creating alternative master pages for specific devices.

Updating Site Themes

A site theme in SharePoint 2013 defines the colors, imagery, fonts, and page layout for the SharePoint environment. Whether in SharePoint Foundation or SharePoint Server, individuals granted the Design or Full Control permission level have the ability to change site themes. There is a default set of site themes available for selection and update, and a SharePoint interface designer, in conjunction with a site collection administrator, has the ability to create and deploy custom themes as well.

To update the theme for a site, do the following:

1. Navigate to the site where you want to change the theme.

2. On the site's home page, select the Site Settings option from the Settings menu.

3. On the Site Settings page, select the Change the Look option from the Look and Feel section.

4. On the Change the Look page, select the theme to use as the starting point for the new site layout.

5. On the Change the Look configuration page, seen in Figure 3-16, the selected theme can be adjusted to meet virtually any needs. The changes that can be made to the theme include the following:

    a. The background image can be changed. Click the Change link below the image thumbnail and select a new image to use as the background for the theme. If your browser supports HTML5, as does Internet Explorer 10, you can also drag the new image over the thumbnail to upload the file. If you wish to remove the background image entirely, click the Remove link below the thumbnail image.

    b. The color scheme for the theme can be updated. Use the Colors drop-down and select the desired color combination.

    c. The site layout can be selected. The site layout identifies the page layout the site will use. By default, there are two available page layouts: Oslo and Seattle. The Oslo layout does not include the Quick Launch area and has the navigation bar positioned below the site title. The Seattle layout includes the Quick Launch area and places the navigation bar above the site title.

    d. The font family for use in the site can be selected. Select the font listing from the Fonts drop-down list.

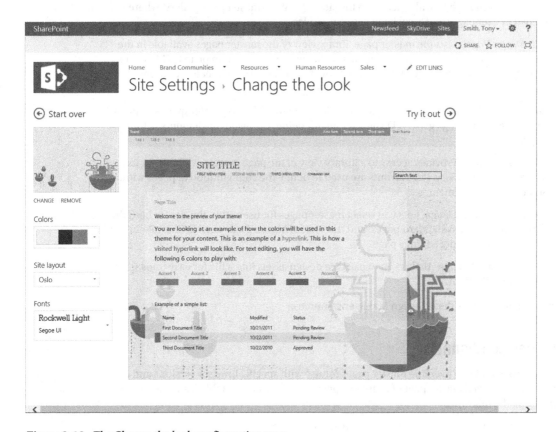

Figure 3-16. *The Change the look configuration page*

6. Once any changes to the theme's background image, colors, site layout, and fonts have been made, the theme can be tested by clicking the Try It Out link. Clicking this link will generate a preview of the look. You see the layout as it will appear within the site.

7. On the Preview page, decide whether the look is complete.

   a. Clicking the No, Not Quite There option returns you to the Change the Look configuration page, where additional alterations to the look and feel can be made.

   b. Clicking the Yes, Keep It option saves the theme as the new look for the site and returns you to the Site Settings page.

Working with Design Manager

When SharePoint Server Standard or SharePoint Server Enterprise is used, Design Manager is available. Design Manager organizes the SharePoint layout management tools in a single place to make it easier to manage the look and feel of the SharePoint environment. Design Manager allows management of the following:

- *Manage Device Channels*: Allows you to define master pages to use with specific browsers and devices.

- *Upload Design Files*: Provides access to the site collections master page gallery, where you can upload master pages and associated css and js files.

- *Edit Master Pages*: Lists the master page library view of the master pages available in the system for edit. This area also provides a link that will allow selection of an HTML file for conversion to a master page. A link is also provided to allow you to create a new minimal master page.

- *Edit Display Templates*: Provides access to a library view of the display templates available within the master page gallery. Display templates define the layout of elements within the environment.

- *Edit Page Layouts*: Provides access to a library view of the page layouts available for use in the master page gallery. Page layouts are used to define the configuration of pages within the SharePoint environment.

- *Publish and Apply Design*: Lets you select master pages for use within the site for both the Site Master Page, used in standard pages, and the System Master Page, used in SharePoint system pages, such as the Site Settings page.

- *Create Design Package*: Allows you to package design assets into a file for easy transport to other site collections.

The next section discusses these Design Manager resources.

Managing Device Channels

Device channels give the ability to define master pages for use with specific browser versions and devices. They allow for the creation of specialized master pages for use on specific devices such as tablets and smart phones. To create device channels, do the following:

1. From the Settings menu, select the Design Manager option.

2. From the Design Manager: Welcome page, select the Manage Device Channels option from the left-hand navigation.

3. On the Manage Device Channels page, click the Create a Channel link.

4. In the Device Channels New Item window, enter the following information:

    a. Name: specifies a name for the channel

    b. Alias: specifies a single word to identify the channel for access through code. It is advisable to make the Alias similar to the Name for identification purposes.

    c. Description: lists an optional description that can be used to describe the new channel.

    d. Device Inclusion Rules: includes the set of rules that specify when the channel should be used to identify the master page instead of using the default master page.

    e. Active: specifies whether the channel should be actively used. Inactive channels do not impact the master page used in the environment.

    f. Once all the information is entered, click the Save button to save the new channel.

The new device channel will be created, and you will be returned to the Manage Device Channels page. You can then edit existing device channels by doing the following:

1. On the Manage Device Channels page, click the Edit or Reorder Existing Channels link.

2. On the Device Channels page, click the item to edit from the list of device channels, and select the Edit Item option from the Items ribbon.

3. On the Device Channel Edit Item screen, make any needed changes to the device channel details, and click the Save button to save the changes made.

The specified changes are made to the channel, and you are returned to the Device Channels page.

Selecting a New Site Design

Design Manager can be used to select and configure new site designs. Design Manager allows selection of a site design package. Such a package can include layouts created by designers using other design tools, such as Dreamweaver. To upload a new design package, do the following:

1. Navigate to the Site Settings page from any site within the site collection.

2. On the Site Settings page, select Design Manager from the Look and Feel section

3. On the Design Manager page, select the Upload Design Files option from the Quick Launch area.

4. On the Upload Design Files page, follow the instructions to map a drive to the site collection's master page gallery.

5. Use the mapped drive to upload design files into the master page gallery.

Edit an Existing Site Design

Master page designs that already exist in the environment can be edited through Design Manager by doing the following:

1. Navigate to the Site Settings page from any site within the site collection.

2. On the Site Settings page, select Design Manager from the Look and Feel section.

3. On the Design Manager page, select the Edit Master Page option from the Quick Launch area.

4. On the Edit Master Pages page, click the ellipsis points (. . .) next to the name of the page and select the Open option from the document's hover window.

In the Page Preview window, the layout of the master page is presented. On this page you can update the preview page, view the status of the master page configuration (including identification of any configuration and layout errors), and access the Snippet Gallery to configure SharePoint objects for injection into the master page. To access the Snippet Gallery, do the following:

1. In the Page Preview window, click the Snippets option from the top of the page (see Figure 3-17).

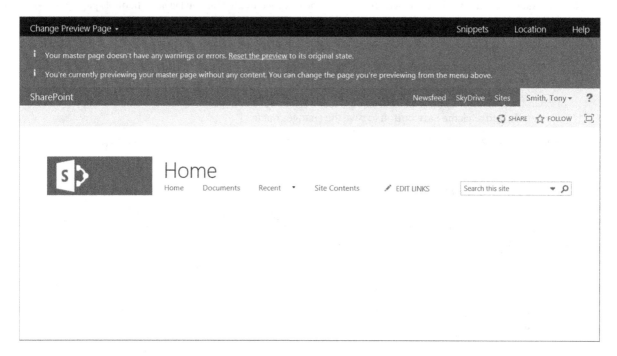

Figure 3-17. *Page Preview window*

2. On the Component Configuration page, seen in Figure 3-18, select the needed component from the Design ribbon tab. This will show the component details in the body of the page.

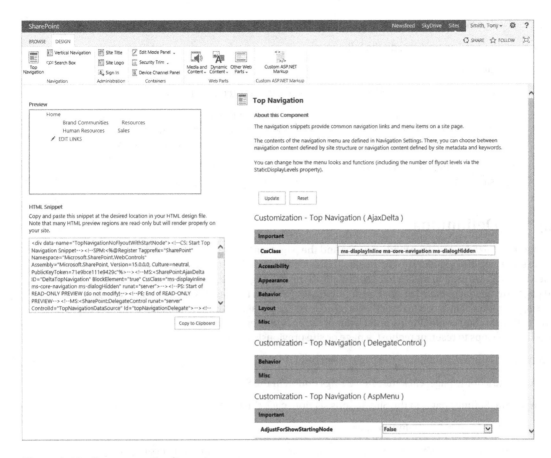

Figure 3-18. *Component Configuration page*

3. In the component customization section, make the appropriate selections to set the configuration of the selected component.

4. Once all needed changes have been made to the component, click the Update button to refresh the component preview and preview the changes made.

5. Once the preview is confirmed, clicking the Copy to Clipboard button below the HTML Snippet section will copy the component with the current configuration to the clipboard for copying into the master page.

Snippet code can be copied into a master page to inject the SharePoint components into the master page file.

Managing Page Layouts

Page templates are used to define the layout of a page within a site. They define the zone configuration of the content and whether standard items, such as Quick Launch navigation, are included. Page layouts are dependent on the site's master page, which dictates the overall style and layout of the site. To manage page templates, do the following:

1. Navigate to the Site Settings page from any site within the site collection.

2. On the Site Settings page, select Design Manager from the Look and Feel section.

3. On the Design Manager page, select the Edit Page Layouts option from the Quick Launch area.

4. On the Edit Page Layout page, do the following:

   a. To create a new page layout,

      i. Select the Create a Page Layout option above the master page listing.

      ii. In the Create a Page layout window, enter a name for the new layout; then select the master page the layout will be associated with and the content type identifying the page layout type to create. Click the OK button to create the page.

   b. To edit an existing page layout, open the page layout to edit it and make any necessary changes.

Resetting Site Definitions

Over time, many customizations may be made to a site and the pages within the site. Some of these customizations are made to the site's look and feel to meet specific needs. Tools, such as SharePoint Designer, are available to make these changes. When the tools are used to make changes directly to the site pages, the pages can become unghosted—that is, the edited pages are no longer based on the site definition that defines the page's standard configuration and layout. Resetting the site definition allows you to reset the pages to leverage the site definition and allows the site pages to again conform to the standard configuration and layout of the environment.

Use the following steps to reset, or reghost, a page or site previously customized.

1. Navigate to the site containing the pages to be reset.

2. On the site's home page, click the Site Settings option in the Settings menu.

3. On the Site Settings page, in the Site Actions section, click the Reset to Site Definition link.

4. On the Reset Page to Site Definition page:

   a. To reset a specific site page, select Reset Specific Page to Site Definition Version, and type the URL of the page to reset.

   b. To reset all pages in the site, select Reset All Pages in This Site Definition Version.

   c. Once the appropriate options are selected, click the Reset button.

The site page or entire site is reset, or reghosted, and you are returned to the Site Settings page.

Controlling Access to Page Layouts and Site Templates

SharePoint Server gives site owners the ability to control page layouts and site templates used for creating pages and subsites within a site when the SharePoint Server Publishing site collection feature is enabled. For page layouts, you can choose to let people create new pages from any available layout or allow only specific page layouts to be made available for use. You can also decide whether subsites under the current site will be limited to the specified page layout. This capability is useful in situations where the site should contain only a specific type of content, such as press releases.

Site templates have abilities similar to those of page layouts in that you can decide whether subsites created under the current site can leverage any available site templates or just specified ones. You can also determine whether the settings should be inherited by the current site's subsites. These capabilities are useful if you need to delegate site creation rights to users but want to restrict their options—for example, if you have an Enterprise Projects site under which users create a site to manage each project. You create a template for project sites that includes resources that are to be part of a project site. Then you restrict the available site templates in the Enterprise Projects site to the template you created. This ensures all project sites created will be based on the appropriate template.

This section also provides the ability to specify default settings to use when new pages are created in the site. These settings include the default page template and URL. You have the ability either to inherit the settings from the parent site or to select them here. While the site layout and URL can be changed after the page is created, it is good practice to set these defaults appropriately to minimize changes needed as new pages are created.

Follow these steps to update page layout and site template settings:

1. Navigate to the Site Settings page for the site where you wish to update the page layout and site template settings.

2. On the Site Settings page, in the Look and Feel section, click the Page Layouts and Site Templates link.

3. On the Page Layout and Site Templates Settings page, do the following:

   a. In the Subsite Templates section, select "Subsites inherit site templates from parent site," "Subsites can use any site template," or "Subsites can only use the following site templates." Then choose the templates that should be made available. You can also indicate whether you want to reset all subsites to inherit the preferred subsite template settings.

   b. In the Page Layouts section, select "Pages inherit preferred layouts from parent site," "Pages in this site can use any layout," or "Pages in this site can only use the following layouts." Then choose the layouts to be made available. You can also indicate whether you want all subsites reset to inherit the preferred page layout settings.

   c. In the New Page Default Settings section, select "Inherit default page layout from parent site" or "Select the default page layout," and select the appropriate layout from the list. If you want, you can also reset all subsites to inherit these new page settings and convert blank spaces in page names to dashes.

   d. Once all options are appropriately updated, click the OK button.

The page layout and site template settings are saved, and you are returned to the Site Settings page.

Identifying Master Pages and Style Sheets for a Site

As discussed, master pages define the general structure and layout of SharePoint. SharePoint pages are designed to leverage master pages so that sets of pages can have the same structure and layout and so that any changes to this structure and layout can be made in a central place. The changes made will apply to all associated pages. When you alter a master page, such as by adding a logo or changing the page format, that change is reflected across all of the site pages associated with that master page.

Style sheets are used in conjunction with master pages to define the specified color scheme, fonts, and backgrounds used in site pages. Site managers are able to modify a site's style sheet to change those colors, fonts, and backgrounds. Thus, site managers can easily update SharePoint to conform to their organization's corporate identity.

The master page and style sheet for a site in SharePoint Server with the SharePoint Server Publishing site feature enabled can be updated by doing the following:

1. Navigate to the Site Settings page for the site where you wish to update the master page or style sheet.

2. On the Site Settings page, in the Look and Feel section, click the Master Page link.

3. On the Site Master Page Settings page, make the following selections:

   a. In the Site Master Page section, either inherit the master page from the parent site (available in subsites only) or choose a master page for this site, and select whether all subsites will inherit this site's master page setting.

   b. In the System Master Page section, either inherit the master page from the parent site (available in subsites only) or choose a master page to form and view pages within the site, and select whether all subsites will inherit this system master page setting.

   c. In the Theme section, identify whether subsites of the current site will inherit the current site's theme.

   d. In the Alternate CSS URL section, inherit the alternative style sheet from the parent site (available in subsites only) and specify whether the default style sheet or an alternative style sheet is to be used for the site. If you specify an alternative style sheet, you must specify the file to reference and whether you want to reset all the site's subsites to use the defined alternative. Alternative style sheets alter the master page styling within the site.

   e. Once all the necessary changes have been made, click the OK button

   The changes you made are saved, and you are returned to the Site Settings page.

Managing Site Templates

As discussed earlier in this chapter, in creating a new site or subsite, you select a template as part of the creation process. The site template defines the initial set of components included in the new site and defines the layout of its components. The template also defines the structure and configuration of the components within the site and whether any content, such as list values and documents, should be added as part of the new site.

Creating Site Templates

The templates discussed in Chapter 2 are default templates provided in SharePoint Foundation and SharePoint Server. Once you create a new site based on one of the available templates and tailor it to meet your specific needs, you can save the updated site as a new template to be used when additional sites are created. Any user assigned the full control permission level in a site can create templates from the site. The templates you create will be available for selection when sites are created within the same site collection where the site template was created.

Here is an example of how site templates are used. Say that you have a site called Budget Planning that contains a subsite called 2012 Budget. You update the 2012 Budget site to reflect the layout needed to support yearly budget planning. (Creating components and editing page layouts are discussed in Chapters 4 through 12.) Once the 2012 Budget site includes the desired structure and content, you save it as a template. This template is then available when other new sites are created. By saving the 2012 Budget site as a template, you save yourself and others the effort of duplicating the customizations made to the 2012 Budget site when additional yearly budget sites are required. Also, you provide others a starting point for creating yearly budget sites that include the layout and components they will need in their sites. This helps ensure that all yearly budget sites have a consistent structure that contains the resources needed to properly support the budget planning process.

■ **Note** If your SharePoint environment contains multiple site collections, templates created within a site collection will be available only within that collection unless a SharePoint technical administrator registers the template for use across collections or unless the template is copied into each site collection's solutions gallery.

To create a site template for use in the current site collection, follow these steps:

1. Navigate to the site you wish to save as a site template.

2. On the site's home page, click the Site Settings option from the Settings menu.

3. On the Site Settings page, in the Site Actions section, click the Save Site as Template link.

4. On the Save Site as Template page, enter the following:

    a. In the File Name section, enter the name to be used to save the template.

    b. In the Name and Description section, enter the template name. This is the name that will appear on the templates tab when a new site is created. You can also enter an optional description for the template.

    c. In the Include Content section, specify whether content within the selected site is to be included in the template. Content includes any document and list data that exist in the selected site. To include the content in the template, check the Include Content check box.

    d. Once all necessary information is entered, click the OK button.

5. On the Operation Completed Successfully page, click the OK button.

A copy of the site is saved as a template, and you are taken to the site's home page. The new site template is added to the Solutions gallery and activated, making it available to users creating sites.

■ **Note**　The Save Site as Template option is not available in a site where the SharePoint Server Publishing site feature is enabled.

Editing Site Templates

To edit a site template, simply edit the site you originally used to create the site template or create a new site from the existing template and make the edits to that site. Once the changes have been made to the site, create the new template by following the steps described previously. Then deactivate and delete the old template from the Solutions Gallery. Deleting templates is discussed in the next section.

Deleting Site Templates

While you cannot remove the default site templates provided, by executing the following steps, you can delete any custom site templates created:

1. Navigate to the root site in the site collection.

2. On the site's home page, click the Site Settings option from the Settings menu.

3. On the Site Settings page, in the Web Designer Galleries section, click the Solutions link.

4. On the Solution Gallery page, hover over the template to delete, click the down arrow to present the item's context menu, and select Deactivate.

5. In the Deactivate Solution window, click the Deactivate command from the View ribbon.

6. On the Solution Gallery page, hover over the template to delete, click the down arrow to present the item's context menu, and select Delete.

7. On the delete confirmation window, click the OK button.

The template is deleted, and the Solution Gallery is updated to reflect the deletion.

Managing Site Content and Structure

SharePoint Server introduces administrative tools that allow site owners to view their SharePoint site, list, and library resources in a single tree structure. These resources can also be managed directly from this same location. This is done through the use of the Site Content and Structure management screen shown in Figure 3-19.

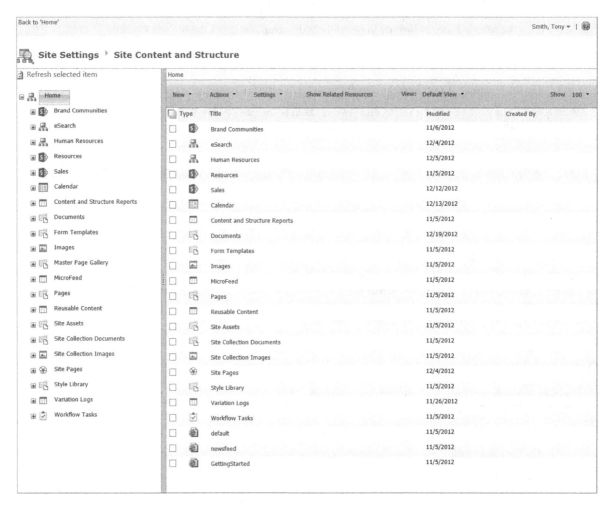

Figure 3-19. *The Site Content and Structure page*

Access the Site Content and Structure page as follows:

1. Navigate to the Site Settings page for the site you wish to manage.

2. On the Site Settings page, in the Site Administration section, click the Content and Structure link.

You are taken to the Site Content and Structure page. This page, which provides a comprehensive tree view of the site collection hierarchy, lists all sites, lists, and libraries within the environment. From here, you can manage the following site activities:

-   Navigate to any of the listed sites.

-   Elect to create new sites, lists, or libraries within a specific site.

-   Delete a listed site.

-   Copy a listed site to a specified location.

-   Move a listed site to a specified location.

-   View the site's recycle bin.

-   Access the site's management resources, including Site Settings, People and Groups, Advanced Permissions, and General Settings.

All of these options are available as selections on the listed site's drop-down menu, as shown in Figure 3-20.

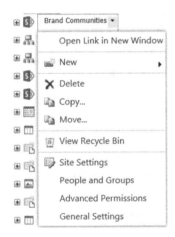

Figure 3-20. *The site's drop-down menu on the Site Content and Structure page*

From the Site Content and Structure page, there are also several management options available for managing lists and libraries:

-   Navigate to the default view of a list or library.

-   Create a new entry in a list, upload a new document in a library, or create a new folder in a library.

-   Delete a list or library.

-   Access a list's or library's properties page.

All of these options are available as selections on the list's or library's drop-down menu, as shown in Figure 3-21.

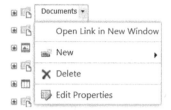

Figure 3-21. *The list's drop-down menu on the Site Content and Structure page*

Managing Site and Site Collection Features

Along with all of the other site capabilities discussed, you also have the ability to enable and disable specific site features within the SharePoint sites and the ability to enable and disable specific site collection features in the overall site collection. (The features available in SharePoint Foundation and SharePoint Server are discussed in Chapter 2.)

Managing Site Features

Site features are made available within a site by activating them. Activating a feature makes the functionality associated with the feature available. To activate or deactivate site features, do the following:

1. Navigate to the site where the feature needs to be managed.

2. On the site's home page, click the Site Settings option from the Settings menu.

3. On the Site Settings page, in the Site Actions section, click the Manage Site Features link.

4. On the Site Features page, click the Activate/Deactivate button to activate or deactivate a feature.

The feature status is changed, and the associated feature capabilities are enabled or disabled.

Managing Site Collection Features

Site collection features are capabilities that, when activated, are available within all sites in the collection. To activate or deactivate site collection features, do the following:

1. Navigate to the root site in the site collection where the feature needs to be managed.

2. On the site's home page, click the Site Settings option from the Settings menu.

3. On the Site Settings page, in the Site Collection Administration section, click the Site Collection Features link.

4. On the Site Collection Features page, click the Activate/Deactivate button to activate or deactivate a feature.

The feature status is changed, and the associated feature capabilities are enabled or disabled.

Managing Content Variations

Organizations that operate globally often need to publish resources in several languages to properly support all users. The process of creating the various translations or variations of the content can be time consuming and difficult to manage.

SharePoint Server gives site owners the ability to define site variations and define primary and variation locations for content needing to be translated. Changes made to the primary location can be automatically or manually propagated to the associated variations. The variation capabilities can be integrated with SharePoint work flows that drive the updating process for variations. These work flows can also be integrated with the SharePoint 2013 translation services to automate the actual creation of the translated versions.

When users access a site that participates in a variation set, they are automatically taken to the variation supporting their language. SharePoint Server makes this determination based on the web browser's language preferences. If no variation supporting users' browser language preferences exist, they are taken to the primary site page for the variation set.

To use the SharePoint Server variation capabilities, configure the variation settings within the site collection. These settings include identifying the source location where variations are to be created and configuring variation creation management and notification settings. To configure the variation settings for the site collection, follow these steps:

1. Navigate to the Site Settings page for the root site in the site collection.

2. On the Site Settings page, in the Site Collection Administration section, click the Variations Settings link.

3. On the Variations Settings page, follow these steps:

   a. In the Site, List, and Page Creation Behavior section, specify whether variations are to be created for all new elements or the user will be able to choose which language sites, if any, the new content should be synchronized to.

   b. In the Recreate Deleted Target Page section, specify whether target pages are to be re-created when the source page is republished.

   c. In the Update Target Page Web Parts section, indicate whether changes to web parts in the source page are to carry through to the target pages.

   d. In the Notification section, specify whether an e-mail will be sent to the contact person for the target when a new subsite or page is created or when a target page is edited.

   e. Once all settings have been properly configured, click the OK button to save the information.

The information is saved, and you are returned to the Site Settings page.

Variation Labels

You can create multiple variations of information in SharePoint. Variation labels are the names given to the variants of an item so that they can be uniquely identified. For example, if you have a site that contains information that needs variants created in Spanish and French, each of these alternative versions will be provided a label uniquely identifying it. Follow these steps to create a new variation label.

1. Navigate to the Site Settings page for the root site in the site collection.

2. On the Site Settings page, in the Site Collection Administration section, click the Variation Labels link.

3. On the Variation Labels page (see Figure 3-22), click the New Label link.

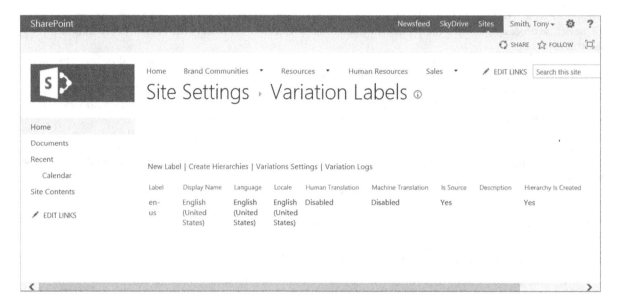

Figure 3-22. *The Variation Labels page*

4. On the Configure Your Target Label page, enter the following:

    a. In the Language section, identify the language for the variation label.

    b. In the Locale section, select the locale for the variation.

    c. Click the Continue button.

5. On the Name Your Target Label page, enter the following:

    a. In the Label Name and Description section, enter a name for the label (you can also enter an optional description).

    b. In the Display Name section, enter the display name for the label. The display name is the friendly name used in displaying the label.

    c. In the Hierarchy Creation section, select the part of the source hierarchy that will be copied for the variation label.

    d. Click the Continue button.

6. On the Translation Options page, identify the following:

    a. In the Create Translation Package section, whether human content translation should be allowed.

    b. In the Machine Translation section, whether machine content translation should be allowed.

    c. Click the Continue button.

7. On the Target Label Behavior page, identify the following:

    a. In the Page Update Behavior section, whether variations should be synchronized manually or automatically.

    b. In the Label Contact section, contacts for the source variation site.

    c. Click the Continue button.

8. On the Review Label Settings page, review the options selected. To make changes, click the link for the option to navigate back to the associated page. Once all information is accurate, click the Finish button.

The variation label is created, and you are returned to the Variation Labels page.

You can edit the variation labels by hovering over a listed label and selecting the Edit option from the drop-down menu. To delete variation labels, hover over a label and select the Delete option.

After the variation settings are configured and variation labels have been created, you need to create the variation hierarchy. The variation hierarchy is the tree structure needed under the identified root variation site to store and manage the site variations. To create the variation hierarchy, click the Create Hierarchies link on the Variation Labels page, as shown in Figure 3-22. Clicking this link will cause SharePoint to create the necessary site hierarchy to support the variant configuration under the root variation site.

Translatable Columns

Site collection administrators are able to identify list and library columns that need to be translated when they appear in a variant site. This identifies elements to translate as part of the variation management workflow process. To update the translatable column settings, do the following:

1. Navigate to the Site Settings page for the root site in the site collection.

2. On the Site Settings page, in the Site Collection Administration section, click the Translatable Columns link.

3. On the Translatable Column Settings page, check the box in front of each column name that must be translated, and click the OK button.

The translatable column settings are saved, and you are returned to the Site Settings page.

Variation Logs

The variation log presents an operational log listing the variation process details. This log can be used to review the status and health of the variation process. To view the variation logs, do as follows:

1. Navigate to the Site Settings page for the root site in the site collection.

2. On the Site Settings page, in the Site Collection Administration section, click the Variation Logs link.

As displayed, the Variation Logs page lists the logged events for the variation process.

Managing Help Information

SharePoint 2013 allows site collection administrators to identify the help collection to be used when help links are clicked within the site. By default, only one help collection is listed by default. This collection contains the standard SharePoint help details. To replace this default collection, a SharePoint developer or administrator must create a new collection and make it available for selection.

To manage help collections, do the following:

1. Navigate to the root site in the site collection.

2. On the site's home page, click the Site Settings option from the Settings menu.

3. On the Site Settings page, in the Site Collection Administration section, click the Help Settings link.

4. On the Help Settings page, do the following:

    a. Select the help collections to be made available. By default, there are four help collections available, including Central Administration Help, SharePoint Help, Student Help, and Teacher Help, with the Central Administration Help and SharePoint Help options selected.

    b. Once the appropriate selections have been made, click the OK button.

Using SharePoint Designer for Site Management

SharePoint Designer is a client tool that can be used to create, extend, and deploy SharePoint solutions. SharePoint 2013 includes the ability to identify whether SharePoint Designer can customize site collection components. Through the SharePoint Designer Settings, you can specify the following:

- Whether to allow SharePoint Designer to be used to edit the site collection.

- Whether site administrators can detach pages from the original site definitions and unghosting the pages.

- Whether site administrators can customize master pages and layouts through SharePoint Designer.

- Whether site administrators can change the hidden URL structure of their sites through SharePoint Designer.

To update SharePoint Designer settings for a site collection, do as follows:

1. Navigate to the root site in the site collection.

2. On the site's home page, click the Site Settings option from the Settings menu.

3. On the Site Settings page, in the Site Collection Administration section, click the SharePoint Designer Settings link.

4. On the SharePoint Designer Settings page, specify the SharePoint Designer management preferences, and click the OK button.

The SharePoint Designer settings are updated, and you are returned to the Site Settings page.

CHAPTER 4

■ ■ ■

Pages, Apps, and Web Parts

Pages, apps, and web parts are used to organize and present information and to introduce business functionality into SharePoint sites. Pages are used to create organized views of information. The information provided in SharePoint pages can be text, images, and videos organized to support information access and management needs. This information can also include the contents of lists or libraries showing the details of the information stored in SharePoint or applications providing other business capabilities to the site. Apps and web parts are used to provide the access to list and library content as well as any application functionality.

In this chapter we discuss the different types of pages available within SharePoint and how to create and manage these pages. We also discuss apps and web parts and how they can be used to present content stored within the sites and introduce additional business application capabilities into your SharePoint sites.

Pages

SharePoint pages are the tools used within sites to organize and present information. When a SharePoint site is created, it typically contains a single SharePoint page that acts as the site's home page. Three types of pages can be created in SharePoint 2013, each with its own capabilities designed to satisfy different needs. These types of pages include the following:

- Web Part pages
- Wiki pages
- Publishing pages

Web Part Pages

The most basic type of page that can be created in SharePoint 2013 is the web part page. A web part page contains web part zones, in which apps and web parts can be added and configured. Web part zones are organized within pages based on the pages' defined layouts. Web part zones are designed to store apps and web parts that are functional components adding application functionality to pages within SharePoint. We discuss apps and web parts in more detail later in this chapter.

Web part pages are best used when you, as the site administrator, need to add a page that contains specific functionality yet would not need to be managed by general site users and would not need significant standard textual content in the page. This type of page allows addition of only apps and web parts to the defined zones.

Creating Web Part Pages

In SharePoint 2013 web part pages are created by default within the Site Pages library. This library is also used to create wiki pages, which we discuss later in this chapter. You can also add the ability to create web part pages in other libraries if you desire.

The Site Pages library is added to a site through the activation of the Wiki Page Home Page feature. Activating this feature will also update the site's home page so that it is based on a wiki page instead of the default web part page. To activate the Wiki Home Page feature, do the following:

1. Navigate to the site where you want to enable the Wiki Page Home Page feature.

2. On the site's home page, select the Site Settings option from the settings menu.

3. On the Site Settings page, select the Manage Site Features option from the Site Actions section.

4. On the Site Features page, click the Activate option for the Wiki Page Home Page feature.

The Wiki Page Home Page feature is activated, creating the Site Pages library and reconfiguring the site's home page so that it is based on a new page, named Home.aspx, created in the Site Pages library.

There are times when you will not want to enable the Wiki Page Home Page feature within a site because you do not want to make the ability to create wiki pages available within the site or want the home page of the site to be updated to a wiki page. When this is the case, you can make the web part page content type available in a different library within the site, allowing web part pages to be created within the library. To make web part pages available in a library, do the following:

1. Navigate to the site where you need to make web part pages available.

2. If it does not yet exist, create the document library where you want to store created web part pages.

3. Navigate to the library where you want to be able to save web part pages.

4. On the library home page, select the Library Settings option from the Library ribbon tab.

5. On the Settings page, select the Advanced Settings option from the General Settings page.

6. On the Advanced Settings page in the Content Types section, select Yes for "Allow management of content types" option, and click the OK button.

7. On the Settings page for the library in the Content Type section, select the "Add from existing site content types" option.

8. On the Add Content Types page, select the Web Part Page option from the Available Site Content Types section, click the Add button to add the item to the Content Types to Add section, and click the OK button.

With the ability to add web part pages now available in the library, you can create web part pages in that library. Whether you decide to create web part pages in the Site Pages library or provide the ability to add web part pages to a different library in the site, you create web part pages by doing the following:

1. Navigate to the library where you want to create the web part page.

2. On the library view page, select the Web Part Page option from the New Document drop-down menu, located on the Files ribbon tab.

3. On the New Web Part page, do the following:

   a. In the Name section, select the name for the new page.

   b. In the Layout section, select the layout for the page. The layout identifies the zone configuration for the new page being created. The standard web part page layouts are listed in Table 4-1.

Table 4-1. *Default Web Part Page Layouts*

Template	Description	Layout
Header, Footer, 3 Columns	Contains a header zone that spans the width of the page, followed by a row of three zones and then below that zone row a footer zone that also spans the width of the page.	
Full Page, Vertical	Includes a single web part zone that spans the page.	
Header, Left Column, Body	Includes a header spanning the width of the page, followed by a row containing a thin left column and wider right column.	
Header, Right Column, Body	Includes a header spanning the width of the page, followed by a row containing a wide left column and a thin right column.	
Header, Footer, 2 Columns, 4 Rows	Contains a header zone spanning the width of the page, followed by a row containing three zones and then below that zone row a footer zone spanning the width of the page.	

(*continued*)

Table 4-1. (*continued*)

Template	Description	Layout
Header, Footer, 4 Columns, Top Row	Includes a header zone spanning the width of the page, followed by a row containing a central set of zones having two full-height right and left columns, with a central area having a full-size zone with two zones located below it. At the bottom is a footer zone spanning the width of the page.	
Left Column, Header, Footer, Top Row, 3 Columns	Includes a full-height left zone and a set of zones to the right that includes two zones spanning the remaining page width, with a set of three zones below this area and a bottom zone below that zone row.	
Right Column, Header Footer, Top Row, 3 Columns	Includes a full-height right zone and a set of zones to the left that includes two zones spanning the remaining page width, with a set of three zones below this area and a bottom zone below that zone row.	

     c.   Click the Create button to create the new page.

The new page is created. You will be navigated to it, and you can then configure the page by adding to it any needed web parts.

Viewing Web Part Pages

Users having access to a site may not initially be aware of pages other than the site's home page. Page visibility is dependent on the configuration of the navigation within the site and the inclusion of page references in the navigation areas. Several methods can be used to make sites accessible within SharePoint. Some of the most common approaches are the following:

- Add a link to a page on the navigation bar of the site.
- Add a link to the Quick Launch menu of the site.
- Create a view on the home page to the web part pages available in site libraries.

Editing Web Part Pages

Web part page editing consists of adding and configuring web parts in the pages. To edit web part pages, do the following:

1. Navigate to the page you want to edit.
2. On the web part page, select the Edit Page option from the Page ribbon tab.

3. With the web part page in Edit mode, select the Add a Web Part link in the zone where you want to add the web part, as seen in Figure 4-1.

Figure 4-1. *Web part page in Edit mode*

4. In the web part selection area (see Figure 4-2), select the web part to add to the zone, and click the Add button.

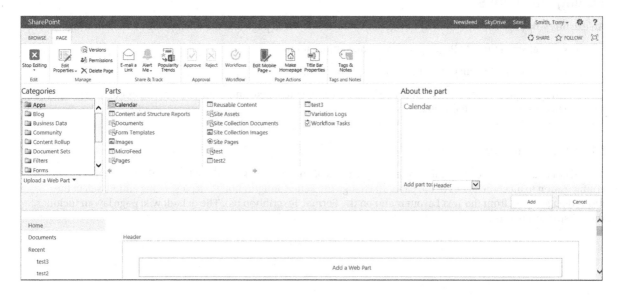

Figure 4-2. *Web part page selection area*

The web part is added to the zone and can be configured. Configuring and managing web parts are discussed later in this chapter. With the items on the page, you can move them into the appropriate location by dragging the items within the zone to the desired location.

Wiki Pages

A wiki page is another type of page that can be created within SharePoint sites. Wiki pages are managed within a site's Site Pages library. While web part pages have zones where apps or web parts can be placed, wiki pages have zones that can contain apps, web parts, rich text content, references to images and videos, HTML elements (like tables and bulleted lists), and code (such as JavaScript) to further manipulate information within the page. These elements can be integrated within the page in any combination.

Create a wiki page when you want to provide full creative control of the page to content contributors within the site. Like web part pages, wiki pages have different page layouts available, and a page's layout can be updated after the page has been created.

Creating Wiki Pages

Wiki pages are created within a site's Site Pages library. This library is made available within a site by activating the Wiki Page Home Page feature (activating this feature is discussed in the "Creating Web Part Pages" section, above). To create a wiki page, do the following:

1. Navigate to the site where you want to create the wiki page.

2. On the site's home page, select the Add a Page option from the Settings menu.

3. In the Add a Page window, enter the name of the new page to create, and click the Create button.

The page is created. You are navigated to the page, and it is placed in Edit mode to allow changes to be made.

Editing Wiki Pages

An existing wiki page can be edited by navigating to the desired wiki page and then doing one of the following:

*   Selecting the Edit Page option from the Settings menu.

*   Selecting the Edit option from the Page ribbon tab.

When a wiki page is edited, several characteristics can be managed, and elements can be added and configured. These elements include the following.

Managing the Page Layout

The layout of a wiki page can be edited after the page has been created. This is done to alter the wiki zone configuration to meet the needs of the page. To change the zone configuration for a page being edited, select the desired page layout from the Text Layout menu on the Format Text ribbon tab. The default wiki page layout includes those listed in Table 4-2.

Table 4-2. *Default Wiki Part Page Layouts*

Template	Description	Layout
One Column	Contains a single column spanning the entire page.	
One Column with Sidebar	Contains a two-column layout, with a large left column and a smaller right column.	
Two Columns	Includes two columns in a side-by-side configuration.	
Two Columns with Header	Includes a single column spanning the width of the page, with two columns in a side-by-side configuration below it.	
Two Columns with Header and Footer	Includes a single column spanning the width of the page, with two columns in a side-by-side configuration below it and a full-width column at the bottom.	
Three Columns	Contains three side-by-side columns making up the page.	
Three Columns with Header	Includes a single column spanning the width of the page, with three columns in a side-by-side configuration below it.	
Three Columns with Header and Footer	Includes a single column spanning the width of the page, with three columns in a side-by-side configuration below it and a full width column at the bottom.	

Editing Text

Wiki pages let you enter text to be presented on the page. Rich text content is added to the page much as you would add content to a Word document. When text is added to the page, it is formatted with the format controls on the Format Text ribbon tab, as seen in Figure 4-3.

Figure 4-3. *Format Text ribbon tab*

Adding Tables

HTML tables, which allow the formatting of content into a table structure, can also be added to the page. A table is added by selecting the row and column configuration from the Table drop-down menu on the Insert tab of the page, as seen in Figure 4-4.

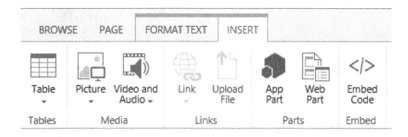

Figure 4-4. *Insert ribbon tab*

Once the table is added to the page, you can select the desired table layout and choose to show or hide grid lines for the table on the Design ribbon tab. You can also specify table and cell width, height, and layout properties on the Table Layout ribbon tab. Tables are used to style text and objects within a page to create the desired information layout.

Adding Pictures

You can add images to wiki pages in order to show them within the page. Pictures can be added using any of three different approaches.

- Approach 1: If the image to be displayed on the page is not yet in SharePoint and you want to upload the image and display it on the page, select the From Computer option from the Picture drop-down on the Insert ribbon tab (see Figure 4-4). You can then pick the file and an upload location. The file is placed in the identified location and referenced on the page.

- Approach 2: If the image to be referenced is already located in SharePoint, you can select the From SharePoint option from the Picture drop-down on the Insert ribbon tab. When the Select an Asset window appears, you pick an item to reference from a location within the site collection. The selected item is referenced on the page.

- Approach 3: If the image to be displayed on the page is in a location outside the site collection from which it will be referenced, you can select the From Address option from the Picture drop-down menu on the Insert ribbon tab. You can then identify the URL of the image to reference.

Adding a Video or Audio File

Video and audio files can be added directly to a wiki page, allowing them to play in place on that page. As with pictures, video and audio files can be added whether they are on your local computer or already in SharePoint or some other web-addressable location.

- Approach 1: If the video or audio file is located outside the SharePoint environment—on your local computer, for example—and needs to be uploaded to the environment, select the From Computer option from the Video and Audio drop-down on the Insert ribbon tab. Then select the file to upload and the library to upload it to. The file is uploaded to the designated location and referenced within the page.

- Approach 2: If the video or audio is in a web-accessible location and needs to be referenced from its current location through an embedded object reference, identify the file by selecting the Embedded option from the Video and Audio drop-down menu on the Insert ribbon tab. The Embed window, which then appears, allows entry of the object reference.

- Approach 3: If the video or audio file is stored in the SharePoint environment, reference it by selecting the From SharePoint option from the Video and Audio drop-down menu of the Insert ribbon tab. Then select the file to reference from the SharePoint site collection.

- Approach 4: If the video or audio file exists in a web-accessible location and can be referenced through a standard URL, reference the file by using the From Address option of the Video and Audio drop-down menu of the Insert ribbon tab. Then enter the URL for the audio or video file.

Adding Links

Link references can be added to wiki pages to create references to other web resources, such as to items that exist in other locations within your SharePoint environment or to web resources external to it. Two approaches can be used to add links to the page.

- Approach 1: If the item you want to create a reference to exists in your SharePoint site collection, select the From SharePoint option from the Link drop-down of the Insert ribbon tab. Then select the item to reference, and the link is added to the page.

- Approach 2: If the item to reference does not exist within your SharePoint environment, reference it by selecting the From Address option from the Link drop-down of the Insert ribbon tab. Then enter the URL of the item and the text to display for the item.

Adding App Parts or Web Parts

App parts and web parts add business functionality to SharePoint sites. They are added to a wiki page to introduce functionality to it. You can add an app part or web part to a page by selecting the appropriate option from the Insert ribbon tab. Then select the app part or web part to add to the page. Once on the page, the item can be configured. Managing app parts and web parts is discussed later in this chapter.

Adding Embedded Code

Just as standard web objects can be embedded in SharePoint pages, if you wish to add script logic to a page, you can embed code directly in the page. Embed an item by selecting the Embed Code option from the Insert ribbon tab, and then enter the code to be placed on the page.

Publishing Pages

The last type of page available in SharePoint is the publishing page. It is not available in SharePoint Foundation, only as part of SharePoint Server Standard or Enterprise. Publishing pages contain web part zones, like web part pages, and rich text entry zones, like wiki pages. Use publishing pages when you want to control the overall layout of the page but want to provide page editors the ability to manage content within the structure. This type of page is commonly used to create standard templated pages, such as press releases or case studies, where you want a consistent layout for each of the items created.

Enabling Publishing Pages

In order to use publishing pages within a site, the publishing features need to be enabled. By default these features are available in publishing sites but need to be enabled in other site types. To enable the use of publishing pages in a site along with the other publishing capabilities of SharePoint, you need to activate the SharePoint Server Publishing Infrastructure feature, and then enable the SharePoint Server Publishing feature within the site where you want to use publishing pages.

To enable the SharePoint Server Publishing Infrastructure site collection feature, do the following:

1. Navigate to the root site in the site collection.

2. On the root site home page, select the Site Settings option from the Settings menu.

3. On the Site Settings page, select the Site Collection Features option from the Site Collection Administration section.

4. On the Site Collection Features page, select the Activate option for the SharePoint Server Publishing Infrastructure site collection feature.

The site collection feature is activated. With this done, you then need to activate the SharePoint Server Publishing feature within the site where you want to use publishing pages. To activate this feature, do the following:

1. Navigate to the site where you want to use publishing pages.

2. From the site's home page, select the Site Settings option from the Settings menu.

3. On the Site Settings page, select the Manage Site Features option from the Site Actions section.

4. On the Site Features page, select the Activate option for the SharePoint Server Publishing feature.

The now active publishing features will allow you to create SharePoint publishing pages.

Creating Publishing Pages

SharePoint Server publishing pages are managed within the site's Pages library. This library is created when the SharePoint Server Publishing feature is enabled. To create a new publishing page, do the following:

1. Navigate to the site where you want to create the page.

2. On the site's home page, select the New option from the Page ribbon tab.

3. In the New Page window, enter the name for the page, and click the Create button.

The page is created, and you are navigated to the new page in Edit mode.

Editing Publishing Pages

Users with Contribute right or higher within the site can create and manage publishing pages. To edit a publishing page do the following:

1. Navigate to the publishing page you want to edit.

2. On the page, select the Edit Page option from the Settings menu.

3. Make your updates to the page, and once done, click the Save option from the Format Text ribbon tab.

4. Publish the page. Other users see the changes by selecting the Publish option from the Publish ribbon tab.

You can make several types of changes to publishing pages when editing them. Changes that can be made to these pages include determining page layout, creating and managing content, and configuring apps and web parts. Publishing pages include two types of zones, along with other elements focused on configuring web-based content. The zone types in a publishing page include the following:

- *Wiki zones* allow management of rich text content, pictures, videos, apps, web parts, and other content (see the "Wiki Page" section, above).

- *Web Part zones* allow inclusion of web parts and app parts that can be added to and configured within these zones.

- *Page Image* allows identification of an image to be displayed on a page in the identified location.

- *Rollup Image* allows identification of an image to be used in other site pages that reference the page using the content query web part or other page rollup tools.

- *Summary Links* is an area within the page containing one or more Summary Links web parts. This area allows identification of links to be displayed on the page.

Within these different zones, related content can be added and managed.

Changing a Page Layout

The page layout defines the number and configuration of zones within a page. When a publishing page is initially created, its layout is based on the Body Only article page layout, which includes a content area and rollup image, as seen in Figure 4-5.

Figure 4-5. Body Only article page layout

To change the page layout for a publishing page while viewing the page in Edit mode, select the desired page layout from the Page Layout drop-down menu on the Page ribbon tab. The available layouts include the following:

- ***Article Pages***
  - *Body Only*: This type of page includes a single content area covering the full page. It also contains a Rollup Image section where you can reference an image used when the page is listed in other areas of the site (see Figure 4-5).
  - *Image on Left*: This page layout is similar to the Body Only layout in that it contains the full-page content area and the Rollup Image section. As Figure 4-6 shows, this page also includes a page image that is listed in the upper left area of the page. Article Date and Byline fields are also listed.

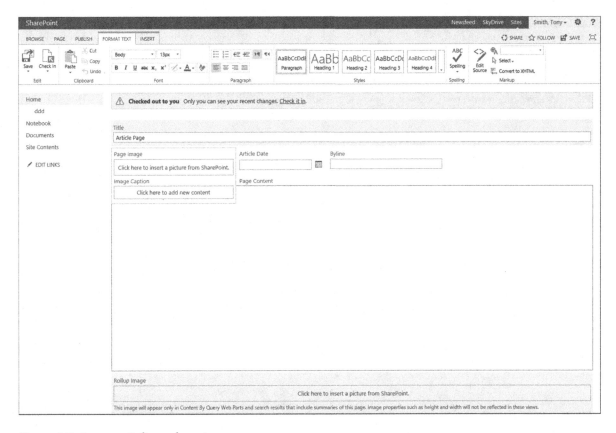

Figure 4-6. *Image on Left page layout*

- *Image on Right*: This page layout and the Image on Left layout contain the same elements, the only difference being that the page image is located to the right of the content area instead of the left.

- *Summary Links*: This layout and the Image on Right layout contain the same structure, but in place of the page image is a Summary Links web part allowing management of a set of related links (see Figure 4-7).

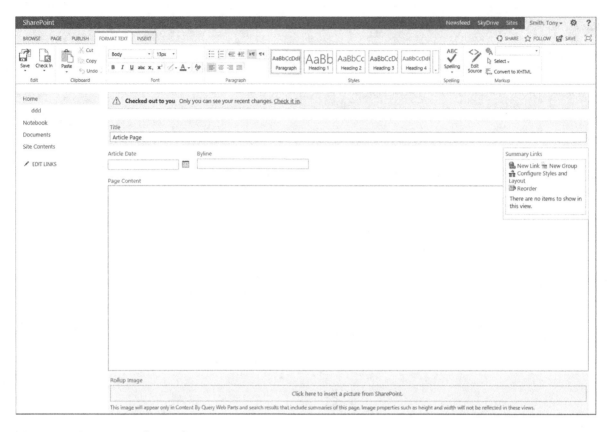

Figure 4-7. *Summary Links page layout*

- ***Catalog Item Reuse***
  - *Blank Catalog Item*: This page layout is used to show Catalog content. It can reference the catalog item and has a series of web part zones, including the Table of Contents web part (see Figure 4-8), with which to manage content.

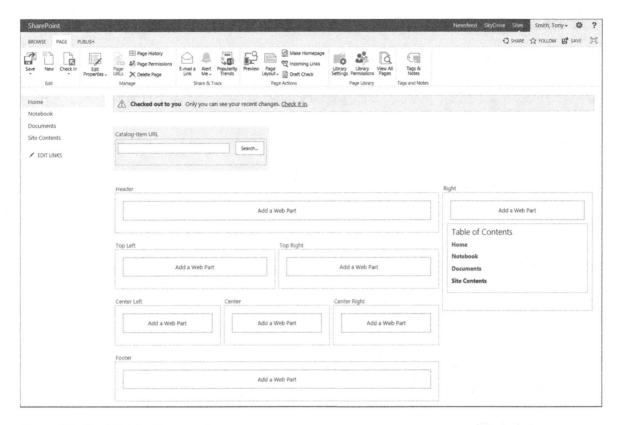

Figure 4-8. *Blank Catalog Item page layout*

- *Catalog Item Image on Left*: This layout allows selection of the catalog item to reference within the page.

- **Enterprise Wiki Page**

  - *Basic Page*: This layout is the only wiki page layout in the Publishing Page layouts. It includes a single wiki zone, like those described in the Wiki Pages section, above. The page also includes a rating option and has the ability to categorize the page.

- **Error Page**

  - *Error*: This type of page includes only a byline, a page content area, and a rollup image.

- **Project Page**

  - *Basic Project Page*: This layout includes a single wiki zone, with an area to the right that allows configuration of metadata about the project to be associated with the page (see Figure 4-9).

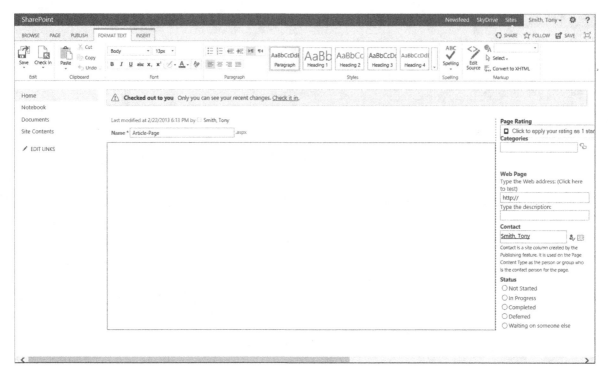

Figure 4-9. *Basic Project Page layout*

- ***Redirect Page***
  - *Redirect*: This type of page has a field that identifies the URL to navigate to when the page is accessed. This page can be any URL and does not need to be located within SharePoint (see Figure 4-10).

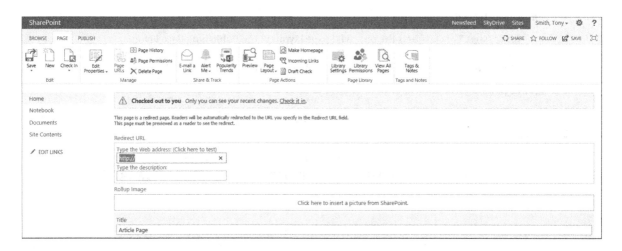

Figure 4-10. *Redirect Page layout*

- *Welcome Page*
  - *Blank Web Part Page*: This page layout includes a full-page wiki zone area for adding content, followed by a series of web part zones for inclusion of web parts within the page (see Figure 4-11).

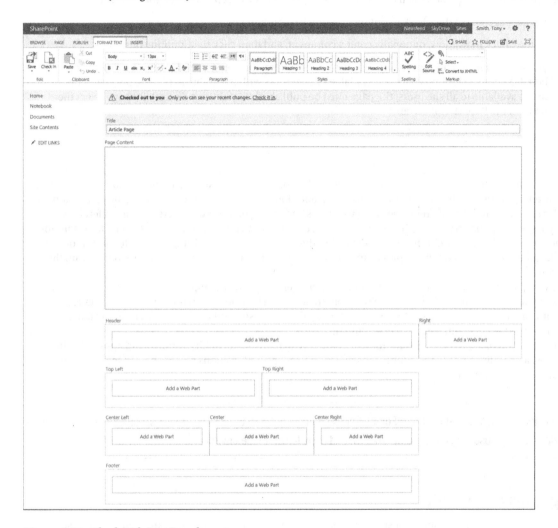

Figure 4-11. *Blank Web Part Page layout*

- *Splash*: This layout can include an image and a set of links, followed by a set of web part zones.

- *Summary Links*: This layout is similar to that of the Blank Web Part Page. It contains the page image area and the page content area. Below the content area, however, this layout also contains a pair of Summary Links web parts that can be used to configure links on the page. Below this pair of web parts is a set of additional web part zones for adding web parts and app parts to the page.

Checking In and Publishing Pages

The publishing pages library, created when the SharePoint Server Publishing feature is activated, has versioning enabled by default. Versioning requires that you check in pages after edits are made and publish the pages before changes become available to general site users. To check in a page that has been edited, do the following:

1. On the page, select the Check In option from the Page ribbon tab.

2. In the Check In window, optionally enter a comment, and then click the Continue button.

The page is checked in as a minor version. For example, if the previous version of the page was 1.0, the new version will be 1.1. Minor versions of a page are available only to users with the ability to edit the page. In order to make the changes available to all site users, the page must be published. To publish a SharePoint page select the Publish option from the Publish ribbon tab.

Apps

In previous versions of SharePoint, when you wanted to add business logic or customized information views to site pages, you used web parts. In SharePoint 2013, apps are an additional option for introducing this type of functionality.

In order to understand the difference between web parts and apps, you need to understand the different ways these two types of components work. Web part solutions are deployed into an environment as either a farm solution or a sandbox solution. Farm solutions have full trust within the SharePoint farm and are available for activation in all the site collections. Sandbox solutions, deployed into a specific site collection, are available for use only within that site collection.

Where web parts are deployed in the SharePoint farm to leverage resources, apps are stand-alone applications. This isolates their execution and allows them to run from their own web locations. SharePoint apps are made available from an online SharePoint App Store that is managed by Microsoft and from internal corporate app catalogs that can be managed from within your own environment.

With the addition of apps comes the addition of being able to manage the ability to download apps, selecting apps to deploy, and adding apps to the appropriate pages for use. The next sections discuss how to manage and use apps within your SharePoint sites.

> ■ **Note** It is the responsibility of the SharePoint technical administrator to create app catalogs, configure connections to app catalogs, and set users' security rights to download apps to use in the environment.

Adding Apps to Your Site

For apps to be available within a SharePoint site, a site manager must first add the app to SharePoint for use. A site manager's ability to add apps to SharePoint depends upon the app management settings defined by the SharePoint technical administrator, who can select from the following options to determine site managers' ability to manage apps.

- *Do not allow users to add apps.* This option allows site managers to work only with apps that have already been added to the SharePoint environment for use. The only apps addable to pages are the app parts for lists and libraries contained in the site.

- *Allow users to request apps.* This option allows site owners to access the app store to identify apps they are interested in adding. They can create a request for a desired app that then must be approved by a SharePoint technical administrator, who will download the app. This allows centralized management of apps and controls app purchases while letting site administrators identify and select apps they feel will meet their business needs.

- *Allow users to add apps.* This option allows site owners to access the app store and add apps to their SharePoint sites without the involvement of the SharePoint technical administrator. This gives site administrators complete control over app management in their sites.

Adding Apps Directly

As already discussed, your ability to add apps to SharePoint depends on settings configured by your SharePoint technical administrator. When the environment is configured to allow site owners to add apps, you can add apps from your corporate app repository or from the online SharePoint app store. To add an app from the online app store or from your corporate app repository, do the following:

1. Navigate to the site where you want to add the app.

2. From the Settings menu of the site, select the Add an App option.

3. On the Your Apps page (see Figure 4-12), select the SharePoint Store option from the Quick Launch area.

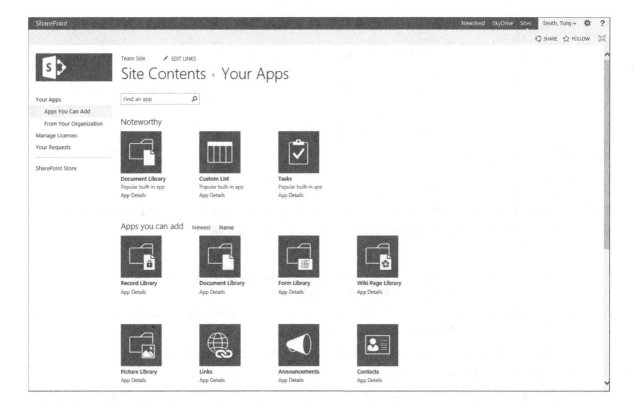

Figure 4-12. *Your Apps page*

4. On the SharePoint Store page (see Figure 4-13), select the app to install. In this example, the World Clock and Weather app has been selected.

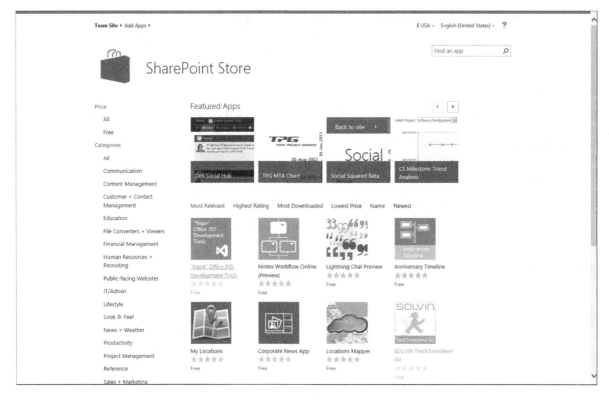

Figure 4-13. *SharePoint Store page*

■ **Caution**   Some apps in the app store are free, but others must be purchased. Note the app's cost before downloading it. Also, some apps are free previews of products that must later be purchased for continued use.

---

5. On an app's detail page, review details about the app, including the description and user ratings, and then choose the Add It option to add the app.

6. On the Market Place page, log on to the online store using your Microsoft account (this is the same as your Windows Live ID).

7. On the "Confirm that you wish to add the app" page, click the Continue option.

8. On the App Added confirmation screen, click the Return to Site option.

The app is added for use in your site from within the Your Apps page. As discussed earlier, you can then add the app to the appropriate SharePoint pages.

Requesting Apps to Add

When your SharePoint technical administrator has configured the environment so that site owners can request apps but not install apps directly, you will need to get the administrator's approval for apps you want to install. To request an app, do the following:

1. Navigate to the site where you want to add the app.

2. From the Settings menu of the site, select the Add an App option.

3. On the Your Apps page (see Figure 4-12), select the SharePoint Store option from the Quick Launch area.

4. On the SharePoint Store page (see Figure 4-13), select the app to install. In this example, the World Clock and Weather app has been selected.

5. On the app's detail page, review the app's details, and select the Request It option.

6. In the App Request window, identify the following:

   a. Enter the user license details: specify the number of users the request is for or note that the request is for the entire organization.

   b. Enter a justification for the request. That is, identify why the app is needed.

   c. Click the Request button to complete the request.

Viewing Your App Requests

After you have placed a request for an app, you can track its status through the Site Content area as follows:

1. Navigate to the site collection where you made the request.

2. From the Settings menu, select the Add an App option.

3. On the Your Apps page, select the Your Requests option from the Quick Launch area.

4. On the Your Requests page, view the details for the identified request, as shown in Figure 4-14.

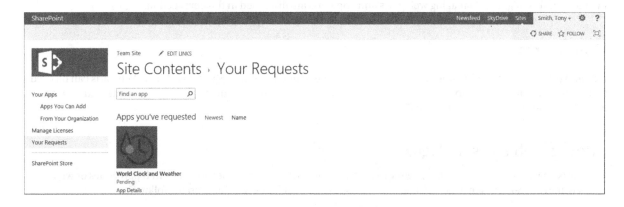

Figure 4-14. *Your Requests page*

Once the SharePoint technical administrator approves the request and adds the app, it is available for use in your SharePoint site.

Removing Apps

Apps that have been added to the SharePoint environment can later be removed if needed. To remove an app, do the following:

1. Navigate to the site collection where you want to remove the app.

2. On the home page of the site, select the Site Contents option.

3. On the Site Contents page click the " ... " option next to the app to remove.

■ **Note** The default apps installed in the SharePoint environment will not have the " ..." option and cannot be removed.

---

4. On the apps hover panel, select the " ..." option, and choose the Remove option.

5. On the deletion confirmation screen, select the OK button to remove the application.

The app is removed, and you are returned to the Site Content page.

Adding App Parts to Pages

Once apps have been added to the environment, they can be added to site pages. To add an app to a page, do the following:

1. Navigate to the page where the app is to be added.

2. On the page, select the Edit option to edit the page.

3. Within the Edit mode of the page, select the location to place the app, and from the ribbon select the App Part option from the Insert tab.

4. On the Parts list, select the app to add to the page, and then select the Add button.

The app part is added to the page, and you can configure it as necessary. App parts have different configurations depending on the configuration needs of the app, and they are managed and configured just as web parts are managed and configured. Managing web parts and app parts are discussed in the next section.

Web Parts

Like app parts, web parts add information views and business functionality to SharePoint sites. Web parts can be used to display details in lists and libraries, implement process, interface with outside databases or systems, and provide any other application solution functionality.

Adding Web Parts to Pages

Web parts can be added to any of the pages discussed previously. They are added to either web part zones or wiki zones within SharePoint site pages. To add a web part to a web part zone in a page, do the following:

1. Navigate to the web part or publishing page to be edited.

2. Place the page into Edit mode (how to do this was explained earlier in this chapter).

3. Click the Add a Web Part link in the web part zone where you want to add the web part.

4. Select the web part to add from the Parts list (see Figure 4-15), and click the Add button.

Figure 4-15. *SharePoint page Parts list*

The web part is added to the page in the top of the web part zone where the Add a Web Part link was clicked. You can drag and drop this web part into the appropriate position in the zone.

To add a web part to a wiki page zone, do the following:

1. Navigate to the wiki or publishing page to be edited.

2. Place the page into Edit mode.

3. Place the cursor in the wiki zone where you want to add the web part.

4. From the Insert ribbon tab, select the Web Part option.

5. Select the web part to add from the Parts list (see Figure 4-15), and click the Add button.

The web part is added to the page in the location where the cursor was placed.

Editing Web Parts

Web parts have properties that govern their configurations. These properties including display settings, connectivity details, and business capability definitions. To edit a web part's properties, do the following:

1. Navigate to the page containing the web part to be configured.

2. Place the page into Edit mode.

3. From the web part drop-down menu, select the Edit Web Part option (see Figure 4-16).

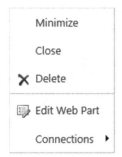

Figure 4-16. *Edit Web Part options menu*

4. In the Web Part Properties window, update the web part's properties, and click the Apply button to save them.

The properties of a web part are specific to the purpose and configuration needs of the web part itself. There are also some common properties available across most web parts to—manage, as Figure 4-17 shows.

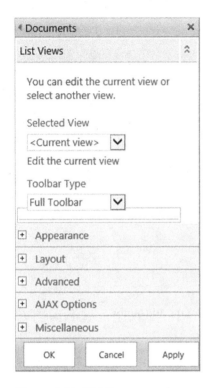

Figure 4-17. *Web Part properties screen*

Common properties include the following:

- *Appearance*: These settings are used to identify properties that manage the appearance of the web part.

  - *Title*: specifies the text displayed in the web part's title bar.

  - *Height*: specifies the height of the web part. The default option is to adjust the height based on the content's needs. However, you can also specify a fixed height for the web part.

  - *Width*: specifies the width of the web part. The default option is to adjust the width based on the width of the zone and the contained content. However, you can also specify a fixed width for the web part.

  - *Chrome State*: determines whether the web part is minimized by default.

  - *Chrome Type*: specifies whether to display the title bar and border for the web part.

- *Layout*: These settings identify the general web part display properties.

    - *Hidden*: specifies whether the web part is hidden on the page. If it is, it is still part of the page but is not visible to site users.

    - *Direction*: allows control of the direction in which the content within the web part is displayed.

    - *Zone*: specifies the zone the web part is located within when it is part of a web part page.

    - *Zone Index*: determines the order of the web part in the zone relative to other web parts in the same zone when it is part of a web part page.

- *Advanced*: These settings allow you to determine which web part capabilities are made available to site users.

    - *Allow Minimize*: specifies whether the web part can be minimized on the page.

    - *Allow Close*: specifies whether page users can close a web part located within a web part page.

    - *Allow Hide*: specifies whether the web part can be hidden within a page located within a web part page.

    - *Allow Zone Change*: specifies whether the web part can be moved to another zone within a page located within a web part page.

    - *Allow Connections*: specifies whether the web part is allowed to be connected to other web parts.

    - *Allow Editing in Personal View*: specifies whether the web part can be edited when the page is in a personal view.

    - *Title URL*: specifies whether the title of the web part can be clicked to navigate to an associated URL and identifies the web address to navigate to.

    - *Description*: identifies the hover text to be displayed when the mouse hovers over the title of the web part.

    - *Help URL*: identifies the URL to navigate to when the Help option is selected from the web part context menu.

    - *Help Mode*: specifies how the help pages are displayed to the users.

    - *Catalog Icon Image URL*: allows display of an image for the web part when it is added to the pages.

    - *Title Icon Image URL*: allows display of an image in the title bar of the web part.

    - *Import Error Message*: specifies the message to display to users if there is a problem when attempting to display the web part.

    - *Target Audiences*: specifies whether the web part is to be targeted to a specific user or group.

Removing Web Parts

Web parts listed on a page can be removed if they are no longer needed. Remove a web part by doing the following:

1. Navigate to the page to be edited.

2. Place the page into Edit mode.

3. From the web part drop-down menu (see Figure 4-16), select the Delete option.

4. In the deletion confirmation window, select the OK button.

The web part is removed from the page.

Connecting Web Parts

Many of the web parts available in SharePoint can be connected to other web parts. This allows details in one web part to be used to filter content in another. Web part connections are made between provider web parts and consumer web parts. These connections pass identified information from the provider web part to the consumer web part.

SharePoint filter web parts are specifically designed to act as provider web parts that can be connected to other web parts, such as list or library views, in order to filter them. For example, you could add a date filter to a page to filter the details in a calendar list to show just those items falling on the identified date. To create a connection between a provider and consumer web part, do the following:

1. Navigate to the page containing the web parts to be connected.

2. Place the page into Edit mode.

3. On the filter web part, select the Connections option, then Send Filter Values To, and then the consumer web part from the web part menu, as shown in Figure 4-16.

4. On the Web Part Dialog Choose Connection page, click the Configure button.

5. On the Web Part Dialog Configure Connection page, select the column that the provider web part is to supply and the column that the consumer web part is to apply the connection against. Then click the Finish button.

The connection is established between the web parts, and the consumer web part is filtered based on the provider web part.

Exporting and Importing Web Parts

Once a web part has been added to a page and properly configured, you may want to export it so that it can be imported into other pages. Doing so allows an exact copy of the web part to be created within other pages.

Exporting a web part creates an XML file containing configuration details for the part. To export a web part, do the following:

1. Navigate to the page containing the web part to be exported.

2. Place the page in Edit mode.

3. From the web part menu, select the Export option.

4. Select where you want to save the exported file.

An exported web part file can be imported into a SharePoint page, where it can be added to the information already displayed. The page will import the exact configuration the web part had when exported. To import a web part into a page, do the following:

1. Navigate to the page where you want to add the web part.

2. Place the page in Edit mode.

3. Select to add a new web part to the page.

4. In the Parts list under the Categories section, select the Upload a Web Part option.

5. In the Upload Web Part box, browse to the file you want to upload, and click the Upload button.

6. Select to add a web part to the page.

7. On the web part selection screen from the Imported Web Parts category, select the uploaded web part, and click the Add button.

The web part is added to the page. Use this approach when you only need to upload the web part into a specific page. It is also possible to upload a web part so that it appears in one of the available web part configurations in the parts list. Over time, the web part can be added to multiple pages within your environment by uploading it into the web part gallery. To import a web part to the web part gallery, do the following:

1. Navigate to the root site in the site collection.

2. Select the Site Settings option from the settings menu.

3. On the Site Settings page, click the Web Parts link under the Galleries section.

4. On the Web Part Gallery page, select the Upload Document command from the New group on the Document ribbon tab.

5. In the Upload Web Part window, click the Browse button.

6. In the Choose File dialog, browse to the exported web part file, and select it. Then click the Open button.

7. In the Upload Web Part window, click the OK button.

8. In the Edit Item window, edit the name, title, and description loaded from the file, and then select a group and optional recommendation settings to determine how the web part is organized and presented to users.

9. Click the Save button.

The web part is added to the Web Part Gallery and is made available when adding web parts to pages within the site collection.

Standard SharePoint Web Parts

There are a variety of default web parts available within SharePoint. These default web parts provide a variety of capabilities to SharePoint sites and allow you to take advantage of many of the SharePoint services, including search, Excel services, PerformancePoint services, and others. These web parts are organized into the following categories and include the following web parts.

Apps

The Apps category lists the app parts available within the environment. App parts available by default include references to each of the lists and libraries available in the current site (apps were discussed earlier in the chapter).

List View App Part

An instance of the List View app part is available in each of the site's lists and libraries. This app part is used to display list information on the page with one of the list's views. You can also create a custom view to display the information from the list or library. Users can be given the ability to view and manage content within the list through this app part. An example of this app part is shown in Figure 4-18.

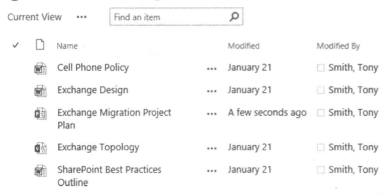

Documents

⊕ new document or drag files here

Current View ⋯	Find an item 🔍		
✓ 🗋 Name		Modified	Modified By
📄 Cell Phone Policy	⋯	January 21	☐ Smith, Tony
📄 Exchange Design	⋯	January 21	☐ Smith, Tony
📄 Exchange Migration Project Plan	⋯	A few seconds ago	☐ Smith, Tony
📄 Exchange Topology	⋯	January 21	☐ Smith, Tony
📄 SharePoint Best Practices Outline	⋯	January 21	☐ Smith, Tony

Figure 4-18. *List View app part*

The options available to configure List View app parts include the items in Table 4-3.

Table 4-3. *List View App Part Properties*

Property	Description
Selected View	Allows selection of the list view to display within the app part. This includes a list of all views available within the list as well as the Summary View. The Summary View is the default view for the type of list the app part is being used to display. In this section you can also select the Edit the Current View option to customize the selected view.
Toolbar Type	Allows selection of the toolbar configuration for the app part. Options available for the toolbar selection include Full Toolbar, Summary Toolbar, No Toolbar, and Show Toolbar.

Blog

The Blog category lists web parts used to display details about blogs. All web parts in this category are available in all versions of SharePoint and are designed to be used within blog sites. The default set of web parts available in this category includes the following:

Blog Archives

The Blog Archives web part provides a set of references to old blog posts located in the current blog site.

Blog Notifications

The Blog Notifications web part can be added to a blog site. It provides registration links for the site's RSS feed or alerts to site activities. Like the Blog Archives part, this part includes no special configuration capabilities beyond standard SharePoint web part configurations.

Blog Tools

The Blog Tools web part provides a set of links for managing a blog site. This web part also has no custom configurations.

Business Data

The Business Data web part category is not available in SharePoint Foundation. Some of its web parts are available only in SharePoint Server Enterprise, while others are available in both SharePoint Server Standard and Enterprise. The Business Data category includes web parts for managing different forms of data to be integrated into site pages. The web parts within this category include the following:

Business Data Actions

The Business Data Actions web part, available only within SharePoint Server Enterprise, provides a list of business data connectivity actions that can be performed. When added to a page, this web part must be configured to connect to the appropriate external content type. Table 4-4 lists the configuration options for the Business Data Actions web part.

Table 4-4. *Business Data Actions Web Part Properties*

Property	Description
Type	Used to identify the external content type for which business data actions are to be displayed.
Item	Used to identify the item or items for which business data actions are to be displayed.
Actions	Allows selection of actions to display and specifies whether new actions are to be displayed by default.
Style	Identifies the styling for the list of actions, with styles including Bulleted List, List, and Tool Bar.

Business Data Connectivity Filter

The Business Data Connectivity Filter web part, also available only in SharePoint Server Enterprise, is used to permit filtering of content returned through data connections.

Business Data Item

Available only in SharePoint Server Enterprise, the Business Data Item web part is used to present a single item from a defined data source. and is used in conjunction with the Business Data Item Builder to identify the item to be presented. Table 4-5 includes the configuration options for the Business Data Item web part.

Table 4-5. Business Data Item Web Part Properties

Property	Description
Type	Used to identify the external content type for which business data actions are to be displayed.
View	Allows selection of the external content type view to use for selecting the business data item.
Item	Used to identify the item or items for which business data actions are to be displayed.
Display Animation While Loading	Allows specification whether an animation is to be displayed when the content is loaded in the web part.
Fields	Allows specification of fields to display for the selected item.
Actions	Allows selection of actions to display and specifies whether new actions are to be displayed by default.
XSL Editor	Used to customize the view of the business data item being displayed.

Business Data Item Builder

The Business Data Item Builder web part is used to identify a data item from a data connection based on parameters passed into the page through the query string. This identified item can then be presented through the Business Data Item web part. The Business Data Item Builder web part is available only in SharePoint Server Enterprise.

Business Data List

The Business Data List web part, available only in SharePoint Server Enterprise, is used to present a list of items from an identified data connection. This web part is used in conjunction with such data retrieval web parts as the Business Data Connectivity Filter or the Business Data Related List to identify the items to be presented (see Figure 4-19).

Business Data List

Actions ▾

CustomerName	CustomerCRMID	CustomerAddress
Datalan Corporation	123A_NY	12 Water St. White Plains, NY
Pen Corporation	156C_CT	2001 RidgeField Rd. Stamford, CT
MAC Corporation	122A_NY	123 Park Ave. NY, NY

Figure 4-19. Business Data List web part

Table 4-6 lists the options available to configure the Business Data List web part.

Table 4-6. *Business Data List Web Part Properties*

Property	Description
Type	Used to identify the external content type for which business data actions are to be displayed.
View	Allows selection of the external content type view to use for selecting the business data item.
Display Toolbar	Specifies whether the toolbar is to be displayed for the presented list.
Display Animation While Loading	Specifies whether an animation is to be displayed when the content is loaded in the web part.
XSL Editor	Used to customize the view of the business data item being displayed.

Excel Web Access

The Excel Web Access web part, available in both SharePoint Server Standard and Enterprise, is used to show content in an Excel workbook within the web page (see Figure 4-20).

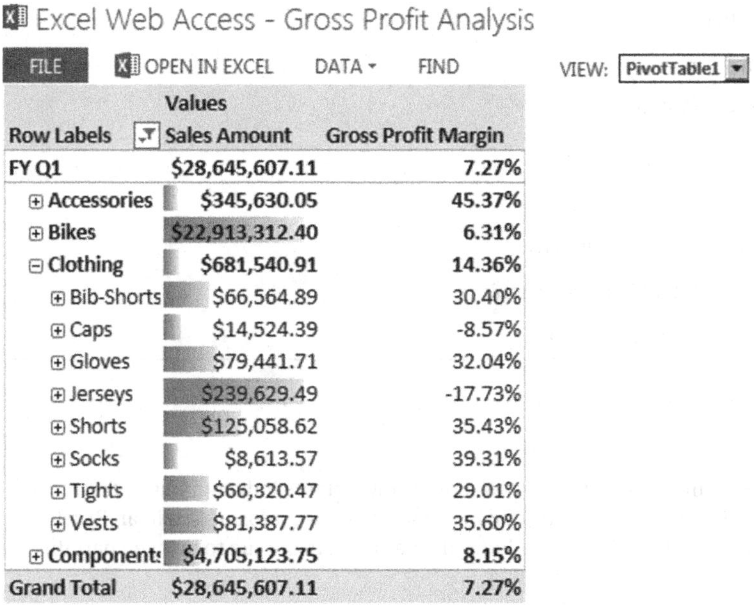

Figure 4-20. *Excel Web Access web part*

The Excel Web Access web part has several properties that need to be configured. These configurations include the items listed in Table 4-7.

Table 4-7. *Excel Web Access Web Part Properties*

Property	Description
Workbook	Identifies the Excel document to be referenced.
Named Item	Identifies the named item in the Excel document to be displayed. This can be any named object, such as a PivotTable or Chart, or a named range.
Title Bar	Specifies whether the web part title and the web part title URL are to be automatically generated.
Type of Toolbar	Specifies whether the toolbar is to be Full, Summary, Navigation Only, or None.
Toolbar Menu Commands	Specifies which menu commands are to be available and allows selection of the following: • Open in Excel, Download, Download a Snapshot • Refresh Selected Connection, Refresh All Connections • Calculate Workbook • Named Item Drop-Down List
Navigation	Specifies whether navigation hyperlinks are to be included.
Interactivity	Allows selection of the type of interactivity with the Excel data the web part is to support. The options available for selection include the following: • All Workbook Interactivity • Typing and Formula Entry • Parameter Modifications • Display Parameters Task Pane • Sorting • Filtering • All PivotTable & PivotChart Interactivity • Periodically Refresh if Enabled in Workbook • PivotTable & PivotChart Modification

Indicator Details

Available only in SharePoint Server Enterprise, this web part is used to show a single status indicator based on information retrieved through a data connection, information located in a SharePoint list, information in an Excel workbook, or information in an Analysis Services KPI. Table 4-8 includes the parameters unique to the web part that need to be configured.

Table 4-8. *Indicator Details Web Part Properties*

Property	Description
Status List	Identifies the list against which the Indicator Detail web part is to be configured.
Status Indicator	Identifies the item in the list to base the indicator on.
Change Icon	Identifies the icon to use for the status indicator, with the options being Default, Checkmarks, Flat, and Traffic Lights.

Status List

The Status List web part shows status indicators, or KPIs, to represent important measures. This web part is available only in SharePoint Server Enterprise. The web part is configured through the management of the options listed in Table 4-9.

Table 4-9. *Status List Web Part Properties*

Property	Description
Indicator List	Identifies the list against which the Status List web part is to be configured.
Change Icon	Identifies the icon to use for the status indicator, with the options being Default, Checkmarks, Flat, and Traffic Lights. Also, identifies which icon and toolbar properties to include, selecting from the following: • Show Only Status Icon • Show Only Problems • Hide the Toolbar • Display edit toolbar in View mode
Display multiple indicators columns	Used to determine whether multiple columns are to be displayed in the web part.
Status Indicator	Specifies the item in the list to be the indicator for the web part.
Column or Dimension	Specifies the column to use for the indicator.
Hierarchy	Identifies the hierarchy for the web part.
Members to Display	Identifies the items from the hierarchy items to be included.

Visio Web Access

The Visio Web Access web part, used to show the contents of a Visio diagram file in a SharePoint page (see Figure 4-21), is available in both SharePoint Server Standard and Enterprise.

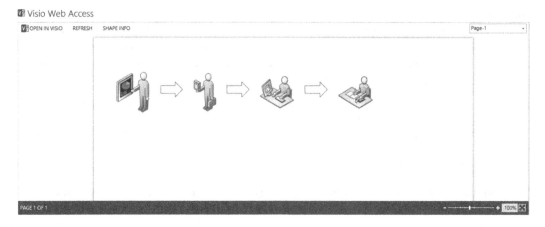

Figure 4-21. *Visio Web Access web part*

The Visio Web Access web part has several properties that need to be configured, including the items listed in Table 4-10.

Table 4-10. *Visio Web Access Web Part Properties*

Property	Description
Web Drawing URL	Identifies the Visio document to reference.
Force raster rendering (applies to VDW files only)	Determines whether raster rendering is to be forced to occur for the web part display.
Automatic Refresh Interval (in minutes)	Identifies how frequently the diagram display is to be refreshed.
Fit all shapes in view	Determines whether the diagram is to be sized to fit in the display of the web part in the page.
Index of the initial page to show	Identifies which page in the Visio diagram to display when the web part is initially accessed.
Expose the following shape data items to web part connections	Specifies whether any of the objects in the Visio diagram configured with data connection display are to be manageable through web part connections (connecting web parts is discussed later in this chapter).
Toolbars and User Interface	Identifies user interactivity with the Visio menus to be made available in the web part, including the following options: • Show Refresh • Show Open in Visio • Show Page Navigation • Show Status Bar • Show the Shape Information Pane • Show default background

(*continued*)

Table 4-10. (*continued*)

Property	Description
Web Drawing Interactivity	Specifies whether the diagram interactivity is to be restricted within the web part by disabling diagram interaction options, including the following: • Disable Zoom • Disable Pan • Disable Hyperlink • Disable Selection

Community

The Community category of web parts includes items used to support community sites within the environment. All of the web parts listed in this category are available in both SharePoint Server Standard and Enterprise but not in SharePoint Foundation.

About the Community

The About the Community web part displays the general community details for a site with the community features enabled. This includes information such as the community description and the date the community was established. The web part does not include any custom configuration options to be managed.

Join

The Join web part allows individuals who access the community site to join the community. This makes them members of the community.

My Membership

The My Membership web part lists membership details, including reputation details, for the person currently visiting the site. Community reputation is discussed in more detail in Chapter 12.

Tools

The Tools web part lists a set of community management feature links for the community site.

What's Happening

The What's Happening web part lists a summary of the activities occurring within the current community site, including how many members have joined, the number of discussions within the site, and the total number of replies made against those discussions, as shown in Figure 4-22.

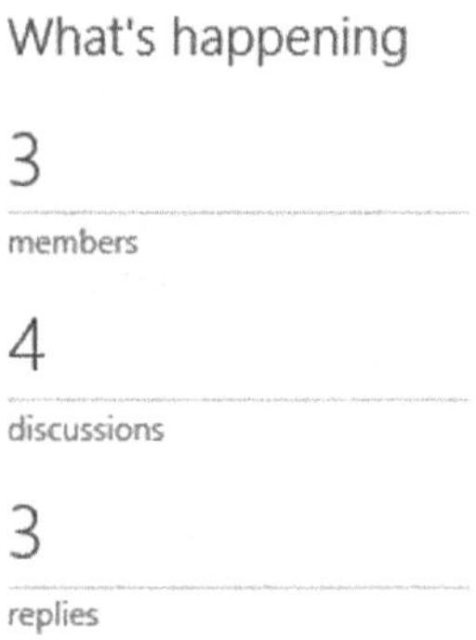

What's happening

3
members

4
discussions

3
replies

Figure 4-22. *What's happening web part*

Content Rollup

The Content Rollup category of web parts includes a set of web parts designed to organize and present information managed within SharePoint. Content in lists and libraries throughout the environment can be organized into logical groupings for site users. This category contains web parts available across the various versions of SharePoint.

Categories

The Categories web part is used to display the category details listed in the site directory of the current site collection. This web part is available in SharePoint Server Standard and Enterprise and can be configured to present the site directory details in different ways. The web part is configured through its web part properties. Table 4-11 displays the properties available to be configured.

Table 4-11. *Categories Web Part Properties*

Property	Description
Header Text	Identifies text to present in the top of the web part to act as the header for the information being displayed.
Header Style	Identifies the style for the header information, with the choices being Default, Large Text, Small Text, Banded, Centered, Separator, and Whitespace.
Level 1 Style	Identifies the style for top level items in the category listing, with options including Vertical, Vertical with boxed title, Vertical with large title, Vertical with small title, Horizontal, Horizontal with boxed title, Horizontal with large title, and Horizontal with small title.
Level 2 Style	Identifies the style for the second tier level of items within the site category to be listed, with the style options being the same as those listed for the Level 1 style.
Level 3 Style	Identifies the style for the third tier level of items, with the style options being the same as those for the Level 1 and 2 styles.
Source List	Identifies the list within the site collection that contains the site directory information.
Source View	Identifies the view from the source list to use as the source for the information to display in the web part, with the web part respecting the sorting and filtering defined in the view.

Content Query

The Content Query web part is used to identify content from across the site collection that you want to consolidate into a single information view. This web part, available in both SharePoint Server and Enterprise, allows environment-wide content selection based on content type and metadata details. Figure 4-23 shows an example of the Content Query web part layout consolidating announcements from across sites in a single site collection.

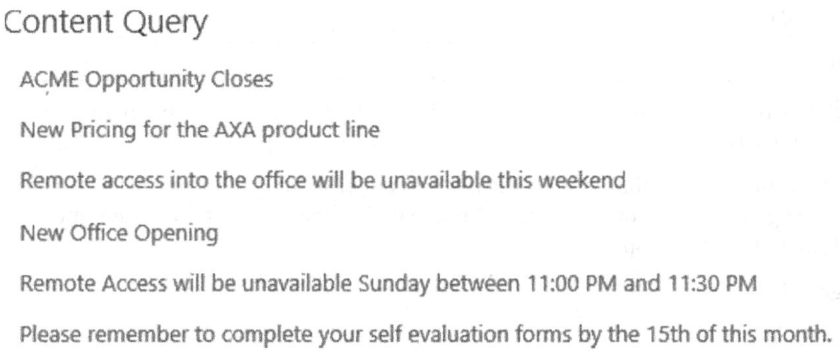

Content Query

ACME Opportunity Closes

New Pricing for the AXA product line

Remote access into the office will be unavailable this weekend

New Office Opening

Remote Access will be unavailable Sunday between 11:00 PM and 11:30 PM

Please remember to complete your self evaluation forms by the 15th of this month.

Figure 4-23. *Content Query web part*

To define the details for the content to be displayed, several properties need to be configured for the Content Query when it is added to a page. These properties are described in Table 4-12.

Table 4-12. *Content Query Web Part Properties*

Property	Description
Source	Identifies the source location for items to be included in the view. Items can come from across the entire site collection, from a specific site location within the site collection, or from a specific list.
List Type	Identifies the type of list from which to take items.
Content Type	Used to identify the source content type on which the content query is to be based and to allow selection of the content type group and content type. You can also specify whether the view is to include content types based on the selected type.
Audience Targeting	Specifies whether information is to be filtered based on audiences and, if it is, whether items not targeted to an audience are to be included.
Additional Filters	Identifies whether the information to be presented is to be further filtered and, if it is, what the filter criteria are to be.
Grouping and Sorting	Specifies whether displayed information is to be grouped and, if it is, by what details, how it is to be sorted and by what column, how many columns the information is to be listed in, and whether any item display limits are to be enforced.
Fields to Display	Identifies the displayed field that is to represent a link to the associated item, the column containing the image to use as the thumbnail image in the view, and the title and description details.
Feed	Identifies whether the content query is to be listed as an RSS feed and, if it is, what details to use as the title and description fields in the feed.

Content Search

Like the Content Query web part, the Content Search web part is used to identify resources to be shown within the current page. The content displayed can be any information crawled by the SharePoint search services and will be organized and displayed based on configuration details, as defined in Table 4-13. This web part is available in SharePoint Server Standard and Enterprise.

Table 4-13. *Content Search Web Part Properties*

Property	Description
Search Criteria	Identifies the search query used to locate items to be displayed and the number of items to include in the display.
Display Templates	Identifies the display control that formats the items to be presented and allows selection of List, List with Paging, or Slideshow. You can also specify the item format for the elements displayed from the following options: • Diagnostic • Large Picture • Picture on left, 3 lines on right • Picture on left, 3 lines on bottom • Recommended Items: Picture on left, 3 lines on right Finally, this property also identifies what is to be displayed when no results are returned.
Property Mappings	Identifies whether the mapping of the managed properties is to be changed from the defaults, with the properties that can be changed including the following: • Picture URL • Link URL • Original Path • SiteID • Line 1 • Line 2 • Line 3
Settings	Specifies where the query results are to be provided and what result table is used to display them. You can also specify the starting item for the results and whether an alternative error message is to be displayed if the query generates an error.

Project Summary

The Project Summary web part lists a summarized view of the task details for the site (see Figure 4-24) and is available in SharePoint Server Enterprise. This web part can be configured to point to any task list within the site through the management of the configuration item listed in Table 4-14.

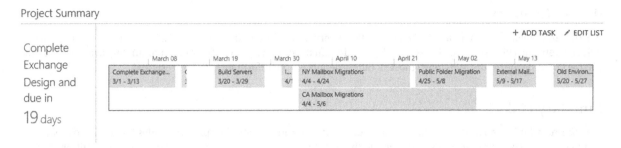

Figure 4-24. *Project Summary web part*

Table 4-14. *Project Summary Web Part Properties*

Property	Description
Primary Task List	Identifies the task list to configure the web part against.
Headlines	Identifies the fields to include in the display.

Relevant Documents

The Relevant Documents web part, available in all versions of SharePoint, lists documents contained within the site that were created or edited by the person currently visiting the site.

RSS Viewer

The RSS Viewer web part, available in SharePoint Server Standard and Enterprise, is used to show the details within an RSS feed. The web part is configured through the web part properties listed in Table 4-15.

Table 4-15. *RSS Viewer Web Part Properties*

Property	Description
RSS Feed URL	Lists the URL to the RSS feed to be displayed within the page.
Feed refresh time (in minutes)	Specifies the interval in which the web part will be refreshed.
Feed Limit	Identifies the item limit for items returned.
Show feed title and description	Specifies whether title and description fields for the feed are to be presented.
Data View Properties	An XSL Editor allowing management of the layout of the RSS data returned.

Site Aggregator

The Site Aggregator web part is used to show documents and tasks located within identified sites assigned to the current user. It is available in SharePoint Server Standard and Enterprise and has no configuration beyond the standard web part configuration options. Web part content is managed by adding tabs within the web part body, using the Add New Tab button and then specifying the URL to add to the site and a title to appear on the new tab.

Sites in Category

The Sites in Category web part, available in SharePoint Server Standard and Enterprise, lists sites in the site directory of the current site collection that are assigned to an identified category. The configuration parameters available for the web part include the ability to manage the XSL Editor details for the information to be presented.

Summary Links

The Summary Links web part, available in SharePoint Server Standard and Enterprise, provides the ability to create a set of formatted web links to allow navigation to the web-based resources. Links can be configured in multiple formats, with bulleted lists and images used to represent the links. They can also be configured to allow the selected item to be opened in the current browser window or in a new window. The configuration of the summary links web part is handled directly within the web part interface by individuals who are able to edit the page (see Figure 4-25).

Figure 4-25. *Summary Links web part management options*

Table of Contents

The Table of Contents web part shows the navigation hierarchy for the current site, including contained sites, lists, and libraries. This web part is available in both SharePoint Server Standard and Enterprise and is configured through the properties defined in Table 4-16.

Table 4-16. *Table of Contents Web Part Properties*

Property	Description
Start From	Identifies the site within the collection from which to start the table of contents view.
Levels to show	Specifies the number of item levels to show in the table of contents.
Show pages	Defines whether pages are to be listed in the table of contents.
Include hidden pages	Defines whether hidden pages are to be listed in the table of contents.
Include hidden sites	Identifies whether hidden sites are to be listed in the table of contents.
Header Text	Specifies the text to show as the table of contents header.
Header Style	Identifies the style for the listed header, with the options including Default, Large Text, Small Text, Banded, Centered, Separator, and Whitespace.
Level 1 Style	Identifies the style for the top level items listed in the table of contents, with style options including Vertical, Vertical with boxed title, Vertical with large title, Vertical with small title, Horizontal, Horizontal with boxed title, Horizontal with large title, and Horizontal with small title.

(continued)

Table 4-16. (*continued*)

Property	Description
Level 2 Style	Identifies the style for the second level items listed in the table of contents, with the style options being the same as those in the Level 1 Style.
Level 3 Style	Identifies the style for the third level items listed in the table of contents, with the style options being the same as those in the Level 1 and 2 Styles
Organization	Identifies the sorting approach for the items listed and allows sorting as in the navigation or based on sorting fields and the direction configured.

Term Property

The Term Property web part shows an identified property from a selected term in the term store. This web part, available in SharePoint Server Standard and Enterprise, must be configured in the page through the web part's properties, which are detailed in Table 4-17.

Table 4-17. *Term Property Web Part Properties*

Property	Description
Term	Used to identify whether the page context term is to be used or a different term is to be selected.
Render Property	Identifies the property to be displayed, the choices being Name, Description, Path, and ID (a custom property can also be entered).

Timeline

The Timeline web part, available in all versions of SharePoint, shows a timeline view of task details within a defined task list (see Figure 4-26).

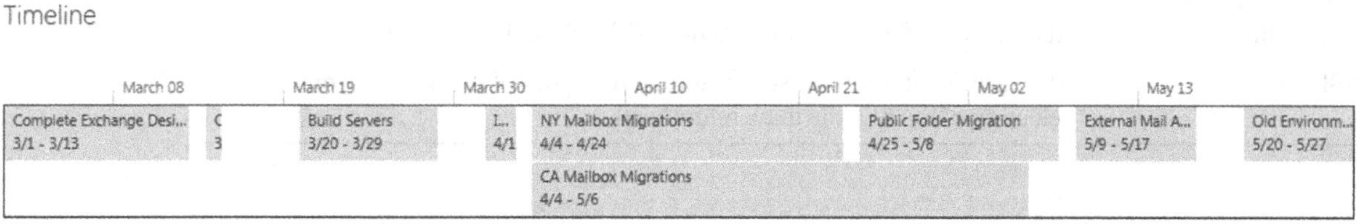

Figure 4-26. *Timeline web part*

The task list to associate with the timeline is identified through the web part properties, which are defined in Table 4-18.

Table 4-18. *Timeline Web Part Properties*

Property	Description
Web URL	Identifies the URL to the web site containing the list.
Type	Specifies the type of object to be identified, with the only option being List.
Source	Allows selection of the task list to base the timeline on.
View Name	Identifies the view within the list to base the timeline on.

WSRP Viewer

The WSRP Viewer web part is available in SharePoint Server Enterprise and can be used to consume WSRP data. The WSRP source to connect with is identified through the properties of the web part listed in Table 4-19.

Table 4-19. *WSRP Web Part Properties*

Property	Description
Producer	Selects the WSRP data producer control.
User Identification	Identifies whether the control uses anonymous access or whether the current user's credentials are to be used.

XML Viewer

The XML Viewer web part is available in all versions of SharePoint and allows the presentation of XML data using XSL to format the information. The web part properties listed in Table 4-20 are used to configure the XML source and the XSL layout for the web part.

Table 4-20. *XML Viewer Web Part Properties*

Property	Description
XML Editor	Allows entry of the XML or selection of the XML file to be referenced.
XSL Editor	Allows entry of the XSL used to define the layout of the information or selection of the XSL file to be referenced.

Document Sets

The Document Sets category of web part includes web parts used to display document set details. All of the web parts in this category are available in both SharePoint Server Standard and Enterprise and allow interaction with document sets and document set content.

Document Set Content

The Document Set Content web part shows the items included in a specified document set. This web part is typically used when navigating within a library into a selected document set.

Document Set Properties

The Document Set Properties web part shows the properties associated with the current document set. This web part, like the Document Set Content web part, is typically used when navigating within a document set.

Filters

Web parts within the Filters category are used to introduce filter restrictions against data displayed within the page. All of the web parts in this category are available only in SharePoint Server Enterprise. Filter web parts are connected to other web parts on a page that support connections. This is done by selecting the Connections option from the web part drop-down, as was discussed earlier in this chapter.

Apply Filters Button

When the go web part is listed on a page, other filters will not be applied to their connected content until this button is pressed. If this button is not on a page, filters are automatically applied to connected content when a value is entered or selected. Use this button when you have multiple filters to apply and want to allow them to be applied at the same time. This web part is configured through the web part properties defined in Table 4-21.

Table 4-21. *Apply Filters Button Web Part Properties*

Property	Description
Show Apply Filters Button	Specifies whether the button is to be displayed and, if it is, what the button text should be. You can also define the button's alignment on the page: left, center, or right.
Allow users to save filter choices	Identify whether the user can save the choices made against the available filter options.

Choice Filter

The Choice Filter web part places a list of choices on the page to be used to filter connected content. The configuration options available for this web part are listed in Table 4-22.

Table 4-22. *Choice Filter Web Part Properties*

Property	Description
Filter Name	Lists a name for the filter.
Choices	Lists selection options for the Choice Filter, along with an optional description.
Control Width	Allows identification of the width of the choice control.
Require user to choose a value	Specifies whether the selection of a choice is required.
Default Value	Identifies the default value, if any, for the choice filter.
Show "(Empty)" value	Defines whether an empty option is to be included in the choice control's list of options.
Allow multiple selections	Specifies whether multiple choices can be selected.

Current User Filter

The Current User Filter web part places on the page a hidden filter on the page that can be used to filter connected content by current user details. The details to be used to filter connected content are configured through the properties listed in Table 4-23.

Table 4-23. *Current User Filter Web Part Properties*

Property	Description
Filter Name	Lists a name for the filter.
Select value to provide	Specifies whether the current user name is passed or a specific profile value for the current user is to be used.
Send Empty if there are no values	Specifies whether an empty value is to be passed if there is no value for the defined user details.
When handling multiple values	Defines how to handle the passing of information if there are multiple values for the filter value. You can choose to send only the first value or all the values or to combine them into a single value separated by a defined character.
Text to insert before values	Allows identification of any text to be inserted into the front of the values to be passed by the filter.
Text to insert after values	Allows identification of any text to be inserted at the end of the values to be passed by the filter.

Date Filter

The Date Filter web part allows selection of a date value against which to filter connected content. This web part is configured by managing the web part properties defined in Table 4-24.

Table 4-24. *Date Filter Web Part Properties*

Property	Description
Filter Name	Lists a name for the filter.
Default Value	Identifies the default value for the filter when presented. The value can be none, a specific date, or a date based on an offset value from the current date. For example, you could identify the default value as always two days after today.
Require user to choose a value	Specifies whether a value for the filter must be selected.

Page Field Filter

The Page Field Filter web part allows selection of details about the current page for use as filter criteria for connected content. This web part is configured by managing the web part properties defined in Table 4-25.

Table 4-25. *Page Field Filter Web Part Properties*

Property	Description
Filter Name	Lists a name for the filter.
Select a column from the list in which the current page is stored	Identifies the page property by which to filter the contained content.
Send Empty if there are no values	Determines whether an empty value is to be sent to the consuming web parts if there is no value for the selected property.
When handling multiple values	Identifies how to handle page fields supporting multiple values, with the options being to send only the first value or send all values or to combine the values into a single value, with items separated by a defined character.

Query String (URL) Filter

The Query String (URL) filter uses details in the query string for the page to filter connected content within the page. This web part is configured by managing the web part properties defined in Table 4-26.

Table 4-26. *Query String (URL) Filter Web Part Properties*

Property	Description
Filter Name	Lists a name for the filter.
Query String Parameter Name	Identifies the parameter from the query string variable to be used to identify the filter value.
Default Value	Specifies whether there is to be a default value for the filter and, if there is, what that value is to be.
Send Empty if there are no values	Determines whether an empty value is to be sent to the consuming web parts if the selected property has no value.
When handling multiple values	Identifies how to handle query string elements containing multiple values, with the options being to send only the first value or send all values or to combine the values into a single value, with items separated by a defined character.

SharePoint List Filter

The SharePoint List Filter web part uses the information contained in a list to filter connected content. The properties in Table 4-27 identify the configuration options for the web part.

Table 4-27. *SharePoint List Filter Web Part Properties*

Property	Description
Filter Name	Lists a name for the filter.
List	Allows selection of the list to filter the content by.
View	Identifies the view against the list to use for the filter.
Value Field	Identifies the field from the list to use as the filter value.
Description Field	Identifies the field to use as the description for selecting the value.

SQL Server Analysis Services Filter

The SQL Server Analysis Services Filter web part allows use of information in an SQL Server Analysis Services cube to filter connected content. The properties in Table 4-28 identify configuration options for the web part.

Table 4-28. *SQL Server Analysis Services Filter Web Part Properties*

Property	Description
Filter Name	Lists a name for the filter.
Pick a data connection from	Identifies the source of the data connection. Allows selection from a status list, data connection file, or a connection in a SharePoint data connection library.
Dimension	Identifies the element to use as the dimension for the filter.
Hierarchy	Identifies the hierarchy element for the filter.
Encode selected values as a set	Determines whether the selected values are to be treated as a set of values.
Control Width	Allows identification of the width of the control.
Require user to choose a value	Specifies whether the selection of a choice is to be required.
Default Value	Identifies the default value, if any, for the filter.

Text Filter

The Text Filter web part adds a text field to the page where text can be entered to filter connected content. The properties in Table 4-29 identify configuration options for the web part.

Table 4-29. *Text Filter Web Part Properties*

Property	Description
Filter Name	Lists a name for the filter.
Maximum number of characters	Identifies how many characters to allow in the text field.
Default Value	Identifies the default value, if any, for the filter.
Require user to choose a value	Specifies whether the entry of a value is required.
Control Width	Allows identification of the width of the choice control.

Forms

The Forms category contains web parts that allow the introduction of forms to the page.

HTML Form Web Part

The HTML Form web part, used to define an HTML-based form for entry of needed information, is present in all SharePoint versions. The HTML Form is configured through the web part properties using the Source Editor option.

InfoPath Form Web Part

The InfoPath Form web part is used to show a browser-enabled InfoPath form on the page where it can be filled out. This web part, available in both SharePoint Server Standard and Enterprise, is configured through the web part properties detailed in Table 4-30.

Table 4-30. *InfoPath Form Web Part Properties*

Property	Description
List or Library	Identifies where the InfoPath form is located.
Content Type	Identifies the content type of the form.
Display a read-only form (lists only)	Identifies whether the form is to be displayed in read-only mode.
Show InfoPath Ribbon or toolbar	Determines whether the InfoPath form management options are to be made available.
Send data to connected Web Parts when page loads	Identifies whether the form data is to be sent to any connected web parts when the page loads.
Views	Identifies the default view used to display the InfoPath form.
Submit Behavior	Specifies what action occurs when the Submit button is selected.

Media and Content

The Media and Content category includes web parts used to create content to be added to pages or to reference existing SharePoint-based content for inclusion on the page.

Content Editor Web Part

When added to a page, the Content Editor web part allows direct entry of enhanced rich text content. Wiki pages allow both text and components, making the Content Editor web part unnecessary, but the part is useful on web part pages when text content is needed. Once added, you can edit the content introduced into the web part within the part itself, just as you would on a wiki page. However, you can also configure the web part to display the content, based on the information in a text file, by identifying the Content Link option in the properties of the web part. The content editor web part is available in all versions of SharePoint.

Get Started with Your Site Web Part

The Get Started with Your Site web part shows a set of links that guide you through managing a site (see Figure 4-27). This web part, available in all versions of SharePoint, is part of the default home page for team sites.

Figure 4-27. Get Started with Your Site web part

Image Viewer Web Part

The Image Viewer web part lets you select an image to display on the page. This part is available in all versions of SharePoint. Configure the image to be presented in the web part through the part properties (see Table 4-31).

Table 4-31. Image Viewer Web Part Properties

Property	Description
Image Link	References the image file to be displayed.
Alternative Text	Specifies the text displayed when hovering over the image file.
Image Vertical Alignment	Specifies the image's alignment: to the top, the middle, or the bottom of the web part area.
Image Horizontal Alignment	Specifies the image's alignment within the web part area: left, center, or right.
Web Part Background Color	Identifies the color to use behind the presented image in the web part.

Media Web Part

The Media web part lets you specify a video or audio file to be embedded in the page. Table 4-32 identifies properties used to configure the web part to display the desired media content. This web part is available in SharePoint Server Standard and Enterprise.

Table 4-32. Media Web Part Properties

Property	Description
Preview Image URL	References an image that can be used as the preview picture for the audio or video file.
Media URL	Identifies the audio or video file to be included in the page.

Page Viewer Web Part

The Page Viewer web part lets you identify a web page to be displayed within the web part on the current SharePoint page. The referenced page can be content within SharePoint or some other site. Identify the page to be displayed within the web part space in the web part properties detailed in Table 4-33. The page is placed in an inline frame (iframe) within the page.

Table 4-33. *Page Viewer Web Part Properties*

Property	Description
Type of item to Display	Used to select a web page, folder, or file.
Link	Identifies the item to be displayed.

Picture Library Slideshow Web Part

The Picture Library Slideshow web part rotates through a set of images in an identified picture library within the page. This web part is available in all versions of SharePoint. Identify the library containing the images to be displayed and the display properties by configuring the options in the web part properties defined in Table 4-34.

Table 4-34. *Picture Library Slideshow Web Part Properties*

Property	Description
Duration to Show Picture (seconds)	Identifies the length of time to present an image before transitioning to the next image.
Picture Library	Identifies the picture library where the images are located.
Library View	Specifies the library view used to identify the images to be included in the display.
Picture Display Mode	Specifies whether the items are to be displayed in a random order or in a sequence based on the selected view.
Display With	Identifies details about the image along with the image and the layout of this information, with options including No Title or Description, Title only below image, Title and Description below image, and Title and Description beside image.
Show Toolbar	Specifies whether to display the items toolbar with the images.

Script Editor Web Part

The Script Editor web part, available in all versions of SharePoint, allows direct injection of HTML code or JavaScript into the page. Once added, the code is entered by selecting the Edit Snippet option listed within the web part. This will open the Embed window, where the script can be entered.

Silverlight Web Part

The Silverlight web part, used to display an identified Silverlight application, is available in all versions of SharePoint. When the part is added to a page, you are prompted to identify the URL the application is to reference. The URL can later be updated in the web part properties.

PerformancePoint

The PerformancePoint category includes web parts used to display and interact with PerformancePoint resources. All of the web parts in this category are available only within SharePoint Server Enterprise.

PerformancePoint Filter

The PerformancePoint Filter web part lets you select a PerformancePoint filter value to connect to other PerformancePoint web parts. This web part is configured through the web part properties, where you can select the list location of the filter.

PerformancePoint Report

The PerformancePoint Report web part lets you identify a PerformancePoint report to display within the page. As with the PerformancePoint Filter web part, the PerformancePoint Report web part is configured through the web part properties by selecting the location of the report.

PerformancePoint Scorecard

The PerformancePoint Scorecard web part lets you identify a PerformancePoint scorecard to display within the page. This web part is configured through the web part properties by selecting the location of the scorecard.

PerformancePoint Stack Selector

The PerformancePoint Stack Selector web part is used to stack and make selectable all PerformancePoint web parts contained in the zone.

Search

The Search category includes a selection of web parts that allow integration with the SharePoint Search services.

Find by Document ID

The Find by Document ID web part can be used when the SharePoint Document ID Service site collection feature is enabled in SharePoint Server Standard or Enterprise. It lets you use the search service to locate a document by its automatically generated document ID created through the Document ID Service.

Refinement

The Refinement web part, which introduces refiners on the page to work in conjunction with search results, allows further refinement of listed results. It is available across all versions of SharePoint. The web part is configured through the properties listed in Table 4-35.

Table 4-35. *Refinement Web Part Properties*

Property	Description
Refinement Target	Identifies the target to be refined using the web part.
Refiners	Specifies whether to manage the refinement options through a term set or directly through the web part.
Control	Identifies the layout of the refiner controls.
Alternate Error Message	Identifies the optional alternative error message text to present if there is an error in the web part.

Search Box

The Search Box web part adds a search box to the page to allow searching against content crawled by the SharePoint search service. This web part, available in all versions of SharePoint, is configured through the web part properties listed in Table 4-36.

Table 4-36. *Search Box Web Part Properties*

Property	Description
Which search results page should queries be sent to?	Identifies whether the search box is to submit the query to other parts on the page or to direct it to a specific search URL.
Show suggestions	Identifies whether search suggestions are to be listed within the search box as users type queries,
Show people name suggestions	Identifies whether suggestions are to include user name suggestions as users type queries.
Number of query suggestions	Allows selection of the number of suggestions to list at a time.
Minimum number of characters	Identifies the number of characters to be typed before suggestions are displayed.
Suggestions delay (in milliseconds)	Specifies the delay in typing before suggestions are presented.
Show personal favorite results	Identifies whether personal favorite results are to be displayed and, if they are, how many.
Show preferences link	Identifies whether the preferences option is to be made available on the search box.
Show advanced link	Specifies whether the advanced option, allowing search users to navigate to an advanced search page, is listed with the search box. Also specifies the URL the advance search page is to use.
Search box control Display Template	Identifies the search box display template defining the layout of the search box, with the default option being the Default Search Box or Site Search Box, and allows customization of the template if needed.
Make the search box have focus when the page is loaded.	Specifies whether the cursor is to default into the search box when the page initially loads and thus allow immediate typing, without the need to click into the field first.

Search Navigation

The Search Navigation web part lets users navigate between search verticals. It is available in all versions of SharePoint. With the web part added, you can identify the web part containing the query and the maximum number of links before the web part is considered to overflow.

Search Results

The Search Results web part, which displays the results of an executed search, is available in all versions of SharePoint and is configured through the web part properties listed in Table 4-37.

Table 4-37. *Search Results Web Part Properties*

Property	Description
Search Criteria	Identifies the search query provider and the query text.
Display Template	Identifies the display template for the search results displayed.
Results Settings	Identifies the number of results per page and whether any of the following result management tools are to be displayed: • Show ranked results • Show promoted results • Show "Did you mean?" • Show personal favorites • Show View Duplicates link • Show link to search center
Results control settings	Specifies whether the advanced link is to be displayed and, if it is, lists the link to the advanced search page. The settings also identify whether the following items are to be presented: • Show result count • Show language drop-down • Show sort drop-down • Show paging • Show preferences link • Show AlertMe link

Taxonomy Refinement Panel

The Taxonomy Refinement Panel web part allows refinement of the search results presented based on information in a defined term set. This web part is configured through the web part properties listed in Table 4-38.

Table 4-38. *Taxonomy Refinement Panel Web Part Properties*

Property	Description
Query	Identifies the Refinement Target and the associated Refiner.
Presentation	Determines the sort order for the results, along with the templates for the controls and filters.

Search-Driven Content

The Search-Driven Content category of web parts includes resources that take advantage of the search service to present various types of information crawled by the search service. All of the web parts in this category are available in SharePoint Server Standard and Enterprise.

Category-Item Reuse

The Category-Item Reuse web part allows presentation of content in an identified catalog. To configure the web part, update the properties listed in Table 4-39.

Table 4-39. *Category-Item Reuse Web Part Properties*

Property	Description
Search Criteria	Identifies the search query and the number of items to be presented.
Property Mappings	Identifies whether to alter the managed properties for the field to display and what field is to be used if they are.
Settings	Allows selection of where query results are to come from and of the result table to use to present the results.

Items Matching a Tag

The Items Matching a Tag web part shows query results associated with a defined term value. Table 4-40 lists the properties within the web part properties area that can be used to configure the web part.

Table 4-40. *Items Matching a Tag Web Part Properties*

Property	Description
Search Criteria	Identifies the search query and the number of items to be presented.
Display Template	Identifies the control and item template for the presentation of information and, when no results are returned, whether anything is to be presented.
Property Mapping	Identifies whether the mappings of managed properties are to be changed and, if they are, what fields are to be mapped to the Picture URL, Link URL, and Line 1, Line 2, and Line 3 elements.
Settings	Allows selection of where query results are to come from and of the result table to use to present the results.

Pages

The Pages web part is used to list a set of items based on the Pages content type. Table 4-41 lists the properties within the web part properties area that can be used to configure the web part.

Table 4-41. *Pages Web Part Properties*

Property	Description
Search Criteria	Identifies the search query and the number of items to be presented.
Display Template	Identifies the control and item template for the presentation of information and, when no results are returned, whether anything is to be presented.
Property Mapping	Identifies whether the mappings of managed properties are to be changed and, if they are, what fields are to be mapped to the Picture URL, Link URL, and Line 1, Line 2, and Line 3 elements.
Settings	Allows selection of where query results are to come from, of the result table to use to present the results, and of the result number to start displaying results from.

Pictures

The Pictures web part is used to list a set of items based on the Picture or Image content type. Table 4-42 lists the properties within the web part properties area that can be used to configure the web part.

Table 4-42. *Pictures Web Part Properties*

Property	Description
Search Criteria	Identifies the search query and the number of items to be presented.
Display Template	Identifies the control and item template for the presentation of information and, when no results are returned, whether anything is to be presented.
Property Mapping	Identifies whether the mappings of managed properties are to be changed and, if they are, what fields are to be mapped to the Picture URL, Link URL, and Line 1 and Line 2 elements.
Settings	Allows selection of where query results are to come from, of the result table to use to present the results, and of the result number to start displaying results from.

Popular Items

The Popular Items web part will show a set of the items that have been recently viewed by the most users. Table 4-43 lists the properties that can be used to configure the web part.

Table 4-43. *Popular Items Web Part Properties*

Property	Description
Search Criteria	Identifies the search query and the number of items to be presented.
Display Template	Identifies the control and item template for the presentation of information and, when no results are returned, whether anything is to be presented.
Property Mapping	Identifies whether the mappings of managed properties are to be changed and, if they are, what fields are to be mapped to the Picture URL, Link URL, and Line 1, Line 2, and Line 3 elements.
Settings	Allows selection of where query results are to come from, of the result table to use to present the results, and of the result number to start displaying results from.

Recently Changed Items

The Recently Changed Items web part shows the set of the most recently modified items. Table 4-44 lists the properties used to configure the part.

Table 4-44. *Recently Changed Items Web Part Properties*

Property	Description
Search Criteria	Identifies the search query and the number of items to be presented.
Display Template	Identifies the control and item template for the presentation of information and, when no results are returned, whether anything is to be presented.
Property Mapping	Identifies whether the mappings of managed properties are to be changed and, if they are, what fields are is to be mapped to the Picture URL, Link URL, and Line 1, Line 2, and Line 3 elements.
Settings	Allows selection of where query results are to come from, of the result table to use to present the results, and of the result number to start displaying results from.

Recommended Items

The Recommended Items web part shows content recommended to the current user based on usage patterns. Table 4-45 lists the properties used to configure the part.

Table 4-45. *Recommended Items Web Part Properties*

Property	Description
Search Criteria	Identifies the search query and the number of items to be presented.
Display Template	Identifies the control and item template for the presentation of information and, when no results are returned, whether anything is to be presented.
Property Mapping	Identifies whether the mappings of managed properties are to be changed and, if so, what fields are to be mapped to the Picture URL, Link URL, and Line 1, Line 2, and Line 3 elements.
Settings	Allows selection of where query results are to come from, of the result table to use to present the results, and of the result number to start displaying results from.

Videos

The Videos web part is used to show a set of items based on the video content type meeting search criteria. Table 4-46 lists the properties within the web part that can be used to configure the part.

Table 4-46. *Videos Web Part Properties*

Property	Description
Search Criteria	Identifies the search query and the number of items to be presented.
Display Template	Identifies the control and item template for the presentation of information and, when no results are returned, whether anything is to be presented.
Property Mapping	Identifies whether the mappings of managed properties are to be changed and, if they are, what fields are to be mapped to the Picture URL, Link URL, Line 1, File Extension, View Count, and Video File URL elements.
Settings	Allows selection of where query results are to come from, of the result table to use to present the results, and of the result number to start displaying results from.

Web Pages

The Web Pages web part is used to list a set of web pages based on the Page content type meeting search criteria. Table 4-47 lists the properties within the web part that can be used to configure the part.

Table 4-47. *Web Pages Web Part Properties*

Property	Description
Search Criteria	Identifies the search query and the number of items to be presented.
Display Template	Identifies the control and item template for the presentation of information and, when no results are returned, whether anything is to be presented.
Property Mapping	Identifies whether the mappings of managed properties are to be changed and, if they are, what fields are to be mapped to the Picture URL, Link URL, and Line 1, Line 2, and Line 3 elements.
Settings	Allows selection of where query results are to come from, of the result table to use to present the results, and of the result number to start displaying results from.

Wiki Pages

The Wiki Pages web part is used to list a set of items that meet search criteria based on the Wiki Page content type. Table 4-48 lists the properties within the web part that can be used to configure the part.

Table 4-48. *Web Pages Web Part Properties*

Property	Description
Search Criteria	Identifies the search query and the number of items to be presented.
Display Template	Identifies the control and item template for the presentation of information and, when no results are returned, whether anything is to be presented.
Property Mapping	Identifies whether the mappings of managed properties are to be changed and, if they are, what fields are to be mapped to the Picture URL, Link URL, and Line 1, Line 2, and Line 3 elements.
Settings	Allows selection of where query results are to come from, of the result table to use to present the results, and of the result number to start displaying results from.

Social Collaboration

The Social Collaboration category includes the SharePoint web parts that provide social interaction capabilities to SharePoint.

Contact Details

The Contact Details web part is used to present details about a contact for the page or site. Identify the site contact through the web part properties.

Note Board

The Note Board enables users to leave microblog-like messages within the page (see Figure 4-28). It can be used when the Site Feed features are active within a site. The web part is available in SharePoint Server Standard and Enterprise.

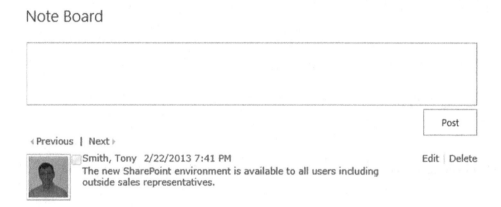

Figure 4-28. *Note Board web part*

Organization Browser

The Organization Browser web part displays the reporting chain for the organization based on the manager details listed in the user profile. As Figure 4-29 shows, users can interact with it. The web part is available in SharePoint Server Standard and Enterprise.

Figure 4-29. *Organization Browser web part*

Site Feed

The Site Feed web part places a microblog feed within the site page. It is available in SharePoint Server Standard and Enterprise.

Site Users

The Site Users web part displays the list of users identified as members of the site. It is available in all versions of SharePoint. The web part is configured through the web part properties described in Table 4-49.

Table 4-49. *Site Users Web Part Properties*

Property	Description
Number of items to display	Identifies the number of items to be displayed in the web part.
Display Type	Identifies whether the web part is to list users permitted to access the site, users in the site's member group, or people in some other identified group.

Tag Cloud

The Tag Cloud web part lists tags associated with content. It is available in SharePoint Server Standard and Enterprise. The web part is configured through the web part properties described in Table 4-50.

Table 4-50. *Tag Cloud Web Part Properties*

Property	Description
Show Tags	Identifies whether to show tags for the current user or all users or just those under the current URL for all users.
Maximum Items	Identifies the maximum number of items to be displayed and whether the number count is to be listed.

User Tasks

The User Tasks web part lists the tasks assigned to the current user within the SharePoint environment. It is available across all versions of SharePoint.

CHAPTER 5

■ ■ ■

Managing Lists and Libraries

SharePoint stores and manages documents and information in lists and libraries. Lists are used to organize and manage sets of data (such as tasks, contacts, and links), and libraries are used to store and manage documents (Microsoft Office files, PDFs, video files, images, etc.). There is a variety of lists and libraries available within SharePoint to allow you to manage all of the different types of information you will need.

Lists are used when you need to store structured data, and they can be tailored to meet the specific needs of the individuals who will manage and consume the information. (The different lists available within SharePoint Foundation and SharePoint Server are discussed in Chapter 6.) Libraries, which can be considered a special type of list, are used to store files in SharePoint. Libraries and lists have many similarities in their creation and management. In this chapter the basic concepts related to managing lists and libraries are discussed, and Chapters 6 and 7 expands on this discussion with a review of the different lists and libraries available in SharePoint and how to manage content within them.

As was just mentioned, in structure and approach to navigation, SharePoint lists and libraries are very similar. Figure 5-1 shows this structure. When you access a list or library in a site, you navigate to its default view. Once within the list or library, the following elements are made available:

- A new link appears at the top of the page that lets you create new items in the list or library.

- A set of views is listed below the new link. You can click on the name of any listed view to update the display of the list or library content based on the definition of that view. You can also modify the view or create a new view from this area as well.

- A search box, located next to the view list, allows you to query the list or library by entering text into the search box and returning the items containing the entered text.

- The content display area, which sits below the listing of views and the search box, presents the content of the list or library as defined by the selected view. From here you can work with the content (as will be discussed in Chapters 6 and 7).

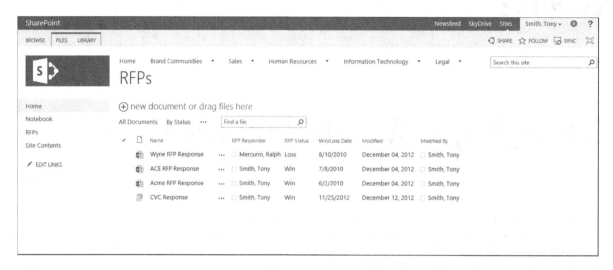

Figure 5-1. *Library view page*

Creating Lists and Libraries

When you create a new site, it will include a default sets of lists and libraries based on the definition of the selected site template. However, you may need to create additional lists and libraries once a site is created in order to manage needed information.

To create a list or library in a SharePoint site, you must have the Manage Lists right, which by default is available as part of the Edit, Design, Manage Hierarchy, and Full Control permission levels. To create a new list or library, do the following:

1. Navigate to the site where you want to create the new list or library.

2. Select the Site Contents option from the Quick Launch or Settings menu.

3. On the Site Contents page, select the Add an App option.

4. On the Your Apps page (see Figure 5-2), select from the Apps You Can Add section the type of list or library to be created.

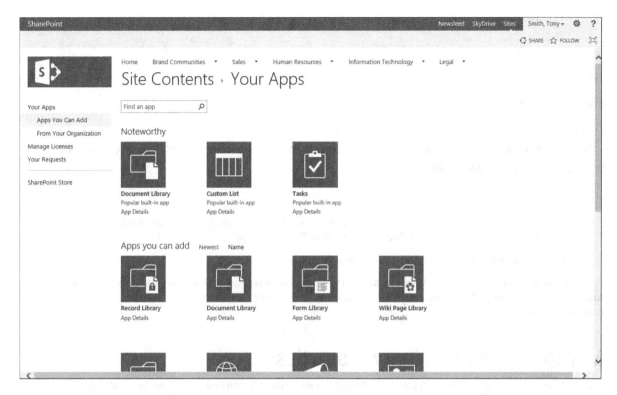

Figure 5-2. Your Apps page

5.   In the Add window, do the following:

   a.   If you want to use the default setup—which includes no description and, for libraries, no versioning—enter the name for the new list or library and click the Create button.

   b.   If you want to change the default settings for the list or library being created, do the following:

      i.   Select the Advanced Options link.

      ii.   On the new screen, enter a name for the new list, enter an optional description, and for libraries, specify whether the library will store versions and what the default document template will be. Then click the Create button.

The new list or library is created, and you are returned to the Site Contents page.

Deleting Lists and Libraries

Whether a list or library was created as part of the creation process of the site or was added later by you or someone else, you can delete any lists or libraries available within the site. You might do this if you created a list in error or wished to remove irrelevant lists or libraries—created during the initial site creation process—to keep users from using them. To delete a list or library within a site, do the following:

1.   Navigate to the list or library to be deleted.

2.   From the List or Library ribbon tab, select the List or Library Settings option (see Figure 5-3).

Figure 5-3. *Library ribbon tab*

■ **Note** In some lists, the List ribbon tab is named differently. For example, in lists created from the Calendar list template, the List tab is named Calendar.

---

3. On the list's or library's Settings page, in the Permissions and Management section, click the Delete This Document Library or the Delete This List option.

4. On the deletion confirmation screen, click the OK button.

The list or library is deleted, and you are taken to the Site Contents page. Deleted lists and libraries are moved to the site's recycle bin and, if necessary, can be restored as long as they remain there (the recycle bin is discussed in detail in Chapter 3).

Managing List and Library Properties

There are several manageable list and library settings that can be used to determine how the list or library is displayed. These settings are managed through the Name, Description, and Navigation Settings section. To manage these settings, do the following:

1. Navigate to the list's or library's Settings page.

2. On the Settings page, select the List Name, Description, and Navigation option from the General Settings section.

3. On the General Settings page, the following areas can be managed:

   a. In the Name and Description section, the name of the list or library can be updated. This is the name used to reference the item in the site. You can also update the list or library's optional description.

   b. In the Navigation section, you can specify whether the list or library is to be included in the Quick Launch area of the site.

   c. Once all information has been updated, click the Save button.

The information is updated, and you are returned to the Settings page.

■ **Note** Changing the name of a list changes only the name displayed, not the underlying system name SharePoint uses for the list. While this does not affect normal use of the list, it matters to developers referencing the list through code.

Metadata Columns

Both lists and libraries allow for the creation of columns of various types to manage information within SharePoint. For lists, the columns store the information being managed. For documents, the columns act as metadata for a document providing details used to describe the document.

Available Columns

Several different types of columns are available in SharePoint Foundation, and additional columns are available when SharePoint Server is in place. The following are types of columns available in SharePoint.

Single Line of Text

The Single Line of Text column is used to store standard text in a single row. Use this column type when you want people adding and working with documents or list data to have complete control over the value entered. It is limited to a single row of text that can contain only up to 255 characters of information. As Figure 5-4 shows, this column is presented as a text box into which text is entered.

Title *

Figure 5-4. *Single Line of Text field*

The Single Line of Text field has the following properties:

- *Column name*: Identifies the name of the column in the list or library. This is the name presented when you view or edit items.

- *Description*: Lists optional description text that, if entered, appears below the column when editing the details. The description field is used when more information is needed to help individuals editing the list understand the purpose or type of information expected to be entered.

- *Require that this column contains information*: Specifies whether the column must contain information in order to save the item.

- *Enforce unique values*: Specifies whether the value entered must be different from the value in this column for all other items in the list or library.

- *Maximum number of characters*: Determines the number of characters that can be entered into the field (the maximum is 255).

- *Default Value*: Specifies whether the column is to automatically contain a value when a new item is created. This option also determines whether the default value will be text identified in the default value text box or will be calculated on the basis of a formula.

- *Column Validation*: Allows entry of a formula used to validate information entered in the field to ensure it contains appropriate data. This section also allows entry of a message presented to the user to identify column data entry requirements. Column validation is discussed in detail in Chapter 6.

Multiple Lines of Text

The Multiple Lines of Text field is used to store the following:

- Larger quantities of text than the Single Line of Text field (limited to 255 characters) allows

- Multiple rows of information (addresses, etc.)

- Richly formatted text (including text with images, colored or bolded text)

This column is represented as a multirow text entry field. Depending on the options selected, it can provide additional ribbon tabs, called Format Text and Insert, that contain options allowing management of text formatting within the column and enabling insertion of additional objects such as images and videos, as seen in Figure 5-5.

Description

Figure 5-5. Multiple Lines of Text field

The Multiple Lines of Text column has the following properties to define the field characteristics:

- *Column name*: Identifies the name of the column in the list or library. This is the name presented when you view or edit items.

- *Description*: Lists optional description text that, if entered, appears below the column when editing the details. The description field is used when more information is needed to help individuals editing the content understand the purpose or type of information expected to be entered.

- *Require that this column contains information*: Specifies whether the column must contain information in order to save the item.

- *Allow unlimited length in document libraries*: This option, available only when configuring Multiple Line of Text fields against document libraries, specifies whether the field is to have a size limitation.

- *Number of lines for editing*: This option identifies how many rows will be visible for the field when editing the item.

- *Specify the type of text to allow*: This option—available only for lists, not libraries—allows specification whether text entered is to allow only plain text (text with no formatting) or enhanced rich text, which supports text formatting, image inclusion, and hyperlinks.

- *Append Changes to Existing Text*: Specifies whether editing information in the field will append the edits to previously entered values or whether updated data will simply replace previously entered details.

Choice (menu to choose from)

This type of column is used to provide a list of choices for setting the value for the column. This column enables selection of a single value or multiple values. It can be presented as a drop-down list or radio buttons when supporting single selections and as check boxes when supporting multiple selections, as seen in Figure 5-6.

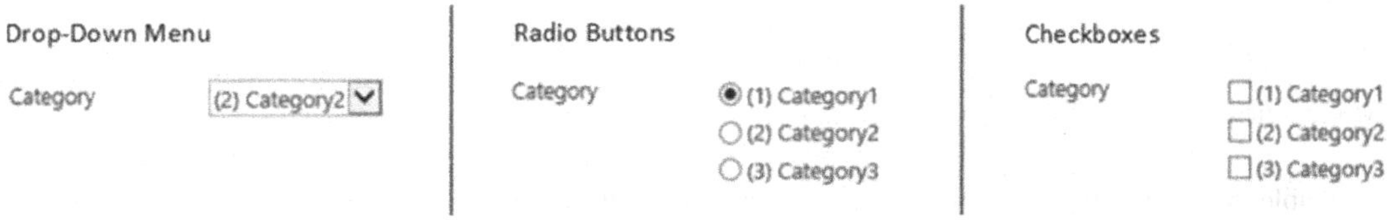

Figure 5-6. *Choice field formats*

The configuration properties available for this field type include these:

- *Column name*: Identifies the name of the column in the list or library. This is the name presented when you view or edit items.

- *Description*: Lists optional description text that, if entered, appears below the column when editing the details. The description field is used when more information is needed to help individuals editing the content understand the purpose or type of information expected to be entered.

- *Require that this column contains information*: Specifies whether the column must contain information in order to save the item.

- *Enforce unique values*: Specifies whether the value entered must be different from the value in this column for all other items in the list or library.

- *Type each choice on a separate line*: This option identifies the choices for the column. Each individual choice should start its own line, or row, in the box. Note that a long choice value will span lines in the list box but will not appear as multiple options in the choice field. When the properties of a list item or document are edited, the choices for the column will appear in the order given here.

- *Display choices using*: Determines the layout of the choices. It allows options to appear as a drop-down list or a set of radio buttons for selection of single values or as check boxes if selection of multiple options is needed.

- *Allow 'Fill-in' choices*: Specifies whether the user is able to manually enter a value for the field. When this option is selected, an additional text field that allows the entry of a separate value appears.

- *Default value*: This option is initially populated with the first item in the list of choices. To exclude a default value, remove it from this box. To change the value, enter the text of the value desired as the default option.

- *Column Validation*: Allows use of a formula to validate information entered in the field to ensure it contains appropriate data. This section also allows entry of a message presented to the user to identify column data entry requirements. Column validation is discussed in detail in Chapter 6.

Number

This column type is used for entry of numerical values. This can include entry and management of integers or decimal numbers, depending on the column's configuration. The number column appears as a standard entry field, as seen in Figure 5-7.

Number

Figure 5-7. *Number field*

Options available for configuring this type of column include the following:

- *Column name*: Identifies the name of the column in the list or library. This is the name presented when you view or edit items.

- *Description*: Lists optional description text that, if entered, appears below the column when editing the details. The description field is used when more information is needed to help individuals editing the content understand the purpose or type of information expected to be entered.

- *Require that this column contains information*: Specifies whether the column must contain information in order to save the item.

- *Enforce unique values*: Specifies whether the value entered must be different from the value in this column for all other items in the list or library.

- *You can specify a minimum and maximum allowed value*: This option allows you to specify optional minimum and maximum values that, when entered, limit the range of numbers allowed in the field.

- *Number of decimal places*: Allows you to specify the number of decimal places to display when presenting the number. Choices can range between 0 and 5 places, 0 meaning only integers are allowed. For example, entering a decimal value of 2 results in the number 8 appearing as 8.00. Also available is an automatic option, where decimal places appear as they did when the number was entered.

- *Default Value*: Specifies whether the column is to automatically contain a value when a new item is created. This column also determines whether the default value will be an entered number or will be calculated based on a formula.

- *Show as percentage*: Selecting this option shows the entered number as a percent value. A percent sign is placed after the number when it is displayed in list or library views.

- *Column Validation*: Allows use of a formula to validate information entered in the field to ensure it contains appropriate data. This section also allows entry of a message presented to the user to identify column data entry requirements. Column validation is discussed in detail in Chapter 6.

Currency

The Currency column allows entry of currency values. It is similar to the Number column but includes currency formatting options. When information is added or edited, the field's layout is the same as the Number column's, seen in Figure 5-7. However, when the entered information is displayed in views, it includes the currency formatting. Options available for configuring this type of column include the following:

- *Column name*: Identifies the name of the column in the list or library. This is the name presented when you view or edit items.

- *Description*: Lists optional description text that, if entered, appears below the column when editing the details. The description field is used when more information is needed to help individuals editing the content understand the purpose or type of information expected to be entered.

- *Require that this column contains information*: Specifies whether the column must contain information in order to save the item.

- *Enforce unique values*: Specifies whether the value entered must be different from the value in this column for all other items in the list or library.

- *You can specify a minimum and maximum allowed value*: This option allows you to specify optional minimum and maximum values that, when entered, limit the range of numbers allowed in the field.

- *Number of decimal places*: Allows you to specify the number of decimal places to display when presenting the number. Choices can range between 0 and 5 places. For example, entering a decimal value of 2 results in the number 8 appearing as 8.00. Also available is an automatic option, where decimal places appear as they did when the number was entered.

- *Default Value*: Specifies whether the column is to automatically contain a value when a new item is created. This column also determines whether the default value will be an entered number or will be calculated based on a formula.

- *Currency format*: Identifies the format used when viewing the field. This includes various country currency formats, any of which can be selected.

- *Column Validation*: Allows use of a formula to validate information entered in the field to ensure it contains appropriate data. This section also allows entry of a message presented to the user to identify column data entry requirements. Column validation is discussed in detail in Chapter 6.

Date and Time

The Date and Time column contains date and optional time values. The field allows selection of a date value and, if time is to be included, a time value. Figure 5-8 shows the layout of the Date and Time column.

Start Date

Figure 5-8. Date and Time field

Options available for configuring this type of column include the following:

- *Column name*: Identifies the name of the column in the list or library. This is the name presented when you view or edit items.

- *Description*: Lists optional description text that, if entered, appears below the column when editing the details. The description field is used when more information is needed to help individuals editing the content understand the purpose or type of information expected to be entered.

- *Require that this column contains information*: Specifies whether the column must contain information in order to save the item.

- *Enforce unique values*: Specifies whether the value entered must be different from the value in this column for all other items in the list or library.

- *Date and Time Format*: Specifies whether the entered value will be only a date or will include both date and time components.

- *Display Format*: This option specifies whether to display the entered date in standard or friendly text format. Standard format uses the standard date layout. The friendly format uses a text phrase relative to the current date and time to represent the information. For example, if the date in the field is the current date, the field shows "Today" instead of the actual date.

- *Default Value*: This option specifies the default value for the field when a new item is created. For date and time columns, you can choose no default value or use the current date, a specified date, or a calculated date value.

- *Column Validation*: Allows use of a formula to validate information entered in the field to ensure it contains appropriate data. This section also allows entry of a message presented to the user to identify column data entry requirements. Column validation is discussed in detail in Chapter 6.

Lookup

This column type lets you populate the column based on the values stored in a different list in the site. The items in the referenced list field appear as the choices for the field in much the same way the Choice column shows options. This column, which appears as a drop-down list of options, allows selection of a value. When the field permits adding multiple options, it appears as a set of two boxes: one shows the options not selected, and the other shows the options selected, as seen in Figure 5-9.

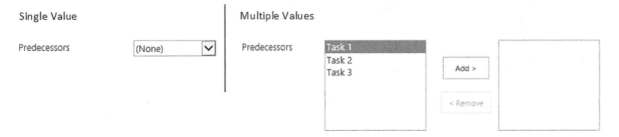

Figure 5-9. *Lookup field*

Options available for configuring the Lookup column include the following:

- *Column name*: Identifies the name of the column in the list or library. This is the name presented when you view or edit items.

- *Description*: Lists optional description text that, if entered, appears below the column when editing the details. The description field is used when more information is needed to help individuals editing the content understand the purpose or type of information expected to be entered.

- *Require that this column contains information*: Specifies whether the column must contain information in order to save the item.

- *Enforce unique values*: Specifies whether the value entered must be different from the value in this column for all other items in the list or library.

- *Get information from*: Identifies the list within the site that is the source for the values. This option includes a drop-down of the lists and libraries available within the site.

- *In this column*: Identifies the column in the selected list used to look up values and allows you to identify whether multiple values can be selected from the list.

- *Add a column to show each of these additional fields*: This option allows you to identify other fields from the lookup list that, based on the value selected, will be viewable in the current list.

- *Relationship*: This option lets you specify whether to enforce relationship behavior between the current item and the lookup item. If you select to enforce the relationship, you can choose either Restrict Delete, which will not allow deletion of the lookup value if it is in use as a lookup item, or Cascade Delete, which deletes the item if the lookup value is deleted.

Yes/No

The Yes/No column provides the ability to have a checked or unchecked value option, as seen in Figure 5-10.

Active   ☑

Figure 5-10.   *Yes/No field*

This type of column includes the following:

- *Column name*: Identifies the name of the column in the list or library. This is the name presented when you view or edit items.

- *Description*: Lists optional description text that, if entered, appears below the column when editing the details. The description field is used when more information is needed to help individuals editing the content understand the purpose or type of information expected to be entered.

- *Default Value*: Requires you to select whether the option should be set to Yes (checked) or No (unchecked) by default.

Person or Group

This column type allows selection of a user or group as the value for the column. By default, SharePoint connects to Active Directory, and in this case the selectable values are the Active Directory user and group values. This column supports selection from any user available in Active Directory or from a limited number of users based on a SharePoint group membership. Individuals adding or editing items within this field are able either to enter a value, choosing whether to validate the user by clicking the validation option, or to search for a user or group with the search interface available within the user search option, as seen in Figure 5-11.

Assigned To | Enter names or email addresses... |

Figure 5-11.   *Person or Group field*

Options available for configuring this field include the following:

- *Column name*: Identifies the name of the column in the list or library. This is the name presented when you view or edit items.

- *Description*: Lists optional description text that, if entered, appears below the column when editing the details. The description field is used when more information is needed to help individuals editing the content understand the purpose or type of information expected to be entered.

- *Require that this column contains information*: Specifies whether the column must contain information in order to save the item.

- *Enforce unique values*: Specifies whether the value entered must be different from the value in this column for all other items in the list or library.

- *Allow multiple selections*: Specifies whether to allow more than one user or group value to be selected and saved in the column.

- *Allow selection of*: Specifies whether just people or both people and groups can be selected for the column values.

- *Choose from*: Specifies whether to allow selection from all available users or whether to limit the list of available users to those contained within a specified SharePoint group.

- *Show field*: Identifies which user details to use to represent the selected value when the column is displayed in views. This option allows the choice of a variety of user profile details to represent the selection. The default option used to represent the field is the name of the user, along with presence awareness details.

Hyperlink or Picture

The Hyperlink or Picture column is used to store web links or web references to pictures. Depending on its format, the column lists either a URL that can be clicked to navigate to the referenced link or a thumbnail of a referenced image for the column. When entering information in this column you are provided with a field for identifying the link and a field for describing the link, as seen in Figure 5-12. You also are given an option to test the entered link to ensure that it navigates to the proper location.

Figure 5-12. *Hyperlink or Picture field*

This column type has the following options available for its configuration:

- *Column name*: Identifies the name of the column in the list or library. This is the name presented when you view or edit items.

- *Description*: Lists optional description text that, if entered, appears below the column when editing the details. The description field is used when more information is needed to help individuals editing the content to understand the purpose or type of information expected to be entered.

- *Require that this column contains information*: Specifies whether the column must contain information in order to save the item.

- *Format URL as*: Specifies whether the entered URL should be treated as a web link or a web reference to a picture.

Calculated

The Calculated column is used to introduce a column whose value is not entered by a user creating or editing an item but instead is calculated automatically based on an entered formula. This field will not appear on the Add or Edit form but can be used within SharePoint views. This type of column includes the following configuration options:

- *Column name*: Identifies the name of the column in the list or library. This is the name presented when you view or edit items.

- *Description*: Lists optional description text for the field.

- *Formula*: The formula, which identifies the calculation used to determine the value for the column, can be computed from values entered in other fields within the list and uses a formula calculation engine similar to Excel's.

- *The data type returned from this formula is*: This option identifies the type of data the formula will generate. Options available for the type of data the calculated field will contain include the following possible formats. Selecting the correct format will allow the column to be used appropriately by search or other services.

    - Single Line of Text

    - Number

    - Currency

    - Date and Time

    - Yes/No

Task Outcome

This type of column stores and tracks values used for workflow task outcomes. This option appears as a drop-down list of the available values, similar to the Choice list drop-down representation seen in Figure 5-6. Options for configuring this column include the following:

- *Column name*: Identifies the name of the column in the list or library. This is the name presented when you view or edit items.

- *Description*: Lists optional description text that, if entered, appears below the column when editing the details. The description field is used when more information is needed to help individuals editing the content understand the purpose or type of information expected to be entered.

- *Require that this column contains information*: Specifies whether the column must contain information in order to save the item.

- *Enforce unique values*: Specifies whether the value entered must be different from the value in this column for all other items in the list or library.

- *Type each choice on a separate line*: This option identifies the choices for the column. Each individual choice should start on its own line, or row, in the box. Note that a long choice value will span lines in the list box but will not appear as multiple options in the choice field. When the first item or document is edited, the choices for the list appear in the order given here.

- *Default value*: This option is initially populated with the first choice in the list of choices. To exclude a default value, remove it from this box. To change the value, enter the text of the value desired as the default option. You can also elect to base the default value on a calculation.

External Data

This column type allows you to create a column that can be connected to an external data source through a Business Connectivity Services (BCS) connection. This connection lets you source information entered in a column from information in some other system. To select the value, search for the information using the filter details configured as part of the BCS connection, as seen in Figure 5-13.

Customer

Figure 5-13. *External Data field*

Options for configuring the External Data column include the following:

- *Column name*: Identifies the name of the column in the list or library. This is the name presented when you view or edit items.

- *Description*: Lists optional description text that, if entered, appears below the column when editing the details. The description field is used when more information is needed to help individuals editing the content understand the purpose or type of information expected to be entered.

- *Require that this column contains information*: Specifies whether the column must contain information in order to save the item.

- *External Content Type*: Allows selection of the BCS connection to associate to the column.

- *Select the field to be shown on this column*: Identifies the field from the selected connection to use as a value for the column.

- *Display the Actions menu*: Allows you to identify whether to display the Actions menu for the column.

- *Link this column to the Default Action of the External Content Type*: Identifies whether the column information, when presented in views, should be configured as a link to the default action defined for the external content type.

Managed Metadata

This type of column is not available in SharePoint Foundation. It uses the term store management capabilities and is available as part of SharePoint Server. A term set can be identified as the source for the values saved in the column. Using a term set as the source for column values allows you to assign a hierarchical tree of terms as the column value. For example, if you have categories that contain products, you can select the category/product combination that best represents the item. When a term set is used to identify the value of a column, the term can be selected when users are editing or adding items, as seen in Figure 5-14.

Product

Figure 5-14. *Managed Metadata field*

Options available when configuring a managed metadata column include these:

- *Column name*: Identifies the name of the column in the list or library. This is the name presented when you view or edit items.

- *Description*: Lists optional description text that, if entered, appears below the column when editing the details. The description field is used when more information is needed to help individuals editing the content understand the purpose or type of information expected to be entered.

- *Require that this column contains information*: Specifies whether the column must contain information in order to save the item.

- *Enforce unique values*: Specifies whether the value entered must be different from the value in this column for all other items in the list or library.

- *Allow multiple selections*: Specifies whether more than one value should be allowed to be saved in the column.

- *Display Value*: This option lets you specify whether you wish the column to show just the label for the selected term or the entire selected path to it.

- *Term Set Settings*: These settings let you specify whether you wish to use an existing term set as the source for the column or a custom term set that you will define in this column settings section.

- *Allow 'Fill-in' choices*: Specifies whether the user should be able to manually enter a value for the field. When this option is selected, an additional text field appears and allows the entry of a separate value.

- *Default Value*: Identifies the value from the term set to be used as the default value for the column when a new item is created in the list or library.

Adding Columns

The different columns available within SharePoint lists and libraries and options available when they are configured have already been discussed. To add a column to a list or library, do the following:

1. Navigate to the list or library where you want to create the column.

2. On the list or library view page, select the Create Column option from the List or Library ribbon tab.

3. On the Create Column screen, do the following:

   a. In the Column Name field, enter the name for the column.

   b. In the Type section, select the field type for the new column.

   c. In the Additional Column Settings section, update the column details. The details to configure are dependent on the column type selected and are described in detail in the "Available Columns" section above.

   d. Once all the information has been entered, click the OK button.

The column is added, and you are returned to the list or library view.

Editing Columns

Existing columns that have been added to a list or library can be edited. To change column details in a list or library, do the following:

1. Navigate to the list or library where you want to edit a column.

2. On the list or library view page, select the List or Library Settings option from the List or Library ribbon tab.

3. In the Columns section on the list's or library's Settings page, select the column to update.

4. On the Edit Column page, make any needed updates to the column properties, and click the OK button to save the changes.

The changes are saved, and you are returned to the list's or library's Settings page.

■ **Note** You can change a column's type only to certain other types. If a column type is changed, you will lose data from the column when the data is not supported by the new column type. For example, changing a Single Line of Text column to a Number column will result in the loss of any values that contain characters other than numbers.

Deleting Columns

Columns that were added to lists or libraries can be deleted if they are no longer needed. To delete an existing column, do the following:

1. Navigate to the list or library where you want to delete a column.

2. On the list or library view page, select the List or Library Settings option from the List or Library ribbon tab.

3. In the Columns section on the Settings page, select the column to delete.

4. On the Edit Column page, click the Delete button.

5. In the delete confirmation window, click the OK button.

You are returned to the Settings page, and the selected column is deleted.

■ **Caution** When a column is deleted, all of the data saved in the column is deleted as well. This information is not placed in the recycle bin, so it cannot be restored if it was deleted in error.

Changing the Order of Columns

The order of columns in a list or library determines their order on the item's view and edit properties pages. To edit column order for a list or library, do the following:

1. Navigate to the list or library where you want to reorder the columns.

2. On the list or library view page, select the List or Library Settings option from the List or Library ribbon tab.

3. In the Columns section on the Settings page, click the Column Ordering link.

4. On the Change Column Ordering page, change the Position from Top values for the listed items to place them in the desired order, and once all items are in the proper order, click the OK button to save the order.

The column order is updated, and you are returned to the Settings page for the list or library. The item order does not affect the order of items within a list or library view. This order is driven by the view itself. Views are discussed later in this chapter.

Setting Column Indexes

Lists and libraries can contain thousands of items. The more items a list or library contains, the longer displaying the list and performing actions such as filtering and sorting of the items in it will take. Creating indexes against columns that are frequently sorted against or filtered on can improve the performance of these activities. To create an index against a list or library column, do the following:

1. Navigate to the list or library where you want to update column indexes.

2. On the list or library view page, select the List or Library Settings option from the List or Library ribbon tab.

3. In the Columns section on the Settings page, click the Indexed Columns option.

4. On the Indexed Columns page, click the Create a New Index link.

5. On the Edit Index page, do the following:

   a. In the Primary Column section, select the column against which the index is to be created.

   b. In the Secondary Column section, select, if you wish, an optional second column for the index.

   c. Click the Create button to create the new index.

The index is created, and you are returned to the Indexed Columns page.

Configuring Keywords

When SharePoint Server is in use, enterprise keyword columns can be added to lists and libraries to make searching for and finding list items easier. The keyword fields will be populated with document tags as they are created. To add an enterprise keywords field to a list or library, do the following:

1. Navigate to the list or library where you want to configure the keywords.

2. On the list or library view page, select the List or Library Settings option from the List or Library ribbon tab.

3. On the Settings page, select the Enterprise Metadata and Keywords Settings option from the Permissions and Management section.

4. In the Enterprise Keywords section on the Enterprise Metadata and Keywords Settings page, check the box next to the "Add an Enterprise Keywords column to this list and enable keyword synchronization" option, and then click the OK button.

The Keyword field is added, and you are returned to the Settings page.

Working with Views

Views present information in lists and libraries to users accessing those lists and libraries. Views allow creation of multiple representations of the information to support its different uses in the list or library. When you first navigate to a list or library, the default view appears. (A list can have multiple views to select from but only one default view.) Figure 5-1 shows a standard document library view, the All Documents view.

Views enable you to organize columns into structures that meet information access needs and allow you to filter and sort information to limit and organize it. You can also run mathematical operations against the columns in a view to include sums, averages, and the like within it. As you will see, a view can be public or private. A public view is available to all site users, whereas a private view is available only to the user that created it.

Types of Views

Six different types of views can be created against SharePoint lists and libraries. Discussion of each of these views and their layouts follows.

Standard View

The standard view is the one most commonly used in SharePoint. Create a standard view when you want to list items in a tabular structure within the list or library itself or on other site pages (see Figure 5-14). This type of view allows grouping, filtering, sorting, and styling of the information presented. People viewing the information will also be able to sort and filter the details displayed. The standard view supports the following:

- Identifying the list or library columns to be included in the view.

- Identifying up to two columns to sort the items by.

- Specifying filter criteria for the view to allow information to be displayed based on the column values.

- Identifying columns to group the presented information by.

- Selecting columns to sum, average, or count.

- Identifying the style for presentation of the information.

Datasheet View

The datasheet view provides an Excel-like display of the information in the list (see Figure 5-15). The interface this view provides allows you to make multiple updates to the information more easily and allows easy navigation between items. This view gives those accessing it the ability to reorder and hide columns, as well as assist with data access and management.

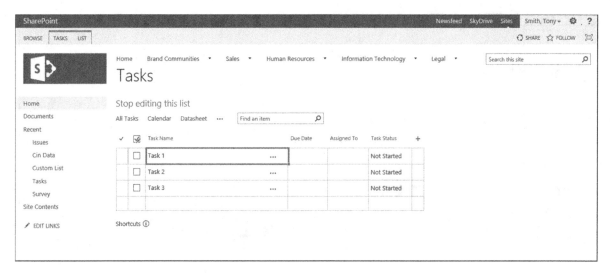

Figure 5-15. *Datasheet view*

The datasheet view allows configuration of many of the options the standard view allows, including the following:

- Identifying the list or library columns to be included in the view.

- Identifying up to two columns to sort the items by.

- Specifying filter criteria for the view to allow information to be displayed based on the column values.

- Selecting columns to sum, average, or count.

Calendar View

The calendar view is used when the information to display needs to be made available in a calendar. This view requires that the columns in the list or library include date fields for the start date and end date for placement on the calendar, as well as fields that can represent the item on the calendar. This view is most commonly used with calendar lists, but it can also be valuable in task lists, issues lists, and others containing date-dependent information. The calendar view allows the following:

- Specifying the date fields used to position the item on the calendar.

- Viewing titles with the columns from the list used to represent the item in the calendar view specified.

- Specifying a default scope that identifies whether the calendar layout initially shows the day, week, or month.

- Setting any filter criteria for the view to allow information to be displayed based on the column values.

The calendar view allows presentation of information in monthly, weekly, and daily displays, any of which can be selected from the Calendar ribbon tab. The monthly display seen in Figure 5-16 shows a single month of information, defaulted to the current month. A month selector, found in the Quick Launch area, can be used to select the desired month.

Figure 5-16. *Calendar in monthly view*

The weekly view shows details for a single week. When first accessed, the weekly view shows the current week. The Quick Launch area includes the same selector seen in the monthly view, but now it is used to select the week to display. Figure 5-17 shows a weekly calendar display.

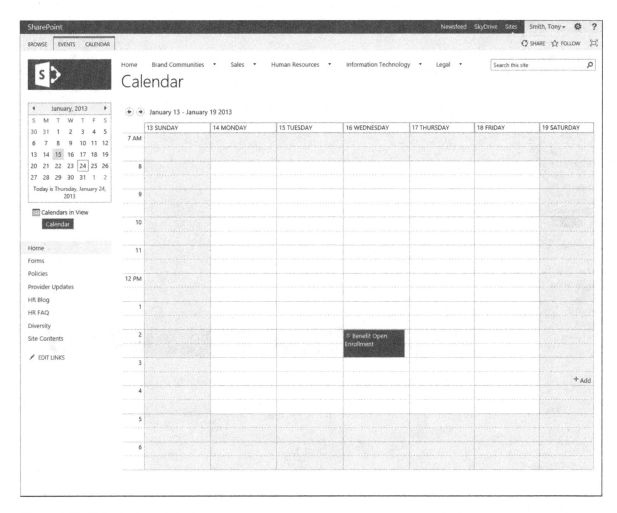

Figure 5-17. *Calendar in weekly view*

The daily view shows items for a single day. When first accessed, the view defaults to the current day. As with the other views, a selector in the Quick Launch area allows selection of a day to view. Figure 5-18 shows the daily view for the calendar.

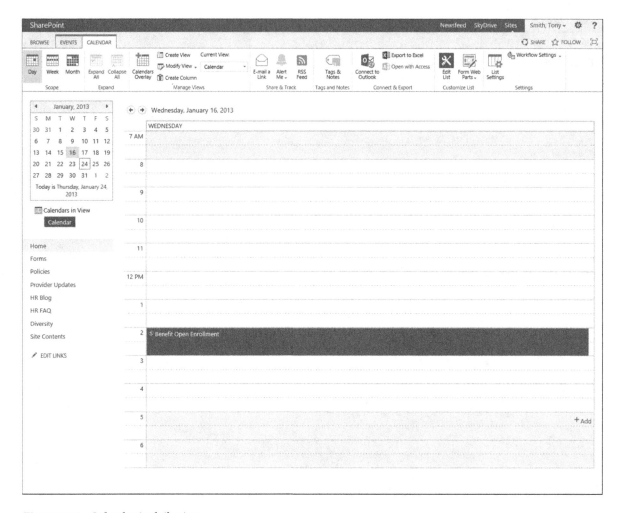

Figure 5-18. *Calendar in daily view*

Gantt View

In the Gantt view, a graphical representation of the information from the list appears in a Gantt chart. This chart shows information in a timeline view. Date fields are required to identify start and end dates for items presented in the Gantt chart. This view is used to track activity over time and is most commonly used with task lists. Figure 5-19 shows the Gantt view.

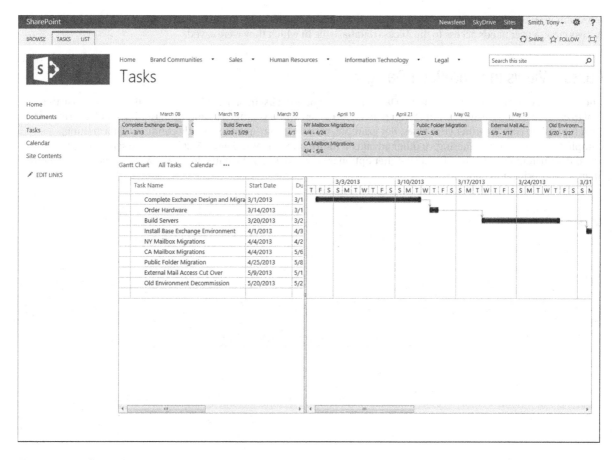

Figure 5-19. *Gantt view*

Configuration of this view requires configuration of the following information:

- Columns to display in the view.

- Gantt columns, including the columns needed to build and display the Gantt chart, among which are a title for the item on the chart, start and end dates, and (optionally) percentage complete and predecessor details.

- Sorting information, to order the items listed in the view.

- Filter details, to refine the list of view items.

- Choice of columns by which to group the presented information.

- Columns to sum, average, or count.

- Choice of a style for the presentation of the information.

- Specification whether the number of items presented should be limited.

Access View

The Access view opens Microsoft Access with a connection to a list letting you create forms and reports based on the information in the list. This view is not available for documents. Access view is used to create a highly formatted representation of information or to permit easy printing of the list details. To see reports or forms created through Access view, a user needs access to the Access database file in which they were saved.

Custom Views in SharePoint Designer

Choosing the Custom View in SharePoint Designer option opens a list in SharePoint Designer that lets you use this tool to create a view. Use SharePoint Designer to create a view when you need a more complex layout of information than is possible with the other view types. For example, your view may need to include conditional formatting, complex styling, complex filtering, or other advanced information layouts. Figure 5-20 shows the screen displayed when the Custom View in SharePoint Designer option is selected. Enter the name for the new view, and then work in SharePoint Designer to configure it.

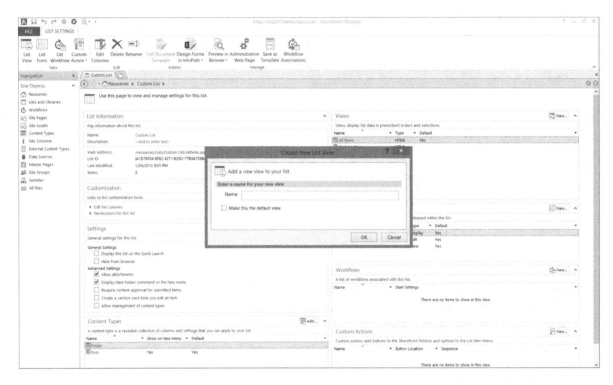

Figure 5-20. *SharePoint Designer Custom View*

Creating Views

To create a new view, first determine the type of view that will best meet your needs. You base this decision on the purpose of the view, and how you want people accessing it to use the information it displays. Once you decide the type of view to create, determine which details from the list or library you want to display in the view and in what order the columns should appear.

■ **Note**   The order of columns in the list itself does not affect the order of columns in the view.

When selecting columns to include in the view, you are shown the standard columns that are part of the list or library, any custom columns you may have added, and a set of special columns that are made available automatically. The special columns are as follows:

- *Attachments*: Used to add a column that shows whether an attachment is associated with the list. This column is available only in lists that support attachments.

- *Modified*: The date and time the list or library item was last modified.

- *Modified By*: The user who last modified the item corresponding to the date information in the Modified column.

- *Checked Out To*: The user to whom the item is checked out if the item is in a checked-out status (available only for items, such as documents, supporting checkout).

- *Content Type*: The name of the content type the item is based on.

- *Created*: The date and time the list or library item was originally created.

- *Created By*: The user who created the item corresponding to the date information in the Created column.

- *Edit (link to edit item)*: An icon that, when clicked, will open the Edit window for the corresponding list item or document.

- *Folder Child Count*: The number of folders contained in the current folder of the list or library.

- *ID*: The unique identifier for the item in the list or library.

- *Item Child Count*: The number of items contained in the current folder of the list or library.

- *Type (icon linked to document)*: An icon representing the type of item that, when clicked, will open the associated list item or document.

- *Version*: The version number of the item. When versioning is not enabled against the list or library, the version number always remains at 1.0.

- *Copy Source*: The URL of the original source document (used when documents are moved within SharePoint).

Once the columns are selected and properly ordered, decide how you want the information in the list or library sorted. Sorting can involve one or two columns in the list or library and allows you to select the primary sort order and one level of subsort ordering. Sort order can be either ascending or descending.

Next, determine whether the view should include all items in the list or library or use conditions to limit the items displayed. To filter items, determine the filtering criteria. Any combination of column criteria available in the list or library can be used.

Once the filter criteria are specified, the next decision is determining whether the information should be grouped by any of the listed columns. Grouping involves a hierarchical display of the information based on the selected columns. You can group by a single column or by two columns and you can choose to show these groups either expanded or collapsed. The expanded grouping keeps all items visible within the view and makes them appear to be contained in the group by columns. As the collapsed grouping shows the group only by values, you must click a plus icon next to a group value to reveal the contained items. With all of these decisions made, you can create the views you need for your lists and libraries.

Creating Standard Views

To create a new standard view, do the following:

1. Navigate to the list or library where you want to create the view.

2. On the list or library view page, select the Create View option from the List or Library ribbon tab, as seen in Figure 5-21.

Figure 5-21. *List ribbon tab*

3. On the View Type page, select the Standard View option from the Choose a View Type section, or select an existing standard view to use as the starting layout for the new view in the "Start from an existing view" section, as seen in Figure 5-22.

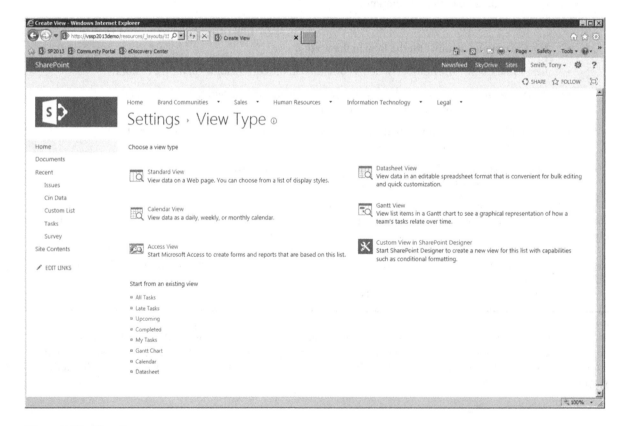

Figure 5-22. *View Type page*

4. On the Create View page, do the following:

a. In the Name section, enter the name for the new view. This name will identify the view in the view selection area of the ribbon and in the views listing at the top of the view page. Also, specify whether the view should be the default view (the view seen when the list or library is initially accessed) for the list or library.

b. In the Audience section, specify whether this will be a personal view (available only to the person creating it) or a public view (available to all visitors to the list or library).

c. In the Columns section, select the columns from the list or library to display, and identify the order to display the columns in.

d. In the Sort section, optionally identify the primary and secondary sort columns, and specify whether the information's sort order is ascending or descending. You can also specify whether all items, including folders, should be sorted in the specified order or listed before the other content items.

e. In the Filter section, optionally define filtering criteria for the items. When specifying criteria, for each filter rule identify the column to filter against and the filtering conditions. You can specify multiple columns to filter on and decide whether the filters are joined with And conditions (i.e., that the content presented must satisfy both listed conditions) or Or conditions (that either item condition will satisfy the filter). The conditions available for use with filters include the items shown in Table 5-1.

Table 5-1. *View Filter Conditions*

Condition	Description
Is Equal To	The value of the column must equal the condition text entered.
Is Not Equal To	The value of the column cannot equal the condition text entered.
Is Greater Than	The value of the column must be greater than the value entered in the condition text. This condition is primarily used with number and date columns.
Is Less Than	The value of the column must be less than the value entered in the condition text. Like the Is Greater Than condition, this condition is primarily used with number and date columns.
Is Greater Than or Equal To	The value of the column must be greater than or the same as the value entered in the condition text.
Is Less Than or Equal To	The value of the column must be less than or the same as the value entered into the condition text.
Begins With	The column value starts with the text entered as the condition text. This condition is primarily used with text values. For example, if "butter" is the text entered, a column value starting with this text, such as "butterfly" or "buttercup," will be included, but a field value such as "coco butter" will not be included.
Contains	The condition text can be found somewhere within the column value. This condition is primarily used with text values. For example if "butter" is the text entered, column values containing this text, such as "butterfly," "buttercup," and "coco butter," will be included.

f. In the Tabular Value section, specify whether you want to allow check boxes for the items. Check boxes (enabled by default) allow selection of multiple items when bulk management tasks are performed. List and library item management is discussed in Chapters 6 and 7.

g. In the Group By section, specify whether the information in the view should be grouped by any column values (one or two levels of column grouping can be chosen). As part of specifying the grouping, identify whether to sort the grouping items in ascending or descending order. Also specify whether grouped items are collapsed (i.e., not visible) and must be expanded to show items within or are expanded by default. Finally in this section, identify the number of items to appear per page in the view.

h. In the Totals section, specify whether any columns are to have a total value calculated and displayed within the view. The type of totaling performed depends on the type of data contained in the column. Table 5-2 shows the type of totaling that can be performed.

Table 5-2. *Totaling Types for Columns*

Totaling Type	Columns Supported	Description
Count	All	Totals the number of items.
Average	Number Date and Time	Calculates the average value for the items in the view.
Maximum	Number Date and Time	Identifies the largest value in the column across all items in the view.
Minimum	Number Date and Time	Identifies the smallest value in the column across all items in the view.
Sum	Number	Adds together all numbers stored in the column across all items in the view.
Std Deviation	Number	Calculates the standard deviation value based on the data in the column.
Variance	Number	Calculates the variance value based on the data in the column.

i. In the Style section, identify the layout that will govern the display of items in the view. Table 5-3 lists the styles available.

Table 5-3. *View Styles*

Style	Description	Example
Basic Table	Lists each item in a single row.	**Type** / **Name** Wyne RFP Response, ACE RFP Response / **RFP Responder** Mercurio, Ralph, Smith, Tony / **RFP Status** Loss, Win
Document Details	Lists document details in a framed section having the document name and each view column listed with one per row; available only in document libraries.	Acme RFP Response — Name: Acme RFP Response; RFP Responder: Smith, Tony; RFP Status: Win
Boxed	Lists items from a list, much as the Document Details view shows documents with a column name and value per row.	Complete Exchange Design and Migration Plan; Smith, Tony; 3/13/2013; 100 %
Boxed, no labels	Shows the list items in the same layout as boxed but without the column names listed.	Task Name: Complete Exchange Design and Migration Plan; Assigned To: Smith, Tony; Due Date: 3/13/2013; % Complete: 100 %
Newsletter	Lists all columns but Multiple Lines of Text fields in a single row, like the Basic Table view, but the Multiple Lines of Text fields sit below this information in a separate row spanning the row's width.	ACE RFP Response, Smith, Tony, Win. The ACE organization has requested assistance with their efforts to introduce a new solution for their AGE system. The XXX solution will be configured to address the need and introduce a new solution.

(continued)

Table 5-3. (*continued*)

Style	Description	Example
Newsletter, no lines	Is the same as the newsletter style but without horizontal line separators between items.	ACE RFP Response — Smith, Tony — Win. The ACE organization has requested assistance with their efforts to introduce a new solution for their AGE system. The XXX solution will be configured to address the need and introduce a new solution.
Shaded	Is the same as the Basic style but with alternate rows shaded.	Type · Name · RFP Responder · RFP Status. Wyne RFP Response — Mercurio, Ralph — Loss. ACE RFP Response — Smith, Tony — Win.
Preview Pane	Includes a three-column display: the first column has title information, the second lists names for the columns in the view, and the third lists the values of the columns.	Wyne RFP Response / ACE RFP Response / Acme RFP Response. Type · Name · RFP Responder · RFP Status → Wyne RFP Response · Mercurio, Ralph · Loss.
Default	As the default view for the current list, is the same as the Basic Table view.	Type · Name · RFP Responder · RFP Status. Wyne RFP Response — Mercurio, Ralph — Loss. ACE RFP Response — Smith, Tony — Win.

j. In the Folders section, specify whether folders will be represented in the view. When selected, this option lists folders within the list or library and shows the items contained in a folder when the folder in the view is clicked on. Alternatively, choosing to show all items without folders will display all list or library items as if the folders did not exist. That is, all items will appear as if stored at the root in the library.

k. In the Item Limit section, specify how many items will appear on a single page in the view and whether the view is to display only that many items or that many items at a time, with paging between groups. By default, a view will show batches of 30 items at a time.

l. In the Mobile section, identify whether to make the view available in the list's or library's mobile views. Mobile views (discussed in detail in Chapter 2) appear when SharePoint is accessed from a mobile device. Also, specify whether the view will be the default for mobile devices accessing the list or library, how many items to display in the view's mobile version, and which field to use in the mobile view simple display.

m. Once all the appropriate information is entered, click the OK button.

The view is created, and you are navigated to the created view.

Creating Datasheet Views

To create a new Datasheet View, do the following:

1. Navigate to the list or library where you want to create the view.

2. On the list or library view page, select the Create View option from the List or Library ribbon tab (see Figure 5-21).

3. On the View Type page, select the Datasheet View option from the Choose a View Type section, or select an existing datasheet view to use as the starting layout for the new view in the "Start from an existing view" section (see Figure 5-22).

4. On the Create View page, do the following:

   a. In the Name section, enter the name of the new view. This name will represent the view in the view selection area of the ribbon and in the views listing at the top of the view page. Also, specify whether the view should be the default view (the view seen when the list or library is initially accessed) for the list or library.

   b. In the Audience section, specify whether this view will be a personal view (available only to the person creating it) or a public view (available to all visitors to the list or library).

   c. In the Columns section, select the columns from the list or library to display, and identify the order to display the columns in.

   d. In the Sort section, optionally identify the primary and secondary sort columns, and specify whether the information's sort order is ascending or descending. You can also specify whether all items, including folders, should be sorted in the specified order or listed before the other content items.

   e. In the Filter section, optionally define filtering criteria for the items. When specifying filter criteria, for each filter rule identify the column to filter against and the filtering conditions. You can specify multiple columns to filter on and decide whether the filters are joined with And conditions (the content presented must satisfy both listed conditions) or Or conditions (either item condition will satisfy the filter). The conditions available for use with filters include the items identified in Table 5-1.

   f. In the Totals section, specify whether any columns are to have a total value calculated and displayed within the view. The type of totaling performed depends on the type of data contained in the column. Table 5-2 shows the type of totaling that can be performed.

   g. In the Folders section, specify whether folders will be represented in the view. When selected this option lists folders within the list or library and shows the items contained in the folder when it is clicked on. Alternatively, choosing to show all items without folders will display all list or library items as if the folders did not exist. That is, all items will appear as if they reside at the root in the library.

   h. In the Item Limit section, specify how many items will appear on a single page in the view and whether the view is to display only that many items or that many items at a time, with paging between groups. By default, a view will show batches of 30 items at a time.

   i. Once all the appropriate information is entered, click the OK button.

The view is created, and you are navigated to the new view.

Creating Calendar Views

To create a new Calendar View, do the following:

1. Navigate to the list or library where you want to create the view.

2. On the list or library view page, select the Create View option from the List or Library ribbon tab, as shown in Figure 5-21.

3. On the View Type page, select the Calendar View option from the Choose a View Type section, or select an existing standard view to use as the starting layout for the new view in the "Start from an existing view" section, as seen in Figure 5-22.

4. On the Create View page, do the following:

    a. In the Name section, enter the name of the new view. This name will represent the view in the view selection area of the ribbon and in the views listing at the top of the view page. Also, specify whether the view should be the default view (the view seen when the list or library is initially accessed) for the list or library.

    b. In the Audience section, specify whether this view will be a personal view (available only to the person creating it) or a public view (available to all visitors to the list or library).

    c. In the Time Interval section, identify the date columns from the list or library to use as the Begin and End date values to determine where the item will appear on the calendar.

    d. In the Calendar Columns section, select the columns from the list or library to display in the calendar view layout. Identify the columns that will represent the month view title, the week view title and subheading, and the day view title and subheading.

    e. In the Default Scope section, identify the default format for the calendar, the format seen when the view is initially accessed. The choices for the default scope include day, week, and month.

    f. In the Filter section, optionally define filtering criteria for the items. When specifying criteria, for each filter rule identify the column to filter against and the filtering conditions. You can specify multiple columns to filter on and decide whether the filters are joined with And conditions (the content presented must satisfy both listed conditions) or Or conditions (satisfying either condition will satisfy the filter). The conditions available to use with filters include the items identified in Table 5-1.

    g. In the Mobile section, identify whether to make the view available in the list's or library's mobile views. Mobile views (discussed in detail in Chapter 2) appear when SharePoint is accessed from a mobile device. Also, specify whether the view will be the default for the list or library when accessed from a mobile device, how many items to display in the view's mobile version, and which field to use in the mobile view simple display.

    h. Once all the appropriate information is entered, click the OK button.

The view is created, and you are navigated to it.

Creating Gantt Views

To create a new Gantt View, do the following:

1. Navigate to the list or library where you want to create the view.

2. On the list or library view page, select the Create View option from the List or Library ribbon tab, as shown in Figure 5-21.

3. On the View Type page, select the Gantt View option from the Choose a View Type section, or select an existing standard view to use as the starting layout for the new view in the "Start from an existing view" section, as seen in Figure 5-22.

4. On the Create View page, do the following:

   a. In the Name section, enter the name of the new view. It will represent the view in the view selection area of the ribbon. Also, specify whether the view should be the default view (the view seen when the list or library is initially accessed) for the list or library.

   b. In the Audience section, specify whether this view will be a personal view (available only to the person creating it) or a public view (available to all visitors to the list or library).

   c. In the Columns section, select the columns from the list or library to display and identify the order to display the columns in.

   d. In the Gantt Columns section, select the columns from the list or library to display on the Gantt chart. Identify the columns that will represent the Gantt chart title, start and due dates, and (optionally) percentage complete and predecessor values.

   e. In the Sort section, optionally identify the primary and secondary sort columns, and specify whether the information's sort order is ascending or descending. You can also specify whether all items, including folders, should be sorted in the specified order or listed before the other content items.

   f. In the Filter section, optionally define filtering criteria for the items. When specifying criteria, for each filter rule identify the column to filter against and the filtering conditions. You can specify multiple columns to filter on and decide whether the filters are joined with And conditions (the content presented must satisfy both listed conditions) or Or conditions (satisfying either item condition will satisfy the filter). The conditions available to use with filters include the items identified in Table 5-1.

   g. In the Group By section, specify whether the information in the view should be grouped by any column values (one or two levels of column grouping can be chosen). As part of specifying the grouping, identify whether to sort the grouping items in ascending or descending order. Also specify whether grouped items are collapsed (i.e., not visible) and must be expanded to show items within or are expanded by default. Finally in this section, identify the number of items to appear per page in the view.

   h. In the Totals section, specify whether any columns are to have a total value calculated and displayed within the view. The type of totaling performed depends on the type of data contained in the column. Table 5-2 shows the type of totaling that can be performed.

   i. In the Style section, identify the layout that will govern the display of items in the view. Table 5-3 lists the styles available.

j. In the Folders section, specify whether folders will be represented in the view. When selected, this option lists folders within the list or library and shows the items contained in a folder when it is clicked on. Alternatively, choosing to show all items without folders will display all list or library items as if the folders did not exist. That is, all items will appear as if they are contained at the root in the library.

k. In the Item Limit section, specify how many items will appear on a single page in the view and whether the view is to display only that many items or that many items at a time, with paging between groups. By default, a view will show batches of 30 items at a time.

l. Once all the appropriate information is entered, click the OK button.

The view is created, and you are navigated to the library or list view you created.

Creating Views in SharePoint Designer

As mentioned earlier, new views can also be created through SharePoint Designer to take advantage of its advanced configurations for view, such as more highly customized layouts and conditional formatting.

To create a new view through SharePoint Designer, do the following:

1. Navigate to the list or library where the view is to be created.

2. From the List or Library ribbon tab on the list or library view page, select the Create View option.

3. On the View Type page, select the Custom View in SharePoint Designer option.

4. In SharePoint Designer in the Create New List View window, enter the name of the new view, specify whether it should be the default view, and click the OK button.

5. In SharePoint Designer on the list or library screen in the Views section, select the newly created view.

6. In SharePoint Designer on the View page, set up the view as appropriate.

The new view will be available in SharePoint when you access the list or library.

Access View

Through the Create View area, Microsoft Access can be used to create forms and reports from lists and libraries and alternate ways to review the information contained in lists and libraries. To take advantage of Microsoft Access for reporting on list and library information, do the following:

1. Navigate to the list or library where the view is to be created.

2. From the List or Library ribbon tab on the list or library view page, select the Create View option.

3. On the View Type page, select the Access View option.

Access will open and connect to the selected list or library. You can then create any needed forms or reports against the list or library.

Editing Existing Views

Existing list and library views can be edited to alter layouts and settings. Views can be edited in SharePoint or SharePoint Designer. Edit a view in SharePoint Designer to alter filtering conditions or change the display in ways not available in the standard SharePoint view management options.

To edit views already created against lists and libraries in SharePoint, do the following:

1. Navigate to the list or library containing the view you want to edit.

2. On the list or library view page, select the view you want to edit from the view list.

3. On the list or library view page, click on the Modify View option from the List or Library ribbon tab.

4. On the Edit View page, update the view details as needed, and once done, click the OK button.

The view will be edited, and you will be navigated to the updated view.

As mentioned, you can also edit existing views in SharePoint Designer. Doing so allows you to take advantage of SharePoint Designer's extended view management capabilities, even on views initially created within SharePoint itself. To edit an existing view in SharePoint Designer, do the following:

1. Navigate to the list or library containing the view you want to edit.

2. On the list or library view page, select the view from the view list that you want to edit.

3. On the list or library view page, click the down arrow next to the Modify View option, and choose the Modify in SharePoint Designer (Advanced) option from the List or Library ribbon tab.

4. In SharePoint Designer, make any needed changes to the view and save the changes.

The view is updated based on the changes made.

Delete Existing Views

You can delete existing views for lists and libraries (except for the default view). To delete a view defined as the default view, first select a new view as the default, and then the former default view can be deleted. To delete a view that is not the default view in SharePoint, do the following:

1. Navigate to the list or library containing the view you want to edit.

2. On the list or library view page, select the view from the view list that you want to edit.

3. On the list or library view page, click on the Modify View option from the List or Library ribbon tab.

4. On the Edit View page, click the Delete button.

5. In the delete confirmation window, click the OK button.

The view is deleted, and you are returned to the list or library.

RSS Feed Settings

An RSS feed (RSS stands for "really simple syndication") is a way of publishing information in a standard format that can be consumed by RSS readers. SharePoint allows you to publish lists and libraries as RSS feeds consumable by RSS reader programs. Publishing lists and libraries as RSS feeds lets you make announcement lists and other information available on mobile phones and other devices, in a program such as Outlook, and on alternative web solutions and interfaces.

To configure RSS settings within a SharePoint list or library, do the following:

1. Navigate to the list or library where you need to configure RSS settings.

2. On the list or library view page, select the List or Library Settings option from the List or Library ribbon tab.

3. On the Settings page, select the RSS Settings option from the Communications section.

4. On the Modify RSS Settings page, do the following:

    a. In the List RSS section, specify whether the list should support RSS.

    b. In the RSS Channel Information section, specify whether Multi-Line of Text fields should be truncated and specify the title, description and image to be used to refer to the list through the RSS feed.

    c. In the Columns section, select the columns from the list or library to expose through the RSS feed and the order in which those columns will appear in the feed.

    d. In the Item Limit section, specify the maximum number of items and days of information to include in the feed.

    e. Click the OK button to save the RSS details.

When a list or library is configured to support RSS, each view within it has an RSS version. RSS views are accessed by navigating to the associated list view and selecting the RSS Feed option from the List or Library ribbon tab.

Managing List and Library Permissions

Chapter 3 discussed managing security within sites and how to control who has access to sites and the content they contain, including their lists and libraries. To further refine security within a SharePoint site, you can change permissions of individual lists and libraries. Managing permissions directly against a list or library causes security for the list and its content to be driven by the updated permissions instead of the overall site permissions. You will want to change a list's or library's permissions when access to it needs to be more restricted than access to the site or when individuals that need to edit its content and those that can edit other site content are different. When changing list permissions, if you configure them such that some site users lack access to the list, references to it within the site will also be unavailable to those users. That is, the list will appear not to exist to users without access rights to it.

Updating List and Library Inheritance Settings

To manage list or library security directly, first update the permission inheritance settings. Removing permission inheritance against a site's list or library allows its security to be managed separately from that of the site as a whole. To update this permission inheritance, do the following:

1. Navigate to the list or library whose permission inheritance is to be updated.

2. On the list or library view page, select the List or Library settings option from the List or Library ribbon tab.

3. On the Settings page, select the Permissions for This Document Library option.

4. On the Permissions page, update the list or library inheritance options as follows:

    a. If the list or library currently inherits permissions from the site, do the following:

        i. On the Permissions ribbon tab, select the Stop Inheriting Permissions option.

        ii. In the confirmation window, click the OK button.

    b. If the list or library does not currently inherit permissions from the site, do the following:

        i. On the Permissions ribbon tab, select the Delete Unique Permissions option.

        ii. In the confirmation window, click the OK button.

The permission inheritance settings are updated, and the permissions page is updated accordingly. If you stopped permission inheritance, a copy of the permissions applied to the site are made for the list or library, and the permission management options are made available in the list's or library's Permissions page. If you deleted unique permissions, the list or library permissions are marked as inherited. They are managed by the site, and any changes made to the permissions of the list or library are lost.

Changing List and Library Permissions

When a list or library does not inherit permissions, update its permissions by doing the following:

1. Navigate to the list or library where you wish to update permissions.

2. On the list or library view page, select the List or Library settings option from the List or Library ribbon tab.

3. On the Settings page, select the Permissions for This List (or Document Library) option from the Permissions and Management section.

4. On the Permissions page, do the following:

    a. To add permissions:

        i. Select the Grant Permissions option from the Permissions ribbon tab.

        ii. In the Share Documents window, enter the user's name or e-mail and select the user from the type-ahead list. If permissions to be added are other than edit, click the Show Options link to show permission levels, and choose the appropriate ones from the drop-down. Then click the Share button.

    b. To edit existing user or group permissions:

        i. Click the box next to the user or group whose permissions are to be updated, and then choose the Edit User Permissions option from the Permissions ribbon tab.

        ii. On the Edit Permissions page, select the appropriate permission levels, and then click the OK button.

    c.   To delete existing user or group permissions:

          i.   Click the box next to the user or group whose permissions are to be deleted, and then select the Remove User Permissions option from the Permissions ribbon tab.

         ii.   In the deletion confirmation window, click the OK button.

The user permissions for the list or library are appropriately updated.

File Plan Reporting

Lists and libraries come with the ability to generate file plan reports. A report lists details about the list or library and its content. Figure 5-23 shows a standard file plan report.

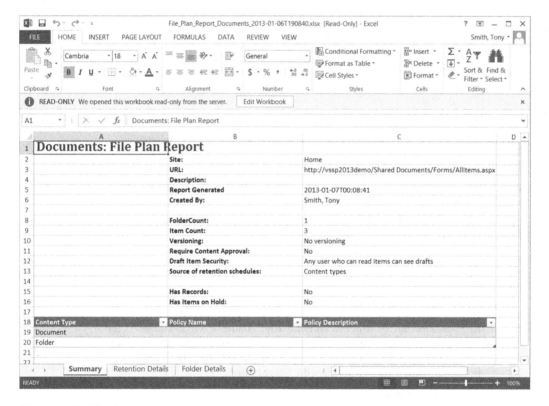

Figure 5-23. *File plan report*

The statistics presented in a list or library file plan report include the following:

- location of the list or library

- number of folders and items

- versioning configuration

- content approval requirements

- security and records management details

To create a file plan report for a list or library, do the following:

1. Navigate to the list or library where you wish to create the report.

2. On the list or library view page, select the List or Library settings option from the List or Library ribbon tab.

3. On the Settings page, select the Generate File Plan Report option from the Permissions and Management section.

4. On the File Plan Report page, identify where you want to save the report, and click the OK button.

The file plan report is generated and presented to you.

List and Library Office Integration

Microsoft Office Excel and Access can be used to view and manage information in lists and libraries. These tools can create advanced views of the information and make it available even when you are not connected to SharePoint.

Excel SharePoint Integration

There are several ways Excel can enhance list and library capabilities and take further advantage of the details in lists and libraries.

Exporting Lists or Libraries to Excel

When list or library information is exported to Excel, the information in the list or library columns can be viewed in Excel. To export a list or library to Excel, do the following:

1. Navigate to the list or library whose information you want to export.

2. On the list or library view page, select the Export to Excel option from the List or Library ribbon tab.

3. When prompted to open or save the file, select the Open option.

4. If prompted with an Excel security notification, click the Enable button.

   If Excel is not open when the Export to Excel option is selected, Excel opens, and the information from the list appears. If Excel is already open when Export to Excel is selected, the Import Data screen appears. On this screen, do the following:

   a. In the "How to view the data" section, select to open the list as a table, PivotTable Report, or chart.

   b. In the "Where do you want to put this data" section, specify an open worksheet, a new worksheet, or a new workbook.

   c. Click the OK button to run the export.

The list or library information opens in Excel and can be managed within the sheet. The information is configured as an External Data Source within Excel (see Figure 5-24).

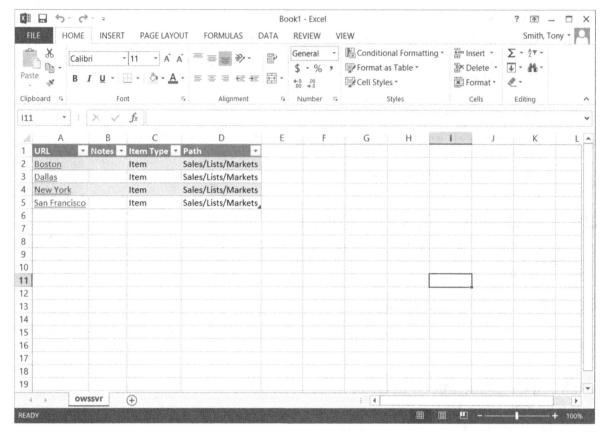

Figure 5-24. *List information in Excel*

Identifying the details in Excel that are part of the external data source is easy since they are outlined in a border. Opening a list in Excel lets you use tools like PivotTables and charts to create needed representations of the data. While you can use Excel to format and manipulate list information, you cannot publish content changes back to the list.

Excel has several data integration options for use in working with external data. This information is available on a Design ribbon tab added to Excel when a cell is highlighted within the exported data set. The more commonly used options include the following:

- *Refresh*: This option, which reloads the details from the list into Excel, provides an accurate representation of current information in the list.

■ **Note** Refreshing the information in Excel causes any edits made to it in Excel to be lost.

- *Open In Browser*: This option opens the web browser and navigates you to the default view of the list.

- *Unlink*: This option, which disconnects Excel from the details in the list, makes the copy of the data in Excel independent of the list.

Importing a Spreadsheet into Excel as a List

An earlier section in this chapter explained how to create lists and libraries in SharePoint with the Add an App interface. This method works well for creating new empty lists. However, sometimes the information you want in a new SharePoint list already exists. In this case you can use Excel as a mechanism to create the list and add the existing information to it by using the Import Spreadsheet option to create a new custom list in your SharePoint site. To create a new custom list based on the information in an Excel spreadsheet, do the following:

1. Navigate to the site where you want to create the list.

2. Navigate to the Site Contents page for the site.

3. On the Site Contents page, click the Add an App option in the Lists, Libraries, and Other Apps section.

4. On the Your Apps page, select the Import Spreadsheet option.

5. In the new window, do the following:

    a. In the Name and Description section, enter a name for the new list and an optional description.

    b. In the Import from Spreadsheet section, select the file to import.

    c. Click the Import button to complete the import.

6. In the opened Excel window, select the cell range to import, and click the Import button.

The list is created, and the data from the Excel document is imported.

To initiate the creation of the custom list and the data import from Excel through the Excel interface, do the following:

1. Open the Excel document with the information needed to create the list.

2. Highlight the range of values to include.

3. Select the Format as Table option from the Styles group of the Home ribbon tab, and select a style.

4. In the Format as Table dialog, click the "My table has headers" check box if the values include column headers.

5. Click the OK button.

Once the values are formatted as a table, the details can be used as the basis for a custom list. To publish the list, do the following:

1. Select the Excel table.

2. Select the Export command from the External Table Data group of the Table Tools Design ribbon tab, and select the Expert Table to SharePoint List option.

3. In the Export Table to SharePoint Site dialog, enter the URL of the SharePoint site where the list is to be created.

4. In the Export Table to SharePoint List Step 1 box, do the following:

    a. In the Address section, enter the URL to the site where the list is to be created, and specify whether a read-only connection is to be established.

    b. In the Name field, specify the name of the new list.

    c.   In the Description field, enter an optional description.

    d.   Click the Next button.

5.   In the Export Table to SharePoint List Step 2 box, click the Finish button.

6.   In the confirmation window, click the OK button.

The list is created in the site meant to contain the data from the source Excel document.

Access SharePoint Integration

Besides being able to manage list and library content in Excel, Microsoft Access can work with list information. Access is used to work with list data since it allows you not only to manage the information but also to create reports based on the information (Access cannot be used, however, to manage library data). A key difference between Excel, as discussed earlier, and Access in managing list data is that while Excel cannot update information in the list, Access can push changes made in it back to the SharePoint list.

To work with a SharePoint list in Access, do the following:

1.   Navigate to the list to be opened in Microsoft Access.

2.   On the list view page, select the Open with Access option from the List ribbon tab.

3.   In the Access window, enter a file name and location for the Access database file. Also, specify whether to link the database to the list or export information from the list.

The list is made available in Access. If you link to the list, any changes made in Access are pushed to SharePoint as well. If you export the list, then a copy of it is made in Access. Since the copy is not directly related to the list itself, changes made after export in Access or in the list are not reflected in the other environment.

Synchronizing List and Libraries for Offline Access

Since SharePoint sites can be synchronized with your local computer, you can access information even without a connection to the SharePoint environment. The method used to synchronize site content depends on the version of Microsoft Office installed on your computer. With Microsoft Office 2010, content is synchronized using the SharePoint Workspace product. With Microsoft Office 2013, SharePoint libraries are synchronized locally using SkyDrive Pro.

Synchronizing Lists and Libraries with SharePoint Workspace

SharePoint Workspace enables you to work with SharePoint lists and libraries within the SharePoint Workspace program. To synchronize SharePoint content with SharePoint Workspace 2010, do the following:

1.   Navigate to the site containing the content to be synchronized.

2.   On the site home page, select the Sync option.

3.   SharePoint Workspace opens and prompts you to confirm synchronization of the items.

Once synchronized with SharePoint Workspace, the content can be used within that environment. Synchronized content will be kept current with the corresponding information in the list as long as SharePoint Workspace is able to connect to the SharePoint content.

Synchronizing Libraries with SkyDrive Pro

SkyDrive Pro lets you synchronize document library content with your local computer and makes it accessible within your local file system:

1. Navigate to the site containing the content to be synchronized.

2. On the site home page, select the Sync option.

3. On the security message click the Allow button.

4. In the SkyDrive Pro window, confirm the library connection and the local storage location, and then click the Sync Now button.

The content is synchronized with the identified local location. This content is kept current as long as the computer can connect to the SharePoint environment. Synchronization allows use of the content whether the machine can or cannot connect to the environment.

CHAPTER 6

Working with Lists

Lists are used to store structured sets of information in SharePoint. Whether you need to track tasks, store contacts, or summarize products, you can use lists to store, manage, and share their information. In Chapter 5 how to create and configure lists and libraries is discussed. This chapter discusses the different types of lists available in SharePoint 2013 and how to create and manage content within them.

Types of Lists

As was discussed in Chapter 5, when you create a new list, you base it on an available template. SharePoint 2013 has several default list templates available to use for creating new SharePoint lists. These templates are considered apps and are found in the app management tools. Available default list templates include the following.

Announcements

Announcements lists, which are used to store and share messages and news, provide a structure and layout to support this type of content. They include a set of features to enhance the management of news. Announcements lists have the structure defined in Table 6-1.

Table 6-1. *Announcements List Columns*

Column	Required	Type	Properties
Title	Yes	Single Line of Text	
Body	No	Multiple Lines of Text	Enhanced Rich Text 15 Lines for Editing
Expires	No	Date and Time	Date Only Standard Format

An Announcements list is often added to the home page of a site to relay key messages to site users. The web part representing the list when it is added to pages within the site includes the layout shown in Figure 6-1.

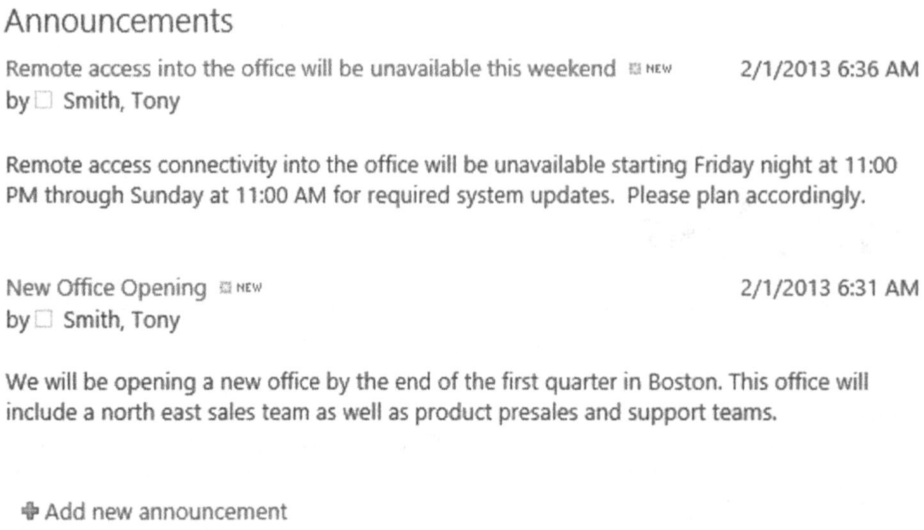

Announcements

Remote access into the office will be unavailable this weekend ⊠ NEW   2/1/2013 6:36 AM
by ☐ Smith, Tony

Remote access connectivity into the office will be unavailable starting Friday night at 11:00 PM through Sunday at 11:00 AM for required system updates. Please plan accordingly.

New Office Opening ⊠ NEW   2/1/2013 6:31 AM
by ☐ Smith, Tony

We will be opening a new office by the end of the first quarter in Boston. This office will include a north east sales team as well as product presales and support teams.

✚ Add new announcement

Figure 6-1. *Announcements list web part*

The default web part layout for an announcement list varies from a standard list view in that it includes a title showing the date and time the announcement was last modified, along with the name of the person modifying the announcement, in a customized format. When announcement lists are initially created, they contain a single view called the All Items view. This view, a standard SharePoint list view, displays all the items in the announcements list sorted in descending order by Modified date and includes the following fields:

- Title (linked to item with edit menu)
- Modified

Announcement lists have the same management and access capabilities as other lists in SharePoint but with an additional advanced capability: announcement lists are among the few list types that support incoming e-mail.

Incoming E-mail Capabilities

Announcement lists can be configured with an e-mail address allowing users to send e-mail messages directly to the list. In the list these e-mail messages become announcements mapping the following details from the Outlook message to the SharePoint announcement:

- E-mail subject becomes the announcement Title.
- E-mail body becomes the announcement Body.
- E-mail From address becomes the announcement Created By.
- E-mail attachments become attachments against the announcement list.

■ **Note**   Before a SharePoint list's incoming e-mail capabilities can be utilized, your SharePoint technical administrator will need to configure your environment to support inbound e-mail.

Once incoming e-mail capabilities have been configured against your SharePoint environment, your SharePoint announcements lists can be configured to support incoming e-mail. To configure incoming e-mail settings against your announcements list, do the following:

1. Navigate to the Announcements list where you want to configure incoming e-mail.

2. On the list view page, select the List Settings option from the List ribbon tab.

3. On the Settings page, select the Incoming E-mail Settings option from the Communications section.

4. On the Incoming E-mail Settings page, make the following selections:

   a. In the Incoming E-mail section, select Yes for the Allow This List to Receive E-mail option, and enter the e-mail address for the library.

   b. In the E-mail Attachments section, specify whether e-mail attachments are to be saved to the list.

   c. In the E-mail Message section, specify whether the original e-mail message is to be saved.

   d. In the E-mail Meeting Invitations section, specify whether meeting invitations sent to the list are to be created as announcements.

   e. In the E-mail Security section, specify whether e-mail messages are to be accepted only from e-mail addresses associated with users that have access to the library or from any e-mail address.

   f. Once all information has been entered, click the OK button to save the settings.

The inbound e-mail configuration is saved, and you are returned to the Settings page.

Contacts

Contacts lists are used to maintain details about people. These lists can be used to track contacts for projects, departments, initiatives, and any other efforts. Contacts lists include the fields necessary to track all key details about people, including the details listed in Table 6-2.

Table 6-2. *Contacts List Columns*

Column	Required	Type	Properties
Last Name	Yes	Single Line of Text	
Last Name Phonetic	No	Single Line of Text	
First Name	No	Single Line of Text	
First Name Phonetic	No	Single Line of Text	
Full Name	No	Single Line of Text	
Email Address	No	Single Line of Text	
Company	No	Single Line of Text	
Company Phonetic	No	Single Line of Text	
Job Title	No	Single Line of Text	
Business Phone	No	Single Line of Text	

(continued)

Table 6-2. (*continued*)

Column	Required	Type	Properties
Home Phone	No	Single Line of Text	
Mobile Number	No	Single Line of Text	
Fax Number	No	Single Line of Text	
Address	No	Multiple Lines of Text	Plain Text 2 Lines for Editing
City	No	Single Line of Text	
State/Province	No	Single Line of Text	
ZIP/Postal Code	No	Single Line of Text	
Country/Region	No	Single Line of Text	
Web Page	No	Hyperlink or Picture	Format: Hyperlink
Notes	No	Multiple Lines of Text	Rich Text 6 Lines for Editing

When contact lists are added to pages within SharePoint, the default view presented is a standard list layout (see Figure 6-2) with the following fields:

- Attachments
- Last Name
- First Name
- Company
- Business Phone
- Home Phone
- E-mail Address

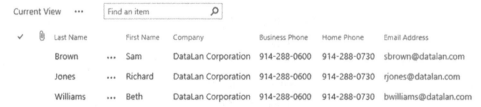

Contacts

⊕ new item or edit this list

	Current View •••	Find an item 🔍					
✓ 📎	Last Name		First Name	Company	Business Phone	Home Phone	Email Address
	Brown	•••	Sam	DataLan Corporation	914-288-0600	914-288-0730	sbrown@datalan.com
	Jones	•••	Richard	DataLan Corporation	914-288-0600	914-288-0730	rjones@datalan.com
	Williams	•••	Beth	DataLan Corporation	914-288-0600	914-288-0730	bwilliams@datalan.com

Figure 6-2. *Contacts list web part*

When a contacts list is created, it contains only a single list view, called All Contacts. This list view presents the following fields from the contacts list, with items sorted by Last Name and First Name:

- Attachments
- Last Name (linked to item with Edit menu)

- First Name

- Company

- Business Phone

- Home Phone

- Email Address

SharePoint contacts lists and Outlook contact lists are similarly structured to help support special integration between SharePoint and Outlook. This integration includes the ability to export SharePoint contacts so that they can be saved to Outlook and the ability to synchronize SharePoint contacts lists with Outlook.

Exporting Contacts

Contacts in a SharePoint contacts lists can be exported to be saved as contacts in Outlook. Exporting a contact creates a copy in Outlook. To export a contact in a SharePoint contacts list, do the following:

1. Navigate to the contacts list from which you want to export the contact.

2. On the contacts list view page, select the Export Contact option from the contact's context menu, as seen in Figure 6-3.

Figure 6-3. *Contact Context Menu*

3. When prompted to open or save the file, choose the Open option.

4. If Outlook is installed, a New Contact window will open. Make any desired updates to the contact information, and click Save & Close to save the contact as an Outlook contact.

The contact is saved to Outlook.

■ **Note**   Once a contact is exported from SharePoint and imported into Outlook, any changes to the contact in one program will not affect the contact in the other.

Connecting Contacts Lists to Outlook

While exporting contacts from SharePoint and importing them into Outlook creates a separate copy of the contact, connecting contacts lists to Outlook will keep the information in Outlook and the list synchronized. Many times when you want SharePoint contacts to be available in Outlook, you also want to be able to continue managing and working with the contacts in SharePoint. Likewise, having them available in Outlook lets you easily e-mail the contact and have access to the details even while not connected to your SharePoint environment. Synchronizing contacts lists enables you to use and manage this information in both environments. To connect a SharePoint contacts list to Outlook, do the following:

1. Navigate to the contacts list you want to synchronize with Outlook.

2. On the contacts list view page, select the Connect to Outlook option from the List ribbon tab.

3. In the Allow the Web Site to Open a Program window, select the Allow button.

4. In the Connect this SharePoint Contact List to Outlook message, click the Yes button.

The contacts list is connected to Outlook and made available on the Outlook Contacts tab. The list of contacts is also cached locally so that you can access them from Outlook when you are not connected to your SharePoint environment.

Calendar

SharePoint calendars let you store details about meetings and other types of events. Unlike most other list types, a calendar list has a completely different set of default views, most being calendar layout views (see Figure 6-4).

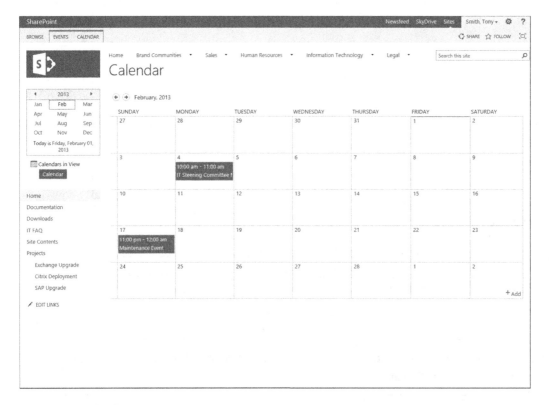

Figure 6-4. *Calendar view*

When calendar lists are created, they include a set of fields necessary to track the details about events. This set of fields includes the items in Table 6-3.

Table 6-3. *Calendar List Columns*

Column	Required	Type	Properties
Attendees	No	Person or Group	Allows both people and groups
Check Double Booking	No	Check Double Booking	
Title	Yes	Single Line of Text	
Location	No	Single Line of Text	
Start Time	Yes	Date and Time	
End Time	Yes	Date and Time	
Description	No	Multiple Lines of Text	
Free/Busy	No	Free/Busy	
Resources	No	Resources	
Category	No	Choice	Display as Drop-Down Menu Allow Fill-in Choices Choices include • Meeting • Work hours • Business • Holiday • Get-together • Gifts • Birthday • Anniversary

Calendar lists have several default views providing different options for displaying and managing the included details. These are the default views:

- *Calendar*: The Calendar view, the default view for the calendar list, shows the details in the list within a calendar layout. This layout defaults to a month view format, but it can be changed to week and day view formats. The following columns are listed in this view:

  - Time Interval Values

    - Begin: Start Time

    - End: End Time

  - Calendar Columns

    - Month View Title: Title

    - Week View Title: Title

    - Week View Sub Heading: Location

    - Day View Title: Title

    - Day View Sub Heading: Location

- *All Events*: The All Events view is a standard list view that lists all the events in the list sorted by the event start time. This view can be used to manage the list details just as the information in other lists is managed. This view shows recurring events as single items in the list and allows management of the recurring items instead of listing each occurrence separately (recurring events are discussed later in this chapter). The fields presented in the view include the following:

  - Recurrence

  - Workspace

  - Title (linked to item with Edit menu)

  - Location

  - Start Time

  - End Time

  - All Day Event

- *Current Events*: Like the All Events view, the Current Events view is a standard list view. However, recurring events in the Current Events view have a listing for each occurrence of the event. This view provides a list of all event occurrences based on the saved items in the list and presents the following details about the item:

  - Recurrence

  - Workspace

  - Title (linked to item with Edit menu)

  - Location

  - Start Time

  - End Time

  - All Day Event

Calendar lists have a unique capability: they allow integration of the details in a calendar with other SharePoint calendar lists, as well as with Microsoft Outlook calendars.

Recurrence

Another unique capability of a calendar list is that events can be marked as recurring. A recurring event is an event occurring more than once over time on a defined schedule. When creating a new list item or editing an existing item in a calendar, you can determine if it should be a recurring item. To create a recurring event, do the following:

1. Navigate to the calendar list in which to create the recurring event.

2. On the calendar view page, select the New Event option from the Events ribbon tab.

3. On the New Item form, do the following:

   a. Enter a title for the event.

   b. Optionally, enter a location for the event.

   c. Enter a start time and end time for the event.

   d. Enter an optional description for the event.

e.   Optionally, select an event category.

f.   Specify whether the event is to be listed as an all-day event.

g.   Identify that the event is a repeating event to show the repeating event options.

h.   In the Recurrence Pattern area, identify the recurrence approach as daily, weekly, monthly, or yearly, and then update the recurrence details. These details vary based on the pattern selected and are defined in Table 6-4.

Table 6-4. *Recurring Time Periods and Patterns*

Time Period	Pattern
Daily	Every X days or every weekday
Weekly	Recur every X weeks on the specified days
Monthly	Day X of each Y months or the X day of the week of every Y months
Yearly	On a specific day or on day X of a specified month

i.   In the Date Range section, identify the start date for the event, and define the end date as no end date (the event recurs endlessly), end after a defined number of occurrences, or stop repeating at a specific date.

j.   Once all the information is entered, click the Save button.

The recurring event is saved to the calendar.

When a recurring event is displayed in the All Events view, it contains an icon identifying it as a recurring item, as shown in Figure 6-5.

Figure 6-5. *All Events view with recurring items*

In the All Events view, the recurring events are listed only once, representing the event series. However, the Current Events view shows each instance of recurring events.

When you create new views in a calendar list, you can select an additional type of view, called the Standard View with Expanded Recurring Events. Views created from this type display each instance of recurring events, much like the Current Events view. A standard view represents recurring events as a single item within the list, as the All Events view does.

Calendar Overlays

The first special capability available in SharePoint calendars is the calendar overlay feature. A calendar overlay lets you layer the contents of multiple calendars onto a single calendar view. Use it when you are managing more than one calendar in your SharePoint environment but want to create a consolidated view of all events across these calendars. For example, you might use it if you have department sites. In these sites each department maintains its own calendar, but you might also want a company calendar to consolidate the view of all the department calendar details. To configure a calendar overlay, do the following:

1. Navigate to the calendar list on top of which you wish to overlay other calendar events. Ensure you are viewing a Calendar view of the list.

2. On the calendar view page, select the Calendars Overlay option from the Calendar ribbon tab.

3. On the first Calendar Overlay Settings page, click the New Calendar link.

4. On the second Calendar Overlay Settings page, enter the details about the calendar to overlay, including the following:

   a. In the Name and Type section, enter a name for the calendar and the type of calendar. If the calendar is in SharePoint, select SharePoint as the calendar type. If you want to include an Exchange calendar, then select Exchange.

   b. In the Calendar Overlay Settings section, do the following:

      i. Add an optional description for the calendar, to appear when the cursor hovers over the calendar's name in the calendars view section of the Quick Launch.

      ii. Identify the color to be used for items from the selected calendar.

      iii. If SharePoint is the selected calendar type, enter the URL to the site where the calendar is located, and click the Resolve button. This updates the list drop-down to include calendar lists in the selected site. Selecting the appropriate calendar updates the list view drop-down with the calendar views for the selected list. Select the appropriate view to include in the overlay.

      iv. If Exchange is the selected calendar type, enter the Outlook Web Access URL to the calendar.

      v. Specify whether the overlay is always to be included on the calendar or users viewing the list can remove the overlay.

      vi. Once the information is entered, click the OK button.

Follow the above steps to include up to ten calendars overlays. Each calendar included is listed in the calendar view seen in Figure 6-6.

Figure 6-6. *Calendar with overlay*

Group Calendars

Group Calendars are configurable within calendar lists to let you identify whether a calendar is to be used to share members' schedules. This configuration creates a calendar based on a different content type and includes calendar views different from those in a standard calendar. These views allow you to add people to the view in order to show events by person. These additional views, called the Day Group and Week Group views, are shown in Figures 6-7 and 6-8. Calendar lists are configured to take advantage of group calendar options as follows:

1. Navigate to the calendar list where you want to enable the group calendar options.

2. On the list view page, select the List Settings option from the Calendar ribbon tab.

3. On the Settings page, select the List Name, Description, and Navigation option from the General Settings section.

4. On the General Settings page in the Group Calendar Options section, set the "Use this calendar to share member's schedule?" option to Yes, and click the Save button.

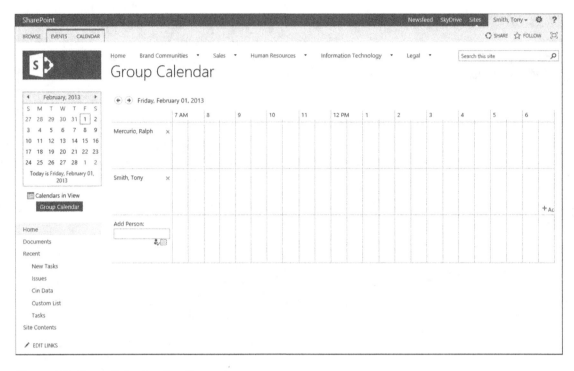

Figure 6-7. *Group Calendar: Day Group view*

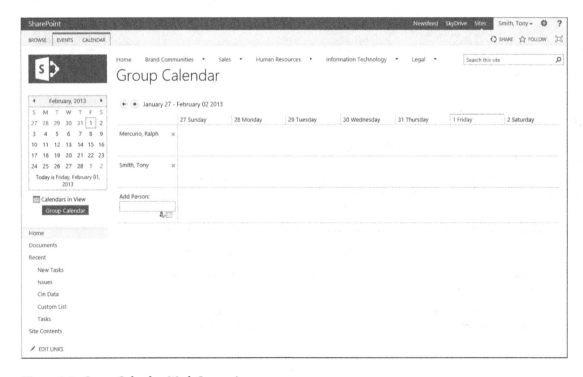

Figure 6-8. *Group Calendar: Week Group view*

Exporting Events

Calendar lists allow users to export items from a list and import them into Outlook as Outlook calendar events. Any list event can be imported into Outlook, with recurring events exportable one instance at a time. To export an event, do the following:

1. Navigate to the calendar list view for the calendar containing items to be exported.

2. On the calendar view page, select the event you want to export.

3. On the item view page, select the Export Event option from the Custom Commands ribbon tab.

4. When prompted to open or save the file, select the Open button.

5. A new Outlook appointment window is opened for the selected item.

6. In the appointment window, make any needed updates to the item, and select the Save and Close option from the Appointment ribbon tab.

The item is saved and added to your Outlook calendar. Once the export to Outlook is complete, the relationship between the items is severed. Changing one does not affect the other.

Connecting Calendar Lists to Outlook

Another advanced feature of calendar lists is the ability to connect them to Outlook. When a SharePoint calendar list is connected to Outlook, it appears as an Outlook calendar and allows the calendar to be used in both SharePoint and Outlook, with changes made in one environment reflected in the other. To connect a calendar list in SharePoint to Outlook, do the following:

1. Navigate to the calendar list you wish to connect to Outlook.

2. On the calendar view page, select the Connect to Outlook option from the Calendar ribbon tab.

3. In the Allow Access window, select the Allow button.

4. In the Connect the SharePoint Calendar to Outlook window, click the Yes button.

The SharePoint calendar is listed in Outlook on the Calendar screen. Edits to the calendar in either environment update the list. Outlook caches a local copy of a calendar, so it is available even when your computer cannot connect to the SharePoint environment.

Incoming E-mail Capabilities

Calendar lists, like Announcement lists, can accept incoming e-mail messages. When a meeting request is sent to a calendar, the details in the request are used to create a new event in the SharePoint calendar.

■ **Reminder** Before a SharePoint list's incoming e-mail settings can be utilized, a SharePoint technical administrator must configure your SharePoint environment to support incoming e-mail.

In a SharePoint environment where incoming e-mail has been configured, you can update your list to support incoming e-mail by doing the following:

1. Navigate to the list where you want to configure inbound e-mail.

2. On the calendar view page, select the List Settings option from the Calendar ribbon tab.

3. On the Settings page, select the Incoming E-mail Settings link from the Communications section.

4. On the Incoming E-mail Settings page, enter the following:

   a. In the Incoming E-mail section, select Yes for the "Allow this list to receive e-mail" option, and enter the e-mail address to use for the list.

   b. In the E-mail Attachments section, specify whether attachments of sent e-mails are to be saved to the list item as attachments.

   c. In the E-mail Security section, select the e-mail security policy identifying whether the list should accept e-mails just from e-mail addresses of known users of the list or from any e-mail address.

   d. Once the information has been updated, click the OK button to save the settings.

The list is updated to accept e-mail messages, and you are returned to the list's settings page.

Discussion Boards

A discussion board, used to manage discussion posts and replies, allows you to host discussion threads for related topics within your SharePoint sites. Discussion board lists contain two separate content types. The first type is used to create the initial discussions, and the second is used to manage replies to the discussion. The column structure that supports the creation of the initial discussions includes the columns in Table 6-5.

Table 6-5. *Discussion Board: Discussion Columns*

Column	Required	Type	Properties
Subject	Yes	Single Line of Text	
Body	No	Multiple Lines of Text	Enhanced Rich Text 15 Lines for Editing
Question	N/A	Yes/No	
Last Reply By		Person or Group	Hidden from form

The second content type, used to create replies to the discussions, called messages, contains the columns listed in Table 6-6.

Table 6-6. *Discussion Board: Message Columns*

Column	Required	Type	Properties
Subject	Yes	Single Line of Text	
Body	No	Multiple Lines of Text	Enhanced Rich Text 15 Lines for Editing
Parent Item Editor		Person or Group	Hidden from form

Discussion lists, by default, are presented to users in a threaded format. Discussion lists include three initial views, which can be used to view and manage discussion information. These views include the following:

- *Subject*: The Subject view, the default view for the overall discussion itself, shows discussions available within the list. Sort is based on when the discussion was created and lists the following details (see Figure 6-9):

    - Subject

    - Body

    - Created By

    - Created

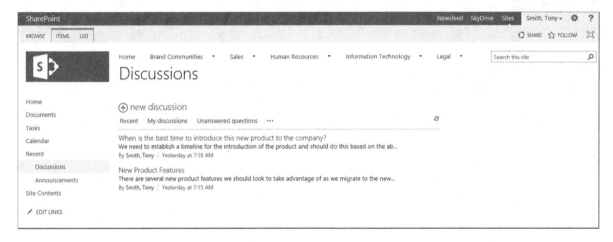

Figure 6-9. *Discussion list subject view*

- *Featured Discussions*: The Featured Discussions view lists only those discussion items marked as Featured Discussions (making a discussion a featured discussion is covered later in this chapter). This view includes the following fields:

    - Subject

    - Body

    - Created By

- *Management*: The Management view is used to manage the discussions within the discussion list. This is the only view that includes the standard Item and List ribbon tabs containing all of the standard list management options. This view includes the following fields:

    - Subject (listed as Title)

    - Body

    - Created By

    - Created

    - Replies

    - Is Featured Discussion

- *Flat*: This view is used to show the details for a specific discussion, including the original post and all replies made (see Figure 6-10). This view includes the following fields for each item:

    - Created By

    - Body

    - Created

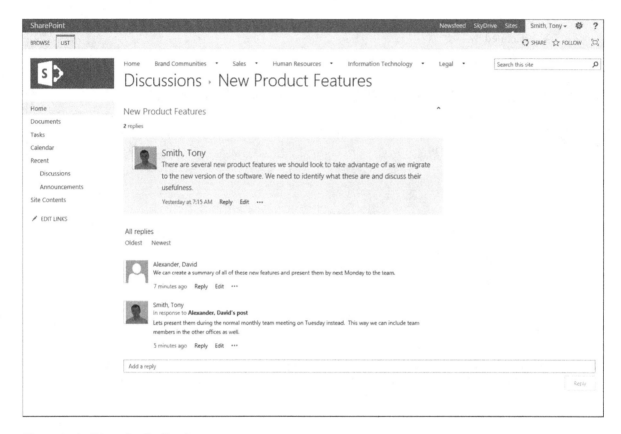

Figure 6-10. *Discussion list flat view*

- *Threaded*: The threaded view and the flat view display similar information, but the threaded view is formatted with replies indented under the parent item, representing the hierarchy of the discussion, as shown in Figure 6-11. This view includes the following columns for each item:

    - Created

    - Created By

    - Body

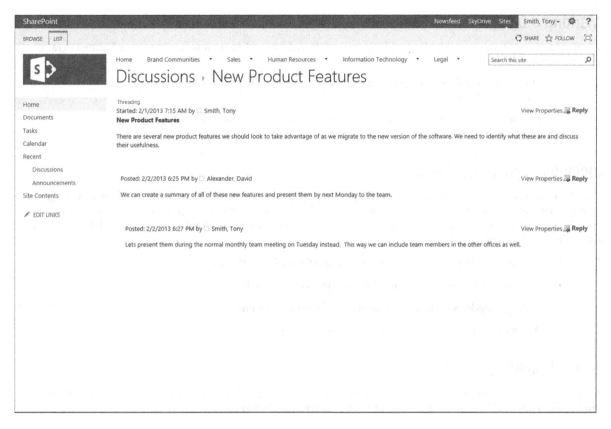

Figure 6-11. *Discussion List threaded view*

Managing Discussions

Management of discussion board content is different from that of other lists. Instead of list items for management being created, content is meant to develop organically as the discussion matures. To create a new discussion in a discussion list, do the following:

1. Navigate to the Discussion Board where you want to create the new discussion.

2. On the Discussion list view page, select the New Discussion option.

3. On the New Discussion form, enter the subject and body for the discussion, and identify whether it is a question. Then select the Save button to save the new item.

Once a discussion is available in a discussion list, people with appropriate rights can reply to content. Reply to a discussion by doing the following:

1. On the Discussion list view page, click the title of the discussion.

2. On the discussion thread view page, click the Reply option for the item that you want to create the reply for.

3. In the Reply box, type the reply text into the box, and click the Reply button to save the reply.

The discussion view is updated to include the new reply.

Marking a Discussion As Featured

Featured discussions appear in the Featured Discussion view of the list. Discussions are flagged as featured to raise their importance in the list.

1. On the Discussion list view page, select the Management view from the view drop-down on the List ribbon tab.

2. On the Management view for the list, check the box in front of the item to mark it as featured, and then select the Mark as Featured option from the Moderation ribbon tab.

Incoming E-mail Capabilities

The Discussion Board is another list that can accept incoming e-mail messages. When discussion lists are configured to support incoming e-mail, messages sent to the list are added as discussions and replies to discussions. This allows contributions to discussions through e-mail. When an e-mail is sent to a discussion list, the following information is used to create the new discussion or reply:

- The subject of the e-mail becomes the Subject field value in the list.

- The body of the e-mail becomes the Body field value in the list.

- The From address of the e-mail becomes the Created By value.

- Attachments to the e-mail become attachments to the list item.

Issue Tracking

An issue tracking list is designed to store and manage related issues against which action needs to be taken. A list created from the Issues Tracking List template has the structure shown in Table 6-7.

Table 6-7. *Issue Tracking List Columns*

Column	Required	Type	Properties
Title	Yes	Single Line of Text	
Assigned To	No	Person or Group	Allow both People and Groups
Issue Status	No	Choice	Options include: • Active • Resolved • Closed Format: Drop-Down Menu Default option: Active
Priority	No	Choice	Options include • (1) High • (2) Normal • (3) Low Format: Drop-Down Menu Default option: (2) Normal
Description	No	Multiple Lines of Text	Rich Text 6 Lines for Editing

(continued)

Table 6-7. (*continued*)

Column	Required	Type	Properties
Category	No	Choice	Options include • (1) Category1 • (2) Category2 • (3) Category3 Format: Drop-Down Menu Default option: (2) Category2
Due Date	No	Date and Time	Includes Date & Time Standard Display Format
Related Issues	No	Lookup	Lookup to Title column in the current list Allow multiple values
Comments	No	Multiple Lines of Text	Rich Text 6 Lines for Editing

When the issues list is created and the view of the list is placed on a page, it has a standard list view, as defined in Figure 6-12.

Issues

⊕ new item or edit this list

✓	Issue ID	Title		Assigned To	Issue Status	Priority	Due Date
	1	Server remote access performance ✻	···	☐ Smith, Tony	Active	(2) Normal	3/1/2013 12:00 AM
	2	User connectivity cutover script errors ✻	···	☐ Mercurio, Ralph	Active	(2) Normal	4/1/2013 12:00 AM
	3	Project time overlap with company sales meeting ✻	···	☐ Smith, Tony	Active	(2) Normal	3/5/2013 12:00 AM

Figure 6-12. *Issue tracking list view*

The default set of views available against an issue tracking list when it is initially created include the following:

- *All Issues*: The All Issues view, the default view for the list, provides a standard view of all items stored in it. This view is sorted in ID and includes the following columns:

  - Issue ID (linked to item)

  - Title (linked to item with Edit menu)

  - Assigned To

  - Issue Status

  - Priority

  - Due Date

- *My Issues*: This view, which displays all the issues assigned to the current user and is sorted by ID, lets the person viewing the list see just those items he or she is responsible for. The view contains the following columns:

  - Issue ID (linked to item)

  - Title (linked to item with Edit menu)

- Issue Status

- Priority

- Due Date

- *Active Issues*: The Active Issues view shows the items in the list with an Issue Status of Active. The view lists all issues still requiring attention. The issues are sorted by ID, and the view includes the following fields:

    - Issue ID (linked to item)

    - Title (linked to item with Edit menu)

    - Assigned To

    - Priority

    - Due Date

E-mail Notifications

Items in an issues list can be configured so that e-mail notifications are sent to users assigned to the issue. Thus, assigned users can be made aware of the assignment and be informed of changes made to the issue. To enable e-mail notifications for an issues list, do the following:

1. Navigate to the Issue Tracking list where you want to enable e-mail notifications.

2. On the list view page, select the List Settings option from the List ribbon tab.

3. On the Settings page, select the Advanced Settings option from the General Settings section.

4. On the Advanced Settings page in the E-mail Notification section, select Yes for the "Send e-mail when ownership is assigned?" option, and click the OK button.

Links

The links list template is used to create lists that contain web links. These can be links to internal or external web resources or web references to pictures. Use links lists when you need to manage and share references to web sites and other web-referenceable resources. Links lists include the columns shown in Table 6-8.

Table 6-8. *Links List Columns*

Column	Required	Type	Properties
URL	Yes	Hyperlink or Picture	Format: Hyperlink
Notes	No	Multiple Lines of Text	Plain Text 6 lines for editing

The links list contains a single view, the All Links view, that includes all the items in the list and displays the following columns:

- Type (icon linked to document)
- Edit (link to Edit item)
- URL (URL with edit menu)
- Notes

When the list is added to a page within a site, it has a special view that creates a bulleted list of the items contained within the list, as shown in Figure 6-13.

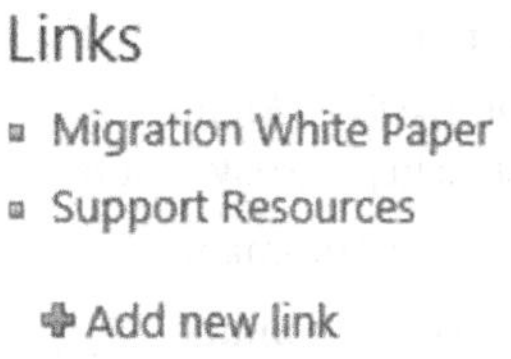

Links

▫ Migration White Paper

▫ Support Resources

✦ Add new link

Figure 6-13. Links list view

Changing List Item Order

link lists permit items to be manually sorted allowing the order to be determined by the manager of the links. To manually set the order of the items in a link list, do the following:

1. Navigate to the links list in which you want to reorder the items.

2. On the list view page, select the Change Item Order option from the Items ribbon tab.

3. In the Change Item Order window, change the order of the listed items by changing the Position from Top numbers. Once the items are in the correct order, click the OK button.

The link order is updated based on the selections made.

■ **Note** Since clicking a link in a links list navigates the current browser window to the referenced URL, doing so also causes you to leave the SharePoint environment.

Promoted Links

The promoted links list is used to create a set of links that are presented as a set of tiles. It functions much as the Get Started with Your Site web part, seen in the Team Site, does. As with the links list, use the promoted links list when you want to manage a list of intranet or Internet links but want to present them in a more stylized fashion and with more navigation control than the normal links list allows.

The promoted links list contains a structure designed to help manage the presentation of the stored links, as seen in Table 6-9.

Table 6-9. *Promoted Links List Columns*

Column	Required	Type	Properties
Title	Yes	Single Line of Text	
Background Image Location	No	Hyperlink or Picture	Format: Hyperlink
Description	No	Multiple Lines of Text	Plain Text 6 Lines for Editing
Link Location	Yes	Hyperlink or Picture	Format: Hyperlink
Launch Behavior	Yes	Choice	Choices <ul><li>In page navigation</li><li>Dialog</li><li>New tab</li></ul>Display: Drop-Down Menu Default Value: In page navigation
Order	No	Number	Decimal Places: Automatic
Background Image Cluster Horizontal Start	No	Number	Decimal Places: Automatic
Background Image Cluster Vertical Start	No	Number	Decimal Places: Automatic

When you create a new promoted link item, specify the details for the link to be created, including the URL to connect to, as well as the details for the imaging used to represent the link, among which are identifying the title and description of the item and the background image to use for the link. Also specify the order in which the link is to be listed and the launch behavior desired when the link is clicked.

The promoted links list initially includes two views.

- *Tiles*: The default view for the list, Tiles view presents the list of items in a tiled fashion (see Figure 6-14) and includes the following details:

    - Background Image Location: Displaying the referenced image as the background for the tile.

    - Title: overlaid on the tile image.

    - Description: Added to the overlay on the image when the mouse hovers over the image.

    - Link Location: Identifying the URL to navigate to when the tile is clicked.

    - Launch Behavior: Identifying the approach for navigating to the URL.

Figure 6-14. *Tiles view*

- *All Promoted Links*: This view, which displays all items in the list in a standard list view order based on the Order column value, is used to manage the items in the list. The view includes the following columns:

  - Title

  - Background Image Location

  - Description

  - Link Location

  - Launch Behavior

  - Order

When a promoted links list web part is added to a page within the site, it includes the use of the Tiles view, shown in Figure 6-14.

Survey

Survey lists let you configure and manage survey questions and track survey answers. While survey lists store and manage data as other lists do, they include a highly customized interface for management of the list itself, as well as for responding to surveys and viewing results. Instead of viewing the list column structure itself when accessing the list settings, the survey Settings page is used to create and manage questions for inclusion in the survey. To configure a survey by adding questions, do the following:

1. Navigate to the created survey where you need to add questions.

2. On the survey view page, select the Add Questions option from the Settings menu.

3. In the New Question window, do the following:

   a. In the Question and Type section, enter the question text and choose the question type.

   b. In the Additional Question Settings section, do the following:

      i. If the question type is Single Line of Text, then specify whether the field is required, whether unique values are to be enforced, what the maximum number of characters is, and whether there is to be a default value.

      ii. If the question type is Multiple Lines of Text, then specify whether the field is required, how many lines to display for editing, and whether the field is to include plain or rich text.

      iii. If the question type is Choice, then specify whether the item is required, whether unique values are to be enforced, the question choices and the display format for the choices, and whether there is to be a default value.

      iv. If the question type is Rating Scale, then specify whether the item is required, the list of subquestions to rate, the number range for the rating, and the range text, and whether an N/A ("not applicable") option is to be included.

      v. If the question type is Number, specify whether the item is required, what unique values are to be enforced, whether there are minimum or maximum values, how many decimal places to show, and whether the item is to be shown as a percentage.

      vi. If the question type is Currency, specify whether the item is required, what unique values are to be enforced, whether there are minimum or maximum values, how many decimal places to show, and whether there is to be a default value.

    vii.   If the question type is Date and Time, specify whether the item is required, whether unique values are to be enforced, what the date format is, and whether there is to be a default value.

    viii.   If the question type is Lookup, specify whether the item is required, what unique values are to be enforced, what list and field to obtain values from, and which values to include in the display.

    ix.   If the question type is Yes/No, identify the default value.

    x.   If the question type is Person or Group, specify whether the item is required, whether unique values are to be enforced, whether multiple values are to be allowed, whether only people or both people and groups are to be selectable, whether selections can be made from all users or just from a selected SharePoint group, and which field to show.

    xi.   If the question type is External Data, specify whether the item is required, what external content type and field to use, and whether the actions menu is to be displayed and whether the column is to be linked to the default action of the content type.

    xii.   If the question type is Page Selector, there are no other options. This simply identifies whether a page separator is to be placed in the current location to divide up the survey questions.

    xiii.   If the question type is Managed Metadata, specify whether the item is required, whether unique values are to be enforced, and what term set to use.

    c.   If you have more questions to enter, click the Next Question button. If you have no more questions to enter, then click the Finish button.

The questions added are made part of the survey. Once they are added to the survey, you can add branching logic, which enables the survey to jump to different questions based on answers to prior questions. To set branching logic within the survey, do the following:

1.   Navigate to the created survey where you need to add branching logic.

2.   On the survey view page, select the Survey Settings option from the Settings menu.

3.   On the Settings page, select the question whose answers are to result in question branching.

4.   On the Edit Question page in the Branching Logic section, identify the value, and jump to question combinations. Once done, click the OK button.

Question branching is established, and you are returned to the list's Settings page.

Responding to a Survey

Responding to a survey works the same way as adding items to a list. To respond to a survey, do the following:

1.   Navigate to the survey view page.

2.   On the survey view page, click the Respond to This Survey link.

3.   On the Survey Response page, enter the responses to the questions. Once completed, click the Finish button.

If you wish to stop taking a survey partway through, click the Cancel button to leave the survey response page. If you have completed answers to previous survey pages when you click the Cancel button, you are prompted either to save the answers to the questions already answered or to remove previously entered information. You can also choose the Close button on a page to save the questions entered and close the survey response at the current point.

When you complete a survey response, you are taken to the survey list page (see Figure 6-15), which lists the summary of entered responses and enables you to display a graphical summary of the responses. Clicking the graphic summary option updates the view of the results to a graphical representation, as shown in Figure 6-16.

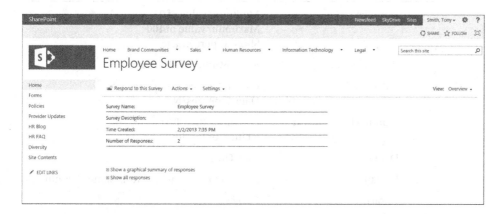

Figure 6-15. *Survey results summary*

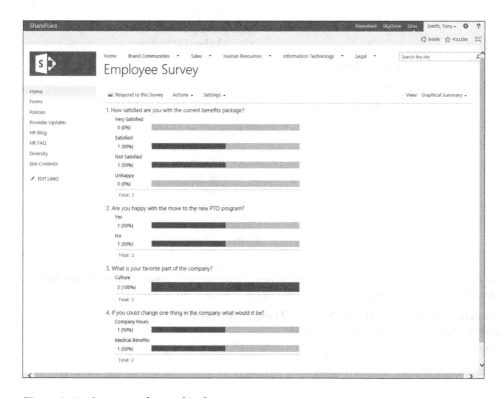

Figure 6-16. *Survey results graphical summary*

Tasks

The tasks list is one of the most commonly used lists in SharePoint. Use it to assign and manage activities to be performed and to track progress against them. The tasks list has the column structure defined in Table 6-10.

Table 6-10. *Tasks List Columns*

Column	Required	Type	Properties
% Complete		Number	Minimum value of 0 Maximum value of 100 Show as percentage
Assigned To		Person or Group	Allow Multiple Selections
Completed		Calculated	Calculation: [% Complete] >= 1 Data Type: Yes/No
Description		Multiple Lines of Text	Enhanced Rich Text 6 Lines for Editing
Due Date		Date and Time	Date Only
Predecessor		Lookup	Lookup to Current List, Task Name Column
Priority		Choice	Choices • (1) High • (2) Normal • (3) Low Display: Drop-Down Menu Default Value: (2) Normal
Related Items		Related Items	
Start Date		Date and Time	Date Only
Task Name		Single Line of Text	
Task Status		Choice	Choices • Not Started • In Progress • Completed • Deferred • Waiting on someone else Display: Drop-Down Menu Default Value: Not Started

A tasks list, when created, has an initial set of views designed to assist in managing the included tasks. This initial set available within the list includes the following views:

- *All Tasks*: The default view for the tasks list. It shows all tasks in the list in a standard SharePoint list view and includes the following details:
  - Completed
  - Task Name (linked to item with Edit menu)

- Due Date

- Assigned To

- *Late Tasks*: The Late Tasks view lists tasks that have not been completed and whose due date has passed and orders them by Due Date and Priority. Doing so allows you to understand which tasks are the least and the farthest overdue. This view and the All Tasks view list the same fields.

- *Upcoming*: The Upcoming view lists all tasks that have not been completed. It includes the same columns as the All Tasks and Late Tasks views.

- *Completed*: The Completed view lists all tasks identified as 100% complete and shows just those tasks that do not require additional work. This view also shows the same columns as the All Tasks view.

- *My Tasks*: The My Tasks view lists all tasks assigned to the current logged-on user. It shows the tasks that need to be completed and includes the same columns as the previous task views.

- *Gantt Chart*: The Gantt Chart view takes the information in the tasks list and organizes it into a Gantt chart, where the overall timeline for the listed activities is displayed. This view lists the following columns:

  - Task Name (linked to item with Edit menu)

  - Start Date

  - Due Date

  - Completed

  - Predecessors

  - Assigned To

  - GUID

- *Calendar*: The Calendar view displays the tasks within a calendar and represents the tasks as activities within that calendar.

Along with these default views, tasks lists can also be viewed with the timeline web part, which displays the activities within a timeline chart that lists the tasks by duration and contains percent complete details. Select needed tasks to navigate to them (Figure 6-17 shows the timeline view). Adding and configuring web parts is discussed in Chapter 4.

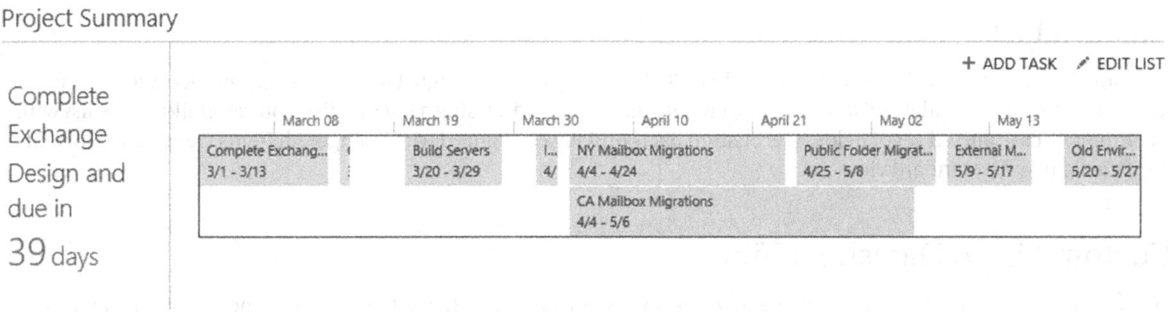

Figure 6-17. Tasks timeline view

Connecting Tasks Lists with Outlook

As with contact and calendar lists, tasks lists can be connected to Outlook to allow access to the SharePoint tasks from within Outlook. When a tasks list is connected to Outlook, the tasks are available in the Outlook Tasks section, and so you can view and manage SharePoint tasks from within Outlook. To connect a tasks list to Outlook, do the following:

1. Navigate to the tasks list you want to connect to Outlook.

2. On the tasks list page, select the Sync to Outlook option from the List ribbon tab.

3. In the Sync Tasks with Microsoft Outlook window, check the Sync Tasks option, and click the OK button.

As Outlook caches a local copy of the tasks list, you can access the information even when you do not have direct access to the SharePoint environment itself.

Open a Tasks List in Project

SharePoint tasks lists can be opened in Microsoft Project. This lets you view and manage tasks within the Project environment and presents the tasks list as a standard project plan. To open a tasks list in Microsoft Project, do the following:

1. Navigate to the tasks list to be opened in Microsoft Project.

2. On the tasks list view page, select the Open with Project option from the List ribbon tab.

3. In the Open File Confirmation window, click the Yes button.

The tasks list opens in Microsoft Project.

External List

SharePoint technical managers can use SharePoint Designer to create external lists. An external list is used to create a list based on a Business Connectivity Services (BCS) connection to information in an external data source, such as a Microsoft SQL Server database. This list, once created, shows the information in the external database as if it were a standard list in SharePoint. The BCS connection can be configured as a read-only connection to the source information or as a read/write connection. In a read-only connection, items in the external list cannot be edited, and the list is read-only for all users. A read/write connection allows you to edit list details, just as you would edit them in any other SharePoint list.

Custom List

A custom list is created with only a single field, the Title field, which is a Single Line of Text column. A custom list is used when the other available list types do not meet your list's needs. Using a custom list, you can build a new list with a completely customized set of fields. The custom list is initially configured with a single All Items view, which formats the Title field in the standard view.

Custom List in Datasheet View

Like the custom list, the custom list in datasheet view is used when the other list templates do not meet the needs of your list. It has the same columns and structure as the custom list. The only difference between the two views is that in the custom list created using the Custom List in Datasheet View option, information is presented in the datasheet layout instead of in a standard layout.

Working with List Items

SharePoint lists are used to store and manage structured data. You can work with lists to track and manage a variety of types of information.

Adding Items to a List

To add new items to a SharePoint list, do the following:

1. Navigate to the list where you want to add the information.

2. On the list view page, click the New Item link above the data being presented.

3. On the list item Add page, enter the details for the new item, making sure to populate all required fields. Once the information has been entered, click the Save button to create the new list item.

The item is added to the list, and you are returned to the list view page.

Editing Items in a List

There are a couple of different options available for editing items in a SharePoint list. To edit individual items in a list, do the following:

1. Navigate to the list where you want to edit the information.

2. On the list View page for the item you wish to edit, select the item menu option, and then from the Hover menu options, select the Edit Item option (see Figure 6-18).

Figure 6-18. *List Item menu*

3. On the Edit Item page, make the changes to the details for the item, and then click the Save button to save the changes.

The information is saved to the list, and you are returned to the list view. An alternative approach for editing items in a list involves doing the following:

1. Navigate to the list where you want to edit the information.

2. On the list view page, click the selection option next to the item to edit, and then select the Edit Item option from the Items ribbon tab.

3. In the Edit Item window, make updates to the listed information, and then click the Save button to save the changes.

The updates to the list are saved, and you are returned to the list view page. If you want to make multiple edits to a list all at once, you can use the Quick Edit option.

Using Quick Edit

The Quick Edit mode uses the datasheet view to allow you to edit multiple items in a list. As Figure 6-19 shows, Quick Edit provides an Excel-like interface to perform list edits.

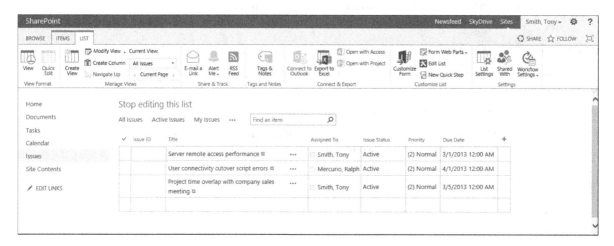

Figure 6-19. *Quick Edit view*

To open a list in the Quick Edit view, do the following:

1. Navigate to the list that you want to edit.

2. On the list view page, select the Quick Edit option from the List ribbon tab.

The list is presented in the Quick Edit view. In Quick Edit mode, you can make changes to information in the list as you would if you were editing data in Excel. Once all edits have been made, you can return to the list's standard view by selecting the View option from the Library ribbon tab or the Stop Editing This List option from above the list view.

Deleting Items in a List

To delete items from a SharePoint list, do the following:

1. Navigate to the list where you want to delete items.

2. On the list view page, click the item's context menu, and select the Delete Item option.

3. In the Delete Confirmation window, click the OK button.

The item is deleted, and the list of items is updated appropriately. If you want to delete multiple items all at once, do the following:

1. Navigate to the list where you want to delete the items.

2. On the list view page, check the box next to the items to be deleted. From the Items ribbon tab, select the Delete Item option.

3. In the Delete Confirmation window, click the OK button.

Working with Attachments

A list can be configured to attach files to items saved in it. By default, a new list added to SharePoint is configured to allow attachments to be added. This feature can be enabled against any type of list in SharePoint.

Enable or Disable List Attachments

If you do not want to let users attach files to a list item, you can disable this option. To change a list's attachment options, do the following:

1. Navigate to the list where you want to update the list's attachment settings.

2. On the list view page, select the List Settings option from the List ribbon tab.

3. On the list's Settings page, select the Advanced Settings option from the General Settings section.

4. On the Advanced Settings page, update the attachment settings as follows:

    a. In the Attachments section, select either Disabled or Enabled to disable or enable the attachment settings.

    b. Click the OK button to save the changes.

The attachment settings are updated.

Adding Attachments to a List Item

When attachments are enabled within a list, you can easily add attachments to the items in the list by doing the following:

1. Navigate to the list where you want to add attachments.

2. On the list view page, check the selection option next to the item to be edited, and then select the Edit Item option from the Items ribbon tab.

3. On the Edit Item page, select the Attach File option from the Edit ribbon tab.

4. In the Attach File window, select the file to attach, and click the OK button.

5. On the Edit Item page, click the Save button.

The file will be attached to the item. You can also attach a file to an item by checking the box next to the item and selecting the Attach File option from the Items ribbon tab. Then select the file to upload. Once attachments are added to a list item, an icon identifying that an attachment is included appears in front of the item's name in the list item view. Clicking on the icon opens the attachment.

Removing Attachments from a List Item

Attachments added to a list item can be removed by doing the following:

1. Navigate to the list where you want to remove attachments.

2. On the list view page, check the selection option next to the item to be edited, and then select the Edit Item option from the Items ribbon tab.

3. On the Edit Item page, click the delete option next to the attachment to be deleted.

4. In the Delete Confirmation window, click the OK button.

5. On the Edit Item page, click the Save button.

The attachment is deleted from the item.

Filtering and Sorting List Items

As lists can contain hundreds or even thousands of items, it is important to have a way to organize and locate information specific to your needs. Filtering a list allows you to limit the items presented to those that contain identified column values. Sorting allows you to identify the order of the items presented based on the values of an identified list column.

You can filter a list based on the values in the columns in the presented view. To filter items in a SharePoint list, do the following:

1. Navigate to the list view page for the list to be filtered.

2. On the list view page, hover over the title for the displayed column header to be used as a filter, and select the value(s) to filter by from the drop-down menu.

When the list view is refreshed, the items presented are limited to those containing the selected filter value, and the column header is updated to include a filter icon to identify that the list is being filtered by the column. You can filter a list by more than one column if you need to.

To clear a filter applied against a list column on the list view page, click the title of the column with the filter, and click the Clear Filters option from the drop-down menu. The filter is removed, and the list view is updated to reflect the removal of the filter.

Besides filtering items within a list, you can also sort list items based on the content in a displayed column. The sort can be in either ascending or descending order by the listed columns. To sort the items within a list by a listed column, click on the column header that you want to sort the list by. Clicking the header once will sort the information in ascending order. Clicking it a second time will sort the column in descending order.

Metadata Navigation

A second method by which to filter the information in a list or library is to use the list's or library's metadata navigation settings to define columns to include as filter options in list views. Metadata navigation lets a list's users easily filter its details to locate needed information.

To leverage metadata navigation within a list, the capabilities must first be enabled within the site where the list is located. This is done as follows:

1. Navigate to the site where you want to use metadata navigation.

2. On the site's home page, select the Site Settings option from the Settings menu.

3. On the Site Settings page, select the Manage Site Features option from the Site Actions section.

4. On the Site Features page, click the Activate option next to the Metadata Navigation and Filtering feature.

Metadata navigation and filtering is activated, and the metadata navigation and filtering options are available within the site's lists. With this feature active, you can configure metadata navigation options against a list or library. To configure metadata navigation options against a specific list or library, do the following:

1. Navigate to the list or library where you want to configure metadata navigation.

2. On the list or library view page, select the List or Library Settings option from the List or Library ribbon tab.

3. On the Settings page, select the Metadata Navigation Settings option from the General Settings section.

4. On the Metadata Navigation Settings page, do the following:

   a. In the Configure Navigation Hierarchies section, select the fields that you want to appear as a hierarchy in the Metadata Navigation section for filtering the items. Hierarchy items are presented as a tree in the Quick Launch area, where the available values that can be filtered by are listed (see Figure 6-20).

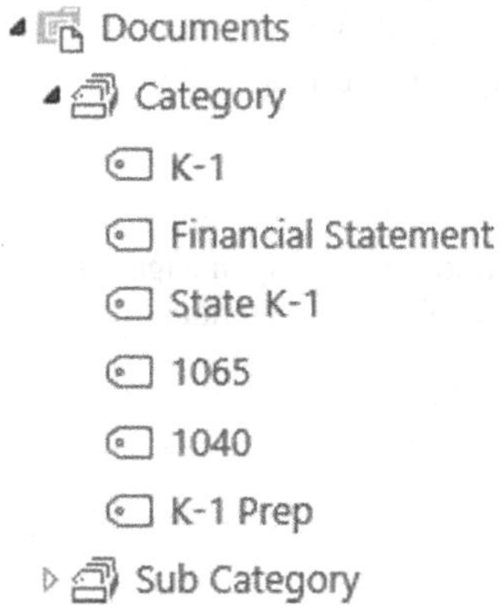

▲ 🔲 Documents
   ▲ 🗐 Category
      ▢ K-1
      ▢ Financial Statement
      ▢ State K-1
      ▢ 1065
      ▢ 1040
      ▢ K-1 Prep
   ▷ 🗐 Sub Category

Figure 6-20. Metadata navigation: Navigation hierarchies

   b. In the Configure Key Filters section, identify the fields to allow filtering against. These fields will be listed below the navigation hierarchies in the Quick Launch area. The values or ranges of values that can be entered will depend on the field type (see Figure 6-21).

Figure 6-21. *Metadata navigation: Key Filters*

    c.   In the Configure Automatic Column Indexing for this List section, specify whether list or library indexes are to be automatically configured based on the options selected for filtering or are not to be modified by the Metadata Navigation Settings options.

    d.   Click the OK button to save the settings.

The metadata navigation options are saved and added to the list view. With these options saved, the navigation hierarchy selected is listed below the Quick Launch options, and the Key Filters are listed below the metadata navigation options, as Figure 6-22 shows.

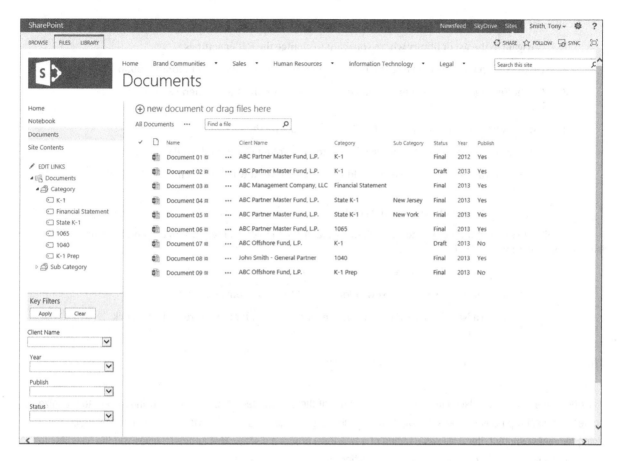

Figure 6-22. *List view with metadata navigation options*

The Navigation Hierarchy section lists the fields identified for use. As you select values in the Navigation Hierarchy and Key Filters, the displayed view is appropriately updated. Any applied filters can be cleared by clicking the Clear button, which will update the list view and return it to its default state.

Using Views

List views are used to create presentations of list data to meet the various needs of the users of the list (how to create and manage views is discussed in Chapter 5). To change the view of a list being presented, navigate to the list you want to view, and on the list view page, do one of the following:

- Select the desired view from the Current View drop-down menu on the List ribbon tab.

- Click on the view name at the top of the list view.

Working with Folders

Folders can be created in any list or library as long as they are enabled within that list or library. In libraries, folders are enabled by default, while in lists they are initially disabled. Folders can be used to group and organize content into a set structure. They can be nested into any desired hierarchy to meet needs within the list and are best used when security differences must be maintained across the content in the list or library.

To allow or disallow folders in a list or library, do the following:

1. Navigate to the list or library where you want to change the folder settings.

2. On the view page, select the List or Library Settings option from the List or Library ribbon tab.

3. On the Settings page, select the Advanced Settings option from the General Settings section.

4. On the Advanced Settings page in the Folders section, do the following:

    a. If you want to enable folders, set the Make New Folder Command Available to Yes.

    b. If you want to disable the use of folders, set the Make New Folder Command Available to No.

    c. Click the OK button to save the changes.

The ability to use folders against the list is made available. With folders enabled, you can create folders within the list. To create new folders, do the following:

1. Navigate to the list where you want to create the folders.

2. On the list view page, select the New Folder option from the Items ribbon tab.

3. In the Create a New Folder window, enter the name of the folder to be created, and click the Save button.

The folder is created, and you are returned to the list view.

■ **Note** When items are placed in a folder, the structure of the content becomes rigid. Thus, using folders to organize content for display purposes is less desirable than using the grouping capabilities in views to create these structures. Using two fields to group items allows creation of a two-level grouped display. This approach gives you the flexibility to create multiple views that organize information in different ways.

Managing Item Level Security

As is discussed in previous chapters, you can manage security against sites and lists. However, you are also able to manage security directly against items stored in lists and libraries. This includes list items, documents, and folders. When items are initially created in a list or library, they inherit the permissions of that list or library. This inheritance, however, can be broken, and permissions can be applied directly to the items.

Managing Permission Inheritance

Before you can change the permissions on a list item, you must configure the item so that it no longer inherits permissions from the list that contains it. To break inheritance on an item in a list, do the following:

1. Navigate to the list view showing the item whose permissions you want to manage.

2. On the list view page, click the item to be managed, and then select the Share With option on the Items ribbon tab.

3. In the Shared With window, select the Advanced option.

4. On the Permissions page, update the permission inheritance settings for the item by doing the following:

    a. To stop inheriting permissions, select the Stop Inheriting Permissions option from the Permissions ribbon tab. In the confirmation window, click the OK button.

    b. To reestablish inheritance between the list and the item, select the Delete Unique Permissions option from the Permissions ribbon tab. In the confirmation window, click the OK button.

The permission inheritance is updated to reflect the selections made.

Editing Item Permissions

Once a folder or list item's inheritance settings have been broken, you can update the item's security rights. Do so as follows:

1. Navigate to the list view showing the item whose permission inheritance has been removed and whose permissions you want to update.

2. On the list view page, check the selection box next to the item, and then select the Shared With option on the Items ribbon tab.

3. In the Shared With window, select the Advanced option.

4. On the Permissions page, do the following:

    a. To add user permissions:

        i.   Select the Grant Permissions option from the Permissions ribbon tab.

        ii. On the Share screen, enter the accounts to which permissions are to be added. If providing permissions other than Edit, click the Show Options item, and then select the desired permission level. Once the appropriate permissions are set, click the Share button.

    b. To edit user permissions:

        i.   Check the box next to the item to be edited, and select the Edit User Permissions button from the Permissions ribbon tab.

        ii. On the Edit Permissions page, select the appropriate permissions, and click the OK button.

    c. To delete user permissions:

        i.   Check the box next to the item to be deleted, and select the Delete Unique Permissions option from the Permissions tab.

        ii. In the Delete Confirmation window, click the OK button to delete the item.

Once the permission updates are complete, you are returned to the Permissions page, and the changes to the permissions are reflected.

Versioning List Items

Lists in SharePoint can be configured to maintain a history of the changes made to items contained in them so that all item iterations over the course of time are recorded. Versioning becomes available when it is activated within a list. Once active, versioning records all item changes and enables content owners to view, manage, and restore earlier versions of items.

Enabling Versioning within a List

To enable versioning within a SharePoint list, do the following:

1. Navigate to the list where you want to enable versioning.

2. On the list view page, select the List Settings option from the List ribbon tab.

3. On the Settings page, select the Versioning Settings option from the General Settings section.

4. On the Version Settings page, do the following:

    a. In the Content Approval section, specify whether the item requires content approval.

    b. In the Item Version History section, select Yes to create versions. Optionally select whether to limit the number of versions tracked and how many to maintain. Also, optionally identify whether to limit the number of approved versions maintained and how many.

    c. In the Draft Item Security section, specify whether all users, only editors, or only approvers can see draft items.

    d. Click the OK button to save the version settings.

The version settings are saved, and you are returned to the List Settings page.

Accessing Version History

Once versioning has been enabled in a list, you can work with the versions. In a list with versioning enabled, you can view items' previous versions. Version History options can be accessed by doing the following:

1. Navigate to the list where you want to review the version history.

2. On the list view page, select the list item's menu, and then select the Version History option from the item's hover menu.

Alternatively, you can access this information by doing as follows:

1. Navigate to the list where you want to review the version history.

2. In the list view, click the box next to the item to view version history, and then select the Version History option from the Item ribbon tab.

The Version History window (see Figure 6-23) is presented. This window provides access to all the version details for the selected item.

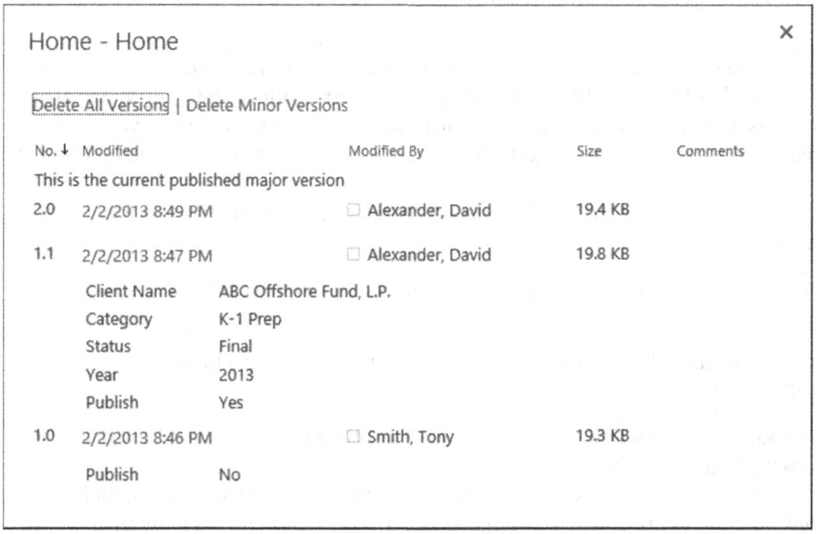

Figure 6-23. *Version History window*

From the Version History window you can do the following:

- View previous versions.

- Restore a previous version of the item to be the current version.

- Delete a previous version.

View Previous Versions of an Item

To view a previous version of a list item from the Version History window, select the View option from the version item's drop-down menu. This will open the details for the selected version.

Restore Previous List Item Versions

When you restore a previous version of a list item, that version becomes the item's current version, the one available to all users accessing it. Restore a previous version when changes were made in error and you need to reset the item to an earlier state. To restore a previous version of a list item, select the Restore option from version item's drop-down menu, and select the OK button in the confirmation window. Doing this creates a new version of the item, one that is an exact copy of the version you chose to restore.

Delete a Previous Version

Versions listed in the version history can be deleted by individuals with appropriate rights. To delete a previous version of a list item, select the Delete option from the version item's drop-down menu, and then click the OK button in the confirmation window. To delete all versions of a list item, in the Version History window, click the Delete All Versions link, and then click the OK button in the confirmation window.

Content Approval

An additional element of item version management is content approval. When a list has content approval enabled, new items are added in a draft state. They will not be available to the list's general users until content approvers give their consent (enabling content approval is discussed earlier in this section). Use content approval when you want multiple users to be able to add or change content but want that information to be reviewed and approved before it is made generally available.

When a list has content approval activated and an item in it is updated, that item is saved with a Pending approval status. Do as follows to approve the item:

1. Select the item's context menu, and from the hover panel menu select the Approve/Reject option.

2. In the Approve/Reject window, update the approval status for the item, optionally add a comment, and click the OK button.

The approval status of the item is updated to reflect the selection made. If approved, content becomes visible to general site users. If rejected, it remains unavailable to them.

Users who have added items to the list can select the My Submissions view to see the current status of their items submitted for approval. This view presents all items each user has created and categorizes them by their approval status. If a content approver rejects an item, any comments the approver entered are also displayed in the My Submissions view in the Approver Comments column, so that the submitter can understand why the rejection occurred. Each time an item in a list where content approval is enabled is edited, its status is set to Pending, and it must be approved again before the changes become available to users.

Item Validation

SharePoint can perform basic validation against list information being created or edited to ensure that it meets a set of business rules based on data constraints. An entire list or specific columns in it can have validation rules enabled. To configure validation rules, do the following:

1. Navigate to the list where you wish to configure validation settings.

2. On the list view page, select the List Settings option from the List ribbon tab.

3. On the Settings page, select the Validation Settings option from the General Settings section.

4. On the Validation Settings page, do the following:

   a. In the Formula section, define the rules to use to validate the information added to the list.

   b. In the User Message section, enter the message to be presented to users to help them understand what they need to do to save information in the list.

   c. Once the information is entered, click the OK button to save it.

The validation settings for the list are now configured. Individual columns can also be configured when rules are specific to them. To configure a list column's validation, do the following:

1. Navigate to the list where you wish to add validation to columns.

2. On the list view page, select the List Settings option from the List ribbon tab.

3. On the Settings page in the Columns section, click the title of the column to which you wish to add validation settings.

4. On the Edit Column page, do the following:

a. Select the Column Validation option to expand the column validation settings.

b. In the Formula box, enter the formula to use to validate information entered in the column.

c. In the User Message box, enter the text that will show users what the needs of the column are.

d. Click the OK button to save the column validation rules.

Rating List Content

Lists can be configured to allow users to rate items in them. Content rating lets individuals see the value that others with access to the information perceive in it. In SharePoint 2013 content rating can be formatted either as star ratings, where content is rated on a five star scale (see Figure 6-24), or as Likes placed against the content (see Figure 6-25). Liking content and other social features are discussed in detail in Chapter 12.

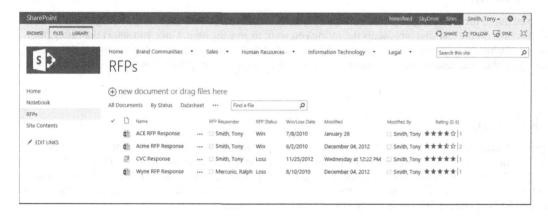

Figure 6-24. *Star ratings*

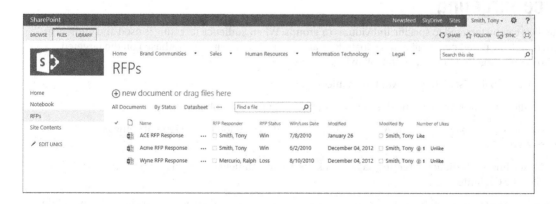

Figure 6-25. *Like ratings*

To use ratings, they must be activated within a list. To activate them, do as follows:

1. Navigate to the list where you want to activate ratings.

2. On the list's view page, select the List Settings option from the List ribbon tab.

3. On the Settings page, select the Rating Settings option from the General Settings section.

4. On the Rating Settings page, do the following:

    a. For the "Allow items in this list to be rated" option, select Yes.

    b. For the "Which voting/rating experience you would like to enable for this list" option, select Star Ratings if you want to manage ratings through a five star rating scale, or select Likes if you want to allow people to rate content by Liking it.

    c. Click the OK button to save the changes.

The ratings for the list will be enabled.

Using Star Ratings

When a list is configured for star ratings, visitors are able to specify, on a five star scale, their item ratings. To rate an item within a list, click on the star that represents the rating you want to give the item. Once you select the rating, the item is updated to include your rating. That is, your rating is included in the item's overall rating average and the total number of ratings. If the same user rates the item a second time, the previous rating applied is replaced by the newly selected rating.

Using Like Ratings

When ratings are configured to let users Like the content, items are presented with Like details listed. The Like details, besides including the number of Likes an item has received to date, allow you to Like the item, if you have not yet done so, or Unlike the item, if you have already Liked it. To Like a listed item, click the Like link. This will update the item to include your Like and permit you to Unlike the item. If you choose to Unlike the listed item, clicking the Unlike option removes your Like and returns the ability to you to Like the item again.

Audience Targeting

Items within lists can be targeted to specific individuals or groups. When audience targeting is used and audiences are configured, web parts and personalization capabilities are able to filter the list details based on the targeted audiences. To enable targeting in a list, do the following.

1. Navigate to the list where you want to enable targeting.

2. On the list view page, select the List Settings option from the List ribbon tab.

3. On the Settings page, select the Audience Targeting Settings option in the General Settings section.

4. On the Enable Audience Targeting page, check the Enable Audience Targeting option and click the OK button.

When audience targeting is enabled in a list, an additional field, Target Audiences, appears in the list item Edit form. That field allows you to select users and groups, and SharePoint groups as target audiences for the information.

CHAPTER 7

Working with Libraries

Libraries are used to store and manage files within SharePoint. Whether you want to manage Microsoft Office documents, PDF files, images, videos, or some other type of file, you use libraries to store, track, and manage these resources. Chapter 5 discusses how to create and configure lists and libraries. This chapter discusses the different types of libraries available in SharePoint 2013 and how to create and manage content within them.

Types of Libraries

There are several default library templates available in SharePoint 2013 that can be used to create new libraries in your sites. Several different types of libraries can be created to store and manage a variety of file types. Default libraries available in SharePoint 2013 include the following.

Document Libraries

The document library is the most general-purpose and commonly used type of library in SharePoint. Document libraries can store documents that need to be managed, edited, and shared within SharePoint, including Microsoft Office files, PDF files, and others (managing content in document libraries is discussed later in this chapter). Document libraries can be created in any version of SharePoint, and when created they contain only a single metadata column, which is used to store the document's title. Document libraries can be updated after their creation to include tracking of details that need to be associated with the document to organize, manage, and present it (configuring library columns and creating and managing views are discussed in Chapter 5).

When document libraries are created, they include only a single view, the All Documents view. Views are used to organize and present documents within a library and the All Documents view lists all documents contained within the library. By default this view shows the following details for each document:

- Type (linked to document)
- Name (linked to document with Edit menu)
- Modified
- Modified By

When document libraries are added to pages within the site using their app parts, the information is presented in a standard library view (see Figure 7-1). From this view you can perform all of the same management tasks available when working directly within the library.

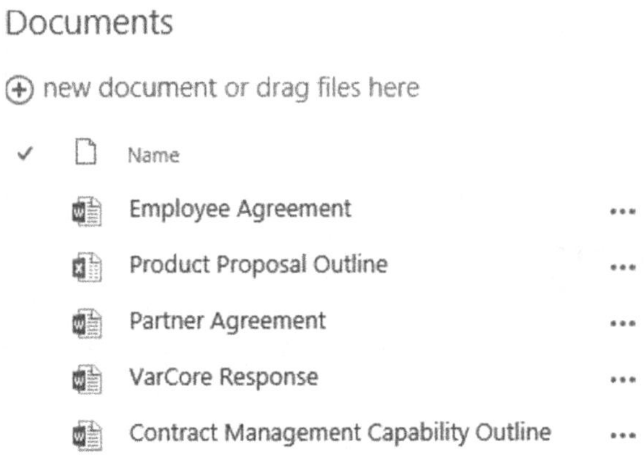

Documents

⊕ new document or drag files here

✓ 　▢　 Name

　　📄 Employee Agreement ・・・

　　📄 Product Proposal Outline ・・・

　　📄 Partner Agreement ・・・

　　📄 VarCore Response ・・・

　　📄 Contract Management Capability Outline ・・・

Figure 7-1. *Document library web part*

As with some of the lists discussed in Chapter 6, document libraries support some extended capabilities that are not available across all libraries or lists. The advanced capabilities of document libraries include the following.

Incoming E-mail Capabilities

A document library can be configured with an e-mail address. This allows e-mail message to be sent to the document library where the message and attachments to the e-mail can be stored. Incoming E-mail routing is also useful when you have systems that generate documents and are capable of distributing them via e-mail. These systems can be configured to e-mail the documents they generate to a SharePoint library for users to access and incorporate into workflow processes. Inbound e-mail routing can be configured to store documents attached to e-mail messages in the associated library or to store the e-mails themselves. When routed to a library, documents maintain their original name.

■ **Note** Before incoming e-mail capabilities can be configured within a library, your SharePoint technical administrator will need to configure your environment to support inbound e-mail.

To configure a document library to support incoming e-mail, do the following:

1. Navigate to the document library where you wish to configure incoming e-mail capabilities.

2. On the document library view page, select the Library Settings option from the Library ribbon tab.

3. On the Settings page, select the Incoming E-mail Settings option from the Communications section.

4. On the Incoming E-mail Settings page, make the following selections:

    a. In the Incoming E-mail section, select Yes for the "Allow this document library to receive e-mail?" option, and enter the e-mail address for the document library.

b. In the E-mail Attachments section, identify how attachments in e-mails sent to the library are handled. Also, identify how files added to the location having the same name as items already there are handled by specifying whether these files are to be overwritten when new items with the same name are added. Options for handling attachments include these:

  i.   *Save all attachments in root folder*: This option will cause attachments to be placed in the root folder of the library.

  ii. *Save all attachments in folders grouped by e-mail subject*: This option will place e-mail attachments within a folder named for the subject of the e-mail message.

  iii. *Save all attachments in folders grouped by e-mail sender*: This option will place e-mail attachments within a folder named for the sender of the e-mail message.

c. In the E-mail Message section, identify whether the e-mail itself is to be saved to the library. If you select Yes, the e-mail message will be saved as an EML file. If you select No, only the e-mail's attachments will be saved to the library.

d. In the E-mail Meeting Invitations section, identify whether meeting invitation messages are to be saved to the library if sent to it.

e. In the E-mail Security section, specify whether e-mail messages are to be accepted into the library from any e-mail address or only from e-mail addresses associated with users having access to the library.

f. Once all of the details are entered, click the OK button.

The inbound e-mail settings are activated, and e-mail messages sent to the identified address will be added to the library.

Form Libraries

Form libraries allow storage and management of InfoPath forms. They use an InfoPath form as the library template and permit exposure of form fields as columns within the library. Use form libraries when you need to collect information from users in a formatted or structured fashion and want this data saved within the XML-based form file or in a database. This data can then be used for reporting or integrated into related business processes.

For example, forms are valuable when you want to collect monthly expense details from your sales team. The form can be configured to manage the collection of all the necessary details and can then be sent through an approval process in which the submitters' manager approves the expenses. After approval has been given, the information can be populated into the accounting system for payment processing.

When initially created, a form library, like a document library, includes only a Title field. However unlike a document library, a form library includes two default views.

- *All Documents*: This is the default view for a form library. It lists all forms located within the library. This view includes the following columns:

  - Type (icon linked to document)

  - Name (linked to document with edit menu)

  - Modified

  - Modified By

  - Checked Out To

- *My Documents*: This view, which lists the library items created by the user viewing the library, includes the following columns:

  - Type (icon linked to document)

  - Name (linked to document with edit menu)

  - Modified

  - Modified By

Adding Forms

The first step in using a newly created form library is to configure the form to be used. To do so, set the template for the library. A form template identifying information to be populated by users must be added to the library.

Managing Form Templates

The form template for the library defines the structure and functionality provided by the form when it is populated by site users. To edit the form template for the library, do the following:

1. Navigate to the form library where the form needs to be populated.

2. On the library view page, select the Library Settings option from the Library ribbon tab.

3. On the Settings page, select the Advanced Settings option from the General Settings section.

4. On the Advanced Settings page in the Document Template section, select the Edit Template link.

5. In the opened InfoPath form, add the fields, logic, and formatting desired for the new form.

6. Once all updates to the form are made, click the Save button, and select a location to save a copy of the form to. This can be any locally available location.

7. Once the form has been saved, it can be published by selecting the Publish option from the File tab (see Figure 7-2) and then choosing the Quick Publish option.

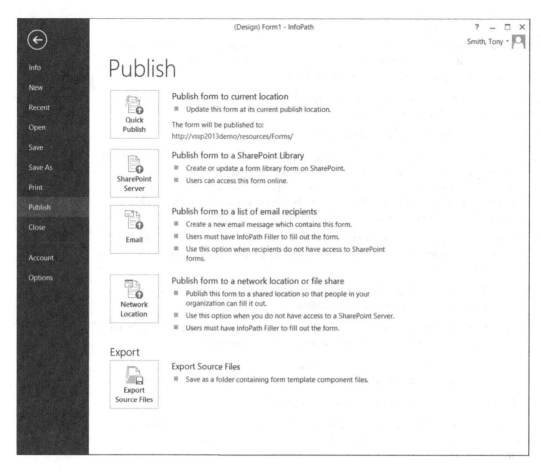

Figure 7-2. *InfoPath Publish option*

8. Once the publishing of the form is complete, select the OK button on the published confirmation window.

Once the form has been published to the library, it is available for use when people using the library select to create a new instance of the form to be populated. Following this approach, you are not prompted to add fields from the form for use as columns in the library. This limits the visibility of the content to when the forms are opened. To override this, you can create the library and the forms for the library directly within InfoPath.

Creating Form Libraries in InfoPath

As you see, creating a form library and customizing the library template through SharePoint requires several separate steps to completely set up the library. The process has limitations in that the form's fields are not included as fields in the library. An alternative method involves creating them in InfoPath and then using the form publishing process in InfoPath to create the form library, publish the form to the library, and expose the desired form fields as columns in the library. To use InfoPath to create a form library and publish a form for use in the library, do the following:

1. Create an InfoPath form containing the desired layout fields and business logic.

2. On the InfoPath File tab, select the Publish option.

251

3. On the Publish page, click the SharePoint Server option.

4. If the form is not yet saved locally, select to save it when prompted and identify a save location. This can be any accessible location. It has no direct relationship with the final form library or template once the item is published.

5. In the first Publishing Wizard window, enter the URL for the SharePoint site where the form is to be created, and click the Next button.

6. In the second Publishing Wizard window, do the following:

   a. Verify that the "Enable this form to be filled out by using a browser" option is clicked. This will render the form to be filled out in the web browser instead of requiring InfoPath to be present on a user's computer to open the form. Rendering the form in the browser leverages SharePoint's Form Services, which are available only in SharePoint Server Enterprise.

   b. Identify the type of object to create in SharePoint using the form. Options include the following. However, we will assume we are selecting the first option, Form Library, to publish our form.

      i. Form Library: This is the most common type of object created. It is used to generate a form library in an identified site.

      ii. Site Content Type: This option creates a content type allowing the form to be associated with multiple form libraries within SharePoint.

      iii. Administrator-Approved Form Template: This option creates an approval request for an administrator to approve to create a new form template.

   c. Click the Next button to continue the publishing process.

7. In the third Publishing Wizard window, either select to create a new form library in the specified site or select an existing form library to update the form template within. Then click the Next button.

8. If you selected to create a new form library, in the fourth Publishing Wizard window, enter the name for the new form library and an optional description, and click the Next button.

9. On the fifth Publishing Wizard screen, identify the fields from the form to include as columns in the library and the fields to be used as parameters for creating connections with other web parts for filtering purposes. Then click the Next button.

10. On the sixth Publishing Wizard page, click the Publish button to publish the form.

11. In the Publish Confirmation window, click the Close button.

The form library is created, the form is made the template of the library, and identified form fields to be included as library columns are exposed to the library.

Filling Out Forms

To fill out a form published in a form library, users will choose to create a new document in the library. Doing this opens a new instance of the form to be filled out. Once the details are entered into the form, it can be saved to the library. An alternative method for completing a form in a library is to upload a completed copy of the form into the library. Adding and uploading documents into libraries are discussed later in this chapter.

Wiki Page Libraries

Wiki page libraries are SharePoint libraries designed to store and manage wiki pages (discussed in detail in Chapter 4). Many sites within SharePoint, such as those created based on the Team Site template, have a wiki page library, the Site Pages library, available by default. A wiki page library is also automatically added to a site when the Wiki Page Home Page feature is activated. You can also introduce wiki pages into sites or add additional wiki pages to sites by selecting to create a new Wiki Page library.

Wiki page libraries, when created through the Wiki Page library template, have a unique view when the library is initially accessed. It navigates the user to the default page in the wiki page library (see Figure 7-3). This initial page describes what wiki libraries are and how to work with them.

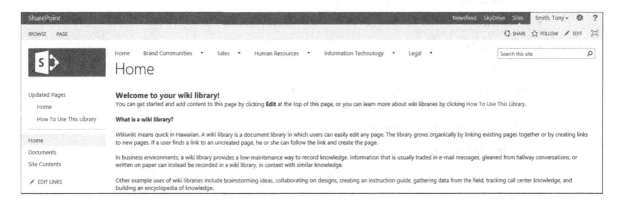

***Figure 7-3.** Wiki page library default page*

When created, wiki pages contain a single column, called the Wiki Content, in which page content details are stored. Also when created, wiki page libraries have several default views to help organize and manage contained wiki pages. These views include the following:

- *All Pages*: The default view for the library, it lists all pages contained within it. Pages are sorted based on when they were last changed and include the following columns in the view:

    - Type (icon linked to document)

    - Name (linked to document with edit menu)

    - Modified By

    - Modified

    - Created By

    - Created

- *Recent Changes*: This view, which contains the same layout and structure as the All Pages view, displays the following columns.

    - Type (icon linked to document)

    - Name (linked to document with edit menu)

    - Modified By

- Modified

- Created By

- Created

- *Created By Me*: This view lists the wiki pages created by the user viewing the library. The view lists the following library columns:

  - Type (icon linked to document)

  - Name (linked to document with edit menu)

  - Modified By

  - Modified

  - Created By

  - Created

- *By Author*: This view groups the wiki pages in the library by who created the pages. Grouped by Created By, the view lists the following columns:

  - Type (icon linked to document)

  - Name (linked to document with edit menu)

  - Modified By

  - Modified

  - Created By

  - Created

- *By Editor*: This view groups the wiki pages by who last modified them. This view, grouped by Modified By, lists the following columns:

  - Type (icon linked to document)

  - Name (linked to document with edit menu)

  - Modified By

  - Modified

  - Created By

  - Created

Picture Libraries

Picture libraries, specifically designed to store and manage image files, include all of the capabilities found in a standard document library, as well as the following additional resources for handling images:

- Generation of thumbnail versions of files added to the library. The thumbnails are used in library views to preview images in the library.

- Preview views that show the thumbnails created from the images. They allow reviewing of image files in the library, as Figure 7-4 shows.

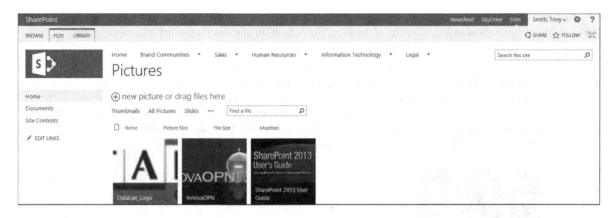

Figure 7-4. *Picture library preview view*

The structure of a newly created picture library includes the fields in Table 7-1.

Table 7-1. *Picture Library Columns*

Column	Required	Type	Properties
Title	No	Single Line of Text	
Date Picture Taken	No	Date and Time	Date and Time
Description	No	Multiple Lines of Text	Plain Text
Keywords	No	Multiple Lines of Text	Plain Text
Created	--	Date and Time	Date and Time Friendly Format Populated by System
Modified	--	Date and Time	Date and Time Friendly Format Populated by System
Created By	--	Person or Group	People Only Populated by System
Modified By	--	Person or Group	People Only Populated by System
Checked Out To	--	Person or Group	People Only Populated by System

A picture library includes views with different displays of the picture details than those provided by other libraries. These views allow easy previewing of the files. The default set of views for picture libraries include the following:

- *Thumbnails*: This view shows the thumbnail previews for the images contained in the library (see Figure 7-4). It is the default view. Hovering over a thumbnail causes the image details—including the title, type, dimensions, and size information—to be shown over the top of the image (see Figure 7-5). Clicking the thumbnail image for a listed image opens the properties display form and shows all of the image properties. From this page you can click on the name or image preview to open the associated image within the browser.

Figure 7-5. *Picture library preview image hover*

- *All Pictures*: This is a standard list view that includes all images in the library sorted by name. It lists the following columns:

    - Type (icon linked to document)

    - Name (linked to document with edit menu)

    - Picture Size

    - File Size

    - Modified

- *Slides*: This is another specialty view for picture libraries. It lists each of the images in the slide library one at a time (see Figure 7-6), and as you scroll through the images, it displays the image and its name.

Figure 7-6. *Picture library slides view*

Asset Libraries

The asset library is the first type we have discussed that is not available in SharePoint Foundation. Found only in SharePoint Server Standard and Enterprise, asset libraries include capabilities specifically designed to support management and sharing of images, audio files, and video files. When initially created, an asset library leverages the Image, Audio, and Video content types to allow collection of appropriate details supporting each media type the library is designed to manage. Table 7-2 lists the details tracked for images, audio files, and videos managed in asset libraries.

Table 7-2. *Asset Library Columns*

Column	Required	Type	Properties	Content Type
Title	No	Single Line of Text		Image, Audio, Video Rendition
Keywords	No	Multiple Lines of Text	Plain Text	Image, Audio, Video Rendition
Comments	No	Multiple Lines of Text	Plain Text	Image, Audio, Video Rendition
Author	No	Single Line of Text		Image, Audio, Video Rendition
Date Picture Taken	No	Date and Time	Format: Date and Time	Image

(continued)

Table 7-2. (*continued*)

Column	Required	Type	Properties	Content Type
Copyright	No	Single Line of Text		Image, Audio, Video Rendition
Preview Image URL	No	Hyperlink or Picture	Format Picture	Audio, Video, Video Rendition
Length (seconds)	No	Integer		Audio, Video, Video Rendition
Description	No	Multiple Lines of Text	Plain Text	Video
Owner	No	Person or Group	People or Groups Allowed	Video
Show Download Link	No	Yes/No	Defaulted to Yes	Video
Show Embed Link	No	Yes/No	Defaulted to Yes	Video
Frame Width	No	Integer		Video, Video Rendition
Frame Height	No	Integer		Video, Video Rendition
People in Video	No	Person or Group	Allow Multiple People or Groups Allowed	Video
Label	No	Single Line of Text		Video Rendition
Bit Rate	No	Integer		Video Rendition
Scheduling End Date	No	Yes/No		
Scheduling Start Date	No	Yes/No		
Created	--	Date and Time	Date and Time Friendly Format Populated by System	
Modified	--	Date and Time	Date and Time Friendly Format Populated by System	
Created By	--	Person or Group	People Only Populated by System	
Modified By	--	Person or Group	People Only Populated by System	
Checked Out To	--	Person or Group	People Only Populated by System	

The asset library, when initially created, includes a set of views designed to help review and manage the image, video and audio files in the library. The views available by default in the asset library include the following:

- *Thumbnail*: This view (see Figure 7-7) previews all items stored in the library sorted by name. Hovering over the thumbnail displays an item's details, which vary based on whether it is an image, audio, or video file.

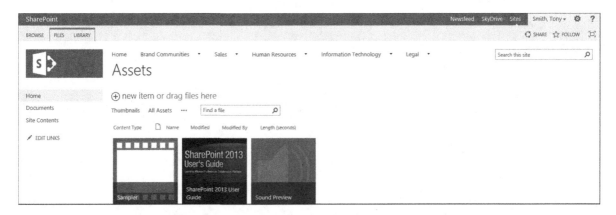

Figure 7-7. *Asset library thumbnail view*

- Clicking on a video file brings you to the video play page, which shows the video's details and plays it in the page (see Figure 7-8).

Figure 7-8. *Video play*

- Clicking an image file brings you to a standard list item properties view for the image files. Hovering over the file displays the image's properties, and clicking on the name or thumbnail opens the image in the browser for viewing.

- Clicking on an audio file brings you to the list item properties view page, which displays the standard audio file properties (see Figure 7-9). Click on the audio file's thumbnail or name to play the file.

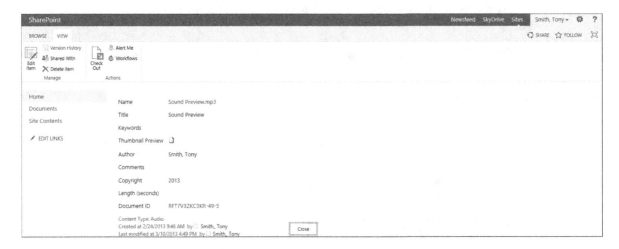

Figure 7-9. *Audio file details page*

- *All Assets*: This standard SharePoint library view includes all of the items in the library sorted by name and displays the following columns:

    - Content Type

    - Type (icon linked to document)

    - Name (linked to document with edit menu)

    - Thumbnail Preview

    - Modified

    - Modified By

    - Length (seconds)

    - Approval Status

    - Scheduling Start Date

    - Scheduling End Date

Record Libraries

The Record Library template is used to create libraries for storing and managing corporate records, documents (such as contracts or financial statements) whose retention must be enforced. This library, like the asset library, is available only in SharePoint Server Standard and Enterprise. Use record libraries when you need to manage documents that must be retained unaltered within defined retention periods. Record libraries are document libraries with major versioning and record retention services enabled so that items added to the library are automatically locked as records. (Records management is discussed in detail in Chapter 10.) Record libraries, like document libraries, by default have no custom fields and include only a single view, the All Documents view, that sorts the documents by name and displays the following columns:

- Type (icon linked to document)
- Name (linked to document with edit menu)
- Modified
- Modified By

Report Libraries

The Report Library template, found only in SharePoint Server Standard and Enterprise, manages web pages and documents that relay analytical information to site users. This type of library has columns for storing metadata to help manage reports and includes two content types, Report and Web Part Page with Status List (see Table 7-3). The Report type can track and manage report files: Excel reports, PDFs, Word files, and others. The Web Part Page with Status List type creates web part pages with a status list web part and can be used to make online scorecards and reports.

Table 7-3. *Report Library Columns*

Column	Required	Type	Properties	Content Type
Title	No	Single Line of Text		Report, Web Part Page with Status List
Report Description	No	Multiple Lines of Text	Plain Text	Report, Web Part Page with Status List
Parent ID	No	Number		Report
Owner	No	Person or Group	People or Groups Allowed	Report
Report Category	No	Choice	Options: Category 1 Category 2 Category 3	Report
Report Status	No	Choice	Options: Final Preliminary Period to Date	Report
Created	--	Date and Time	Date and Time Friendly Format Populated by System	Report, Web Part Page with Status List
Modified	--	Date and Time	Date and Time Friendly Format Populated by System	Report, Web Part Page with Status List
Created By	--	Person or Group	People Only Populated by System	
Modified By	--	Person or Group	People Only Populated by System	
Checked Out To	--	Person or Group	People Only Populated by System	

The report library contains three views for presenting documents within it. These views include the following:

- *Current Reports*: This view shows all Report items within the library and includes the following columns:
    - Type (icon linked to document)
    - Name (linked to document with edit menu)
    - Report Status
    - Report Category
    - Modified
    - Owner
    - Report Description
- *Dashboards*: This view shows all of the Web Part Page with Status List items in the library and includes the following columns:
    - Type (icon linked to document)
    - Name (linked to document with edit menu)
    - Modified
    - Modified By
    - Checked Out To
    - Report Description
- *All Reports and Dashboards*: This view lists all library items and sorts them with the most recently modified at the top. It includes these fields:
    - Type (icon linked to document)
    - Name (linked to document with edit menu)
    - Modified
    - Modified By

In a report library, items managed by Report content type function just as documents in any other document library do. However, the Web Part Page with Status List content type provides a unique approach to creating web part pages to be added to the library. To create a new Web Part Page with Status List item, do the following:

1. Navigate to the Report Library where you want to create a Web Part Page with Status List.

2. On the library view page, select the Web Part Page with Status List option from the New Document drop-down menu on the Files ribbon tab.

3. On the New Web Part Page with Status List screen, do the following:

    a. In the Page Name section, enter the file name, page title, and optional description for the new web part page.

    b. In the Location section, the report library will be listed. You can select this or some other report library in the site. You can also select the folder within the library where the page is to be created.

    c.   In the Create Link in Current Navigation Bar section, specify whether a link to the page is to be created in the navigation bar and, if it is, what heading the link is to be placed under.

    d.   In the Web Part Page with Status List Layout section, select the page layout to use in the web part page from the following choices:

        i.   *Three Column Horizontal Layout*: This creates a page containing two zones, with a larger left zone followed by a full-width page zone and then two sets of three side-by-side zones.

        ii.   *One Column Vertical Layout*: Like the Three Column Horizontal Layout, this one has a set of two zones: a larger left and a single zone, then a single web part zone in the page.

        iii.   *Two Column Vertical Layout*: Like the Three Column Horizontal Layout, this one has a set of two zones: a larger left and a single zone, then a two column web part zone area with the columns listed side by side.

    e.   In the Status Indicators section, identify how a status indicator list is to be added, with options including the following:

        i.   Create a status indicator list for me automatically.

        ii.   Allow me to select an existing status indicator list later.

        iii.   Do not add a status indicator list to the dashboard.

    f.   Once all information has been entered, click the OK button

The new web part page is created in the report library, and you are brought to the page to make any necessary updates.

Data Connection Libraries

Data connection libraries, available only in SharePoint Enterprise, are used to store and manage data connection files for use in Microsoft Office documents, such as InfoPath and Excel, that need to connect to other data. Data connection libraries store Office Data Connection files and Universal Data Connection files. They contain a content type for each of these types of connection files and include the fields listed in Table 7-4.

Table 7-4. *Data Connection Library Columns*

Column	Required	Type	Properties	Content Type
Title	No	Single Line of Text		Office Data Connection File, Universal Data Connection
Description	No	Single Line of Text		Office Data Connection File, Universal Data Connection
Keywords	No	Single Line of Text		Office Data Connection File
UDC Purpose	Yes	Choice	Options: ReadOnly WriteOnly ReadWrite	Universal Data Connection

(*continued*)

Table 7-4. (*continued*)

Column	Required	Type	Properties	Content Type
Connection Type	Yes	Choice	Allow Fill-In Options: SharePointList SharePointLibrary Database XMLQuery XMLSubmit WebService	Universal Data Connection
Created	--	Date and Time	Date and Time Friendly Format Populated by System	
Modified	--	Date and Time	Date and Time Friendly Format Populated by System	
Created By	--	Person or Group	People Only Populated by System	
Modified By	--	Person or Group	People Only Populated by System	
Checked Out To	--	Person or Group	People Only Populated by System	

Data connection libraries initially include five views to manage the files they contain. These views include the following:

- *All Items*: This view lists all files in the library, sorted by Title, and includes the following fields:

  - Type (icon linked to document)

  - Title

  - Name (linked to document with edit menu)

  - Description

  - Modified

  - Document Modified By

  - Keywords

- *By Author*: This view lists all items in the library, grouped by Created By, and includes the following columns:

  - Type (icon linked to document)

  - Title

- Name (linked to document with edit menu)
- Description
- Modified
- Document Modified By
- Created By
- Keywords

- *All Info*: Like the All Items view, this view lists all items in the library. However, it includes all columns used to manage information in the library, including the following:

  - Type (icon linked to document)
  - Title
  - Name (linked to document with edit menu)
  - Description
  - Modified
  - Created By
  - ID
  - Keywords
  - UDC Purpose
  - Connection Type

- *My Submissions*: This view lists items added to the library by the user viewing it, with the items sorted by Title. It includes the following fields:

  - Type (icon linked to document)
  - Title
  - Name (linked to document with edit menu)
  - Description
  - Modified
  - Created By
  - ID
  - Keywords
  - UDC Purpose
  - Connection Type
  - Approval Status
  - Approval Comments

- *Approve/Reject*: This view has a list of all files sorted by Title, with approval details for the items. The columns in this view include these:
  - Type (icon linked to document)
  - Title
  - Name (linked to document with edit menu)
  - Description
  - Modified
  - Created By
  - ID
  - Keywords
  - UDC Purpose
  - Connection Type
  - Approval Status
  - Approval Comments

Unlike most other libraries in SharePoint, data connection libraries do not contain document templates that can be opened in the library and edited directly. Instead, the library supports only the upload of files for storage.

Dashboards Libraries

The Dashboards library template is available only in SharePoint Server Enterprise and when the site has the PerformancePoint Services Site Feature enabled. This library is designed to store PerformancePoint dashboard pages, which are web part pages containing PerformancePoint dashboard elements. The library supports storage and management of both web part pages and general documents. It includes only a single column, Title, associated with either content type, and a single view, the All Items view, which lists all items stored in the library sorted by Title. It includes the following columns:

- Type (icon linked to document)
- Title
- Name (linked to document with edit menu)
- Modified
- Modified By
- Keywords

Within a dashboards library, you are able to create web part pages or upload documents. If you select creating a web part page, you are guided through the standard web part page creation process (creating web part pages is discussed in Chapter 4). A dashboards library has special features to support the creation and management of PerformancePoint dashboards.

Designing Dashboards

Along with standard document uploading and creation of web part pages, dashboards libraries let you design and deploy PerformancePoint dashboards using the Dashboard Designer app, found on the PerformancePoint ribbon tab. The Dashboard Designer allows you to create reusable dashboard, scorecard, and report components that can be organized into different dashboard displays and published for use in dashboards libraries. To create a PerformancePoint dashboard using the Dashboard Designer, do the following:

1. Navigate to the Dashboard library in which you wish to create the dashboard.

2. On the Dashboard view page, select the Dashboard Designer option from the PerformancePoint ribbon tab.

3. If prompted to install the Dashboard Designer app, allow the installation to run.

4. In the Dashboard Designer app (see Figure 7-10), you can create KPI reports, Excel Services reports, strategy maps, and chart or grid reports. This is done through the Create ribbon tab options.

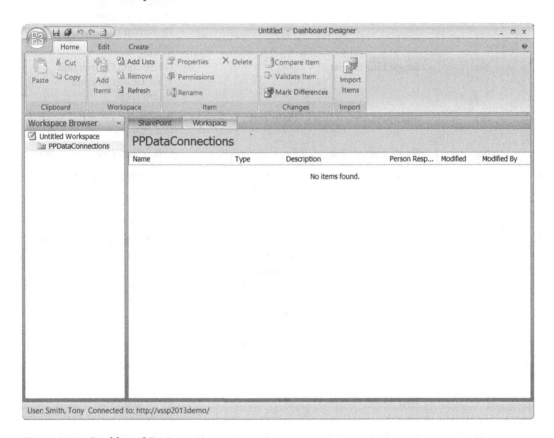

Figure 7-10. *Dashboard Designer*

5. Once the report creation is complete, it can be saved.

The report is created and added to SharePoint.

Data Connections Library for PerformancePoint

The Data Connections Library for PerformancePoint template is used to store and manage data connection files, much as the standard data connections library discussed earlier in this chapter does. However while the standard data connection library allows management of Office data connection files and universal data connection files, the data connections library for PerformancePoint introduces a third content type, PerformancePoint Data Connection, which is used to manage connection files for data contained in PerformancePoint dashboards. This library template, like the Dashboards template, is available only in SharePoint Server Enterprise and only when the PerformancePoint Site Feature is enabled. The structure created from the Data Connection Library for PerformancePoint is detailed in Table 7-5.

Table 7-5. *Data Connection Library for PerformancePoint Columns*

Column	Required	Type	Properties	Content Type
Title	No	Single Line of Text		Office Data Connection Files, Universal Data Connection, PerformancePoint Data Source
Description	No	Single Line of Text		Office Data Connection Files, Universal Data Connection
Description	No	Multiple Lines of Text	Plain Text	PerformancePoint Data Source
Keywords	No	Single Line of Text		Office Data Connection Files
UDC Purpose	Yes	Choice	Options: ReadOnly WriteOnly ReadWrite	Universal Data Connection
Connection Type	Yes	Choice	Allow Fill-In Options: SharePointList SharePointLibrary Database XMLQuery XMLSubmit WebService	Universal Data Connection
Person Responsible	No	Single Line of Text		PerformancePoint Data Source
Display Folder	No	Single Line of Text		PerformancePoint Data Source
Image	No	Hyperlink or Picture	Formatted as Picture	PerformancePoint Data Source

(*continued*)

Table 7-4. (*continued*)

Column	Required	Type	Properties	Content Type
Created	--	Date and Time	Date and Time Friendly Format Populated by System	Office Data Connection Files, Universal Data Connection, PerformancePoint Data Source
Modified	--	Date and Time	Date and Time Friendly Format Populated by System	Office Data Connection Files, Universal Data Connection, PerformancePoint Data Source
Created By	--	Person or Group	People Only Populated by System	
Modified By	--	Person or Group	People Only Populated by System	
Checked Out User	--	Person or Group	People Only Populated by System	

The Data Connection Library for PerformancePoint includes several list views for managing and presenting data connection files. These views include the following:

- *All Items*: This view shows all files within the library, sorted by Title, and lists the following columns:

  - Type (icon linked to document)

  - Title

  - Name (linked to document with edit menu)

  - Description

  - Modified

  - Modified By

  - Keywords

- *My Submissions*: This view lists the library items, sorted by Title, created by the user viewing the library and includes the following columns:

  - Type (icon linked to document)

  - Title

  - Name (linked to document with edit menu)

  - Description

  - Modified

  - Created By

  - ID

- Keywords
- UDC Purpose
- Connection Type
- Approval Status
- Approval Comments

- *Approve/Reject*: This view, which is used to show the approval status for items in the library, sorted by Title, includes the following columns:

  - Type (icon linked to document)
  - Title
  - Name (linked to document with edit menu)
  - Description
  - Modified
  - Created By
  - ID
  - Keywords
  - UDC Purpose
  - Connection Type
  - Approval Status
  - Approval Comments

- *By Author*: This view lists the items in the library, grouped by the Created By information, and includes the following columns:

  - Type (icon linked to document)
  - Title
  - Name (linked to document with edit menu)
  - Description
  - Modified
  - Modified By
  - Created By
  - Keywords

- *By Display Folder*: This view groups the columns in the library by the Display Folder information. It includes the following columns:

  - Type (icon linked to document)
  - Name (linked to document with edit menu)
  - Description

- Modified

- Modified By

- Keywords

- Person Responsible

- Version

- *By Data Source Type*: This view organizes the data connection files by the data source type, or Content Type, field and lists the following fields:

  - Name (linked to document with edit menu)

  - Description

  - Modified

  - Modified By

  - Keywords

  - Person Responsible

  - Version

  - Content Type

As with the dashboard library, the Data Connections Library for PerformancePoint library supports the use of the Dashboard Designer, discussed earlier in this chapter, to create connections and resources for the library.

Working with Documents

Libraries store and manage a variety of types of files, from Microsoft Office documents and PDF files to web pages and data connections. Libraries provide you with the ability to work with the documents so you can locate and manage information you have been given rights to work with.

Adding Documents to Libraries

There are several different approaches available for adding documents to libraries. These options include approaches for uploading documents that already exist as well as approaches for creating new documents.

Uploading Documents

When you want to place existing documents in SharePoint, several options are available for copying the items into the desired library. These options support uploading of individual documents and multiple items at once.

You can upload single files directly to the library using the document upload options available within the SharePoint ribbon. This is the most commonly used approach for uploading documents into a library. It enables you to get not only the document into the library but also populate metadata associated with it. To upload a document to a library using the ribbon upload options, do the following:

1. Navigate to the library where you want to upload the file.

2. On the library view page (see Figure 7-11), click the New Document link at the top of the document view area, and choose the Upload Existing File link from the New Document menu, or click the Upload Document option from the Files ribbon tab.

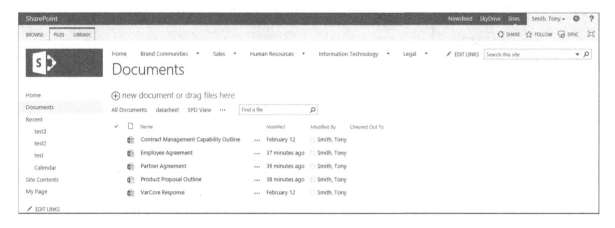

Figure 7-11. *Document view page*

3. In the Add Document window, do the following:

   a. Find the document to add by browsing to it, then select it.

   b. Identify the upload behavior for a document with the same name as a file already in the library. Specify whether to add it as a new version of that file. If you choose not to allow this by unchecking the Overwrite Existing Files option, an error message appears if you try to upload a file with the name of one already in the library.

   c. Once the file has been selected, click the OK button.

4. In the document properties window, identify the content type, if prompted to, and enter any presented metadata. Rename the file being uploaded if you wish to. Once this information is entered, click the Save button.

The document is added to the library, and the identified metadata is assigned to the document.

■ **Note**   If you select Cancel in the document properties window instead of the Save option when there are required fields, the document is added to the library in a checked-out state. You must edit the properties to provide any required data before checking in the document. Since the document has not yet been checked in, it will be available only to the individual that uploaded it.

While uploading documents through the standard ribbon upload options works well for individual documents, at times you may want to upload multiple items all at once. A couple of different approaches can be used to upload multiple documents into a library in this way. The first approach is to upload them through the Windows Explorer view. This view opens the library in an Explorer window, like the one you see when you browse through directories on your local computer. Then you can drag and drop or copy and paste files into the Explorer window. To upload files through Windows Explorer view, do the following:

1. Navigate to the library were you want to upload the files.

2. In the document view window, do one of the following. Select the New Document option or Upload Document option from the Files ribbon tab. Then click either the Upload Files using Windows Explorer option or the Open with Explorer option from the Library ribbon tab.

3.   In the Windows Explorer window, drag and drop or copy and paste files from the other locations into the opened Explorer window.

4.   Once the files are uploaded, edit their properties to assign any required metadata column values, and then check the documents into the library. Editing document properties is discussed later in this chapter.

■ **Note**   The documents are added to the library. When the files are uploaded through the Explorer view to a library that has required properties, the documents are added to the library in a checked-out state. They are not available to site users until the required columns are populated and the document is checked in.

If you use an HTML5-compliant browser such as Internet Explorer 10, a third option can be used to upload documents into a library. This approach allows you to copy files directly over the library view on the page. This can include either the view of the library itself or an app part on a site page showing library content. To upload a document in this way, drag the file over a library view or a library app part. The document will be uploaded to the library in the same way that files are uploaded through the Windows Explorer view. As with the latter method, you will need to edit the file's properties after it is uploaded to populate required column properties.

■ **Note**   There are some restrictions to the types of files that can be uploaded into a library. For example, by default EXE and DLL files are not allowed. The file types not allowed in libraries are managed by your SharePoint technical administrator.

Creating New Documents in a Library

Besides uploading existing documents, you can also create new documents within a library directly. This allows you to generate a document in the desired library and place the new item in that library for management and use. To create a new document in a SharePoint library, do the following:

1.   Navigate to the library where you want to create the new document.

2.   On the document view page, select the type of document to be created from the New Document drop-down menu on the Files ribbon tab. If you click on the New Document drop-down option directly, the default document type will be created.

3.   The document will open in the associated document's editing program.

A document saved from the opened program is saved in the library where you created the file. You will be prompted to enter any associated properties defined in the library.

Using the New Document Menu

Whether you are working in a document library view page or through a library app part listed on a web part or wiki page, SharePoint 2013 has a New Document link at the top of the library information view. This link enables you to easily upload content and create new documents within the library. Clicking this link opens a list of new document activities, including a list of the possible documents that can be created directly in the library and a link to upload a document, as Figure 7-12 shows.

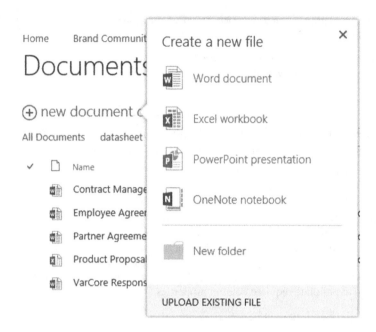

Figure 7-12. *New document menu*

To create a new document in the site through the New Document link, do the following:

1. Navigate to the library where you want to create the new document.

2. Click the New Document link at the top of the library view to show the Create a New File menu.

3. In the Create a New File menu, click the type of document to be created.

4. In the Create a New Document window, enter the name for the new document to be created.

5. In the document's Edit Properties window, enter the document property details, and click the Save button.

The new document is added to the library. You can also use the New Document menu to upload a document to the library. When you select the Upload Existing File option from the New Document menu, you are prompted to identify the file and then the document properties, using the process described in the "Uploading Documents" section earlier in this chapter.

Editing Documents in SharePoint

Once documents are uploaded to SharePoint or added to a SharePoint library directly, the documents and their properties can be edited. Several capabilities exist within SharePoint to help you manage and edit documents.

Checking Documents In and Out

Check a file out of a library when you plan to make edits and do not want others opening the document for editing. Checking out the file locks it so it can be edited only by you until you check it back in. Individuals visiting a library can see whether files are checked out and to whom. For example, you may want to check out a file if you plan to make edits spanning several days. A checked-out file, even when not open in a program such as Word or Excel, will be unavailable for edit by any other individual, and others will not see your changes until the file is checked back into the library.

To check out a document in a library, do the following:

1. Navigate to the library where you want to check out the document.

2. Check the selection box next to the document or documents you wish to check out, and click the Check Out option from the Files ribbon tab (see Figure 7-13).

Figure 7-13. *Library view with Check Out options*

3. On the confirmation screen, click the OK button.

The files are checked out, and the library view is updated. This update includes details about the individual who checked out the file, as well as changing the file's icon to include the checked-out symbol (see Figure 7-14).

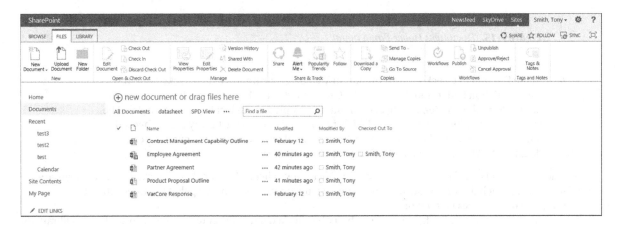

Figure 7-14. *Library view with checked out documents*

There is another method you can use to check out a file:

1. Navigate to the library where the file to be checked out is located.

2. In the library view, select the Hover Panel option.

3. From the document's Hover Panel menu, select the Check Out option (see Figure 7-15).

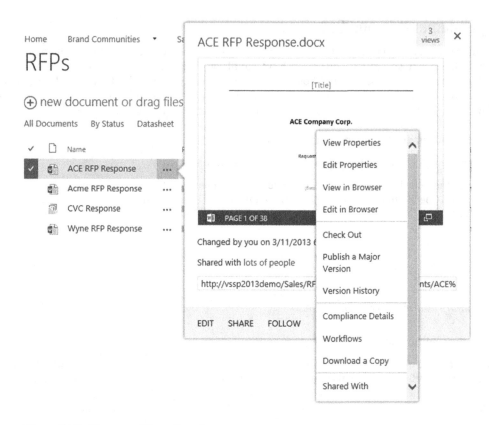

Figure 7-15. *Document Hover Panel menu*

4. In the Document Checkout window, identify whether the item is to be checked out into your local draft folder, and then click the OK button to check out the file. If you choose to use the local draft folder, the checked-out item is copied to the local computer and will be edited from this location once checked out and saved back to the library when checked back in. If you do not choose to use the local draft folder, changes to the checked-out document will be managed within the SharePoint library.

The document is checked out to the current user. Documents checked out are later checked back into a library using the same approach discussed for checking items out, the only exception being that the Check In option is available instead of the Check Out option.

Library managers can require that items in a library be checked out in order to be edited. To configure a library to require items to be checked out for editing do the following:

1. Navigate to the library where checkout is to be required.

2. On the library view page, select the Library Settings option from the Library ribbon tab.

3. On the Settings page, select the Versioning Settings from the General Settings section.

4. On the Versioning Settings page in the Require Check Out section, select Yes for the "Require documents to be checked out before they can be edited" option, and click the OK button.

The library is configured to require documents to be checked out. With this option enabled, when you want to edit a document from a Microsoft Office program, you are prompted to check out the files (see Figure 7-16). Click the Check Out button to check out the associated file.

Figure 7-16. *Microsoft Office Check Out prompt*

Any file checked out to you can be checked back into the library. But if you wish, you can also discard the checkout of a document. When you discard checkout, any changes made to the file since it was checked out are lost, and the file returns to the state it was in when you checked it out. To discard your checkout of a file, do the following:

1. Navigate to the library where the checked-out file exists.

2. Check the box next to the document to discard checkout, and choose the Discard Checkout option from the Files ribbon tab.

3. On the confirmation screen, select the OK button.

The file is checked back into the library, and changes made to it while it was checked out are discarded. Individuals with Full Control rights to the library can not only discard the checkout of files they had checked out but also discard the checkout of items checked out by others. Thus, administrators can override the checkout of these items, making documents checked out by other library users available for edit in their earlier state.

Editing Documents

A document in a SharePoint library is edited by opening the file in its associated program or, for a Microsoft Office document, opening it in Microsoft Office Web Apps. Clicking the name of a file in a library opens that file. A file associated with a program not in Microsoft Office opens in its associated program—for example, a PDF file opens in Adobe Reader. Microsoft Office documents, including Word, Excel, and PowerPoint files, open in either their associated program or in Microsoft Office Web Apps. The way they are opened depends on the document opening settings.

Managing Document Opening Settings

When your SharePoint technical administrator configures Microsoft Office Web Apps within your SharePoint environment, Microsoft Office documents, including Word files, Excel spreadsheets, and PowerPoint presentations, are configured by default to open in Microsoft Office Web Apps instead of their associated Microsoft Office desktop program. You can configure SharePoint libraries to determine the default program in which to open these files. To specify whether a Microsoft Office document is to open in the associated Office program or in Microsoft Office Web Apps, do the following:

1. Navigate to the library where you wish to edit the document opening settings.

2. On the document view page, select the Library Settings option from the Library ribbon tab.

3. On the Settings page, select the Advanced Settings option from the General Settings section.

4. On the Advanced Settings page in the Opening Documents in the Browser section, specify the behavior for opening documents. One option is "Use the server default" (the default), in which the library inherits the document-open settings defined by the SharePoint technical administrator. A second is "Open in browser", which opens files in Microsoft Office Web Apps, letting you view and edit them in the web browser. A third is "Open in client application", which opens files in the associated Office program. Once the setting is configured, click the OK button.

Even when the default opening behavior of files is defined, however, users of the library can still explicitly identify the method they wish to use to open a file.

Opening Documents

You can open a document in a library for viewing or editing by navigating to the library and clicking the name of the document. When this is done, the document opens in the file's default program. For Office documents, files open in either the associated Office program or Office Web Apps, depending on the library settings. You yourself can also determine how to open a document by choosing the opening method.

- *Open in Program*: To open the document in its associated program, display the hover panel, and select the Edit option from the panel.

- *Open in Browser*: To open a Microsoft Office document for editing in Office Web Apps, select the Edit in Browser option from the Hover Panel menu. To open an Office document for viewing only, select the View in Browser option from the Hover Panel menu. This choice opens the document in the Office Web App, as Figure 7-17 shows.

Figure 7-17. *Office Web App*

Office Web Apps give the web browser the full editing capabilities of Microsoft Office Word, Excel, PowerPoint, and OneNote. Use Office Web Apps to open a document when your local computer does not contain a copy of Microsoft Office but you need to edit a document or when your computer's version of Microsoft Office is not Office 2013 and you want to take advantage of capabilities not available in the installed earlier version of Office.

■ **Note** It is not required that you have Microsoft Office 2013 to work with documents in SharePoint 2013. You can manage documents within SharePoint using previous versions of Office, but you will be limited to the features available in your version.

Editing Document Properties

When you work with documents in libraries, you can edit the information in the metadata columns. (How to create columns in lists and libraries to manage metadata of a document in them is discussed in Chapter 5.) To edit the properties of a document, do the following:

1. Navigate to the library containing the document to be edited.

2. On the library view page, check the selection box next to that document, and then select the Edit Properties option from the Files ribbon tab.

3. If the library requires checkout and the document is not checked out, click the OK button in the checkout window.

4. On the document's properties edit page, make any needed changes to the document's details. Once done, click the Save button.

The document properties are updated, and you are returned to the document library view. You can also edit a document's properties by doing the following:

1. Navigate to the library containing the document to be edited.

2. On the library view page, select the Hover Panel option.

3. In the hover panel, open the menu, and select the Edit Properties option (see Figure 7-15).

4. If the library requires checkout and the document is not yet checked out, click the OK button in the checkout window.

5. On the document's properties edit page, make any needed changes to the document's details. Once done, click the Save button.

The document properties are updated, and you are returned to the library view page.

Using Quick Edit

Quick Edit, used to make multiple changes to a document's properties, opens a SharePoint list or library view in a datasheet view resembling Excel (see Figure 7-18).

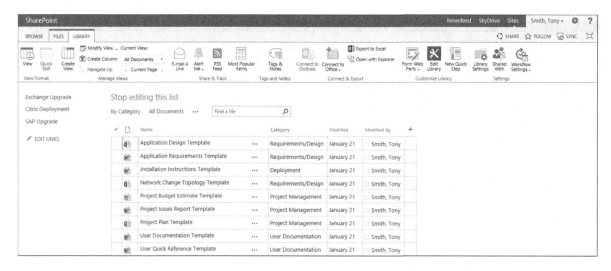

Figure 7-18. *Quick Edit*

To open a library in the Quick Edit view, do the following:

1. Navigate to the library in which you want to edit a file's properties.

2. On the library view page, select the Quick Edit option from the Library ribbon tab.

The library appears in the Quick Edit view, where you can make needed changes to library properties. Changes are made individually, by typing in columns, or through multicell copy-and-paste actions, like those used to edit data in Excel files. Once done, selecting the View option from the Library ribbon tab returns you to the standard view of the library.

Managing Files with No Checked-in Version

When a document is added to a library requiring checkout or is added without entering required metadata, the file is added in a checked-out state and must be checked in by its creator. Until a document is checked in the first time, other users of the library will not see it.

Library managers are able to manage files that have no checked-in versions. That is, they can manage files when their creator is not available to check them in the first time. To manage a file with no checked-in version, a library manager must take ownership of the file. To take ownership of a file with no checked-in version, do the following:

1. Navigate to the library containing the file to be managed.

2. On the library view page, select the Library Settings option from the Library ribbon tab.

3. On the Settings page, select the Manage Files which have No Checked-In Version option from the Permissions and Management section.

4. On the Checked Out Files page (see Figure 7-19), check the box next to the file you wish to take ownership of, and click the Take Ownership of Selection option.

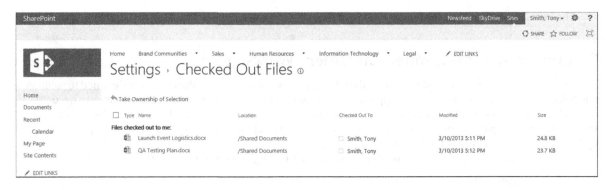

Figure 7-19. *Checked Out Files page*

The file is updated to give the current user control of the checked-out item. Once the control is set, you can edit, check in, or delete the item from the library.

Deleting Documents in a Library

Documents within SharePoint libraries can be deleted by individuals who are able to manage library content. Several different approaches can be used to delete such items. To delete a single item from a library, do the following:

1. Navigate to the library where you want to delete a document.

2. On the library view page, select the Hover Panel option to show the hover panel for the selected item.

3. In the hover panel, select the menu, and choose the Delete option (see Figure 7-15).

4. On the Delete Confirmation screen, click the OK button.

The file is deleted, and the library view is refreshed to reflect the change. The deleted file is moved to the site's recycle bin (the recycle bin is discussed in Chapter 3).

At times you may want to delete multiple documents all at once. In this case, deleting items individually would not be efficient. Deleting multiple items at once from SharePoint libraries is done in one of two ways. The first method is as follows:

1. Navigate to the library containing the documents to be deleted.

2. In the library view, check the box next to each item to be deleted, and then select the Delete Document option from the Files ribbon tab.

3. On the Delete Confirmation screen, click the OK button.

The items are deleted from the library, and the view is updated. The deleted files are moved to the site's recycle bin.

A second method for deleting multiple files is through Windows Explorer. To delete multiple files from a library using Windows Explorer, do the following:

1. Navigate to the library containing the files to be deleted.

2. On the library view, select the Open with Explorer option from the Library ribbon tab.

3. On the Windows Explorer screen, select the files to be deleted, and select to delete the files.

The items are deleted from the library.

Editing Documents through Document Workspaces

A document workspace can be used to manage the editing process of a document through a site designed to facilitate updating, including the management of supporting documents, links, and tasks related to the document's needed edits. When a document workspace is used to manage editing, an editable copy of the document is placed in a workspace. The original document is left in its source location untouched until the workspace copy is appropriately updated and published back to the source.

To create a document workspace to manage a document's editing process, do as follows:

1. Navigate to the library containing the document to be edited.

2. On the document view page, check the box next to the document to be edited in a document workspace. Then select the Create Document Workspace option from the Send To drop-down menu on the Files ribbon tab.

3. On the Create Document Workspace page, click the OK button.

A document workspace is created (see Figure 7-20), and a copy of the selected document is placed in the workspace. You are brought to the workspace, where you can work on the document as well as manage any materials and information related to the edits you make.

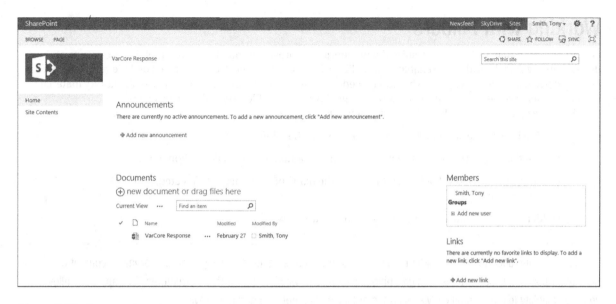

Figure 7-20. *Document workspace*

A document workspace contains a set of resources designed to support the editing of documents, including the following:

- Announcements list

- Calendar list

- Documents library, containing a copy of the document for which the workspace was created.

- Links list

- Team Discussion list

When working in a document workspace, you can use the available lists and libraries and create resources to help make necessary changes to the document. Once the document is appropriately updated, you can publish it back to the original source file by checking the box next to the finalized file in the document workspace and then selecting the Copy to Source option from the Send To drop-down on the Files ribbon tab.

Download a Copy

Users of a SharePoint library are able to download copies of files from the library. That is, users can save copies of documents to another location they have access to, such as the local computer or an accessible network location. To download a copy of a file from a library, do the following:

1. Navigate to the library containing the file to be downloaded.

2. On the library view page, select the Hover Panel option.

3. On the hover panel, choose the Download a Copy option from the Hover Menu.

4. In the "Do you want to save..." message, select Save or Save As and then the Save location.

A copy of the file is saved to the identified location.

Working with Folders

Folders can be used in libraries to organize documents and to provide a container to uniquely secure groups of documents. By default, folders are enabled within libraries. They can be nested into any needed hierarchy. A folder is best used when a set of documents to be stored needs to be secured differently from the rest of the library materials. Both the folder and the documents in it can be updated to reflect the files' special security needs.

To create a new folder in a library, do the following:

1. Navigate to the library where you want to create the folder.

2. On the library view page, select the New Folder option from the Files ribbon tab.

3. In the Create a New Folder window, enter the name of the folder to be created, and click the Save button.

The folder is created, and you are returned to the library view.

■ **Note**   Placing documents in a folder results in a fixed structure. Instead of using folders to organize content for display purposes, it is better to use the grouping capabilities of views to create these structures. This approach allows you the flexibility to create multiple views and to organize documents in different ways.

Folders are most effectively used to secure groups of documents requiring special security. Doing this need not adversely affect the display of the documents in the library. If you configure the library's views to ignore folders, you preserve the security you want, and the documents will be listed as if they are all contained in the root of the library. To configure a view to ignore folders in the display, do the following:

1. Navigate to the library containing the folders to be ignored in the view.

2. Select the library view that you wish to update.

3. On the library view page for that view, select the Modify View option from the Library ribbon tab.

4. On the Edit View page in the Folders section, select the "Show all items without folders" option, and click the OK button.

The library view is updated and shows all content without listing the folders.

Document Sets

At times multiple documents will make up what your organization considers a single piece of business content. For example, an RFP response may consist of a Word document response and a PowerPoint response presentation. Another example is a contract consisting of the original contract and one or more amendment documents. Not uncommonly, such a set of closely related documents need to share metadata properties, go through workflow processes together, or be subject to the same information management policies. A document set is a special kind of folder that allows multiple documents to be managed together and treated as if they were a single item. A document set can have

- Metadata columns that are shared with the documents contained within it.

- Workflow processes that can be run against the document set (workflows are discussed in detail in Chapter 9).

- Information management policies, such as retention or auditing policies, that can be configured within the set itself (information management policies are discussed in detail in Chapter 9).

Being a special content type, a document set must be enabled within a library for it to be used. To configure a library to allow content types and to include document sets, do the following:

1. Navigate to the library where you want to enable document sets.

2. On the library view page, select the Library Settings option from the Library ribbon tab.

3. On the Settings page, select the Advanced Settings option from the General Settings section.

4. On the Advanced Settings page, select Yes for the Allow Management of Content Types option in the Content Types section. Click the OK button.

5. On the Settings page in the Content Types section, select the Add From Existing Site Content Types option.

6. On the Add Content Types page,

   a. Select the Document Sets Content Types option from the Select Site Content Types From drop-down to filter the list of content types to only the Document Set type.

   b. Select the Document Set option from the Available Site Content Types section, and click the Add button to move the content type to the Content Types to Add section.

   c. Click the OK button.

The Document Set content type is added to the library for use. The Document Set content type must next be configured to identify a set's display setting when it is accessed and the column properties that the set will share with its contained documents. To configure a document set in a library where the document set content type has been enabled, do the following:

1. Navigate to the library containing the document set to be configured.

2. On the library view page, select the Library Settings option from the Library ribbon tab.

3. On the Settings page, select the Document Set option from the Content Types section.

4. On the List Content Type page, select the Document Set Settings option from the Settings section.

5. On the Document Set Settings page,

   a. In the Allowed Content Types section, select the content types to be created within the document set.

   b. In the Default Content section, specify materials to be added to the document set when it is created by identifying the content type and then selecting the items to be added. Also, specify whether file names, when added to the set, are to include the document set's name.

   c. In the Shared Columns section, identify the metadata columns in the library to be inherited from the set. Documents added will inherit the values of the columns identified as inherited from the set.

   d. In the Welcome Page View section, identify the document view to be used to display contained documents when the set is first accessed.

   e. In the Welcome Page section, select whether you want to change the layout of the welcome page (the page displayed when you navigate to the document set). A new window will open, in which you can tailor the page layout.

   f. Click the OK button to save the document set settings.

The document set is updated based on the changes made. With the set configured, you can create a new document set within the library. Do this as follows:

1. Navigate to the library where you want to create the document set.

2. On the document view page, select the Document Set option from the New Document drop-down menu on the Files ribbon tab.

3. On the New Document Set page, enter the details for the new document set, and click the Save button.

The new document set is created, and you are brought to its welcome page (see Figure 7-21).

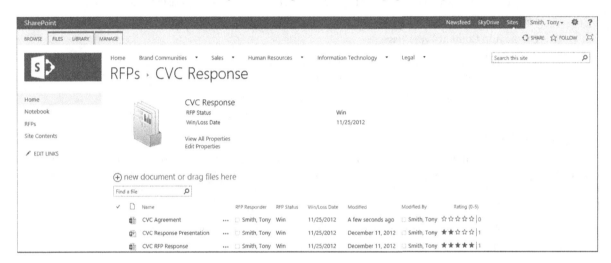

Figure 7-21. *Document Set welcome page*

Working in Document Sets

Once a document set is created, you can add and manage documents within it just as you work with documents in any other library. (The only exception is that column properties inherited by the document set will be prepopulated with the values of the properties defined in the set.) While within a document set, you can view and manage its properties. As discussed earlier, the welcome page initially lists the details identified for display when the set was configured. Clicking the View All Properties link brings you to the set's properties display page, where all the set's details are shown.

When viewing the document set welcome page, you can edit the set's properties. To do this, click the Edit Properties option and make any necessary updates to the details. When updates are made to set properties that are inherited by the documents in it, the properties are updated against the documents contained in the set as well.

Document Set Version Management

When versioning is enabled in a library that contains document sets, you are can create document set versions. Creating a version of a document set identifies the version of each file within the set and ties them to the set version so that you can track and view the state of all the set's materials when the version was created.

To capture a version of the document set, do the following:

1. Navigate to the document set in which you wish to capture the version.

2. On the document set welcome page, select the Capture Version option from the Manage ribbon tab.

3. In the Capture Document Set Version window, do the following:

   a. In the Version Options section, specify whether the version is to include the latest major versions of contained documents or just the most recent version of each, whether it be a major or minor version.

   b. In the Comments section, optionally enter a comment to associate with the version.

   c. Click the OK button to save the version.

The version of the set is saved. To view the captured versions of a document set, navigate to it, and select the Version History option from the Manage ribbon tab. This will show the details for the saved version of the set, including references to the contained document versions (see Figure 7-22).

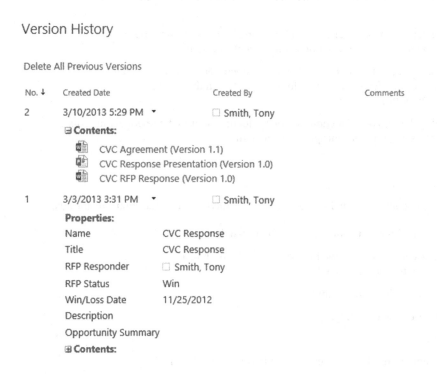

Figure 7-22. *Document set version history*

Managing Item Level Security

As discussed in previous chapters, security can be managed in sites, lists, libraries, and list items. You can also manage security for documents and folders directly within libraries. To manage security for a document or folder in a library, first configure the document or folder to no longer inherit its permissions from the library or folder containing it. You can then manage the document's or folder's permissions directly. Typically, the permissions are edited when you want to restrict access to an item beyond the rights assigned to the library itself.

Managing Permission Inheritance

As just noted, before you can change a document's permissions, you must reconfigure it to stop inheriting its permissions from its library. To break inheritance on a document in a library, do the following:

1. Navigate to the library view showing the document that requires permissions to be managed.

2. On the library view page, click the document whose permissions are to be managed, and then select the Shared With option on the Files ribbon tab.

3. In the Shared With window, select the Advanced option.

4. On the Permissions page, update the permission inheritance settings for the document by doing the following:

    a. To stop inheriting permissions, select the Stop Inheriting Permissions option from the Permissions ribbon tab. In the confirmation window, click the OK button.

    b. To reestablish inheritance between the library and the document, select the Delete Unique Permissions option from the Permissions ribbon tab. In the confirmation window, click the OK button.

Permission inheritance is updated based on your choices. Once a document or folder no longer inherits permissions from the library, you can set the rights appropriate to the item.

Editing Document Permissions

To change the permissions of a document or folder that does not inherit its permissions from the library, do the following:

1. Navigate to the library view showing the document to be updated.

2. On the library view page, check the selection box next to the document, and then select the Shared With option on the Files ribbon tab.

3. In the Shared With window, select the Advanced option.

4. On the Permissions page, do the following:

    a. To add permissions:

        i. Select the Grant Permissions option from the Permissions ribbon tab.

        ii. On the Share screen, enter the accounts to which permissions are to be added. If providing permissions other than Edit, click the Show Options item, and then select the permission level to provide. Once the appropriate permissions are set, click the Share button.

    b. To edit permissions:

        i. Check the box next to the item to be edited, and select the Edit User Permissions button from the Permissions ribbon tab.

        ii. On the Edit Permissions page, select the appropriate permissions, and click the OK button.

    c.   To delete permissions:

        i.   Check the box next to the item or items to be deleted, and select the Delete Unique Permissions option from the Permissions tab.

        ii.   In the Delete Confirmation window, click the OK button to delete the item.

Once the permission updates are complete, you are returned to the Permissions page, where the permissions changes are reflected.

■ **Note**   Resetting a document or folder to inherit permissions from its folder or library removes the security permissions you configured for the item and resets it to those of the folder or library.

Audience Targeting

In a document targeted to specific individuals or groups, web parts and library views can be configured to display the information based on the target details. To enable targeting within a library, do the following:

1.   Navigate to the library where you want to enable targeting.

2.   On the library view page, select the Library Settings option from the Library ribbon tab.

3.   On the Settings page, select the Audience Targeting Settings option in the General Settings section.

4.   On the Enable Audience Targeting page, click the Enable Audience Targeting option, and click the OK button.

When audience targeting is enabled in a library, an additional field, Target Audiences, is listed on the document's Edit Properties form. This field lets you select users, groups and SharePoint groups as target audiences for the information.

Document Versioning

As is discussed with lists in Chapter 6, versioning is used to maintain a record of all changes made to a document over time. This record lets you view the document as it existed at any point in its life cycle to date, along with the date, time, and editor of the document in each version. With versioning enabled, you can also revert a document to a previous version if necessary and compare the current state of the document to that of past versions to identify changes made to it over time.

Enable Versioning

Before using it for documents in a library, versioning must first be enabled. To enable versioning, do the following:

1.   Navigate to the library where you want to enable versioning.

2.   On the library view page, select the Library Settings option from the Library ribbon tab.

3.   On the Settings page, select the Versioning Settings option from the General Settings section.

4. On the Version Settings page, do the following:

    a. In the Content Approval section, select whether the document is to require content approval.

    b. In the Document Version History section, select Yes to create versions. Optionally select whether the number of versions tracked is to be limited and, if it is, how many. Also, optionally identify whether the number of approved versions maintained is to be limited and, if it is, how many.

    c. In the Draft Item Security section, identify whether all users, only editors, or only approvers are to see draft items.

    d. Click the OK button to save the version settings.

The version settings are saved, and you are returned to the Settings page.

Working with Existing Versions

When versioning is enabled in a library and a document's versioning history has been created, you can access details of its past versions. To access the version details for an existing document, do the following:

1. Navigate to the library where you want to review the version history.

2. On the library view page, open the document's hover panel.

3. On the document's hover panel, select the Version History option from the Hover Panel menu (see Figure 7-15).

Alternatively, do the following to access this information:

1. Navigate to the library where you want to review the version history.

2. In the library view, click the box next to the document whose history you want to view, and then select the Version History option from the Files ribbon tab.

The version history window, shown in Figure 7-23, appears. This window provides access to all the version details for the selected document.

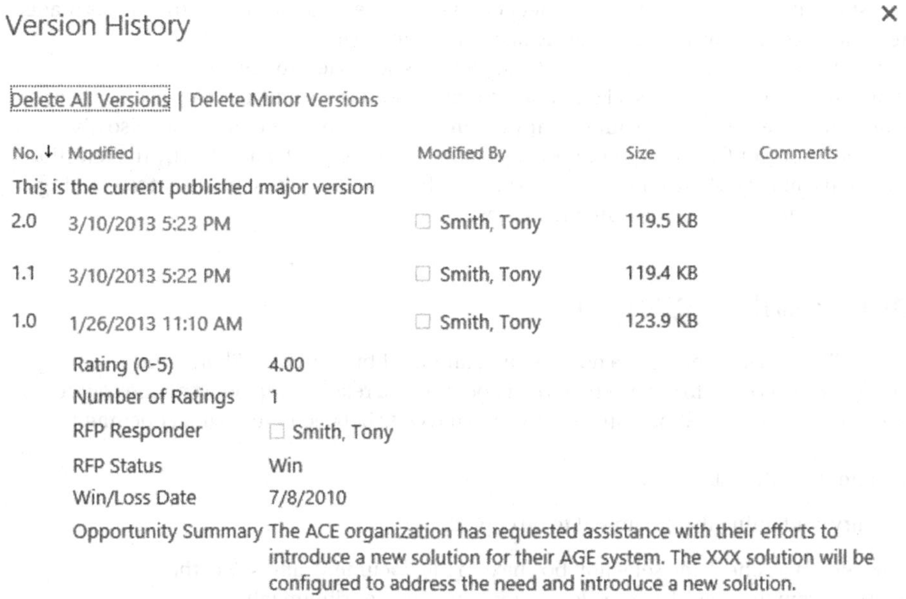

Version History   ✕

Delete All Versions | Delete Minor Versions

No. ↓	Modified		Modified By	Size	Comments
	This is the current published major version				
2.0	3/10/2013 5:23 PM		☐ Smith, Tony	119.5 KB	
1.1	3/10/2013 5:22 PM		☐ Smith, Tony	119.4 KB	
1.0	1/26/2013 11:10 AM		☐ Smith, Tony	123.9 KB	

Rating (0-5)	4.00	
Number of Ratings	1	
RFP Responder	☐ Smith, Tony	
RFP Status	Win	
Win/Loss Date	7/8/2010	
Opportunity Summary	The ACE organization has requested assistance with their efforts to introduce a new solution for their AGE system. The XXX solution will be configured to address the need and introduce a new solution.	

Figure 7-23. *Version history window*

When you access a document's version history details, the version's context menu can be used for the following activities:

- *View Previous Versions*: Selecting the View option opens the selected version for review.

- *Restore Previous Versions*: Restoring a previous version of a document creates a copy of the selected version and makes it the current version. To do this, select the Restore option from the document version's context menu.

- *Delete Previous Versions*: Individuals with appropriate rights can delete specific versions of a file. To delete a version, select the Delete option. To delete all versions, select the Delete All Versions link in the version history window.

Content Approval

Along with versioning, content approval is used to help ensure the integrity of a document and ensure that only approved changes to it are available to its users (enabling content approval is discussed earlier in this section). Content approval lets multiple individuals edit a document but includes a set of people that must approve the changes made by these individuals before the changes to the document are seen by others.

To approve changes made to a document requiring content approval, do the following:

1. Navigate to the library view containing the document.

2. Select the hover panel for the document to be approved or rejected.

3. In the hover panel, select the Approve/Reject option from the Hover Panel menu.

4. In the Approve/Reject window, update the approval status for the document, optionally add a comment, and click the OK button.

The document's approval status is updated to reflect the selection made. If the content was approved, it is made visible to site users. If rejected, the document will not become available to general site users.

A user who has added documents to the library can select the My Submissions view to see the status of documents submitted for approval. This view presents all documents that a user has created and categorizes them by their approval status. If a content approver rejects a document, any comments the approver entered are also displayed in the My Submissions view in the Approver Comments column so that the submitter understands why the rejection occurred. Each time a document in a library where content approval is enabled is edited, its status is set to Pending. It must be approved again before the changes are made available to users.

Copying Documents with Send To

The Send To option in document libraries lets you copy a document to another library in your SharePoint environment. When the Send To option is used to create copies of a document, a relationship between the source document and the copies is established. This relationship allows you to navigate between the original document and its copies.

To create a copy of a document, do the following:

1. Navigate to the library containing the document to be copied.

2. On the document view page, check the selection box next to the document, and select the Other Location option from the Send To drop-down menu on the Files ribbon tab.

3. In the Copy window, do the following:

   a. In the Destination section, enter the URL to the library where you want to copy the file, and specify a name for the file.

   b. In the Update section, identify whether the author of the document is to be prompted to send updates when it is checked in and whether an alert is to be created for the source document so that the user making the copy is kept aware of updates made to the source document.

   c. Click the OK button.

4. In the Copy Progress window, click the OK button.

5. Once the copy is created, click the Done button in the copy progress window.

The file is copied to the identified location. Once copies of a document have been created, you have the ability to view the copies by doing the following:

1. Navigate to the library containing the source document.

2. On the library view page, select the Hover Panel option.

3. In the hover panel, select the View Properties option from the Hover menu.

4. On the document properties view page, select the Manage Copies option from the View ribbon tab.

On the Manage Copies page you can view and select listed copies (see Figure 7-24).

Figure 7-24. *Manage Copies page*

The Manage Copies page allows the following:

- *Edit the properties of a document copy*: Selecting the Edit icon allows editing of the destination location and file name for the copy, as well as whether the author is to be sent an update when the document is checked in. You can also use this option to remove the link to this copy.

- *Create a new copy*: This option allows you to enter details for a new copy, including the destination location and file name, and to identify whether an update is to be sent to the author when the document is checked in.

- *Update existing copies*: This option allows you to identify copies to be updated based on the content of the source.

When viewing a document that is a copy, you can get back to the source file the copy is based upon by selecting the Go to Source Item from the context menu of the document. This will bring you to the source file's document view page.

Item Validation

SharePoint has the ability to validate document properties when a document is added to a library and when the properties are edited. This allows you to add conditional validation requirements to your document's details. To configure validation rules for a library, do the following:

1. Navigate to the library where you wish to configure validation settings.

2. On the library view page, select the Library Settings option from the Library ribbon tab.

3. On the Settings page, select the Validation Settings option from the General Settings section.

4. On the Validation Settings page, do the following:

    a. In the Formula section, define the rules to use to validate the information added to the library.

    b. In the User Message section, enter a message for users to help them understand what is needed to save the information in the library.

    c. Once the information is entered, click the Save button to save the information.

The validation settings for the library are configured. You can also configure validation rules for an individual column in a library when the rules are specific to the column and do not need to reference other columns. To configure validation for individual library columns, do the following:

1. Navigate to the library where you wish to add validation to columns.

2. On the library view page, select the Library Settings option from the Library ribbon tab.

3. On the Settings page in the Columns section, click the title of the column to which you wish to add validation settings.

4. On the Edit Column page, do the following:

    a. Select the Column Validation option to expand the column validation settings.

    b. In the Formula box, enter the formula to use to validate the information entered in the column.

    c. In the User Message box, enter the text to show users to help them identify the needs of the column.

    d. Click the OK button to save the column validation rules.

The validation rule is configured against the updated column.

Document Templates

Document libraries use template files to identify the program and the initial file opened when you select to create a new document in a library. Templates allow you to control the types of documents created within libraries. When you create a document library, as discussed in Chapter 5, you can select from several document templates, including the following:

- *None*: With this choice, the New Document option is not available in the library. Documents can only be uploaded to the library.

- *Microsoft Word 97-2003 Document*: A document created using the New Document option will be a Microsoft Word document (.doc).

- *Microsoft Excel 97-2003 Spreadsheet*: A document created using the New Document option will be an Excel spreadsheet (.xls).

- *Microsoft PowerPoint 97-2003 Presentation*: A document created using the New Document option will be a PowerPoint presentation (.ppt).

- *Microsoft Word Document*: A document created with the New Document option will be a Word document (.docx).

- *Microsoft Excel Spreadsheet*: A document created with the New Document option will be an Excel spreadsheet (.xlsx).

- *Microsoft PowerPoint Presentation*: The New Document option will create a PowerPoint presentation when clicked (.pptx).

- *Microsoft OneNote 2010 Notebook*: With this selected, the New Document option will create OneNote notebook files.

- *Microsoft SharePoint Designer Web Page*: A document created with the New Document option will be a SharePoint page opening in SharePoint Designer for editing.

- *Basic Page*: Generating a new document when this option is selected creates a SharePoint Basic page.

- *Web Part Page*: Generating a new document when this option is selected creates a SharePoint web part page.

After a library has been created, document templates can be edited to establish an appropriate starting point for new documents. For example, if the library will store case studies, the template can include a standard layout and content to all case study documents. To edit the document template for a library, do the following:

1. Navigate to the library where the template needs to be edited.

2. On the library view page, select the Library Settings option from the Library ribbon tab.

3. On the Settings page, select the Advanced Settings option from the General Settings section.

4. On the Advanced Settings page, select the Edit Template option in the Document Template section.

5. In the opened document, make necessary updates to the file, and save the changes.

6. On the Advanced Settings page, click the OK button.

The template is updated. Replacing the template file instead of editing it allows you to use an existing document as the template for a new document created in the library. To choose a document as the template for the library, do the following:

1. Open the library in Windows Explorer view, and ensure that the folder option to show hidden files and folders is in place.

2. Navigate to the Forms folder (a hidden folder) in the Explorer view of the library.

3. Copy the file to use as the template to the Forms folder.

4. On the library view page, select the Library Settings option from the Library ribbon tab.

5. On the Settings page, select the Advanced Settings option from the General Settings section.

6. On the Advanced Settings page, update the file name in the Document Template section to the new file name you chose as the template file. Click the OK button when done.

■ **Note** When a library is configured with content types enabled, you cannot edit the template for the library. With content types enabled, the templates are managed through the content types themselves. Content types are discussed in more detail in Chapter 8.

Rating Library Content

Like lists, libraries can be configured to allow items in them to be rated by site users. Rating lets people declare their general opinion of the files and consolidates these opinions to give an overall evaluation of content. Content rating is configurable as a five star rating model or as Likes placed against items. To use ratings, the rating capability must be activated in the library. Activate ratings by doing the following:

1. Navigate to the library where you want to activate ratings.

2. On the library's view page, select the Library Settings option from the Library ribbon tab.

3. On the Settings page, select the Rating Settings option from the General Settings section.

4. On the Rating Settings page, do the following:

    a. For the "Allow items in this list to be rated" option, select Yes.

    b. For the "Which voting/rating experience you would like to enable for this list" option, select Star Ratings, if you want the five star rating scale, or Likes, if people are to rate content by Liking it.

    c. Click the OK button to save the changes.

Content rating for the library is enabled.

Using Star Ratings

When a library is configured for star ratings, visitors are allowed to specify, on a five star scale, a rating of the document. To rate a document in a library, click on the star that represents the rating you want to give the document. Once you select a rating, the document is updated to include it. That is, your rating becomes part of the document's overall rating average and increases by one the number of ratings counted. If a user rates the document a second time, the previous rating applied is replaced by the newly selected one. Figure 7-25 shows a page with star ratings.

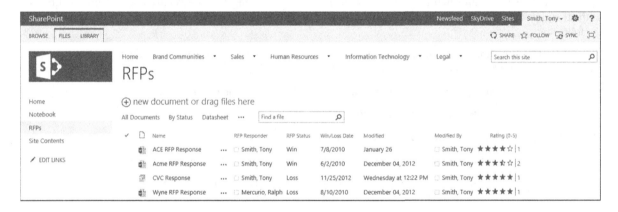

Figure 7-25. *Star ratings*

Using Like Ratings

When ratings are configured to allow users to Like content, documents in the library appear with Like details listed. Like details show the number of Likes the document has received to date. Users can Like a document, if they have not yet done so, or Unlike a document, if they earlier Liked it. To Like a listed document, click the Like link. This updates the document to include your Like. If you decide to Unlike a document, clicking the Unlike option removes your Like and allows you to Like the document again. Figure 7-26 shows a document library with Like ratings enabled.

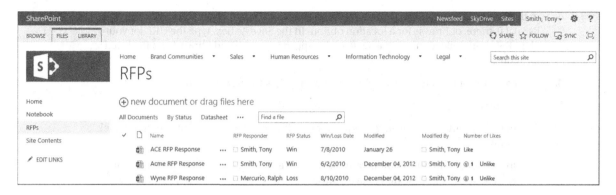

Figure 7-26. *Like ratings*

Document ID Service

The Document ID Service, a feature that can be activated in SharePoint, to provide unique IDs to documents in the site collection. The feature creates a reference to the document that is consistent even if the document is moved around the environment as it matures. The ID is viewable on the document properties page, along with other standard document properties. When this service is active, the document acquires a URL that can be used to access the document regardless of its location. This URL has the following format:

```
http://<SiteCollection>/_layouts/DocIDRedir.aspx?ID=<DocumentID>
```

Once the Document ID Service feature is activated, you can configure the layout of the IDs created and specify the search scope to locate documents based on the ID. To configure the Document ID Service settings, do the following:

1. Navigate to the root site in the site collection.

2. On the site collection home page, select the Site Settings option from the Settings menu.

3. On the Site Settings page, select the Document ID Settings option from the Site Collection Administration section.

4. On the Document ID Settings page, identify the characters to use as a prefix for document IDs and the search scope for locating documents by ID. Then click the OK button to save the Document ID settings.

Working with Documents in Office

There are several capabilities available in Microsoft Office to make working with SharePoint content within Office programs and documents easier.

Saving Documents to SharePoint

Microsoft Office programs can natively save files in SharePoint. When you create a new file in Office or want to save an opened file to SharePoint for the first time, do as follows:

In Office 2010:

1. From the File Menu, select the Save & Send option.

2. On the Save and Send screen, select Save to SharePoint.

3. In the Save to SharePoint area, select the SharePoint location from the Recent Locations list, if it is there, or browse for a location option. In the Save As box, type the URL for your SharePoint site collection, and navigate to the appropriate site and library from the listed locations.

4. Enter a name for the file in the File Name field, and click the Save button.

5. If the library where the file is to be saved has required metadata:

   a. In the presented file warning message, select the Go to Document Information Panel button.

   b. In the Document Information Panel section (see Figure 7-27), enter the document metadata, and click the Retry Save Button.

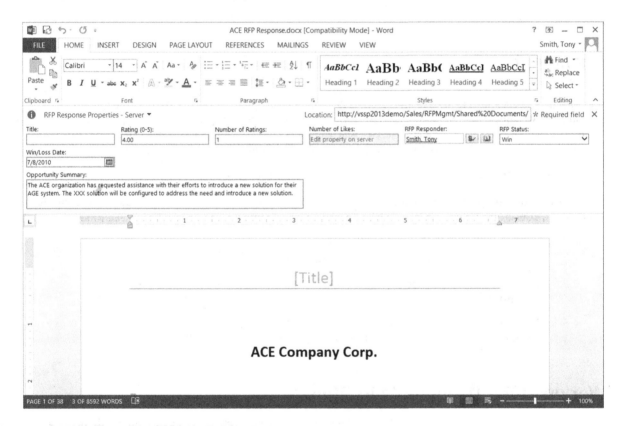

Figure 7-27. *Document Information Panel*

The document is saved to the library.
In Office 2013:

1. From the File Menu, select the Save As option.

2. On the Save As screen, select SharePoint.

3. On the SharePoint screen, select the SharePoint location from the Recent Locations list, if it is there, or browse for a location option. In the Save As box, type the URL for your SharePoint site collection, and navigate to the appropriate site and library from the listed locations.

4. Enter a name for the file in the File Name field, and click the Save button.

5. If the document library where the file is to be saved has required metadata:

    a. In the presented file warning message, select the Go to Document Information Panel button.

    b. In the Document Information Panel section (see Figure 7-27), enter the document metadata, and click the Retry Save Button.

The document is saved to the library.

Editing Document Properties

Document properties managed within SharePoint can be edited directly within Microsoft Office from the Document Information Panel. To edit a document's properties in Office, open the Document Information Panel in either Office 2010 or Office 2013 by selecting the File menu. On the Info page, select the Show Document Panel from the Properties drop-down menu (see Figure 7-28).

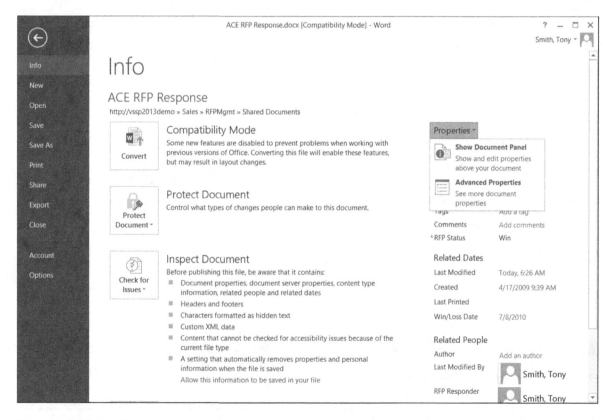

Figure 7-28. *Office File menu*

Accessing Documents While Offline in Outlook

Connecting SharePoint libraries to Outlook makes files accessible in an Outlook folder. When the connection is established, the files in the library are synchronized with Outlook and are available even when you are not connected to SharePoint. This approach works well for a set of documents you need to reference while traveling. For example, if you have a sales team requiring access to marketing materials wherever they are, you can synchronize these files with Outlook. This is done as follows:

1. Navigate to the document library to connect to Outlook.

2. On the library view page, select the Connect to Outlook option from the Library ribbon tab.

3. If a warning message is presented about access to content, click the Allow button.

4. In the confirmation window, click the Yes button to confirm the connection with Outlook.

The library will appear in the SharePoint lists section of Outlook (see Figure 7-29).

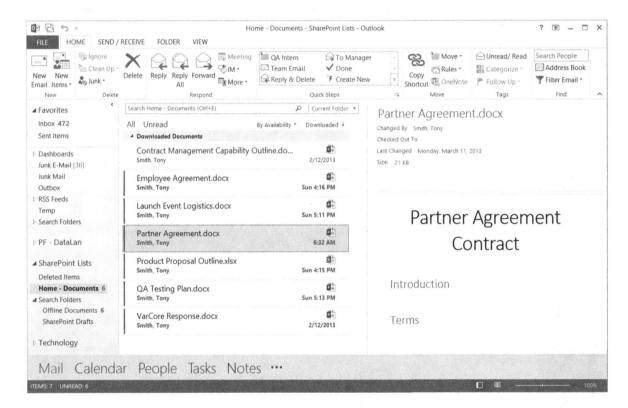

Figure 7-29. *Synchronized library in Outlook*

■ **Note**   When you open a document in the Outlook view, the file is opened for offline editing. Any changes you make to the document from this view must be synchronized with the SharePoint library when the SharePoint server is available.

CHAPTER 8

■ ■ ■

Working with Site Columns, Content Types, and Term Sets

In the first seven chapters we have discussed creating and managing sites, which act as containers for content managed through SharePoint; pages, which present content and information to users; and lists and libraries, which are used to store content managed in SharePoint. In this chapter we discuss site columns, content types, and term sets, all of which are used to standardize and centralize the management of list details and document metadata.

We use site columns to create centrally managed column definitions that can be reused across lists and libraries throughout your portal. Content types combine site columns and other list and library features, including templates, information management policies, and workflows, into reusable definitions applicable across your SharePoint environment. Term sets are centrally managed hierarchical collections that can be used as values in list and library columns.

Site columns, content types, and term sets increase your control over SharePoint lists and libraries. The benefits they offer in managing and working with data include letting you:

- Create information hierarchies as choices for list and library columns. For example, if you manage product-related information and want to track the combined Category, Brand, and Product hierarchy an item is related to, you can make columns that associate each item with the appropriate hierarchy.

- Create columns with choices that are standard across your environment. For example, if you need to track documents' status, you can create a Status column with Draft, Pending Approval, Final, and Archived as choices.

- Associate and combine columns with workflows and content policies to create standard document definitions. For example, to manage contracts across your environment, you can create a Contract document definition that includes standardized columns, workflows to perform contract approvals, and auditing and disposition processes to track and manage the contracts over time.

The aim of this chapter is to make you thoroughly familiar with the creation and use of these capabilities to enhance lists and libraries within your SharePoint environment.

Site Columns

Site columns let you create reusable column definitions in lists, libraries, and content types within SharePoint. There are several scenarios in which you might want to take advantage of site columns to help manage lists and libraries. Site columns are typically used to address these situations:

- You need to use the same column configuration in multiple lists and libraries—for example, a column, Status, that is a choice list with specific values, such as Draft, Pending, Approved, and Expired, across multiple libraries throughout the environment.

- You want to create a column that will look up a list in a site from lists or libraries in other sites. For example, you created a list of departments in the root of your site collection and want lists and libraries throughout the collection to contain a lookup column that uses this departments list as the lookup's source.

- You need to create content types that will contain column definitions. Content type columns must be built from site columns.

Creating Site Columns

Where you create a site column impacts the scope of its availability and usability in lists within the environment. A site column can be created in any site in a site collection hierarchy, but the column will be available only in the site where it is created and in subsites below it. For example, if your site collection has the structure defined in Figure 8-1 and you create a site column in the Information Technology site, the column will be available in the Information Technology site and its subsites, including Projects and Systems, but not in the Human Resources site or its subsites.

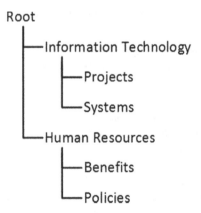

Figure 8-1. Site structure example

To ensure that a site column is available throughout your site collection, create it in the collection's root site. Where a site column is created is also significant when creating reusable lookup columns (how lookup columns can be used to create a column whose values are selected from a list of items in a list or library is discussed in Chapter 5). When you create a lookup column, that column must be created in the same site as the list that is to contain the values to be made available. For example, if you want to make a list of departments available for selection across several sites in your site collection, create a Departments list in the site collection's root. You can then create a site column, also in the root, that references the Departments list. This site column can then be used in lists, libraries, and content types throughout your site collection. (Creating lists and libraries and creating columns in lists and libraries are also discussed in Chapter 5.)

■ **Note** Since creating and managing site columns within SharePoint 2013 requires Manage Lists rights, you must have at least Designer rights within the site to make these adjustments.

To create a site column, do the following:

1. Navigate to the site where the column is to be created. As discussed, this is the site from which the column will be made available to the current site and its subsites. To make it available across your entire site collection, create it in the root site of the collection.

2. On the site's home page, select the Site Settings option from the Settings menu.

3. On the Site Settings page, select the Site Columns option from the Web Designer Galleries section.

4. On the Site Columns page (see Figure 8-2), click the Create option.

Figure 8-2. *Site columns page*

5. On the Create Column screen, do the following:

    a. In the Name and Type section, enter the name it is to be identified as when it is selected for use in lists. Then select the type of column. All the column types and all the same configurations available for creating columns in lists and libraries directly are available here, too (see Chapter 5). A couple of additional types of columns (discussed later in this section) not available for creating standard list columns are available here, however.

      b.   In the Group section, select the site column group in which the site column is to be referenced. The Group selection is used to organize site columns for display in the site columns list and for filtering purposes when site columns are used in lists, libraries, or content types. This selection does not affect availability or functionality of the site columns but is used simply for organizational purposes. By default the Custom Columns group is selected, but you can select some other existing group or create a new group.

■ **Note**   To make site columns easy to find, it is a good practice to organize them into groups that represent their purpose. It is also a good practice not to add your custom site columns to the existing groups in which the standard SharePoint site columns are organized. The purpose is to make it easy to distinguish between standard site columns and those created by users.

---

      c.   In the Additional Column Settings section, specify column-specific information for the column to be created. Optionally create a description for display below the column, and choose whether the column is to be required. Other settings listed vary with the type of column (these settings are discussed in Chapter 5).

      d.   Click the OK button to create the new column.

The site column is created, and you are returned to the Site Columns page.

Additional Column Types for Site Columns

When creating site columns, you have more choices than are available when creating standard columns in lists and libraries (as discussed in Chapter 5). Having more site column choices provides additional options for list and library columns. Among the extra column types are the following:

Full HTML Content with Formatting and Constraints for Publishing

The Full HTML Content with Formatting and Constraints for Publishing column type creates a column that supports full-featured HTML, including the ability to insert tables, links, pictures, video references, and embedded code. This column type, which works much as content zones do in a publishing page, includes no additional column settings when it is created beyond the standard optional description and requirement settings.

Image with Formatting and Constraints for Publishing

The Image with Formatting and Constraints for Publishing column type is used to create columns allowing selection of an image to be displayed in the list item or document details. This type also lacks settings beyond the standard description and requirement settings.

When this type of column is added to a list or library, a link that can be clicked to insert a picture is displayed (see Figure 8-3).

Figure 8-3. *Image with Formatting and Constraints for Publishing column*

Clicking this link brings you to the Edit Image Properties window (see Figure 8-4).

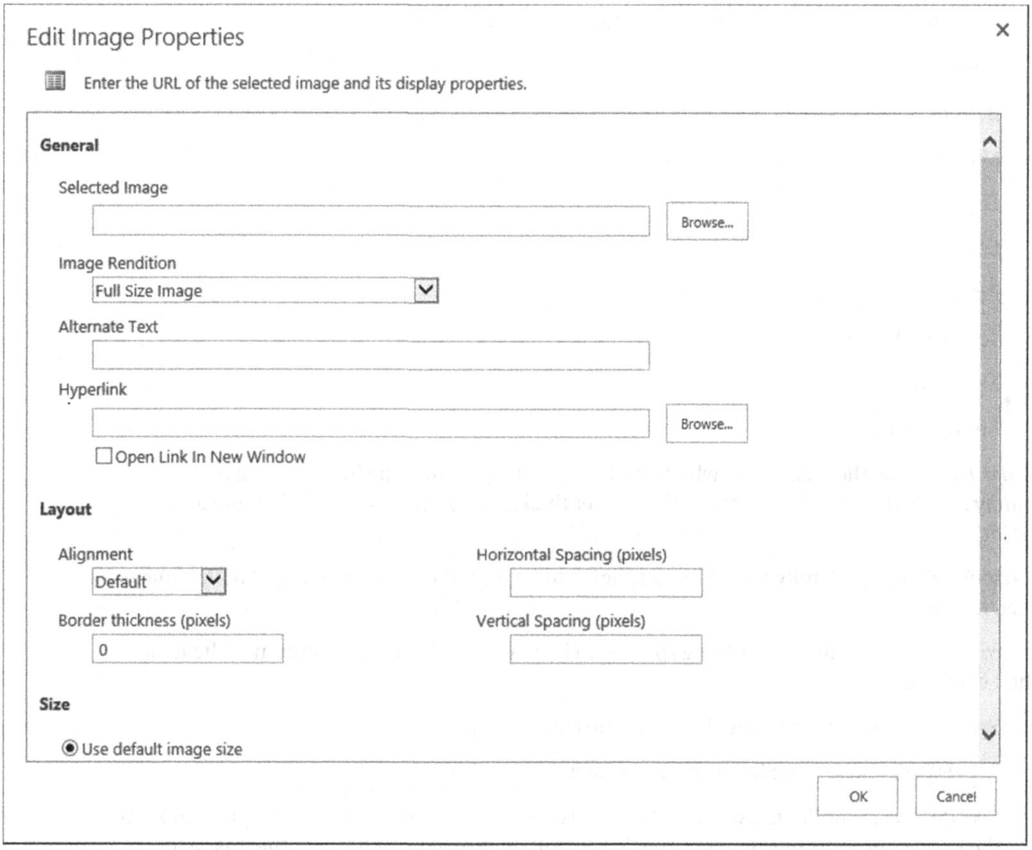

Figure 8-4. *Edit Image Properties window*

The Edit Image Properties window lets you specify the following about the added image:

- *Selected Image*: Choose the image in SharePoint to be displayed in the list item or document details.

- *Image Rendition*: Identify the layout dimensions for the image to be displayed. Default options include these:

  - Full Size Image

  - Display Template Picture 3 Lines (100 × 100)

  - Display Template Picture On Top (304 × 100)

  - Display Template Large Picture (468 × 220)

  - Display Template Video (120 × 68)

- *Alternate Text*: Identify text to be presented when the mouse hovers over the displayed image.

- *Hyperlink*: Enter or select a URL to navigate to when the image is clicked and specify whether the URL is to be navigated to within the current browser window or in a new window.

- *Alignment*: Specify image placement in the item display area. Options are:

  - Default

  - Bottom

  - Middle

  - Top

  - Left

  - Right

  - Top of Text

  - Middle of Text

  - Bottom of Text

- *Border Thickness*: Allow choice of whether a border is to surround the image and, if it is, identify its thickness in pixels (setting the border thickness to 0 pixels will not include a border).

- *Horizontal Spacing*: Identify the padding spacing to be placed to the left and right of the image when it appears.

- *Vertical Spacing*: Identify the padding spacing to be placed to the top and bottom of the image when it appears.

- *Size*: Specify the size of the image display in the column. Options are:

  - *Use default image size*: Shows the image at its actual size.

  - *Specify Size*: Identifies the width or height, using the Maintain Aspect Ratio option to keep the image's proportions intact or specifying both width and height to set the image to a specific size.

Hyperlink with Formatting and Constraints for Publishing

The Hyperlink with Formatting and Constraints for Publishing column type allows creation of hyperlink fields in which you can select a hyperlink to be displayed. This column type has no additional configuration settings beyond the optional description and requirement settings all columns have.

A column created from the Hyperlink with Formatting and Constraints for Publishing column type presents a link for accessing the hyperlink configuration options used to select or enter a URL to add to the list or document properties (see Figure 8-5).

Hyperlink with Formatting	Click to add a new hyperlink

Figure 8-5. Hyperlink with Formatting and Constraints for Publishing field

When you select the "Click to add a new hyperlink" option, the Edit Hyperlink Properties window appears. It allows selection or entry of a URL. In the Edit Hyperlink Properties window, enter the following information:

- *Selected URL*: Allows you to browse to an item in the site collection to reference by its URL or enter a URL to an internal or external web location. You can also specify whether the link opens in the current window or a new one and whether the link display includes the item type icon. For example, if the link is to a Word document, the Word icon would appear with the link.

- *Display Text*: Specifies a name for the URL when it appears to site users.

- *ToolTip*: Identifies any text to appear when the mouse hovers over the hyperlink field.

Summary Links Data

The Summary Links Data column type lets you create site columns that provide the same capabilities seen in the Summary Links web part (discussed in Chapter 4). Like the other columns described, this one has no configuration settings beyond the optional description and requirement details.

With a column in place based on the Summary Links Data field type, while editing items in a list, you have options for managing multiple links in the field (see Figure 8-6).

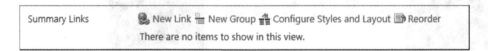

Figure 8-6. *Summary Links Data field*

Within the field you have the following options:

- *New Link*: To add a new link to the field. Clicking the New Link option opens the New Link form, on which you can enter the following details.

    - Create a link either to an item or to a person.

    - If you choose to create a link to a person, enter or select the person the link is to reference.

    - A title for the new link.

    - Optionally a description for the link.

    - Enter the link URL or browse to it.

    - Specify whether the link opens in the current browser window or a new one.

    - Optionally enter a tool tip to appear when hovering over the link.

    - Optionally select an image to associate with the link.

    - Identify a description to be displayed when hovering over the image.

    - Select an optional group within which the link is to be organized.

    - Specify a style for the image and define its layout with style options.

- *New Group*: To create groups under which links can be organized. If you choose this option, identify a name for the group to be created.

- *Configure Styles and Layout*: To define style options for the link's appearance. Choices include the following:

  - The default style for newly created links.

  - The style that any existing links are to be changed to.

  - The style for listed group headers.

  - The number of columns the links are to be presented within.

- *Reorder*: To update the listed items' order by rearranging them as desired.

Rich Media Data for Publishing

The Rich Media Data for Publishing column type permits selection of a video or audio file to be referenced and played in the list or document properties view. A site column created with this column type has no settings beyond the optional description and requirement settings. When added, this column is configured through the "Click here to configure" option (see Figure 8-7).

Figure 8-7. *Rich Media Data for Publishing field*

When this link is clicked the Media ribbon tab appears to allow media configuration settings. These settings let you do the following:

- Identify the media file to reference. You can select a file from the local computer and specify where it is to be placed. You can reference a file already in SharePoint or a file that exists in some other location, or you can remove references to a media file already selected.

- Identify an image preview to represent the audio or video file when it is not playing. You can select a local computer file and specify where to place it, reference a file already in SharePoint or a file existing in some other location, or remove the reference to an already selected preview image.

- Enter the title for the item.

- Identify whether the video is start playing automatically when displayed.

- Identify whether playback is to continually loop or end when done playing.

- Specify either the player's horizontal or vertical size (in pixels) with the aspect ratio maintained or both horizontal and vertical size without maintaining the aspect ratio.

Adding and Configuring Site Columns in Lists and Libraries

Site columns can be added to lists and libraries to manage necessary information. The Departments list example in the "Creating Site Columns" section mentions how to maintain a list of departments in the root of your site collection and then create a site column, also in the root, that is a Lookup column pointing to the Departments list. You can then add this site column to any list or library in any site in the collection. By doing this you create, in any list or library, a Department lookup column that lets you select a department from the items in the Departments list.

To add an existing site column as a column in a given list or library, do as follows:

1. Navigate to the list or library where you wish to add the site column.

2. On the list or library view page, select the List or Library Settings option from the List or Library ribbon tab.

3. On the Settings page in the Columns section, select the Add from Existing Site Columns option.

4. On the Add Columns from Site Columns page, do the following:

   a. Select the group containing the column or columns to be added. This will filter the list of available site columns to only those associated with the selected group.

   b. Select the site columns to add to the list or library from the Available Site Columns, and click the Add button to move the column to the Columns to Add section.

   c. Identify whether the column or columns are to be added to the default view of the list or library.

   d. Click the OK button.

The site column is added to the list or library columns. You can then configure the column settings for the specific list or library by doing as follows:

1. Navigate to the list or library containing the column to configure.

2. On the list or library view page, select the List or Library Settings option from the List or Library ribbon tab.

3. On the Settings page, click the title of the column to be edited in the Columns section.

4. On the Edit Column page, update the column name, description, and requirements settings. Then click the OK button to save the changes.

The column settings are updated. These updates, however, will apply only to the column in the list or library, not to other columns based on the site column in other locations.

Removing a Site Column from a List or Library

If you remove a site column from a list or library, it will no longer be available in that list or library. To remove a site column, do as follows:

1. Navigate to the list or library containing the column to configure.

2. On the list or library view page, select the List or Library Settings option from the List or Library ribbon tab.

3. On the Settings page, click the title of the column to be edited in the Column section.

4. On the Edit Column page, click the Delete button.

5. In the deletion confirmation window, click the OK button.

The column is removed from the list or library. You are returned to the Settings page.

Editing Existing Site Columns

You can edit an existing site column in your SharePoint environment to change its name, group, and specific column type settings. A site column must be edited in the site where it was created. To edit an existing site column, do the following:

1. Navigate to the site where the site column was created.

2. On the site's home page, select the Site Settings option from the Settings menu.

3. On the Site Settings page, select the Site Columns option from the Web Designer Galleries section.

4. On the Site Columns page, click the name of the site column to be edited.

▪ **Note**   If the site column name cannot be clicked, the current site is not where the column was created. In this case, you can identify where the site column was created in the Source column of the view.

---

5. On the Edit Column page, do the following:

   a. Make any necessary updates to the column details.

   b. Identify whether all list columns based on this site column are to be updated to reflect your changes.

   c. Click the OK button to save the changes.

The site column is updated. If you chose to update all columns based on this site column, then all list and library columns using this site column are updated as well.

Deleting Existing Site Columns

Site columns within SharePoint can also be deleted. As when you edit a site column, so too when you delete a site column, do it from the site where the column was created. To delete an existing site column, do the following:

1. Navigate to the site where the site column was created.

2. On the site's home page, select the Site Settings option from the Settings menu.

3. On the Site Settings page, select the Site Columns option from the Web Designer Galleries section.

4. On the Site Columns page, click the name of the site column to be edited.

5. On the Edit Column page, click the Delete button.

6. In the deletion confirmation window, click the OK button.

The site column is deleted, and you are returned to the Site Columns page. Though lists and libraries with the site column still contain the field, you will no longer be able to centralize management of column details or add the column to other lists or libraries.

Content Types

Content types are content definitions used in lists and libraries to specify details about information to be stored, including column definitions for the content, workflows to be run on the content, information management rules defined for the content, and, for libraries, document templates for creating content. Content types also let you store multiple types of content with different content definitions in a list or library, since more than one content type can be associated with a single list or library.

Content types are hierarchical. When you create a content type, you base it upon an existing type. The new content type inherits the settings and properties of the selected parent. In taking advantage of these inheritance settings, you create a hierarchy of content types. Say, for example, that you define a document type called a Customer Document to include Customer as a required field, one that must be entered when new documents of this type are created. This Customer Document content type will be based on the Document content type. It inherits the document definition and adds the Customer field to the definition. You can then create a Project Documents content type and a Sales Documents content type, both based on the Customer content type. For the Project Documents type, you might create a column, Project, to be entered in the document and add it to the required Customer field. For Sales Documents you might require fields identifying the product being sold and include a specific document template to be used when new Sales Documents are created.

Creating and Configuring Content Types

Like site columns, content types can be created at any level of your SharePoint site collection and will be available only in and below the site where it is created. For example, if your site structure is the one seen in Figure 8-8 and we create a content type in the Information Technology site, the content type will be available only in that site and its contained Projects and Systems sites. To have a content type available throughout the site collection, create it in the root site of the collection.

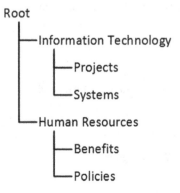

Figure 8-8. Sample site structure

Content types can be shared across site collections through use of Content Type Hubs, SharePoint sites defined as locations with content types shareable across site collections. Your SharePoint technical administrator can identify site collections containing such shareable content types.

To create a new content type within a site, do the following:

1. Navigate to the site where you want to create the new content type.

2. On the site's home page, select the Site Settings option from the Settings menu.

3. On the Site Settings page, select the Site Content Types option from the Web Designer Galleries section.

4. On the Site Content Types page, click the Create option.

5. On the New Site Content Type page, do the following:

    a. Enter the name for the new content type to be created.

    b. Enter an optional description for the content type.

    c. In the Parent Content Type section, select the group containing the content type to use as the parent for the new content type to filter the listed content types by the selected group. Then select the content type to be used as the parent content type for the new one.

    d. In the Group section, identify the group under which to store the new content type, or enter a name for the new group to be created.

    e. Once the information is entered, click the OK button.

The content type is created. You are taken to the Site Content Type page for the newly created content type.

Configuring and Editing an Existing Content Type

Once you create the content type, you need to configure it. Configuring a content type is similar to configuring a list or library and includes doing the following:

- Identifying the site columns to be used in the content type and defining the ordering and requirement settings of the columns.

- Configuring any workflows to be made available to the content type's content.

- Defining any information management policies to be applied to the content type's content.

As your needs for the content type change and mature, you can update the content type details to align with the changing needs.

Editing General Content Type Details

To edit the name, description, and group information entered when the content type was created, do the following:

1. Navigate to the site where the content type was created.

2. On the site's home page, select the Site Settings option from the Settings menu.

3. On the Site Settings page, select the Site Content Types option from the Web Designer Galleries section.

4. On the Site Content Types page, click the name of the content type to be edited.

5.   On the Site Content Type page for the content type to be edited, click the Name, Description, and Group link in the Settings section.

6.   On the Content Type Settings page, update the Name, Description, and Group information as necessary. Then click the OK button.

The general details for the content type are updated, and you are returned to the Site Content Type page.

Configuring Content Type Advanced Settings

Along with general settings, you can also configure advanced settings for the content type. These include changes to the document template and the content type within the library and list pages. To configure these advanced settings for a content type, do the following:

1.   Navigate to the site where the content type was created

2.   On the site's home page, select the Site Settings option from the Settings menu.

3.   On the Site Settings page, select the Site Content Types option from the Web Designer Galleries section.

4.   On the Site Content Types page, click the name of the content type to be edited.

5.   On the Site Content Type page for the content type to be edited, click the Advanced Settings link from the Settings section.

6.   On the Advanced Settings page, do the following:

   a.   When the content type is based on a document-centric content type, the Document Template section will be available. In this section you can enter the URL for a document to be used as the template for the content type or choose to upload a document template to use as the document template for the content type.

   b.   In the Read Only section, specify whether the content type is to be alterable. If the setting is Read-Only, no change to the content type will be permitted.

   c.   In the Update Sites and Lists section, identify whether changes made to the template and read-only settings are to be inherited by all lists and libraries where the content type is in use.

   d.   Once all information has been entered, click the OK button to save the information.

The changes to the document template and the read-only settings are updated. If you chose to update all lists and libraries where the content type is in use, all of these lists and libraries are updated to reflect the changes made.

Manage a Content Type's Workflows

As mentioned earlier in this section, content types can have workflows associated with them for items in the list or library where the content type is in use. To add or edit these workflows, do the following:

1.   Navigate to the site where the content type was created.

2.   On the site's home page, select the Site Settings option from the Settings menu.

3.   On the Site Settings page, select the Site Content Types option from the Web Designer Galleries section.

4.   On the Site Content Types page, click the name of the content type to be edited.

5. On the Site Content Type page for the identified content type, click the Workflow Settings link from the Settings section.

6. On the Workflow Settings page, do the following:

    a. To add a workflow:

        i. Click the Add a Workflow Link.

        ii. On the Add a Workflow page, configure the new workflow, or use SharePoint Designer to create a new workflow for the content type (creating and managing workflows is discussed in Chapter 9).

    b. To edit an existing workflow:

        i. Click the name of the workflow to be edited.

        ii. Edit the details of the workflow (editing workflows is discussed in detail in Chapter 9).

The workflows are appropriately updated for the content type.

Managing a Content Type's Information Management Policies

Information management policies, which define auditing, retention, barcoding, and labeling requirements for items, can be configured for content types. To configure information management policies for a content type or to edit an existing policy, do the following:

1. Navigate to the site where the content type was created.

2. On the site's home page, select the Site Settings option from the Settings menu.

3. On the Site Settings page, select the Site Content Types option from the Web Designer Galleries section.

4. On the Site Content Types page, click the name of the content type to be edited.

5. On the Site Content Type page for the identified content type, click the Information Management Policy Settings link from the Settings section.

6. On the Edit Policy page, configure the information management policy for the content type (configuring information management policies is discussed in Chapter 9).

The information management policies are added and updated appropriately.

Managing Content Type Document Information Panel Settings

When a content type is based on a document parent type, you can also change the document information panel settings for the content type. (Thus, you can change the information panel discussed in Chapter 7 when working with Microsoft Office documents.) You are able to edit the existing information management panel or select a new panel. To manage the information management panel settings for a content type, do the following:

1. Navigate to the site where the content type was created.

2. On the site's home page, select the Site Settings option from the Settings menu.

3. On the Site Settings page, select the Site Content Types option from the Web Designer Galleries section.

4.   On the Site Content Types page, click the name of the content type to be edited.

5.   On the Site Content Type page for the content type to be managed, click the Document Information Panel Settings link in the Settings section.

6.   On the Document Information Panel Settings page, do the following:

   a.   In the Document Information Panel Template section, identify whether the Microsoft Office Document Information Panel is to show the default template, an existing custom template, or a new custom template to be uploaded or created in place.

   b.   In the Show Always section, identify whether the document information panel is to open automatically when the document opens.

   c.   Click the OK button when the document information panel settings updates are complete.

The document information panel settings are saved, and you are returned to the Site Content Type page for the associated content type.

Adding Site Columns to Content Types

Columns for the content type can be defined and changed, though only site columns can be used within content types. You can select existing site columns or create new ones when working within a content type. To add existing site columns to the content type, do the following:

1.   Navigate to the site where the content type was created.

2.   On the site's home page, select the Site Settings option from the Settings menu.

3.   On the Site Settings page, select the Site Content Types option from the Web Designer Galleries section.

4.   On the Site Content Types page, click the name of the content type to be edited.

5.   On the Site Content Type page for the content type to be edited, click the Add from Existing Site Columns link in the Columns section.

6.   On the Add Columns page, do the following:

   a.   In the Select Columns section, select the group in which the site column exists to filter the list of site columns, and then select the desired site column from the Available Columns section.

   b.   Click the Add button to move the selected site columns to the Columns to Add section.

   c.   In the Update List and Site Content Types section, identify whether all content types based on this one are to inherit the site column changes.

   d.   Click the OK button to save the changes.

The content type is updated to include the added site columns. If you chose to update content types inheriting from this one, then these types are also updated to include the newly added site columns.

You can also add not-yet-existing columns as site columns to a content type by creating the new site columns as part of the process of adding them to the content type. To create site columns while updating a content type, do the following:

1. Navigate to the site where the content type was created.

2. On the site's home page, select the Site Settings option from the Settings menu.

3. On the Site Settings page, select the Site Content Types option from the Web Designer Galleries section.

4. On the Site Content Types page, click the name of the content type to be edited.

5. On the Site Content Type page for the content type to be managed, click the Add from New Site Column link in the Columns section.

6. On the Create Column page, do the following:

    a. In the Name and Type section, enter the name for the new Site Column, and select the type for the column.

    b. In the Group section, identify the group under which the site column is to be listed, or enter a name for the new group.

    c. In the Additional Column Settings section, specify the details for the column. They include an optional description and the requirement settings for the column. In this section also list any column-specific settings for the type of column selected (column-specific settings for different column types are discussed in Chapter 5).

    d. In the Update List and Site Content Types section, identify whether the column added is to be inherited by content types inheriting from the current type.

    e. In the Column Validation section, enter any optional column validation rules for the new column being created.

    f. Click the OK button to save the information.

The new site column is created within the current site and added to the content type. You are returned to the Site Content Type page for the associated content type.

Editing Site Column Settings for a Content Type

You can also edit the details for site columns associated with the content type. Do so as follows:

1. Navigate to the site where the content type was created.

2. On the site's home page, select the Site Settings option from the Settings menu.

3. On the Site Settings page, select the Site Content Types option from the Web Designer Galleries section.

4. On the Site Content Types page, click the name of the content type to be edited.

5. On the Site Content Type page for the content type to be edited, click the name of the site column to be edited in the Columns section.

6. On the Change Content Type Column page, do the following to update the site column:

   a. In the Site Column Information section, click the Edit Site Column link to navigate to the Site Column Management page (discussed in the "Site Columns" section, above).

   b. In the Column Settings section, identify whether the column is Required, Optional, or Hidden. Hidden columns do not appear on list or library forms.

   c. In the Update List and Site Content Types section, identify whether all content types inheriting from this type are to include the changes made.

   d. Once the changes have been made, click the OK button.

The changes are made to the column, and you are returned to the Site Content Type page for the associated content type.

Removing Site Columns from a Content Type

Removing a site column from a content type does not delete the column from SharePoint. It is simply no longer available as part of the content type's definition. To remove a site column from a content type, do as follows:

1. Navigate to the site where the content type was created.

2. On the site's home page, select the Site Settings option from the Settings menu.

3. On the Site Settings page, select the Site Content Types option from the Web Designer Galleries section.

4. On the Site Content Types page, click the name of the content type to be edited.

5. On the Site Content Type page for the content type to be edited, click the name of the site column to delete.

6. On the Change Content Type Column page, click the Remove button.

7. On the confirmation window click the OK button.

The site column is removed from the content type.

Changing the Column Ordering of a Content Type

To change the order in which the columns associated with a content type are displayed when editing and viewing content details, do the following:

1. Navigate to the site where the content type was created.

2. On the site's home page, select the Site Settings option from the Settings menu.

3. On the Site Settings page, select the Site Content Types option from the Web Designer Galleries section.

4. On the Site Content Types page, click the name of the content type to be edited.

5. On the Site Content Type page for the content type to be edited, click the Column Order option from the Columns section.

6. On the Column Order page, do the following:

    a. In the Column Order section, change the Position from Top numbers to set the sort order for the columns.

    b. In the Update Sites and Lists section, identify whether the ordering changes are to be inherited by content types based on this type.

    c. Click the OK button to save the changes.

The changes are made, and you are returned to the Site Content Type page for the associated content type.

Deleting Content Types

Content types not in use in lists or libraries can be deleted. If you try to delete a content type that is in use, a message indicating that the type is in use appears, and deletion is not allowed. To delete a content type not in use, do the following:

1. Navigate to the site where the content type was created.

2. On the site's home page, select the Site Settings option from the Settings menu.

3. On the Site Settings page, select the Site Content Types option from the Web Designer Galleries section.

4. On the Site Content Types page, click the name of the content type to be edited.

5. On the Site Content Type page for the selected content type, click the Delete this Content Type link from the Settings section.

6. In the deletion confirmation window, click the OK button.

The content type is deleted, and you are returned to the Site Content Types page.

Configuring Content Types for Lists and Libraries

Once content types have been created and properly configured, they can be configured for use in lists and libraries.

Enable the Use of Content Types in Lists and Libraries

Before enabling a content type for use in a list or library, you must enable the list or library to support the use of content types. To enable the use of content types in a list or library, do the following:

1. Navigate to the list or library where you want to enable content types.

2. On the list or library view page, select the List or Library Settings option from the List or Library ribbon tab.

3. On the Settings page, select the Advanced Settings option from the General Settings section.

4. On the Advanced Settings page in the Content Types section, select Yes for the "Allow management of content types?" option, and click the OK button.

The ability to manage content types within the list or library is enabled, and the Content Type section is added to the Settings page, where you can manage content type details for the list or library.

Adding Content Types to Lists and Libraries

After enabling the management of content types in a list or library, you can add an existing content type for use there. Do so as follows:

1. Navigate to the list or library where you want to add content types.

2. On the list or library view page, select the List or Library Settings option from the List or Library ribbon tab.

3. On the Settings page, click the Add From Existing Site Content Types option in the Content Types section.

4. On the Add Content Types page, do the following:

    a. Select the group in which the content type exists from the group's drop-down in order to filter the list or content types to include only those contained in the selected group.

    b. Select the content type to add in the Available Site Content Types list, and click the Add button to add the selected type to the Content Types to Add section.

    c. Once the desired content type has been added to the Content Types to Add section, click the OK button.

The content type is added to the list or library.

Managing Content Type Defaults and Order in a List or Library

Once content types are added to a list or library, they can be managed. Management of content types includes specifying which of the available ones is the default for the list or library and identifying the order of the listed content types and whether the listed types are visible to users when adding new items. To manage these content types, do the following:

1. Navigate to the list or library where content types need to be managed.

2. On the list or library view page, select the List or Library Settings option from the List or Library ribbon tab.

3. On the Settings page, select the "Change new button order and default content type" option from the Content Types section.

4. On the Change New Button Order page, do the following:

    a. Identify the order of the listed content types by updating the Position from Top value. Placing an item in the first position makes that item the default content type for the list or library.

    b. Identify whether a content type is to be visible. Unchecking the Visible option in front of the item makes it unavailable for selection when creating new items.

    c. Once all changes are made, click the OK button to save the changes.

The updates to the content type ordering and visibility details for the list or library are saved.

Deleting a Content Type from a List or Library

You can remove content types from a list or library as long as at least one content type is left. To remove a content type, do the following:

1. Navigate to the list or library where you want to remove the content type.

2. On the list or library view page, select the List or Library Settings option from the List or Library ribbon tab.

3. On the Settings page, click the name of the content type to delete from the Content Types section.

4. On the List Content Types page, click the Delete this Content Type option from the Settings section.

5. In the deletion confirmation window, click the OK button.

The content type is removed from the list or library, and you are returned to the Settings page.

Configuring Content Type Settings in a List or Library

In a content type available in a list or library, you can configure several content type settings for that instance of the type. Your configuration settings will impact the content type only in that list or library, not in other locations in the environment. Configurable settings for the current list or library instance of a content type include the following:

- *Name and Description*: The name of the content type as it exists in the list or library, along with its optional description.

- *Advanced Settings*: For libraries, the document template available when new documents are created using the content type can be updated. You can also identify whether the content type is read-only in the list or library.

- *Workflows*: Allows you to add, alter, or delete workflows affecting the content type (workflows are discussed in detail in Chapter 9).

- *Information Management Policies*: Lets you create additional information management policies affecting the content type in the current list or library. You can also edit and delete existing policies (information management policies are discussed in detail in Chapter 9).

- *Document Information Panel Settings*: In document libraries, their Microsoft Office application ribbon settings can be managed or altered.

You alter any of these options in the Settings page of the list or library by selecting the appropriate content type to manage and then selecting the appropriate option from the list's or library's Content Type page.

Working with Content Types in a List or Library

With content types enabled in a list or library, you create a new item by clicking the New Item option from the Items ribbon tab or New Document option from the Files ribbon tab. The new item is created based on the default content type in that list or library. If only a single content type is available, it is the default content type. When multiple content types are associated with a list or library, the New Item or New Document option also includes a drop-down menu from which you select the content type to base a new item on. You create a new item in a list or library based on a specific content type by doing the following:

1. Navigate to the list or library where you want to create the new item.

2. On the list or library view page, do the following:

    a. For lists, select the content type from the New Item drop-down menu on the Items ribbon tab.

    b. For libraries, select the content type from the New Document drop-down menu on the Files ribbon tab (see Figure 8-9).

Figure 8-9. *New Document drop-down menu*

The new item is created based on the selected content type.

To upload a document to a library configured with multiple content types, identify the content type on which the document is to be based in the Edit Properties window that appears after the file to upload has been selected (see Figure 8-10).

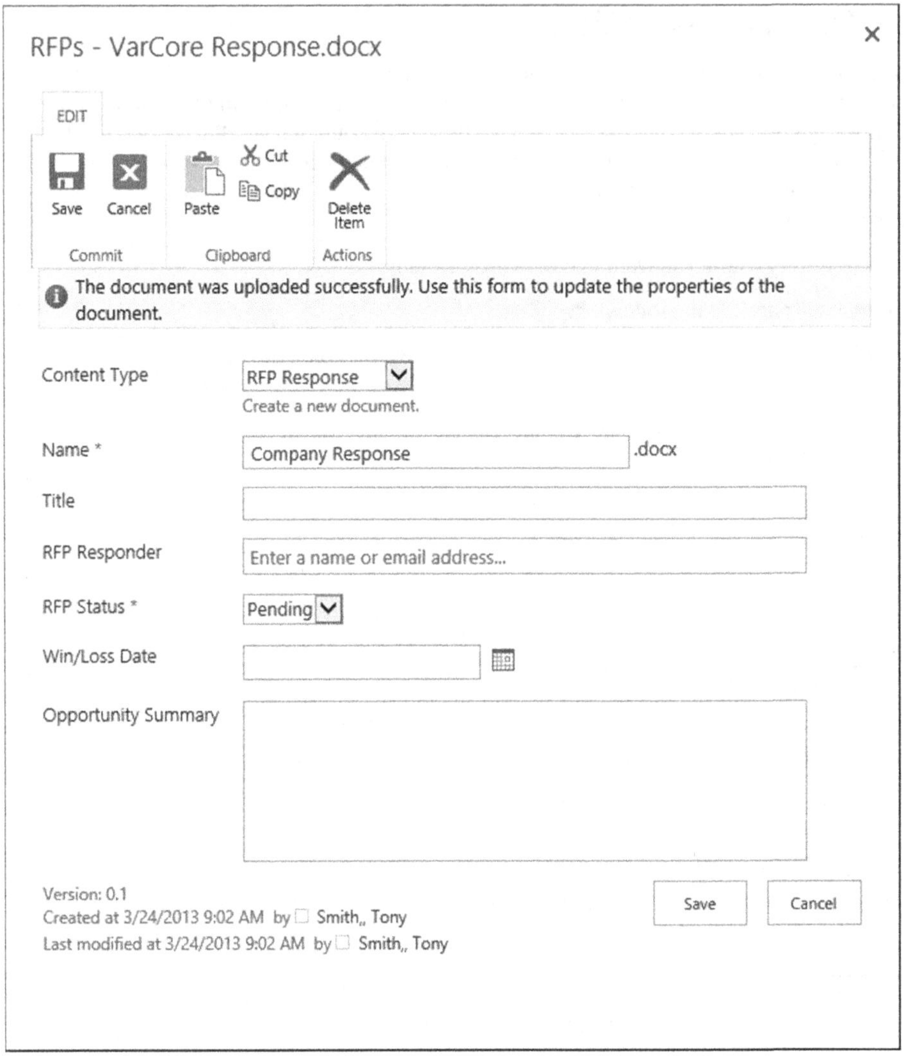

Figure 8-10. Document Edit Properties window

In the Edit Properties window the content type is initially set to the library's default type. To update it, select any available content type. When a type is selected, the listed document properties are updated to reflect those configured for the selected type.

Term Sets

Terms are stored in term sets. Term sets are sets of hierarchical values that allow you to create formal taxonomies within SharePoint. These sets—are managed within term stores. A term store (see Figure 8-11) enables you to manage all aspects of term sets, including structures, contained terms, and security.

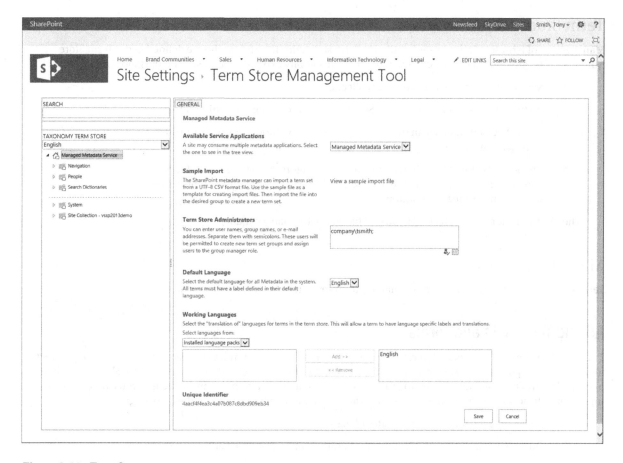

Figure 8-11. *Term Store*

Term sets are used in SharePoint for the following:

- To create a set of standard values for use as metadata in list or library columns.

- To control the site navigation options available in the SharePoint site (navigation management is discussed in detail in Chapter 3).

Term sets can be created to be available within a single site collection or across your SharePoint environment. Making a term set available across site collections must be done by your SharePoint technical administrator. Once created, terms within a set can be managed by anyone with appropriate rights (managing terms is discussed later in this chapter).

Term Store Administration

Management of term sets and terms is handled by term store administrators, who are defined in the Term Store Administration area. To specify which individuals have the ability to manage term sets, do the following:

1. Navigate to the root site in your site collection.

2. On the site's home page, select the Site Settings option from the Settings menu.

3. On the Site Settings page in the Site Administration section, click the Term Store Management option.

4. On the Term Store Management Tool page (see Figure 8-11) in the Term Store Administrators section, add the users who are to get administration rights to the term store. Then click the Save button.

The term store administrators list is updated based on the changes made.

Managing Term Sets

Term store administrators can create and manage term sets and terms within those sets.

Adding Term Sets and Terms

There are two approaches to adding term sets and terms to the term store. You can create term sets and terms directly in the store or import terms by using a CSV file. To import a term set from a CSV file, first create a CSV file having the appropriate structure and information to import. SharePoint includes a sample import file that you can review to understand the format for importing term sets. To access the sample import file, do the following:

1. Navigate to the root site in your site collection.

2. On the site's home page, select the Site Settings option from the Settings menu.

3. On the Site Settings page in the Site Administration section, click the Term Store Management option.

4. On the Term Store Management Tool page, click the View a Sample Import File option from the Sample Import section of the page.

5. On the Open or Save prompt, select the Open option.

The sample term set import file is opened (see Figure 8-12).

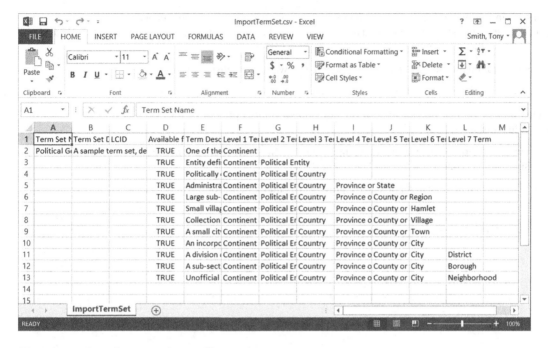

Figure 8-12. *Sample term set import file*

Once you have created and properly configured your term set import file, you can import a term set by doing the following:

1. Navigate to the root site in the collection where you want to create the term set.

2. On the site's home page, select the Site Settings option from the Settings menu.

3. On the Site Settings page, click the Term Store Management option from the Site Administration section.

4. On the Term Store Management Tool page, select the Import Term Set option from the desired group's context menu (see Figure 8-13).

Figure 8-13. *Term store groups context menu*

5. In the Term Set Import window, select the CSV file to import, and click the OK button.

The term set is imported, and you are returned to the Term Store Management Tool page. As mentioned earlier, you can also create term sets and their contained terms directly in the term store management page. To create a term set in the term store, do the following:

1. Navigate to the root site in the collection where you want to create the term set.

2. On the site's home page, select the Site Settings option from the Settings menu.

3. On the Site Settings page, click the Term Store Management option from the Site Administration section.

4. On the Term Store Management Tool page, select the New Term Set option from the desired group's context menu (see Figure 8-13).

5. In the newly created term set box (see Figure 8-14), enter a name for the new term set.

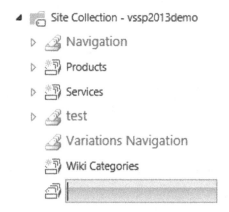

Figure 8-14. *New term set entry box*

6. Select the context menu for the newly created Term Set (see Figure 8-15), and select the Create Term option.

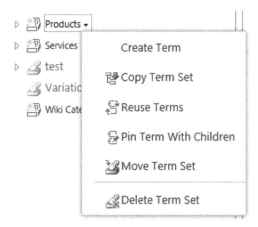

Figure 8-15. *Term set context menu*

7. In the newly created Term box, enter a name for the new term.

8. After each term is entered, a new Term box appears. Continue to enter new term names into the Term boxes until all terms are properly entered, then press Enter in the last empty term box to stop creating new terms.

9. Subterms can be created under existing terms by doing the following:

   a. Select the Create Term option from the existing term's context menu (see Figure 8-16).

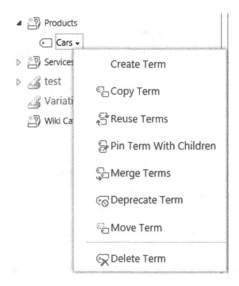

Figure 8-16. *Term context menu*

   b. In the newly created Term box, enter a name for the new term.

   c. After each term is entered, a new Term box appears. Continue to enter new term names into the Term boxes until all terms are properly entered, then press Enter in the last empty term box to stop creating new terms.

Managing Term Set Properties

Once a new term set is created, you can configure its properties by clicking the name of the term set to show its properties screen. On this screen, which is broken down into four tabs, you can manage the following details:

- On the General tab:

  - *Term Set Name*: Changes the term set's name.

  - *Description*: Optionally lets you enter a description for the term set.

  - *Owner*: That is, the owner of the term set—set by default to the person who created the set.

  - *Contacts*: Lets you specify an optional contact e-mail address for the term set.

- *Stakeholders*: Identifies people who are to be notified when changes are made to the term set.

- *Submission Policy*: Lets you configure the term set as closed or open. Closed term sets only have terms added by metadata managers. Open term sets can have terms added by term set users.

- On the Intended Use tab:

  - Identify whether the term set can be used in lists and libraries for metadata assignment to list items and documents.

  - Identify whether the term set can be used for site navigation.

  - Identify whether the terms in the set can be used as reference details to support faceted navigation.

- On the Custom Sort tab:

  - Identify whether terms are to be sorted alphabetically or via a custom sort order using an available label.

- On the Custom Properties tab:

  - Add custom metadata properties and values to be associated with the term set.

In the term set's context menu are other management options that can also be used to manage some of the set's details. Options in the term set context menu (see Figure 8-15) include the following:

- *Create Term*: Enables creation of terms to be contained in the term set (term creation is discussed earlier in this section).

- *Copy Term Set*: Lets you make a copy of the selected term set, including its properties and all of its contained terms.

- *Reuse Terms*: Allows selection of terms for reuse in other term sets. Reuse of a term set permits selection of other term sets where those terms are made available. Any changes to a reused term are reflected in all copies of that term across all term sets that use it. To view the locations where a term is used, select any instance of the term, and view the Member Of area on the General tab of the Term Properties page.

- *Pin Term With Children*: Permits selection of a term set to be pinned within another set. This allows reuse of the terms but also allows them to be managed by different security groups in other term sets.

- *Move Term Set*: Lets you move a selected term set under a different group within the term store.

- *Delete Term Set*: Deletes the selected term set.

Managing Term Properties

Like term sets, terms have manageable properties. To manage the properties of a term, click the term within the Term Store Management Tool page, and the properties page for the selected term appears. Term properties that can be managed include the following:

- On the General tab:

  - Identify whether the term is available when assigning metadata to lists and libraries.

  - Identify the language for the term's labels.

- Optionally enter a description for the term.

- Identify the term's default label, which is initially set to the term name entered when the term was created.

- List any additional labels for the term.

- List term sets that the term belongs to

- On the Custom Properties tab:

  - Identify properties associated with the term that are to be available in all locations where the term is used.

  - Identify properties associated with the term that are to be available only when the term is used in the current term set.

As with term sets, in the context menu for listed terms there is a set of options that allow management of the following details (see Figure 8-16):

- *Create Term*: Provides the ability to create terms contained within the selected term (creating terms is discussed earlier in this section).

- *Copy Term*: Lets you make a copy of the selected term, including its properties and all its contained terms.

- *Reuse Terms*: Allows selection of terms for reuse in other term sets. Reuse of terms permits selection of other term sets where those terms can be used. Any changes to a reused term are reflected in all copies of that term across the term sets that use it. To view the locations where a term is used, select any instance of the term, and view the Member Of area on the General tab of the Term Properties page.

- *Pin Term With Children*: Permits selection of a term to be pinned with another term set. This allows reuse of the terms, but also allows them to be managed by different security groups.

- *Merge Terms*: Lets a selected term be merged into another. The properties of the destination term, including labels, are updated with the selected term's details.

- *Deprecate Term*: Makes the term unselectable when the term set is in use. The term continues to exist and be available for reference if it was previously assigned to content, but it can no longer be assigned to other items.

- *Move Term*: Allows you to move a selected term under a different term set or term within a term set.

- *Delete Term*: Deletes the selected term.

Working with Terms as Metadata

Once configured, term sets and terms can be used as values within Managed Metadata columns in lists and libraries. (Creating columns, including Managed Metadata columns, is discussed in Chapter 5.) When configuring a Managed Metadata column, select an available term set to use as the source for the options in the column. When a Managed Metadata column is edited within a list item's or document property's details, it appears as a text field followed by a term selector (see Figure 8-17).

Services

Figure 8-17. *Managed Metadata column*

You can add values to this field by typing in the text box itself. Take advantage of the type-ahead capability, which will list matching terms below the entered text to allow easy selection of the desired term. You can also add terms by clicking on the Term Selector icon and directly selecting the desired term from the presented term set hierarchy.

CHAPTER 9

Workflows and Information Management Policies

Thus far the various resources available in SharePoint to store and manage information have been discussed. You have seen how to manage media (such as standard documents, videos, and images), structured data (such as contact lists, tasks, and events), and web content (such as web pages). This chapter discusses how process can be introduced into the environment to enhance information, allowing it to be incorporated into associated business processes and to help automate information management. Also discussed is how information management policies can be introduced to control content as it matures and to audit changes to information.

Workflow Overview

One of SharePoint's most significant capabilities is that it can be used to automate business processes through creation of workflow solutions. Automate business processes when you want to do any of the following:

- Reduce the length of time a process takes.

- Ensure consistency through iterations of a process.

- Reduce errors by ensuring information integrity and reducing manual work.

- Provide auditability and oversight of work efforts.

Workflows automate business processes by creating a series of interconnected activities organized to represent the business process. SharePoint 2013 includes two separate workflow platforms. One platform, already present in previous versions of SharePoint, is the Windows Workflow Foundation workflow services, now called the SharePoint 2010 workflow platform. The SharePoint 2010 workflow platform is available by default in SharePoint 2013 as part of the SharePoint installation. It provides the same capabilities available in SharePoint 2010, which is discussed in this chapter.

SharePoint 2013 also includes the SharePoint 2013 workflow platform. It leverages Microsoft's new Workflow Manager Services, which are designed to be used across applications, including SharePoint. Workflow Manager Services are installed and configured separately from standard SharePoint services and so must be specially set up in SharePoint environments. The SharePoint 2013 workflow platform provides the following benefits over the SharePoint 2010 workflow platform:

- Having workflows hosted outside SharePoint allows scaling of workflow services without impacting general SharePoint access and allows workflow services to support multiple applications.

- An integrated Visual Designer is available in SharePoint Designer for creating workflow processes through a Visio-like interface that can be used only when creating workflows for the SharePoint 2013 workflow platform.

- Additional actions are included, such as looping, web service access, and task process management.

Whether you create workflows using the SharePoint 2010 workflow platform or the SharePoint 2013 workflow platform, workflow capabilities are found in all versions of SharePoint 2013, from SharePoint Foundation through SharePoint Server.

Workflow Lists

Before we discuss the different types of workflows and how to create them, we need to discuss the structure of the SharePoint resources that support workflows. Workflow data is managed in the site where the workflow is created, and a set of lists stores information about the running instances of a workflow. A workflow instance is a single execution of the workflow process. You can have multiple instances of a workflow running at any given time in your site. However, only one instance at a time can run on a specific list item or document.

Workflow Tasks List

A workflow tasks list is used to store and manage tasks assigned through workflows. These lists are located in the same site that contains the workflows they support. There can be more than one workflow tasks lists per site, and multiple workflows can save tasks to the same workflow tasks list. The list used by a workflow process is defined as part of the configuration of the workflow. A workflow tasks list's structure varies depending on whether it is created to support SharePoint 2010 or SharePoint 2013 workflows. A workflow tasks list created to support SharePoint 2010 workflow platform tasks contains the structure described in Table 9-1.

Table 9-1. *SharePoint 2010 Workflow Platform Workflow Tasks List*

Column	Required	Type	Properties
% Complete	No	Number	Minimum Value: 0 Maximum Value: 100 Show as Percentage
Assigned To	No	Person or Group	Allow People or Groups
Description	No	Multiple Lines of Text	Allow Rich Text
Due Date	No	Date and Time	Date Format: Date Only Display Format: Standard
Predecessors	No	Lookup	Lookup to current list Title column Allow Multiple Values
Related Items	No	Related Items	
Start Date	No	Date and Time	Date Format: Date Only Display Format: Standard Default Value: Today's Date

(*continued*)

Table 9-1. (*continued*)

Column	Required	Type	Properties
Status	No	Choice	Options: • Not Started • In Progress • Completed • Deferred • Waiting on someone else Default Option: Not Started Display: Drop-Down Menu
Task Group	No	Person or Group	Allow People or Groups
Title	Yes	Single Line of Text	

When a workflow tasks list to support SharePoint 2013 workflow platform processes is created, the list will include the structure shown in Table 9-2.

Table 9-2. *SharePoint 2013 Workflow Platform Workflow Tasks List*

Column	Required	Type	Properties
% Complete	No	Number	Minimum Value: 0 Maximum Value: 100 Show as Percentage
Assigned To	No	Person or Group	Allow People or Groups
Completed	--	Calculated	Calculation: =[% Complete>=1 Return Type: Yes/No
Description	No	Multiple Lines of Text	Allow Enhanced Rich Text
Due Date	No	Date and Time	Date Format: Date Only Display Format: Friendly
Predecessors	No	Lookup	Lookup to current list Task Name column Allow Multiple Values
Priority	No	Choice	Options: • (1) High • (2) Normal • (3) Low Default Option: (2) Normal Display: Drop-Down Menu
Related Items	No	Related Items	
Start Date	No	Date and Time	Date Format: Date Only Display Format: Friendly
Task Name	Yes	Single Line of Text	

(*continued*)

Table 9-2. (*continued*)

Column	Required	Type	Properties
Task Outcome	No	Task Outcome	Options • Approved • Rejected
Task Status	No	Choice	Options: • Not Started • In Progress • Completed • Deferred • Waiting on someone else Default Option: Not Started Display: Drop-Down Menu

While workflow tasks lists are used by the workflow processes to store and manage tasks assigned through the workflow processes, they can also be used to provide visibility into tasks requiring attention and can be rolled up into consolidated task views, such as the My Tasks list available in My Site. These types of views provide visibility into workflow processes and activities. (The My Site Tasks view is discussed in Chapter 12.)

■ **Note**   Tasks associated with the SharePoint 2010 workflow platform processes and tasks associated with the Share-Point 2013 processes cannot exist in the same list since these types have different workflow tasks list structures. When creating workflows, you do not get the option to create SharePoint 2013 workflow tasks in a list created for SharePoint 2010 workflows, and vice versa.

Workflow History List

The second type of list used to support workflow processes is the workflow history list. Like a workflow tasks list, a history list resides in the same site where the workflow executes, and there can be multiple instances of workflow history lists in the same site. These lists are used to track the activities occurring as part of the running workflow instances. The lists contain the running history of actions, outcomes, and comments that can be used to audit a workflow from inception through completion. Workflow history lists are the source for the workflow history details shown when you view workflow interface details, which are discussed later in this chapter.

Unlike workflow tasks lists, which are visible and directly accessible in sites, workflow history lists are hidden and directly accessible only by typing in the path to the list in the web browser. The path is in the format `http://<SiteURL>/Lists/<HistoryList>`, where `SiteURL` is the full path to the site where the workflow resides and `HistoryList` is the workflow history list's name, as it was identified when the workflow was created. By default this list is named Workflow History.

The workflow history list supports a workflow by acting as the log for all the actions that have occurred as part of the workflow. Unlike the workflow tasks list, workflow history lists have the same structure whether they are created to support SharePoint 2010 workflows or SharePoint 2013 workflows. These lists have the structure detailed in Table 9-3.

Table 9-3. *Workflow History List*

Column	Required	Type	Properties
Event Type	Yes	Event Type	
Workflow History Parent Instance	Yes	Single Line of Text	
Workflow Association ID	Yes	Single Line of Text	
Workflow Template ID	Yes	Single Line of Text	
List ID	Yes	Single Line of Text	
Primary Item ID	No	Integer	
User ID	Yes	Person or Group	Allow People or Groups
Date Occurred	Yes	Date and Time	Date Format: Date and Time
Group Type	No	Integer	
Outcome	No	Single Line of Text	
Duration	No	Number	
Description	No	Single Line of Text	
Data	No	Multiple Lines of Text	

While the information in the workflow history lists become available when workflow instance details are viewed, you can also use the lists for reporting sources; that is, to create audit reporting for a specific processes instance.

Creating and Configuring Workflows

There are several approaches for creating workflows that provide different levels of workflow capability and require different levels of workflow creation skills. Approaches for creating workflows include the following:

- *Out of the Box*: Available in SharePoint are several reusable workflows that can be used to create some basic workflow processes. Reusable workflows, configured directly through the web browser, can be created by anyone having Design permissions or higher in a list or library. The available Out of the Box workflows depend on the version of SharePoint you are using. (Out of the Box reusable workflows are discussed later in this chapter.)

- *SharePoint Designer*: SharePoint Designer 2013 is a free downloadable tool that allows creation of comprehensive SharePoint 2010 foundation workflows and SharePoint 2013 foundation workflows. SharePoint Designer includes a series of events, actions, conditions, and steps for defining workflow solution functionality. Like out of the box workflows, these workflows require Design permissions in order to be created. (SharePoint Designer workflows are discussed later in this chapter.)

- *Visual Studio*: Visual Studio is used to create .NET workflows, which leverage the underlying workflow services directly and are created by SharePoint developers as compiled solutions. They must be deployed by a SharePoint technical administrator.

■ **Note**   There are also several third-party solutions available to create workflows in SharePoint. These solutions provide a variety of levels of integration and often include a visual workflow design interface and an extended set of available actions to incorporate into workflow processes.

The methods and capabilities necessary to create workflows depend on the type of workflow you are creating. This section focuses on how to create and configure the available out of the box reusable workflows and how to create and configure workflows in SharePoint Designer.

Creating Out of the Box Workflows

As mentioned earlier, some workflows available in SharePoint can be created directly through the web browser based on a set of reusable workflows. Which reusable workflows are available by default in SharePoint depends on the version of SharePoint in place and the features enabled in the site collection. The following out of the box workflows are available by default in SharePoint 2013.

Three-State Workflow

The Three-State workflow lets you promote a list item or document through three phases. With the move to each stage defined in the workflow the following activities occur:

- A defined task is assigned to an identified individual.

- The individual assigned the task is alerted to it via e-mail.

- The status of the item is moved to the next status once the defined task is marked complete.

The Three-State workflow is the only workflow available in all versions of SharePoint: Foundation, Server Standard, and Server Enterprise. This workflow is based on the SharePoint 2010 workflow foundation. To make this workflow available, you must have the Three-State Workflow site collection feature enabled in the site collection where you want to use it.

Once the Three-State Workflow site collection feature is enabled in your site collection, you can add the Three-State reusable workflow template to your lists and libraries. To create a new Three-State workflow, do the following:

1. Navigate to the list or library where you want to create the Three-State workflow.

2. On the list or library view page, select the Add a Workflow option from the Workflow Settings drop-down menu on the List or Library ribbon tab (see Figure 9-1).

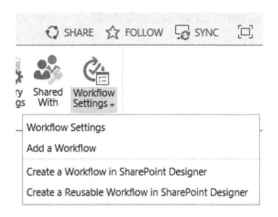

Figure 9-1. Workflow Settings drop-down menu

3. On the Add a Workflow page (see Figure 9-2), do the following:

a. In the Workflow section, select the Three-State option from the Select a Workflow Template list.

b. In the Name section, enter a name for the workflow. This name cannot be the same as that for any other workflow created for the same list or library.

c. In the Task List section, select the workflow task list where tasks generated by it are to be created. All SharePoint 2010 workflow foundation tasks lists in the site are listed, along with a Tasks (new) option. If selected, it creates a new workflow tasks list.

d. In the History List section, select the workflow history list that is to be used to store workflow history details for workflow instances. All workflow history lists in the site are listed for selection, along with a New History List option that can be selected to create a new workflow history list to store the workflow history.

e. In the Start Options section, identify how to initiate the workflow for items in the list or library. Selectable options are these:

- *Allow this workflow to be manually started by an authenticated user with Edit permissions*: Identifies whether to start the workflow manually. In configuring this option, specify whether users with Edit Item permissions can start the workflow or whether they must have Manage List Permissions, such as Designers, to start it.

- *Creating a new item will start this workflow*: Identifies whether the workflow starts automatically when an item is added to the list or library.

f. Once all information is entered, click the Next button.

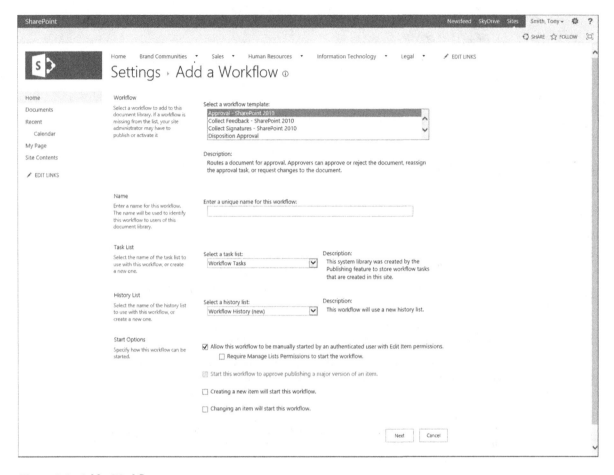

Figure 9-2. *Add a Workflow page*

4. On the Customize the Three-State Workflow page (see Figure 9-3), do the following:

a. In the Workflow States section, identify the field containing the status values the item will be promoted through. This must be a Choice field with at least three value options defined. Once this is selected, identify the three values the item is to be promoted through by identifying the Initial State value, Middle State value, and Final State value.

b. In the "Specify what you want to happen when a workflow is initiated" section, do the following

i. In the Task Details section, identify information to include in the tasks created to support the movement from the first stage to the second stage. Include the following details:

1. Task Title: identifies details to be placed in the task's Title field. This information is created as a concatenation of entered text and an optional field value of the list item or document.

2. Task Description: identifies details to be included in the task's Description field. This information includes entered text, an optional field value from the list item or document, and an optional link to the item.

3. Task Due Date: identifies a date for the task's Due Date field. This date is based on a date field in the item defaulted to the Created date.

4. Task Assigned To: identifies details for the task's Assigned To value. This information can be based on any Person or Group field value associated with the list item or a specifically entered user. The default option is the Created By user value of the item.

ii. In the E-mail Message Details section, do the following:

1. Identify whether an e-mail is to be sent to the individual assigned the task. Identify an e-mail address to send the message to and specify whether you want the e-mail sent to the assigned individual.

2. Identify the subject for the message to be sent and whether to include the task title in the subject line.

3. Identify details for the body of the e-mail message. Specify whether to include a link to the list item or document and what text to include.

c. In the "Specify what you want to happen when a workflow changes to its middle state" section, do the following:

i. In the Task Details section, identify information to include in the tasks created to support the movement from the second stage to the third stage. Include the following details:

1. Task Title: identifies details to place in the task's Title field. This information is created as a concatenation of entered text and an optional field value of the list item or document.

2. Task Description: identifies details to include in the task's Description field. This information includes entered text, an optional field value from the list item or document, and an optional link to the item.

3. Task Due Date: identifies the date for the task's Due Date field based on a date field in the item defaulted to the Created date.

4. Task Assigned To: identifies details for the task's Assigned To value. This information can be based on any Person or Group field value associated with the list item or a specifically entered user. The default option is the item's Created By user value.

ii. In the E-mail Message Details section, do the following:

1. Identify whether an e-mail should be sent to the individual responsible for the task. Identify an e-mail address to send the message to and specify whether you want it sent to the assigned individual.

2. Identify the subject of the message to be sent and whether to include the task title in the message's subject line.

3. Identify the details in the body of the e-mail message. Specify whether to include a link to the list item or document and, if it is included, with what text.

5. Once the information is entered, click the OK button.

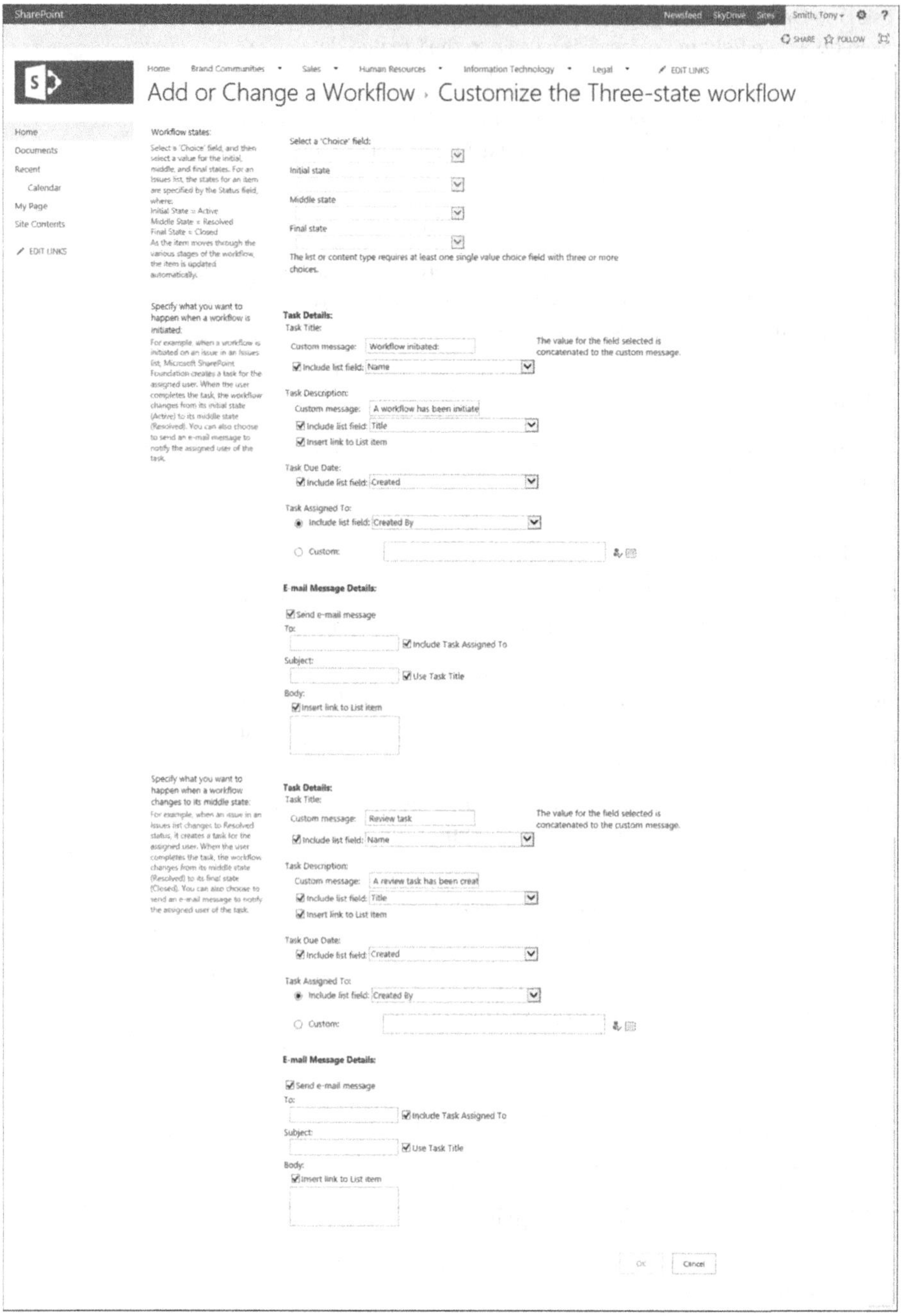

Figure 9-3. *Customize the Three-State workflow page*

The workflow is created, and you are returned to the list or library view page.

Approval — SharePoint 2010 Workflow

Another out of the box reusable workflow based on the SharePoint 2010 workflow platform is the Approval—SharePoint 2010 workflow, which is only in SharePoint Server Standard and Enterprise and requires activation of the Workflows site collection feature before it becomes available. This workflow allows a list item or document to be approved by one or more people in a combination of serial and parallel approval stages. The Approval workflow is one of the most commonly used out of the box workflows in SharePoint.

To create an Approval workflow, do the following:

1. Navigate to the list or library where you want to create the workflow.

2. On the list or library view page, select the Add Workflow option from the Workflow Settings drop-down menu on the List or Library ribbon tab.

3. On the Add Workflow page (see Figure 9-2), do the following:

    a. In the Workflow section, select the Approval — SharePoint 2010 workflow template from the Select a Workflow Template list.

    b. In the Name section, enter a name for the workflow. It cannot be a name used for any other workflow created in the same list or library.

    c. In the Task List section, select the workflow task list where tasks generated by this workflow are to be created. All workflow tasks lists in the site will be of the same type, either SharePoint 2010 workflow or SharePoint 2013 workflow. A Tasks (new) option is also listed. If selected, it creates a new workflow tasks list.

    d. In the History List section, select the workflow history list in which to store workflow history details for the workflow instances. All of the site's workflow history lists are listed for selection, along with a New History List option that can be selected to create a new workflow history list to store the workflow history.

    e. In the Start Options section, identify how to initiate the workflow for items in the list or library. Selectable options are these:

        •   *Allow this workflow to be manually started by an authenticated user with Edit permissions*: Identifies whether to start the workflow manually. In configuring this option, specify whether users with Edit Item permissions can start the workflow or whether they must have Manage List Permissions, such as Designers, to start it.

        •   *Start this workflow to approve publishing a major version of an item*: Available when versioning is enabled in the list or library, it identifies whether to start the workflow when a major version of the item is being published and require it for the publishing to complete.

        •   *Creating a new item will start this workflow*: Identifies whether to start the workflow automatically when an item is added to the list or library.

        •   *Changing an item will start this workflow*: Identifies whether to start the workflow automatically when an item in the list or library is altered.

    f. Once all information is entered, click the Next button.

4. On the Change a Workflow page for the new workflow (see Figure 9-4), do the following:

   a. In the Approvers section, select the users or groups to assign the approval tasks to and identify whether to perform the approvals one at a time (serially) or all at the same time (in parallel). If you wish, add more stages by clicking the Add a New Stage option to assign additional approval tasks, also serially or in parallel.

   b. In the Expand Groups section, identify how to handle groups when they are assigned to perform approvals. Identify whether to assign a task to each member of the group, creating individual tasks for each person, or to the group itself, requiring a group member to take ownership of the task and thus making only one individual responsible for approval.

   c. In the Request section, enter the text for the message sent to task assignees.

   d. In the Due Date for All Tasks section, optionally identify a date on which all the tasks are due.

   e. In the Duration Per Task section identify how many days, weeks, or months to allot each task for completion from the date of assignment.

   f. In the Duration Units section, identify whether the Duration Per Task value is in days, weeks, or months.

   g. In the CC section, identify individuals to be CC'ed on task notifications.

   h. In the End on First Rejection section, identify whether to mark the item rejected if it is rejected by one of the assigned approvers.

   i. In the End on Document Changes section, identify whether to mark the item rejected if it is modified while the workflow is running.

   j. In the Enable Content Approval section, identify whether approval of an item with content approval enabled is to have its content approval status updated based on the workflow outcome.

   k. Once all the information is entered, click the Save button to create the new workflow.

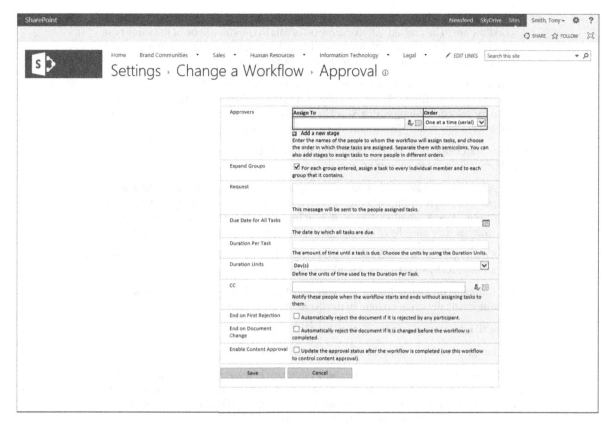

Figure 9-4. *Customize the Approval workflow page*

The workflow is created, and you are returned to the list or library view page.

Collect Feedback — SharePoint 2010 Workflow

The Collect Feedback — SharePoint 2010 workflow, another out of the box SharePoint 2010 workflow, is available in SharePoint Server Standard and Enterprise when the Workflows site collection feature is enabled. This workflow is used to route items to individuals for collecting comments and feedback. Feedback is then compiled and returned to the item's owner.

To create a new Collect Feedback workflow, do the following:

1. Navigate to the list or library where you want to create the workflow.

2. On the list or library view page, select the Add Workflow option from the Workflow Settings drop-down menu on the List or Library ribbon tab.

3. On the Add Workflow page,(see Figure 9-2), do the following:

    a. In the Workflow section, select the Collect Feedback — SharePoint 2010 workflow from the Select a Workflow Template list.

    b. In the Name section, enter a name for the workflow. It cannot be a name used for any other workflow created in the same list or library.

    c.   In the Task List section, select the workflow task list where tasks generated by this workflow are to be created. All workflow tasks lists in the site will be of the same type, either SharePoint 2010 workflow or SharePoint 2013 workflow. A Tasks (new) option is also listed. If selected, it creates a new workflow tasks list.

    d.   In the History List section, select the workflow history list in which to store workflow history details for the workflow instances. All of the site's workflow history lists are listed for selection, along with a New History List option that can be selected to create a new workflow history list to store the workflow history.

    e.   In the Start Options section, identify how to initiate the workflow for items in the list or library. Selectable options are these:

       •   *Allow this workflow to be manually started by an authenticated user with Edit permissions*: Identifies whether to start the workflow manually. In configuring this option, specify whether users with Edit Item permissions can start the workflow or whether they must have Manage List Permissions, such as Designers, to start it.

       •   *Creating a new item will start this workflow*: Identifies whether to start the workflow automatically when an item is added to the list or library.

       •   *Changing an item will start this workflow*: Identifies whether to start the workflow automatically when an item in the list or library is altered.

    f.   Once all information is entered, click the Next button.

4.   On the Change a Workflow page for the new workflow (see Figure 9-5), do the following:

    a.   In the Reviewers section, select the users or groups to assign the review tasks to and identify whether to perform reviews one at a time (serially) or all at the same time (in parallel). If you wish, add more stages by clicking the Add a New Stage option to assign additional review tasks, also serially or in parallel.

    b.   In the Expand Groups section, identify how to handle groups when they are assigned to perform reviews. Identify whether to assign a task to each member of the group, creating individual tasks for each person, or to the group itself, requiring a group member to take ownership of the task and thus making only one individual responsible for the review.

    c.   In the Request section, enter the text for the message sent to task assignees.

    d.   In the Due Date for All Tasks section, optionally identify a date on which all tasks are due.

    e.   In the Duration Per Task section, identify how many days, weeks, or months to give each assignee to complete the task from the date of assignment.

    f.   In the Duration Units section, identify whether the Duration Per Task value is in days, weeks, or months.

    g.   In the CC section, identify individuals to be CC'ed on task notifications.

    h.   In the End on Document Changes section, identify whether to end the workflow process if it is modified while the workflow is running.

    i.   Once all the information is entered, click the Save button to create the new workflow.

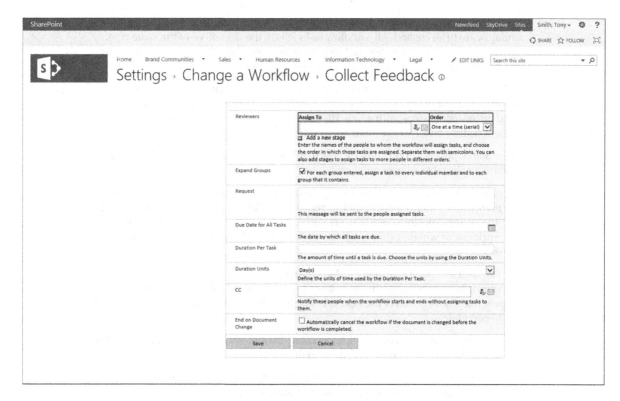

Figure 9-5. *Customize the Collect Feedback workflow page*

The workflow is saved, and you are returned to the list or library view page.

Collect Signatures — SharePoint 2010 Workflow

The Collect Signatures — SharePoint 2010 out of the box reusable workflow can collect a set of digital signatures for Microsoft Office documents. This workflow integrates with the digital signature capabilities of Microsoft Office to allow management of signature collections. As with the other out of the box workflows discussed, the Collect Signatures workflow leverages the SharePoint 2010 Workflow Foundation and is made available in a site collection by enabling the Workflow site collection feature.

To create a Collect Signatures workflow, do the following:

1. Navigate to the list or library where you want to create the workflow.

2. On the list or library view page, select the Add Workflow option from the Workflow Settings drop-down menu on the List or Library ribbon tab.

3. On the Add Workflow page (see Figure 9-2), do the following:

    a. In the Workflow section, select the Collect Signatures — SharePoint 2010 workflow template from the Select a Workflow Template list.

    b. In the Name section, enter a name for the workflow. It cannot be a name used for any other workflow created in the same list or library.

c. In the Task List section, select the workflow task list where tasks generated by this workflow are to be created. All workflow tasks lists in the site will be of the same type, either SharePoint 2010 workflow or SharePoint 2013 workflow. A Tasks (new) option is also listed. If selected, it creates a new workflow tasks list.

d. In the History List section, select the workflow history list in which to store workflow history details for the workflow instances. All of the site's workflow history lists are listed for selection, along with a New History List option that can be selected to create a new workflow history list to store the workflow history.

e. In the Start Options section, identify how to initiate the workflow for items in the list or library. Selectable options are these:

   • *Allow this workflow to be manually started by an authenticated user with Edit permissions*: Identifies whether to start the workflow manually. In configuring this option, specify whether users with Edit Item permissions can start the workflow or whether they must have Manage List Permissions, such as Designers, to start it.

   • *Start this workflow to approve publishing a major version of an item*: Available when versioning is enabled in the list or library, it identifies whether to start the workflow when a major version of the item is being published and require it for the publishing to complete.

   • *Creating a new item will start this workflow*: Identifies whether to start the workflow automatically when an item is added to the list or library.

   • *Changing an item will start this workflow*: Identifies whether to start the workflow automatically when an item in the list or library is altered.

f. Once all information is entered, click the Next button.

4. On the Change a Workflow page for the new workflow (see Figure 9-6), do the following:

   a. In the Signers section, assign users or groups to sign the item, and identify whether to add the signatures one at a time (serially) or all at the same time (in parallel). If you wish, add more stages by clicking the Add a New Stage option to assign additional signing tasks, also serially or in parallel.

   b. In the CC section, identify individuals to be CC'ed on task notifications.

   c. Once all the information is entered, click the Save button to create the new workflow.

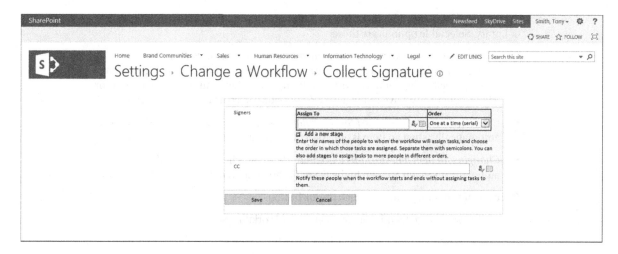

Figure 9-6. *Customize the Collect Signature Workflow Page*

The workflow is saved, and you are returned to the library view page.

Disposition Approval Workflow

The Disposition Approval workflow is used to help manage retention and expiration of content and the approval processes tied to deciding whether to delete or keep content. The Disposition Approval workflow is typically used in conjunction with information management retention policies (discussed in a later section). Like other out of the box reusable workflows discussed so far, the Disposition Approval workflow is built on the SharePoint 2010 workflow foundation. This workflow is made available in sites by activating the Disposition Approval Workflow site collection feature. To create and configure this workflow, do the following:

1. Navigate to the list or library where you want to create the workflow.

2. On the list or library view page, select the Add Workflow option from the Workflow Settings drop-down menu on the List or Library ribbon tab.

3. On the Add Workflow page (see Figure 9-2), do the following:

    a. In the Workflow section, select the Disposition Approval workflow template from the Select a Workflow Template list.

    b. In the Name section, enter a name for the workflow. It cannot be a name used for any other workflow created in the same list or library.

    c. In the Task List section, select the workflow task list where tasks generated by this workflow are to be created. All workflow tasks lists in the site will be of the same type, either SharePoint 2010 workflow or SharePoint 2013 workflow. A Tasks (new) option is also listed. If selected, it creates a new workflow tasks list.

    d. In the History List section, select the workflow history list in which to store workflow history details for the workflow instances. All of the site's workflow history lists can be selected, along with a New History List option that, if selected, creates a new workflow history list.

e.   In the Start Options section, identify how to initiate the workflow for items in the list or library. Selectable options are these:

- *Allow this workflow to be manually started by an authenticated user with Edit permissions*: Identifies whether to start the workflow manually. In configuring this option, specify whether users with Edit Item permissions can start the workflow or whether they must have Manage List Permissions, such as Designers, to start it.

- *Creating a new item will start this workflow*: Identifies whether to start the workflow automatically when an item is added to the list or library.

- *Changing an item will start this workflow*: Identifies whether to start the workflow automatically when an item in the list or library is altered.

f.   Once all information is entered, click the Ok button.

The Disposition workflow is created, and you are taken to the Workflow Settings page.

Creating SharePoint Designer Workflows

When workflows you want to create in SharePoint go beyond what the out of the box workflows offer, SharePoint Designer 2013 is the solution. As mentioned earlier, SharePoint Designer is a freely downloadable tool that lets you create sophisticated workflow processes in SharePoint. You can create three types of workflows using SharePoint Designer: list and library workflows, site workflows, and reusable workflows.

Creating SharePoint Designer List and Library Workflows

The first workflow type that SharePoint Designer 2013 can create is the list and library workflow. This type is similar to an out of the box workflow in that it is configured directly in a list or library and executed in that list's or library's items.
   SharePoint Designer workflows are comprised of a combination of steps, conditions, and actions.

- *Steps*: Steps are used to group and organize conditions and actions. They make it easier to understand and manage the workflow process.

- *Conditions*: Conditions are rules used to determine whether actions are run.

- *Actions*: Actions are activities to be performed in the workflow.

There are several approaches for creating SharePoint Designer workflows in a library. To create a SharePoint Designer workflow in a list or library, do the following:

1.   Navigate to the list or library where you want to create the workflow.

2.   On the list or library view page, select the Create a Workflow in SharePoint Designer option from the Workflow Settings drop-down menu on the List or Library ribbon tab.

3.   If prompted to confirm allowing the web site to open a program on the computer, click the Allow button.

4.   If prompted with a notification that a web site wants to open a program, click the Allow button.

5.   If prompted with a warning that some files may be harmful and asking whether you still want to open the file, click the Yes button.

6. In the Create List Workflow window in SharePoint Designer (see Figure 9-7), enter the following information:

    a. Name of the workflow.

    b. An optional description for the workflow.

    c. Platform Type identifying whether to create the workflow as a SharePoint 2010 Workflow or a SharePoint 2013 Workflow.

    d. Click the OK button.

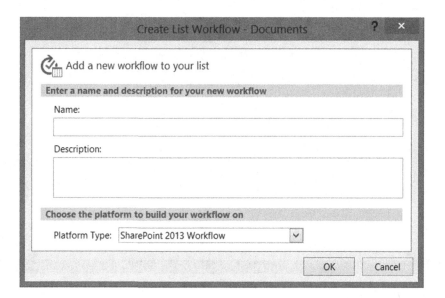

Figure 9-7. *SharePoint Designer Create List Workflow window*

■ **Note** The SharePoint 2013 Workflow option is available when you create a workflow only if the SharePoint 2013 Workflow Platform has been installed and configured for use by a SharePoint technical administrator in your SharePoint environment.

---

7. On the Workflow screen in SharePoint Designer (see Figure 9-8), build the workflow logic by adding necessary actions, conditions, and steps. On the Workflow screen, save the workflow by choosing the Save option from the workflow ribbon tab. Saving the workflow does not make it available to be run; it only saves work completed to date.

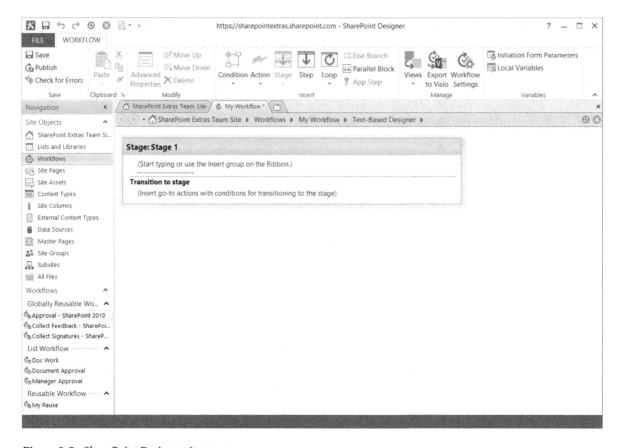

Figure 9-8. *SharePoint Designer site screen*

8. Once the workflow is configured, select the Check for Errors option from the Workflow ribbon tab. This option verifies that there are no syntax or configuration errors in the workflow structure. If there are errors, they are identified. If there are no errors, a message indicating that the workflow contains no syntax errors appears.

9. Once the workflow has no errors, you can publish it by selecting the Publish option from the Workflow ribbon tab. The workflow is published and made available to be run in the list or library.

The created workflow is published for use in SharePoint. We discuss running workflows later in this chapter.

Creating SharePoint Designer Site Workflows

Our discussion so far has concerned creating workflows in lists and libraries. You can also create workflows in sites; for example, when the process you want to run is not directly linked to any one item in a list or library but instead will act on multiple items in a single list or library or across multiple lists and libraries. Say that you have a human resources workflow that calculates employee time-off carryover days. You may want to make it a site workflow, since it does not relate to any one item in a list. Instead it needs to access all items in a list of employee time-off details.

No out of the box site workflows of this sort are available in SharePoint. You would create them using SharePoint Designer by doing as follows:

1. Open SharePoint Designer.

2. Open your site in SharePoint Designer by selecting the Open Site option in the Open SharePoint Site section.

3. On the SharePoint Designer site screen (see Figure 9-8), click the Site Workflow option from the Site ribbon tab.

4. In the Create Site Workflow window, enter the following:

    a. A name for the new site workflow.

    b. An optional description for the workflow.

    c. The workflow's platform type: SharePoint 2013 Workflow or SharePoint 2010 workflow. As mentioned previously, the SharePoint 2013 Workflow option is available only if the SharePoint 2013 Workflow Foundation is installed and configured for use in your SharePoint environment.

    d. Click the OK button.

5. On the Workflow screen in SharePoint Designer (see Figure 9-8), build the workflow logic by adding necessary actions, conditions, and steps. On the Workflow screen, save the workflow by choosing the Save option from the workflow ribbon tab. Saving the workflow does not make it available to be run; it only saves work completed to date.

6. Once the workflow is configured, select the Check for Errors option from the Workflow ribbon tab. This option verifies that there are no syntax or configuration errors in the workflow structure. If there are errors, they are identified. If there are no errors, a message identifying that the workflow contains no syntax errors appears.

7. Once the workflow has no errors, you can publish it by selecting the Publish option from the Workflow ribbon tab. The workflow is published and made available to be run in the site.

The created workflow is published for use in SharePoint. We discuss running workflows later in this chapter.

Creating Reusable Workflows

Along with list and library and site workflows, you can also create reusable workflows in SharePoint. Reusable workflows are workflow definitions, or templates, that are created so that site users can associate them with their lists or libraries, just as they might pick out of the box workflows. How broadly a reusable workflow can be used in your environment depends on how generic you make the logic when you create the workflow. For example, if your workflow references a specific column, only lists and libraries containing that column will work with the reusable workflow.

To create a reusable workflow, do the following:

1. Open SharePoint Designer.

2. Open your site in SharePoint Designer by selecting the Open Site option in the Open SharePoint Site section.

3. On the SharePoint Designer site screen (see Figure 9-9), click the Reusable Workflow option from the Site ribbon tab.

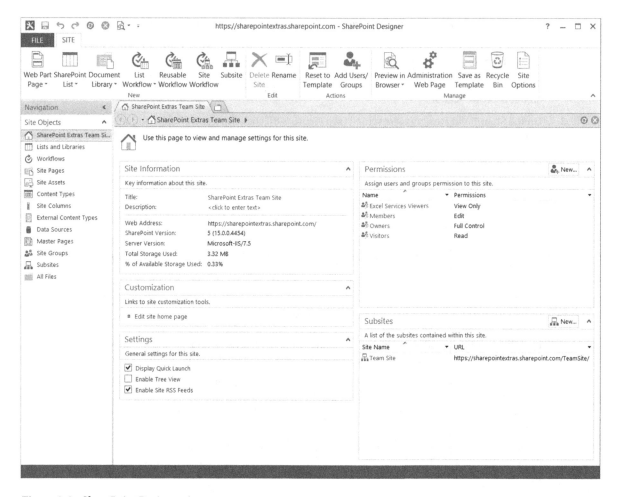

Figure 9-9. *SharePoint Designer site screen*

4. On the Create Reusable Workflow screen, enter the following:

   a. A name for the new reusable workflow. This name will appear on the Add Workflow Screen.

   b. An optional description for the workflow.

   c. The content type the workflow is to be limited to. If you are not limiting the scope of the workflow, select the All option.

   d. The workflow's platform type: SharePoint 2013 Workflow or SharePoint 2010 workflow. As mentioned previously, the SharePoint 2013 Workflow option is available only if the SharePoint 2013 Workflow Foundation is installed and configured for use in your SharePoint environment.

   e. Click the OK button.

5. On the Workflow screen in SharePoint Designer (see Figure 9-7), build the workflow logic by adding necessary actions, conditions, and steps. On the Workflow screen, save the workflow by selecting the Save option from the workflow ribbon tab. Saving the workflow does not make it available to be run; it only saves work completed to date.

6. Once the workflow is configured, select the Check for Errors option from the Workflow ribbon tab. This option verifies that there are no syntax or configuration errors in the workflow structure. If there are errors, they are identified. If there are no errors a message identifying that the workflow contains no syntax errors appears.

7. Once the workflow has no errors, you can publish it by selecting the Publish option from the Workflow ribbon tab. The workflow is published and made available in the site's Add a Workflow area.

The reusable workflow is created and can be selected from the Add a Workflow screen when new workflows are added to lists and libraries. A workflow limited to a specific content type will be available for creation only in locations where that content type is in use.

SharePoint Designer Workflow Activities

When you create workflows in SharePoint Designer, there are a variety of options to ensure workflow processes are robust. The available workflow steps, conditions, and actions vary depending on the type of workflow (SharePoint 2010 workflow or SharePoint 2013 workflow) you are creating. Table 9-4 shows the actions available in SharePoint Designer.

Table 9-4. *Workflow Actions*

Action	Available in SharePoint 2013 Workflows	Available in SharePoint 2010 Workflows	Description
Coordination Actions			
Go to Stage	Yes	No	Promotes the workflow to the next stage.
Start a List Workflow	Yes	No	Starts an identified SharePoint 2010 workflow associated with a list or library.
Start a Site Workflow	Yes	No	Starts an identified SharePoint 2010 workflow associated with a site.
Core Actions			
Add a Comment	Yes	Yes	Adds a comment into the workflow history.
Add Time to Date	Yes	Yes	Adds time details to a date field.
Build Dictionary	Yes	No	Builds a variable composed of a set of key/value pairs.
Call HTTP Web Services	Yes	No	Interacts with a web service.

(continued)

Table 9-4. (*continued*)

Action	Available in SharePoint 2013 Workflows	Available in SharePoint 2010 Workflows	Description
Count Items in a Dictionary	Yes	No	Returns the count of the number of items in an identified dictionary.
Do Calculation	Yes	Yes	Returns the result of a defined calculation.
Get an Item from a Dictionary	Yes	No	Returns a specific value from an identified dictionary.
Log to History List	Yes	Yes	Creates an entry in the workflow history list.
Pause for Duration	Yes	Yes	Delays the workflow execution for a specified time interval.
Pause until Date	Yes	Yes	Delays the workflow processing until a specified date and time.
Send an Email	Yes	Yes	Sends an e-mail to an identified individual.
Set Time Portion of Date/Time Field	Yes	Yes	Stores a date and time in a variable.
Set Workflow Status	Yes	Yes	Updates the status of the workflow.
Set Workflow Variable	Yes	Yes	Sets the value of a workflow variable.
Stop Workflow	No	Yes	Ends workflow.
Document Set Activities			
Capture a version of the Document Set	No	Yes	Creates a version for the document set that includes the current version of all the contained documents.
Set Content Approval Status for the Document Set	No	Yes	Sets the content approval details for a document set.
Start Document Set Approval Process	No	Yes	Starts an approval task against a document set to an identified user.
Send Document Set to Repository	No	Yes	Moves or copies an identified document set to an identified document repository.
List Actions			
Check In Item	Yes	Yes	Check in an identified checked-out list item or document.
Check Out Item	Yes	Yes	Check out an identified checked-in list item or document.

(*continued*)

Table 9-4. (*continued*)

Action	Available in SharePoint 2013 Workflows	Available in SharePoint 2010 Workflows	Description
Copy Document	Yes	No	Creates a copy of an identified document in a different document library.
Create List Item	Yes	Yes	Creates a new item in an identified list.
Declare Record	No	Yes	Sets the current item as a record.
Delete Draft	No	Yes	Deletes the draft version of a list item or document.
Delete Item	Yes	Yes	Deletes an identified list item or document.
Delete Previous Version	No	Yes	Deletes the previous version of a list item or document.
Discard Check Out Item	Yes	Yes	Discards changes made to a checked-out list item or document and checks the item back into the list or library.
Set Content Approval Status	No	Yes	Sets the content approval status for the item.
Set Field in Current Item	Yes	Yes	Sets an identified field value in the current item.
Translate Document	Yes	No	Translates a document to an identified language.
Undeclared Record	No	Yes	Undeclares the current item if it is a record.
Update List Item	Yes	Yes	Updates the field values for a specified list item or document.
Wait for Change in Document Check-Out Status	No	Yes	Pauses the workflow until document checkout status is updated.
Wait for Event in List Item	Yes	No	Pauses the workflow until an identified activity occurs in the list or library.
Wait for Field Change in Current Item	Yes	Yes	Pauses the workflow until an identified column is set to a specific value.
Relational Actions			
Lookup Manager of a User	No	Yes	Gets the manager for an identified user.

(*continued*)

Table 9-4. (*continued*)

Action	Available in SharePoint 2013 Workflows	Available in SharePoint 2010 Workflows	Description
Task Actions			
Assign a Form to a Group	No	Yes	Creates a custom task form and assigns the form to a user.
Assign a Task	Yes	No	Creates a workflow task for identified users.
Assign a To-Do Item	No	Yes	Assigns a to-do task to identified users.
Collect Data from a User	No	Yes	Allows a user to enter data as part of a task in a process.
Start a Task Process	Yes	No	Creates a set of tasks for one or more users.
Start Approval Process	No	Yes	Creates a workflow approval task for the current item.
Start Custom Task Process	No	Yes	Creates a customized task for the current item.
Start Feedback Process	No	Yes	Creates a collect feedback task for the current item.
Utility Actions			
Extract Substring from End of String	Yes	Yes	Sets a variable based on part of a string, starting at an identified character to the end of the string.
Extract Substring from Index of String	Yes	Yes	Sets a variable based on part of a string, starting at an identified character.
Extract Substring from Start of String	Yes	Yes	Sets a variable based on part of a string, starting at the beginning to an identified character.
Extract Substring of String from Index with Length	Yes	Yes	Sets a variable based on part of a string, starting at an identified character until an identified character.
Find Interval Between Dates	Yes	Yes	Calculates the difference between two dates in minutes, hours, or days.
Find Substring in String	Yes	No	Locates a substring in another string and returns the index location for the start of the substring.
Replace Substring in String	Yes	No	Replaces a substring in another string with a different substring.
Trim String	Yes	No	Removes leading and trailing spaces from a string.

Table 9-5 shows the conditions available in SharePoint Designer.

Table 9-5. *Workflow Conditions*

Condition	Available in SharePoint 2013 Workflows	Available in SharePoint 2010 Workflows	Description
If Any Value Equals Value	Yes	Yes	Identifies whether two values are equal.
If Current Item Field Equals Value	No	Yes	Identifies whether a field in the current item equals a value.
Created by a Specific Person	Yes	Yes	Identifies whether an item was created by an identified person.
Created in a Specific Date Span	Yes	Yes	Identifies whether an item was created within an identified date range.
Modified by a Specific Person	Yes	Yes	Identifies whether an item was last modified by an identified person.
Modified in a Specific Date Span	Yes	Yes	Identifies whether an item was last modified within an identified date range.
Person is a valid SharePoint User	Yes	Yes	Identifies whether the person is a valid user in the identified SharePoint location.
The file size in a specific range of kilobytes	No	Yes	Identifies whether a file is within a specific size range.
Title Field contains Keywords	Yes	Yes	Identifies whether the title contains identified words.
The File Type is a Specific Type	Yes	Yes	Identifies whether the file has an identified extension.

Creating a SharePoint 2013 workflow involves a separate set of actions, called loops. These actions allow looping through a set of items to perform needed actions until a condition is met. Table 9-6 shows the looping actions available in SharePoint 2013.

Table 9-6. *Workflow Loops*

Loop	Available in SharePoint 2013 Workflows	Available in SharePoint 2010 Workflows	Description
Loop N Times	Yes	No	Loops through a set of actions an identified number of times.
Loop with Condition	Yes	No	Loops through a set of actions until a condition is met.

Various other capabilities can be leveraged in SharePoint Designer when you create workflows: using variables, creating parallel actions, using form parameters, and others. More information on these and other SharePoint Designer workflow development capabilities can be found on Microsoft's web sites.

Using Visual Designer when Creating Workflows

Visual Designer is a new workflow creation view in SharePoint Designer 2013 for creating a new workflow that will leverage the SharePoint 2013 Workflow Platform. To access this view, select the Visual Designer option from the views drop-down menu to represent the workflow process in a Visio-like design palette, as Figure 9-10 shows.

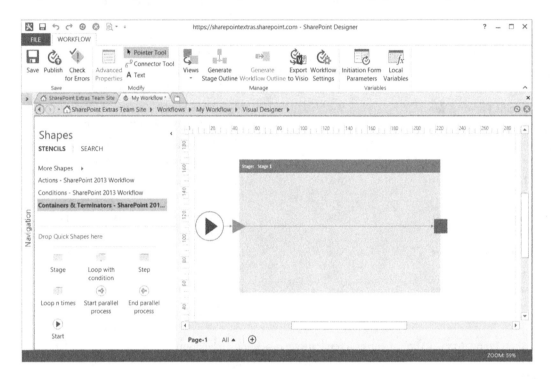

Figure 9-10. *Visual Designer*

In this view you can select actions, conditions, containers, and terminators from the shapes section and drag them on to the palette. You add items to the palette in the order they should be executed in. Once an action is on the palette, configure it by hovering over it and selecting properties from the action's drop-down menu (see Figure 9-11).

Figure 9-11. *Visual Designer action drop-down menu*

Managing Workflows

When workflows are available in lists and libraries in SharePoint, you can view and manage the workflow instances on the list's or library's Workflow Settings page. To access this page, do as follows:

1. Navigate to the list or library containing the workflows.

2. On the list or library view page, select the Workflow Settings option from the Workflow Settings drop-down menu on the List or Library ribbon tab.

The Workflow Settings page (see Figure 9-12) appears. From this page you can:

- View the list of workflows associated with the current list or library.

- View the workflows associated with content types available in the current list or library.

- For all available workflows, see how many running workflow instances are active.

- Modify an existing workflow.

- Remove an existing workflow.

- Disallow new running instances of an existing workflow.

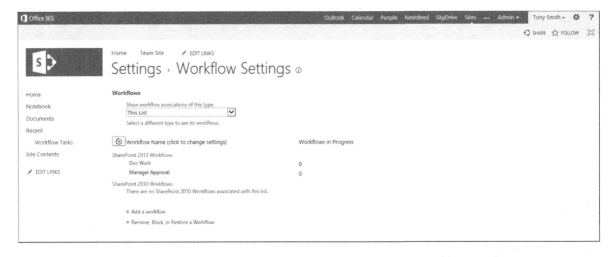

Figure 9-12. *Workflow Settings page*

Viewing Available Workflows

From a list or library Workflow Settings page, you can view all available workflows configured in the list or library or for content types used in the list or library. By default, when this page is accessed, it displays the workflows created in the current list or library and shows the number of running instances of each (see Figure 9-12). If you have SharePoint 2013 Workflow foundation configured in your environment, the workflows are grouped by type, SharePoint 2013 workflows, and SharePoint 2010 workflows.

As discussed earlier, a running instance of a workflow identifies an executing copy of the workflow in progress in one of the items in the list or library. This concept is important to understand if you are planning to update or remove a listed workflow.

To view workflows associated with a content type used in the list or library, selecting the content type from the "Show workflow associations of this type" drop-down list on the Workflow Settings page refreshes the page and shows the workflows associated with the selected content type.

To view available site workflows, navigate to the Site Workflow page by clicking the workflow link from the Site Contents page. This will list all site workflows and allow selection of a workflow to run.

Editing General Workflow Details

Workflows created for a list or library can be edited from its Workflow Settings page. This is done by clicking on the name of the workflow to be edited. Doing this brings you to the Change a Workflow page, where you can update all of the general workflow details, including the following:

- The name of the workflow.

- The workflow tasks list where the workflow's generated tasks are stored.

- The workflow history list, where the workflow activity logging is done.

- The start options for the workflow, where you can identify whether it is to start manually, when new items are created in the list or library, or when items are changed in the list or library.

Both out of the box and SharePoint Designer list and library workflows can have their general details and settings edited in this way. However, after editing an out of the box workflow's general settings, you see the workflow process details that define the workflow. You can then make necessary changes to these details to change the logic of the workflow.

Blocking Workflows

When a workflow is in a list or library or associated with one of a list's or library's available content types, you can configure it so new instances of it cannot be started. This configuration allows any workflow instances already in progress to run through completion. You might want to do this when phasing out an old workflow process in favor of a new one. To block a workflow from having new instances created, do the following:

1. On the Workflow Settings page for the associated list or library, select the Remove, Block, or Restore a Workflow option.

2. On the Remove Workflow page, select the No New Instances option for the workflow to block. Then click the OK button.

New instances of the workflow are restricted from starting, and you are returned to the Workflow Settings page.

Deleting Workflows

A workflow that is no longer relevant should no longer be available. To remove it from a list or library and delete its definition and all its running instances, do the following:

1. On the Workflow Settings page for the list or library containing the workflow, click the Remove, Block, or Restore a Workflow link.

2. On the Remove Workflow page, select the Remove option for the workflow you want to delete, and click the OK button.

The workflow is removed from the list or library, and you are returned to the Workflow Settings page.

Editing Workflows

The business logic for workflows created from out of the box workflow templates and from SharePoint Designer can be edited after their creation to ensure they properly support their associated business processes over time.

Editing Out of the Box Workflows

To edit the workflow process for workflows created from out of the box reusable workflows, do the following:

1. Navigate to the list or library containing the workflow to edit.

2. On the list or library view page, select the Workflow Settings option from the Workflow Settings drop-down menu on the List or Library ribbon tab.

3. On the Workflow Settings page, click the name of the workflow to edit.

4. On the Change a Workflow page, edit the workflow's general details, and then click the Next button.

5. On the second Change a Workflow page, make any further needed changes to the workflow details, and then click the Save button.

The workflow is updated based on the changes made.

Editing SharePoint Designer Workflows

SharePoint Designer workflows (list and library as well as site and reusable workflows) are all editable in SharePoint Designer. Edit them as follows:

1. Open SharePoint Designer.

2. Open your site in SharePoint Designer by selecting the Open Site option in the Open SharePoint Site section.

3. On the SharePoint Designer Site screen, select Workflows from the Site Objects section of the page.

4. On the Workflows screen, click the name of the workflow to edit.

5. On the selected workflow's detail screen, click the Edit Workflow link in the Customization section.

6. On the workflow's edit screen, make any needed changes to the workflow details. Saving your changes saves updates made to the workflow but does not make these updates available to be run until they are published.

7. Once the workflow is configured, select the Check for Errors option from the Workflow ribbon tab. This option verifies there are no syntax or configuration errors in the workflow structure. If there are errors, they are identified. If there are no errors, a message indicating that the workflow contains no syntax errors appears.

8. Once the workflow has no errors, you can publish it by selecting the Publish option from the Workflow ribbon tab. The workflow is published and made available to be run in the site.

The workflow, updated to include the changes made, is published. These changes become part of any new instances of the workflow.

Running Workflows

After you create workflows in your SharePoint environment, you can run them. An instance of a list or library workflow runs in a specific list item or document in the associated list or library. An instance of a site workflow runs directly in the associated site.

Running List and Library Workflows

Workflows configured in a list or library or a content type associated with a list or library start based on configured start options. Workflows configured for manual start can be started by users having at least Edit permissions to the list item or document the workflow is to run against. To start a workflow configured to be started manually, do the following:

1. Navigate to the list or library containing the workflow.

2. On the list or library view page, select the item to run the workflow against, and select the Workflows option from the Items/Files ribbon tab.

3. On the Workflows page, select the workflow to start from the Start a New Workflow section.

4. If the workflow requires input on start, you are prompted to enter any required information before clicking the Start button.

The workflow is started against the selected item, and you are returned to the list or library view page.

A second approach is to start a workflow against items in a list or library through the item's hover menu. Do so as follows:

1. Navigate to the list or library containing the workflow.

2. On the list or library view page, open the hover panel for the list item or document against which you want to start the workflow. Then select the Workflows option from the hover menu (see Figure 9-13).

Figure 9-13. *Item hover menu*

3. On the Workflows page, select the workflow to start from the Start a New Workflow section.

4. If the workflow requires input on start, you are prompted to enter any required information before clicking the Start button.

The workflow is started against the selected item, and you are returned to the list or library view page.

■ **Note** Multiple instances of the same workflow cannot run on a single item at the same time. If a specific workflow is already running, you will not be able to start another instance of it against the same item. However, an item can have more than one workflow running at once.

Workflows configured to start when new items are created in a list or library or when items are edited start automatically when the associated start condition is met.

Running Site Workflows

When your site contains site workflows, run them by doing the following:

1. Navigate to the site containing the site workflow to be run.

2. On the site's home page, select the Site Contents option from the Quick Launch area or from the Settings menu.

3. On the Site Contents page, select the Site Workflows options.

4. On the Workflows page, select the workflow to run.

5. If the workflow requires input on start, you are prompted to enter any required information before clicking the Start button.

The workflow is started in the site.

Working with Workflow Instances

As previously discussed, a workflow instance is a distinct execution against a selected item of the workflow process. You can view and manage these running and completed instances of workflows in the SharePoint environment You can also view their status and execution history, as well as run workflow actions and terminate executing instances.

Viewing Workflow Instance Status and History

When a workflow instance is running and after it is completed, you can view the detailed activities that occurred during the instance. This information is available in the Workflow Status page (see Figure 9-14).

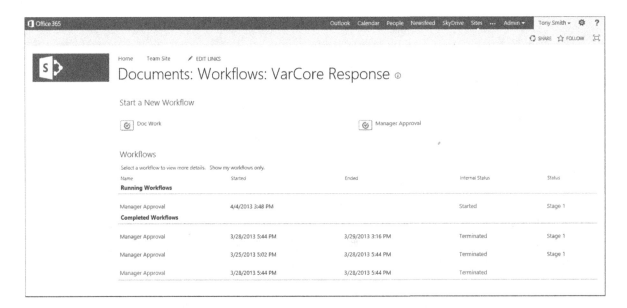

Figure 9-14. *Workflow status page*

The Workflow Status page lists current and completed workflow instances for a selected list item or document. To access the Workflow Status page, do the following:

1. Navigate to the list or library containing the item whose workflow history you want to review.

2. On the list or library view page, select the desired item, and then click the Workflows option from the Items/Files ribbon tab.

3. On the Workflows page, select the running or completed workflow instance whose details you want to view.

The Workflow Status page for the associated workflow instance appears. You can also navigate to the Workflow Status page, where the workflow status column shows the most recent execution of a workflow against an item. When workflows are added to a list or library, a column is added to it that lists the status of the most recent execution of the workflow against the item. This status is shown as a hyperlink. When clicked, you are taken to the Workflow Status page that lists all details associated with that workflow instance. If an item against which the workflow has not yet been run in the list or library, the status details for that item are blank.

■ **Note** To get to a workflow instance via the workflow column, include the column in the displayed list or library view. This column is added automatically to the list's or library's default view the first time a workflow is run. Add it manually to other list or library views as needed.

On the Workflow Status page, you can view the entire logged history for a given workflow instance and view all actions and completed tasks associated with that instance. Select the listed workflow tasks to view their details. This page also lists general workflow instance information, including the following:

- The initiator of the workflow instance.

- When the workflow instance was started.

- The time of the instance's last activity.

- A link to the item with which the workflow instance is associated.

- The internal status of the workflow instance.

- The workflow process status.

Terminating Workflow Instances

A workflow process runs until all of the activities it is to perform as part of the process are completed. At this point the workflow instance is complete. At times you might want to abort a workflow's run and end it at the current point in its execution, prior to completion of all its identified activities. You can do this in the Workflow Status screen.

When you are viewing the details for a running workflow instance, a link, called End This Workflow, appears at the bottom of the Workflow Information section. When you click the link, you are prompted to confirm that you want to terminate the workflow instance. Clicking the OK button on the confirmation message ends the running workflow instance and returns you to the Workflow Status page. There the workflow instance is updated to reflect its termination. In the completed workflows section of the page, its status is marked Cancelled.

Information Management Policies

Information management policies are rules you create to enforce compliance requirements for SharePoint sites and their content. Information management policies help you enforce content retention, management, and audit requirements. They can be configured at multiple levels in the environment:

- *Site Collection*: Policies defined at the site collection level apply in all sites throughout the collection.

- *Content Type*: Policies defined at the content type level apply to the content type wherever in the environment it is used.

- *List or Library Content Type*: Policies defined at this level impact items of a specific content type in a specified list or library.

- *List or Library*: Policies defined at the List or Library level apply to all items in the identified list or library.

Policy Types

Several types of information management policies can be configured in the environment. The policies that can be configured include the following:

Retention

Retention policies allow you to define automated content locking and disposal rules. These policies are created to do the following:

- Ensure the integrity and retention of content based on defined rules.

- Facilitate the removal of content based on defined time frames.

- Enforce the deletion of materials based on defined rules.

Retention rules are defined as multistage processes where in each stage you determine the following (seen Figure 9-15).

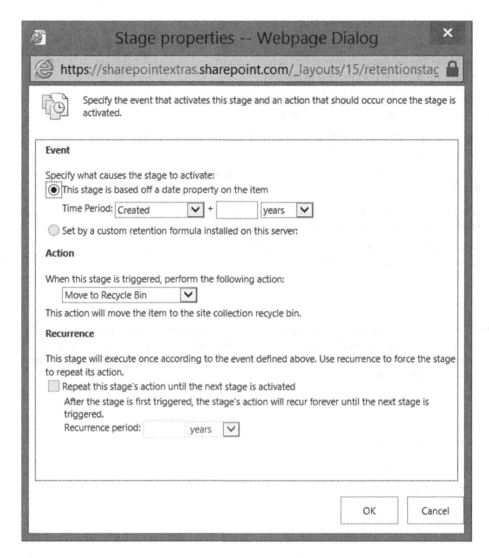

Figure 9-15. *Retention rules management*

- *Event*: The event that triggers the stage. The event is based on date details or a custom retention formula.

- *Action*: The activity to be performed when the event occurs. Options include:

  - *Move to Recycle Bin*: The item is deleted from the list or library, much as items are deleted manually. They are then subject to the recycle bin management rules.

  - *Permanently Delete*: The item is deleted from the list or library. It is not placed in the recycle bin and so is unavailable for restoration.

  - *Transfer to Another Location*: The item is moved to a registered destination location in SharePoint. The location must be configured as a registered destination for it to be available for selection. (Creating registered locations is discussed in Chapter 10.)

- *Start a Workflow*: An identified workflow is started against the item when the event occurs.

- *Skip to Next Stage*: The information management policy transitions to the next defined stage. The associated item is not changed in any way.

- *Declare Record*: The item is locked as a record. This option requires enabling of the In Place Records Management site collection feature in the site collection.

- *Delete Previous Drafts*: Any previous draft versions stored in its version history are deleted. Only published versions remain.

- *Delete All Previous Versions*: All previous versions of the item stored in its version history are deleted. Only the current version remains.

- *Recurrence*: Identifies whether the stage actions are to be repeated while the item is in the stage. If the actions are to be run repeatedly, define how frequently.

Define as many stages as needed to support item retention and removal in SharePoint lists and libraries. Configuring retention policies is discussed later in this chapter.

Auditing

Auditing policies identify activities that you want to track in relation to materials. Auditing settings can be configured globally in a site collection or as part of an information management policy to impact only those items in a specific site, list, or library. When configuring auditing settings as part of an information management policy, you can specify to audit the following options (see Figure 9-16).

- Opening or downloading documents, viewing items in lists, or viewing item properties.

- Editing items.

- Checking out or checking in items.

- Moving or copying items to another location in the site.

- Deleting or restoring items.

☑ Enable Auditing

Caution: This Web application is configured to enable anonymous access. The actions of anonymous users will be audited, but their identities will not be recorded.

Specify the events to audit:

☐ Editing items
☐ Checking out or checking in items
☐ Moving or copying items to another location in the site
☐ Deleting or restoring items

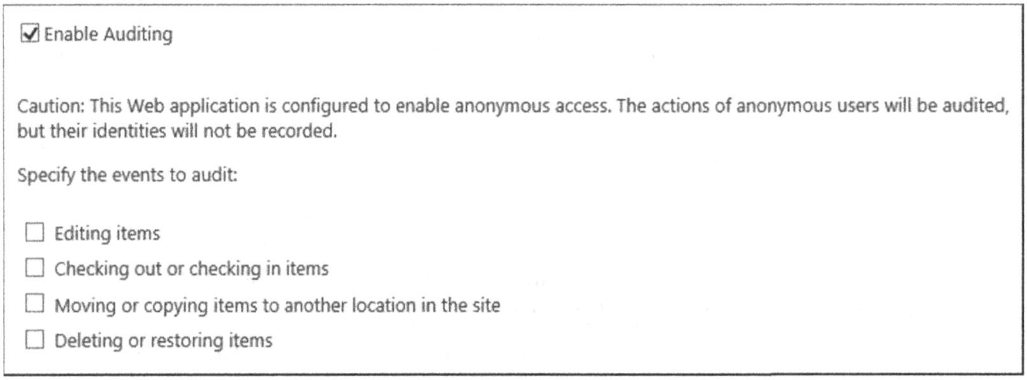

Figure 9-16. Auditing rules management

Barcodes

When barcoding is configured as part of an information management policy, a barcode is assigned to each item. It can track physical, paper-based, copies of the information in relation to electronic counterparts. When configuring this option, you can also specify whether to prompt users to insert barcodes into Microsoft Office documents prior to saving or printing the files.

Labels

Labels let you add watermarks to Microsoft Office documents. When you enable labels, you can configure the following elements (see Figure 9-17):

- Prompt users to insert a label before saving or printing: Prompts the user accessing the document in Microsoft Office to insert the label before the document is saved or printed.

- Prevent changes to labels after they are added: Locks the label from editing after it is created.

- Label format: Defines the format and content of the label's details.

- Appearance: Identifies the font type, size, style, and placement details.

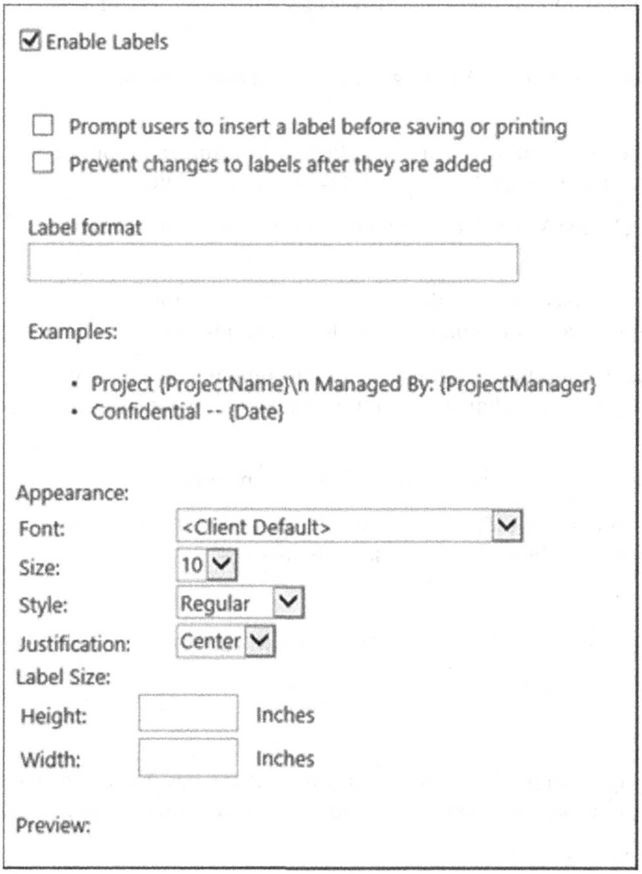

Figure 9-17. Labels rules management

Site Collection Policies

Site collection policies are the broadest policy types configurable in SharePoint. When created, they apply to all content in all sites of the site collection. Create a site collection policy (such as the desire to audit security changes globally) when you want to enforce a policy throughout your environment. To create site collection policies, which can only be created and managed by by Site Collection Administrators, do as follows:

1. Navigate to the root site in your site collection.

2. On the site collection home page, select the Site Settings option from the Settings menu.

3. On the Site Settings page, select the Site Collection Audit Settings option from the Site Collection Administration section.

4. On the Configure Audit Settings page, do the following:

   a. In the Audit Log Trimming section, identify whether to trim the audit log to store only a specific number of days' worth of audit details and, if you do, whether to copy the current audit report to another location before it is trimmed.

   b. In the Documents and Items section, identify the document and list item activities to be audited. Specify any combination of the following options:

      i. Editing Items: Auditing all modifications to existing content or additions of new content.

      ii. Checking Out or Checking In Items: Auditing item check-in and check-out actions.

      iii. Moving or Copying Items to Another Location in the Site: Tracking item copy or move activities performed through the SharePoint Send To capabilities.

      iv. Deleting or Restoring Items: Auditing deletion of items and restoration of items from the recycle bin.

   c. In the Lists, Libraries, and Sites section, identify the site, list, and library level activities to be audited. Specify any combination of the following options:

      i. Editing Content Types and Columns: Audits changes to content types associated with lists and libraries, as well as changes to columns in content types, lists, and libraries.

      ii. Searching Site Content: Audits searches performed in the environment.

      iii. Editing Users and Permissions: Audits changes made to the permissions of sites, lists, libraries, or items, including inheritance settings changes.

   d. Click the OK button.

The site collection auditing options are saved, and the identified activities will be tracked and logged.

Content Type Policies

Content type policies are information management policies defined against content types. These policies are enforced everywhere those content types are in use. To create and manage site content types, do the following:

1. Navigate to the site where the content type was created.

2. On the site's home page, select the Site Settings option from the Settings menu.

3. On the Site Settings page, select the Site Content Types option from the Web Designer Galleries section.

4. On the Site Content Types page, select the content type for which you want to create the information management policy.

5. On the Site Content Type page, click the Information Management Policy Settings option from the Settings section.

6. On the Edit Policy page,

   a. In the Name and Administrative Description section, optionally enter an administrative description of the policy.

   b. In the Policy Statement section, enter the policy statement—that is, the description users see when they open an item subject to the policy.

   c. In the Retention section, identify whether the policy is to contain retention rules. If it is, define the retention stages. (Retention policy options are discussed in this chapter's Retention section.)

   d. In the Auditing section, identify whether the policy includes any auditing requirements. If it does, specify the activities to audit. (Trackable auditing activities are discussed in the "Auditing" section.)

   e. In the Barcodes section, specify whether the policy includes barcoding requirements and whether to prompt the user to insert a barcode before saving or printing a Microsoft Office document.

   f. In the Labels section, identify whether the policy includes document labeling requirements. Then select label configuration and display settings (these options are discussed in the "Labels" section).

   g. Once the information for the policy is entered, click the OK button to save the information management policy.

The information management policy is saved, and you are returned to the Content Type page. Once the policy is configured, you can edit it by returning to the Edit Policy page and making any necessary alterations.

List and Library Content Type Policies

If you want to configure a policy for a content type but only when that content type is used in a specific list or library, you can create a list or library content type policy that is enforced only for items of the identified content type in the selected list or library. To create a list or library content type policy, do the following:

1. Navigate to the list or library where you want to create the policy.

2. On the list or library view page, select the List or Library Settings option from the List or Library ribbon tab.

3. On the Settings page, select the Information Management Policy Settings option from the Permissions and Management section.

4. On the Information Management Policy Settings page, select the content type for which you want to create the policy from the Content Type Policies section.

5.   On the Edit Policy page,

    a.   In the Name and Administrative Description section, enter an optional administrative description for the policy.

    b.   In the Policy Statement section, enter the policy statement—the description users see when they open an item subject to this policy.

    c.   In the Retention section, identify whether the policy is to contain retention rules. If it is, define the retention stages (retention policy options are discussed in this chapter's "Retention" section).

    d.   In the Auditing section, identify whether the policy includes any auditing requirements. If it does, specify the activities to audit. Trackable auditing activities are discussed in the "Auditing" section.)

    e.   In the Barcodes section, identify whether the policy includes barcoding requirements and whether to prompt the user to insert a barcode before saving or printing a Microsoft Office document.

    f.   In the Labels section, identify whether the policy includes document labeling requirements. Then select label configuration and display settings (these options are discussed in the "Labels" section).

    g.   Once the information for the policy is entered, click the OK button to save the information management policy.

The policy is saved, and you are returned to the Information Management Policy Settings page. To modify an existing list or library content type policy, return to the Edit Policy page and make any needed adjustments.

List and Library Policies

At times you might want to create a policy enforced on all items in a specific list or library regardless of content type. To do so, create a list or library policy. These policies support only retention, not audit, barcode, or label policies. To create this type of policy, do as follows:

1.   Navigate to the list or library where you want to create the policy.

2.   On the list or library view page, select the List or Library Settings option from the List or Library ribbon tab.

3.   On the Settings page, select the Information Management Policy Settings option from the Permissions and Management section.

4.   On the Information Management Policy Settings page, click the Change Source option.

5.   On the List Based Retention Schedule page, change the Source of Retention value to Library and Folders.

6.   In the warning message, click OK to accept ignoring any content type retention policies that may be in place.

7.   On the List Based Retention Schedule page in the List Based Retention Schedule section, create a retention policy (described in the "Retention" section). Then click the OK button to save the new schedule.

The retention policy is saved, and you are returned to the Information Management Policy Settings page. To edit or remove the policy, return to the List Based Retention Schedule page and change any of the listed options.

Viewing Compliance Details

After an information management policy is configured, you can view its captured details from the Compliance Details windows (see Figure 9-18).

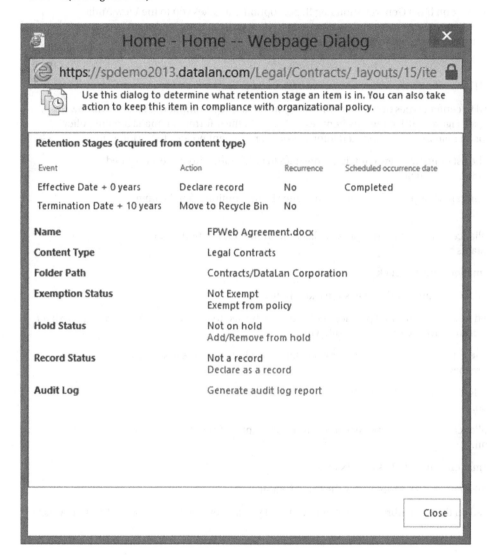

Figure 9-18. *Compliance details window*

The compliance details window includes retention and audit details based on the policies assigned to the item. To access this window, select the Compliance Details option from the context menu of the document, list item, or folder whose details you wish to view.

The compliance details window contains the following information:

- The Retention Stages section lists the retention details that the item has been processed through.

- The Audit Log section has a General Audit Log Report option that takes you to the View Audit Reports page, where you can run a variety of reports to view audit, activity, and security details. (Reporting is discussed in detail in Chapter 13.)

Policy Exemptions

While policies are defined in content types or lists and libraries, you can use the Compliance Details window for a selected item or folder (see Figure 9-18) to identify items excluded from the information management policy.

To exclude a folder or an item from an associated information management policy, do the following:

1. Navigate to the list or library view containing the item to be excluded from the associated information management policy.

2. On the list or library view page, select the Compliance Details option from the item's context menu.

3. In the Compliance Details window, select the Exempt From Policy option in the Exemption Status section.

4. In the confirmation window, click the OK button.

5. In the Compliance Details window, click the Close button.

The item is exempted from the associated policies, and you are returned to the list or library view page. To later remove a policy exemption you have created, do the following:

1. Navigate to the list or library view containing the item to exclude from the associated information management policy.

2. On the list or library view page, select the Compliance Details option from the item's context menu.

3. In the Compliance Details window, click the Remove Exemption from the Exemption Status section.

4. In the confirmation window, click the OK button.

5. In the Compliance Details window, click the Close button.

The exemption placed on the list or library item is removed, and you are returned to the list or library view page.

■ ■ ■

CHAPTER 10

Records Management

A record is a type of information, typically a document, that requires structured retention and management to support either internally defined or externally mandated regulatory requirements. Records management encompasses the process and resources to properly handle the declaration, undeclaration, and removed of materials at the appropriate points in their life cycles. Records management in SharePoint is used for the following:

- Uploading materials to be stored and tracked as records.

- Identifying when items managed through the environment are to be classified and managed as records.

- Determining how long records are to be maintained.

- Archiving and disposing of materials based on defined disposition rules.

Several capabilities available in SharePoint Server Standard and SharePoint Server Enterprise to manage these aspects of records management are not, however, available in SharePoint Foundation. Records management capabilities in SharePoint include the following:

- Content organizer, which is used to collect and organize materials.

- Record retention rules, which define declaration, undeclaration, and removal rules for materials.

- Record centers, which store and organize records.

- Holds created to identify items that need to be retained or exported based on the outcome of external events (typically litigation).

Understanding Records Management

Before the technical tools in SharePoint that support record retention and management are discussed, you need to become familiar with the elements of records management and with the planning to be done to prepare for managing records within your SharePoint environment, including how to manage materials identified by the organization for proactive control and planning for reacting to content retention, or hold, needs to address situational information retention requirements, especially litigation or audit events.

Proactive Records Management Planning

Before you can take advantage of the SharePoint records management features, you need to define your requirements for managing records, including how these features are to be applied to the content managed in SharePoint. This planning should include the following:

- Identifying finalized materials to be uploaded to SharePoint for retention and access purposes.

- Identifying materials to be developed in SharePoint and matured as records.

- Defining records retention rights.

- Determining retention rules records are to adhere to.

- Defining content consumption approaches for the material.

- Defining content archival and expiration rules and approaches.

Identify Records

The first step in records management planning is identifying materials in the environment that are to be managed as records. To determine the materials to be managed (such as contracts, standard operating procedures, product specifications, and so on) and decide whether these materials are to be developed in the environment or added to it after they are created and are ready for maintenance as records. For each type of item, define the following:

- The method to be used to bring the content into the environment. This will be some combination of the following:

  - Uploading the materials in their completed state to store them for retention and consumption.

  - Uploading materials that are to be further developed in the environment and retained as records later in their life cycle.

  - Creating new materials and managing their entire life cycle in the SharePoint environment, including eventual retention as records.

- The details about the items to be tracked. They should include a combination of fields to manage records retention, as well as fields to support targeted searching and content organization requirements. For example, a field needed to manage retention might include the one tracking an effective date for a contract if retention rules leveraged the date to determine when the document should be declared a record.

- Security of items at each point in the life cycle. As materials mature, security may need to be updated to reflect changes to their access. For example, when a proposal document is being developed, sales representatives might have rights to edit it. But once finalized and distributed, it might become read-only for them to protect it from alteration after distribution.

- How content is consumed by site users, including organization for viewing and availability through search. Just as document security may change over time, how documents are exposed to the organization may also change. For example, a contract in development might be seen only by navigating to the library where it exists. But when finalized and executed, the contract might join other executed agreements in being viewable and searchable.

With this information identified, you can determine the record management capabilities required to support the organization's records management needs.

Planning for Content Holds

Unlike records retention processes, which are proactively configured and managed, content holds occur as reactions to events, such as litigation events, that require identification and retention of materials related to a specific topic or activity. Since information retention needs cannot be predetermined, this is a reactionary process, one based on each situation's specific needs. Pre-hold planning can help streamline information discovery and optimize content to make locating it easier based on details most likely to relate to content hold needs. Taking the following planning steps will help you prepare for content holds:

- Identify the most likely scenarios for which content holds will be needed.

- Specify content attributes that represent the details most likely to be used to identify materials needed to support expected hold scenarios. If, for example, you expect to need content holds for product materials, ensure that items associated with a specific product are easy to identify by tracking the product or products an item relates to as part of its properties.

Adding Content with Content Organizer

Adding documents to SharePoint libraries, including methods that support uploading single items and multiple items all at once into an environment, is discussed in Chapter 7. One characteristic of all the methods is that the individual doing the upload has to know where the document must be placed to become available. But at times you will not want to rely on users in the environment to place items in appropriate locations or want items placed in their final store until a specific person or group in the organization reviews them. You might want the records management department, for example, to review a contract before the rest of the organization sees it.

Content organizer is used to allow materials uploaded into a single library, called a Drop Off library, to be automatically routed to a final storage location based on the item's properties when uploaded. Content organizer is an alternative to constructing workflow processes when you want to control routing of documents added to SharePoint. It lets you manage duplicate document uploading and simple document review requirements prior to materials' being made generally available.

Enabling Content Organizer

Content organizer must be enabled in a site before it can be used. Record center sites (discussed later in the chapter) have this feature activated by default. However, all other sites require its enabling as needed. To enable content organizer in a site, do the following:

1. Navigate to the site where you want to enable content organizer.

2. On the site's home page, select the Site Settings option from the Settings menu.

3. On the Site Settings page, click the Manage Site Features option from the Site Actions section.

4. On the Site Features page, click the Activate button for the Content Organizer feature.

With the content organizer feature activated, a Drop Off library is created, and content organizer management capabilities are added.

Configuring Content Organizer

Once content organizer features are active in a site, you can configure its services to identify how content added to the site is handled. To configure content organizer in a site where the feature is enabled, do the following:

1. Navigate to the site where content organizer is enabled.

2. On the site's home page, select the Site Settings option from the Settings Menu.

3. On the Site Settings page, select the Content Organizer Settings option from the Site Administration section.

4. On the Content Organizer Settings page (see Figure 10-1), do as follows:

    a. In the Redirect Users to the Drop Off Library section, identify whether to redirect users of libraries listed as content organizer destinations to the Drop Off library when they upload content.

    b. In the Sending to Another Site section, identify whether content organizer rules can route documents to libraries in a different site.

    c. In the Folder Partitioning section, identify whether to create new folders to route content to once the folder currently in use contains a specified number of files. As part of configuring this option, also specify the number of items to allow before routing to a new folder and the format to use for naming new folders that are created.

    d. In the Duplicate Submissions section, identify the approach for handling an uploaded file with the same name as an existing item in the destination location. You can choose to upload the file as a new version of the existing file or to append unique characters to the uploaded file's name to store it as a new item in the library.

    e. In the Preserving Context Section, identify whether audit log and property details are to be kept with the document as it is routed to its identified final storage location.

    f. In the Rule Manager section, specify who can create content organizer rules and whether such individuals are to get e-mail notifications when items submitted do not meet defined rules or when content is left in the Drop Off library for a designated number of days.

    g. Click the OK button to save the content organizer configuration.

Figure 10-1. Content Organizer Settings page

The overall configuration of the content organizer is saved, and content organizer is ready to have content organizer rules configured.

Configuring Content Organizer Rules

Content organizer rules govern movement of content from the site's Drop Off library to other locations in the current site or in another SharePoint site. To create content organizer rules in a site, do as follows:

1. Navigate to the site where content organizer rules need to be configured.

2. On the site's home page, select the Site Settings option from the Settings menu.

3. On the Site Settings page, select the Content Organizer Rules option from the Site Administration section.

4. On the Content Organizer Rules page, click the New Item option to create a new content organizer rule.

5. On the New Rule page (see Figure 10-2), do the following:

    a. In the Rule Name section, enter the name for the new content organizer rule.

    b. In the Rule Status and Priority section, identify whether the rule is active and, if active, the rule's priority level. Inactive rules are not used to route content. The priority determines the importance of the rule. If more than one rule will impact a document, the rule with the highest priority is applied to the item.

    c. In the Submission's Content Type section, do the following:

        i.   Identify the content type for the rule to act on by selecting the Group the content type is categorized under. Then select the content type.

        ii. Specify whether the content type has alternate names and, if it does, what they are. To specify alternate names, enter them in the Add Alternate Name box, and click the Add button to place the name in the List of Alternate Names section.

    d. In the Conditions section, identify the conditions under which to execute the rule. This includes identifying the property values that will make the item meet the rule's conditions.

    e. In the Target Location section, identify the library to which to move the items meeting the rule and whether to place the items in folders. You can specify the property to base the folder name on and whether the name is to include the name of the property, its value, or both.

    f. Click the OK button to save the rule.

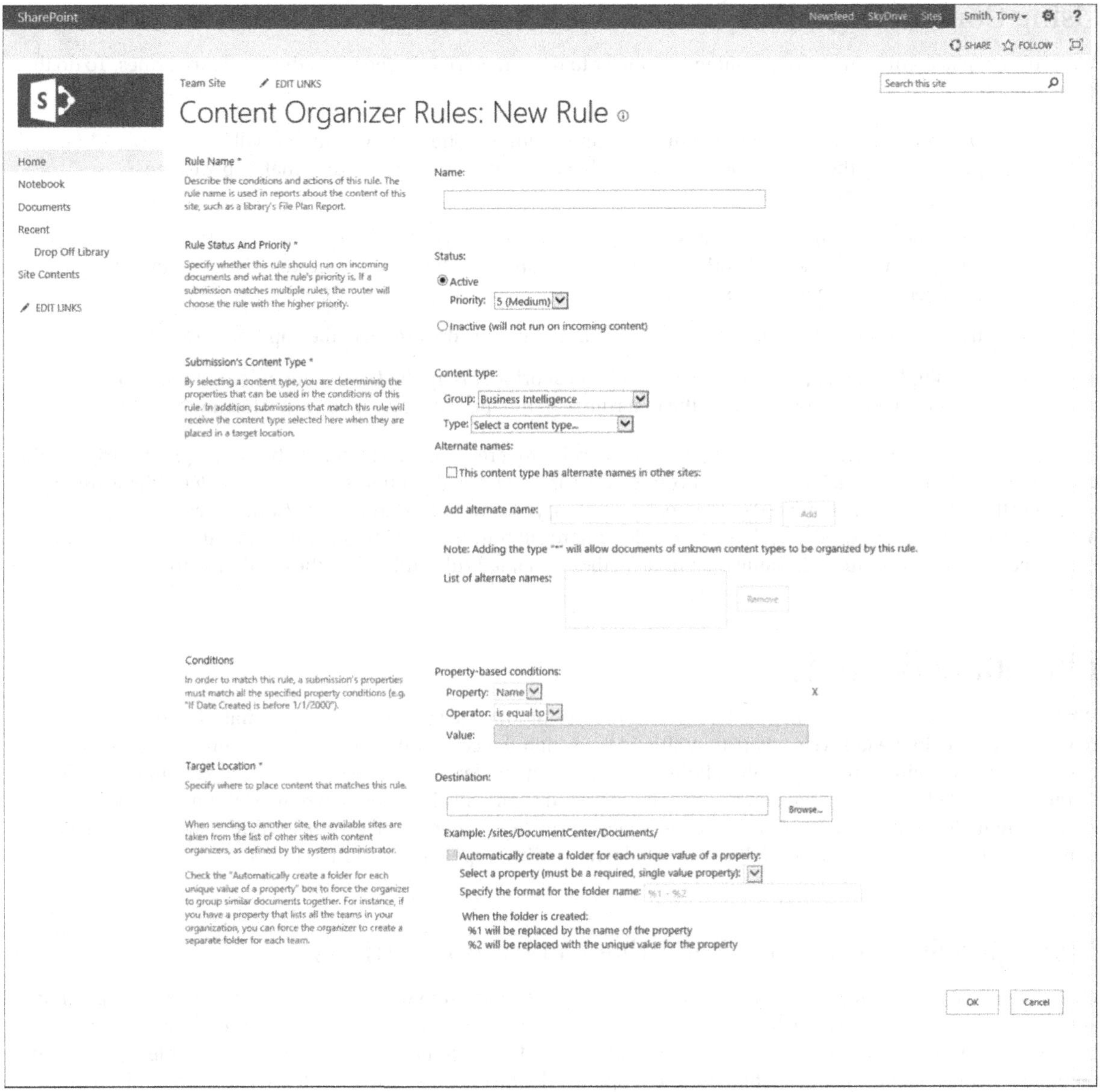

Figure 10-2. *New Rule page*

The rule is created and will be applied to content added to the Drop Off Library. You can add other rules to support content routing. To edit them on the Content Organizer Rules page, select the appropriate rule and then the Edit Item option from the Items ribbon tab.

Using Content Organizer

With rules in place, you can leverage content organizer to route materials based upon the configured rules. To do this, do as follows:

- Upload items into the Drop Off library. Items added to the Drop Off library will be processed by the content organizer, which will identify the rule or rules that apply to the item being added.

- If no rules apply, the document is left in the Drop Off library. If content organizer was configured to send e-mail notifications to rule managers, the e-mail indicates that a document has been added to which no rules apply.

- If a single rule applies, that rule is executed and routes the document to the appropriate location.

- If multiple rules apply, the rule with the highest priority is applied to the document. If multiple rules with equal priority apply, the first rule with that priority is applied to the document.

In working with content organizer, you may create rules that require information to be edited prior to routing the document to a final location. For example, if you allow people to upload contracts but want your legal department to review them before they are routed to the Contracts library, set the rule to run on the Contract content type when a Status field is set to Approved. Legal can access documents in the Drop Off library and update the Status field to Approved. Editing the Status field value then triggers the associated rule and moves the document to the library.

Managing Records

Whether you want to upload content to be saved as records or manage the development of materials that have reached the point in the life cycle where they should be declared records, you can manage the entire process of creating and maintaining records in SharePoint. Materials can be identified as records and locked from modification or removal, routed to different locations as they mature, and eventually be deleted to remove them from the environment. The management of overall record declaration and management settings within a site collection is configured at the site collection level. It can then be refined within specific lists and libraries.

Managing Site Collection Records Declaration Settings

Overall records management settings are configurable for a site collection when the In-Place Records Management site collection feature is activated. In-Place Records Management allows management of records in any list or library in a site collection. Once this feature is activated, record management options become available, and you can configure records management capabilities. These options define the default settings for declaring records in the site's lists and libraries. The settings determine the level of restrictions placed on items declared records, including whether to allow their editing or deletion. The settings are also used to determine whether manual record declaration can be performed and what rights levels users need to manually declare and undeclare records. To manage a SharePoint site collection's record declaration settings, do the following:

1. Navigate to the root site in the site collection.

2. On the home page of the site, select the Site Settings option from the Settings menu.

3. On the Site Settings page, select the Record Declaration Settings option from the Site Collection Administration section.

4. On the Record Declaration Settings page (see Figure 10-3), do as follows:

   a. In the Record Restrictions section, from the following options select access restrictions to associate with documents locked as records:

      - *No Additional Restrictions*: Records will have the same access capabilities as standard items. With this option selected, a record can be edited or deleted like any other SharePoint item.

      - *Block Delete*: Items declared as records cannot be deleted. With this option selected, records can only be edited. To delete an item declared a record, first undeclare it, then delete it.

      - *Block Edit and Delete*: The default option for records. With this option selected, once an item is declared a record, it cannot be edited or deleted. To change a record, first undeclare it, then make the change.

   b. In the Record Declaration Availability section, identify whether the ability to manually declare records is available by default in the site collection's lists and libraries.

   c. In the Declaration Roles section, identify the rights users need to declare and undeclare records. Set independently, these options let you require different rights levels for each activity. With both options configured, security levels available for selection are as follows:

      - *All list contributors and administrators*: The default for record declaration settings, this option specifies that the action can be performed by any individual having at least contribute rights to the list or library.

      - *Only list administrators*: The default for undeclaring records, this option specifies that only individuals with administrative rights to the list or library can perform the activity.

      - *Only policy actions*: Select this option when you do not want to allow any user, regardless of security rights, to declare or undeclare records. With this option selected, only information management policy processes can perform the action.

   d. Once the record declaration settings are appropriately configured, click the OK button to save the settings.

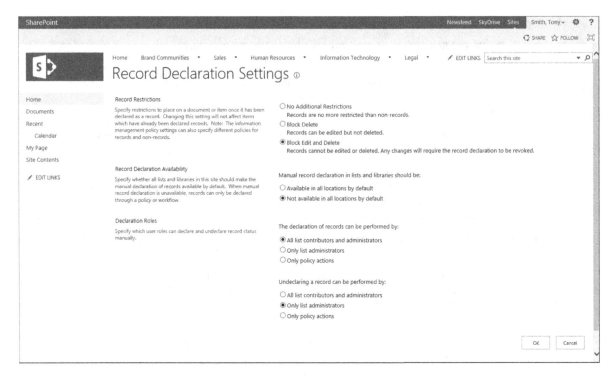

Figure 10-3. *Record Declaration Settings page*

The settings are saved and applied to your entire site collection. You are returned to the Site Settings page.

Managing List and Library Record Declaration Settings

We have discussed how you can define records declaration settings for your overall site collection that impact all lists and libraries in the SharePoint site collection. Many times, however, you will want to be more granular in configuring these capabilities and define only specific locations where manual records management is allowed. You can do this by configuring the record declaration settings for a list or library. These settings let you override, for a specific list or library, configuration settings defined for the site collection. You can determine whether to declare records in the selected list or library and identify whether items added to that location are automatically declared as records. To configure a list's or library's record declaration settings, do the following:

1. Navigate to the list or library where you want to manage record declaration settings.

2. On the list or library view page, select the List/Library Settings option from the List/Library ribbon tab.

3. On the Settings page, select the Record Declaration Settings option from the Permissions and Management section.

4. On the Library Record Declaration Settings page (see Figure 10-4), select the following:

   a. In the Manual Record Declaration Availability section, specify whether to make manual records declaration available in the list or library. Select from the following options:

      • *Use the site collection default settings*: The default for all lists and libraries, this option bases the ability to manually manage records on the records management settings configured for the site collection itself (configuring the site collection's record declaration settings is discussed earlier in the chapter).

      • *Always allow the manual declaration of records*: With this option selected, users can manually declare records in the list or library. Security levels required for declare and undeclare actions are based on the selections made in the site collection's record declaration settings.

      • *Never allow the manual declaration of records*: With this option selected, list or library users are not permitted to declare records in that list or library. Only information management retention policies and workflow processes are able to declare and undeclare records in this location.

   b. In the Automatic Declaration section, identify whether new items added to the list or library are automatically declared records.

   c. Once the record declaration settings for the list or library are configured, click the OK button.

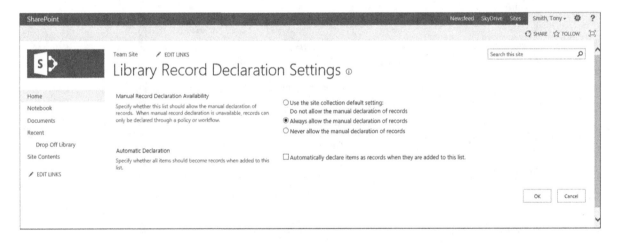

Figure 10-4. Library Record Declaration Settings page

The record declaration settings are saved and applied to the list or library. You are returned to the settings page for the list or library.

Manual Records Declaration

As discussed earlier in this chapter, site collection and list or library records declaration settings are used to establish whether records can be manually declared and undeclared in lists and libraries. At times you will want to enable individuals to manually declare records. For example, your process may not be well enough defined to create automated retention rules, or you may have a group in your organization that is responsible for reviewing and classifying items before they are declared records.

To manually declare records within a list or library where manual records declaration settings are enabled, do the following:

1. Navigate to the list or library where you want to manually declare an item a record.

2. On the list or library view page, select the Compliance Details option from the list item's context menu or the document's hover panel menu.

3. In the Compliance Details window (see Figure 10-5), click the Declare as a Record option in the Record Status section.

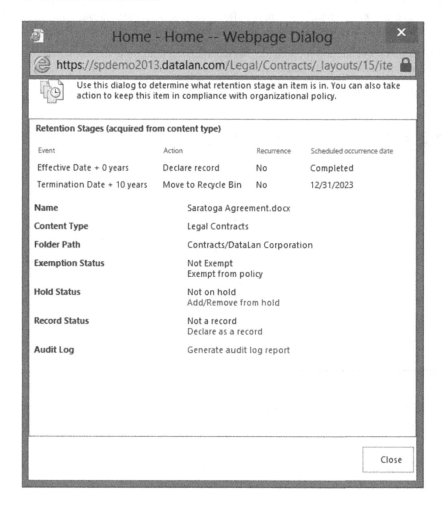

Figure 10-5. *Compliance Details window*

4. In the confirmation window, click the OK button to confirm that the item is declared a record.

5. The Compliance Details window is updated to show the Record Status as Record. Select the Close button to return to the list or library view.

The list or library view is updated to indicate the item is locked as a record (the lock indicator is added to the file's icon, as Figure 10-6 shows). The file also becomes subject to the defined records management restrictions discussed earlier in this chapter.

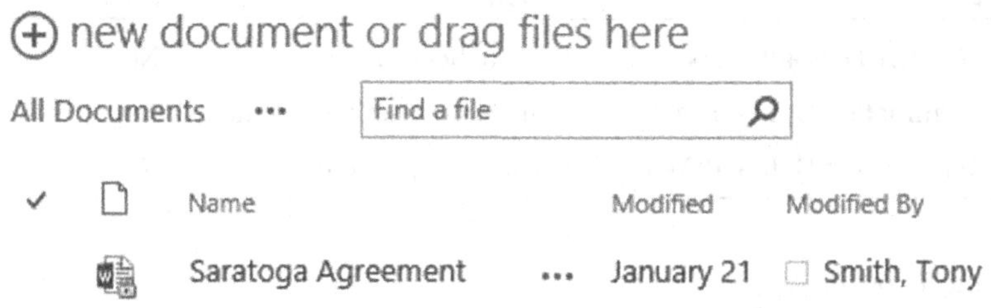

⊕ new document or drag files here

All Documents   ••• | Find a file   ρ |

✓   ☐   Name   Modified   Modified By

☑   Saratoga Agreement   •••   January 21   ☐ Smith, Tony

Figure 10-6. *File locked as a record*

To manually undeclare an item that is currently declared a record, do the following:

1. Navigate to the list or library where you want to undeclare an item a record.

2. On the list or library view page, select the Compliance Details option from the list item's context menu or the document's hover panel menu.

3. On the Compliance Details window (see Figure 10-5), click the Undeclare Record option in the Record Status section.

4. In the confirmation window, click the OK button to confirm that the item is undeclared a record.

5. The Compliance Details window is updated to show the record status as Not a Record. Select the Close button to return to the list or library view.

The item is no longer considered a record, and all record management restrictions are removed from the item.

Managing Records through Record Retention Rules

Record retention rules are defined as part of information management policies configured to automatically declare and undeclare items as records based on the items' properties. These rules allow you to define record declaration and undeclaration settings as part of an item's life cycle. This section covers how to configure retention policies to automatically declare and undeclare records (how to configure information management policies to address document retention and auditing needs is discussed in Chapter 9).

You might want to automatically manage declaration and undeclaration of records when you have materials that have a defined life cycle and need protection to ensure they are not removed or edited once they reach a specific point in their development. For example, these rules may apply in managing contracts. You may have a corporate policy requiring copies of executed contracts to be maintained in the environment from the time they are made effective, the Effective Date, till ten years after they are no longer in effect—the Termination Date. To support this policy, you can create an information management procedure that declares a document a record on the Effective Date, moves the item to an archive location on the Termination Date, and then deletes the item ten years after the Termination Date.

Configuring Retention Policies

Retention policies are configured within information management policies, which include a set of rules organized into stages, each representing a life cycle stage of an item. The stages are defined by property values of the item. To create a retention policy, first identify the details by which the policy stages are to be defined and then the action to be taken when an item reaches that stage. To support the contract management example, let us configure a retention policy similar to the one detailed in Table 10-1.

Table 10-1. *Contract Management Retention Policy Example*

Stage Description	Event	Action	Recurrence
Contract Effective	Effective Date + 0 Years	Declare Record	No
Contract Terminated	Termination Date + 0 Years	Transfer to Another Location	No
10 Years after Contract Terminated	Termination Date + 10 Years	Permanently Delete	No

To configure a retention policy, do the following:

1. Navigate to the list or library where you want to configure the retention policy.

2. On the list or library view page, select the List/Library Settings option from the List/Library ribbon tab.

3. On the Settings page, select the Information Management Policy Settings option from the Permissions and Management section.

4. On the Information Management Policy Settings page, select the content type or library settings option to navigate to the Edit Policy page for the appropriate item (editing content type and library policies are discussed in Chapter 9).

5. On the Edit Policy page, do the following:

   a. In the Retention section, select the Enable Retention option.

   b. With the Enable Retention option selected, the Add a Retention Stage link appears. Click the link to open the Stage Properties window, where you can define the details for the records retention stage.

   c. In the Stage Properties window (see Figure 10-7), enter the following information:

      i. In the Event section, identify a date property to use for that stage of the item and a date offset value to identify when the policy stage is to take effect. For the contract management example discussed earlier in this section, identify a stage as Effective Date + 0 years to create a stage to take effect on the defined Effective Date. Alternatively in this section, choose a custom retention formula (formulas are configured in your SharePoint environment by a SharePoint technical administrator). If none are present, this option is disabled.

      ii. In the Action section, identify the activity that is to occur when the item enters the stage. In our contract's Effective Date example, have the Declare Record option declare the item a record when the Effective Date is reached. Actions available for selection include the following:

- *Move to Recycle Bin*: The item is deleted from the list or library, much as items are deleted manually. The item becomes subject to the recycle bin management rules.

- *Permanently Delete*: The item is deleted from the list or library. Since it is not placed in the recycle bin, it is unavailable for restoration.

- *Transfer to Another Location*: This option moves the item to a registered destination location in SharePoint. It requires configuring the location as a registered destination (how to do this is discussed in Chapter 10).

- *Start a Workflow*: An identified workflow is started when the configured event occurs against the item.

- *Skip to Next Stage*: This option causes the information management policy to transition to the next defined stage. The associated item is not changed in any way.

- *Declare Record*: This option locks the item as a record. It requires you to enable the In Place Records Management site collection feature in the site collection.

- *Delete Previous Drafts*: Any previous draft versions stored in its version history are deleted, leaving only published versions.

- *Delete All Previous Versions*: All previous versions of the item stored in its version history are deleted, leaving only the current version.

■ **Note**   To declare items records as part of a policy, enable the In-Place Records site collection feature. If this feature is not enabled, the Declare Record option is not available for selection.

---

    iii. In the Recurrence section, identify whether to repeat the assigned action for the item while it is in the stage and, if it is repeated, how frequently. The option to repeat the action within a stage is not available for all actions.

    iv. Once the details for the stage are configured, click the OK button.

  d. Once all of the retention stages are properly defined, click the OK button to save the policy.

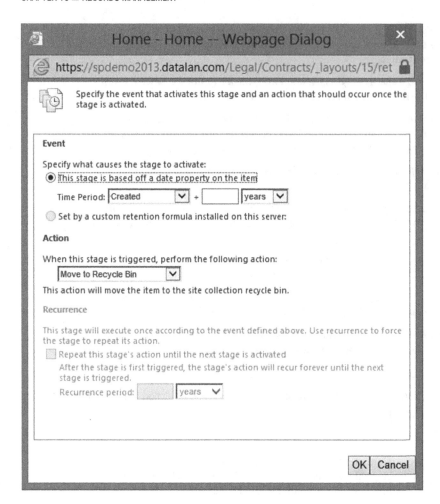

Figure 10-7. *Stage Properties window*

The information management policy is saved, and the defined retention policy is applied to the list or library.

Viewing Item Retention Stage Details

When you configure a retention policy to impact an item in a list or library, you can view the item's status to understand the stages the item has passed through, the stage it is in, and the stages it has not entered. This information appears in the Compliance Details window (see Figure 10-5).

Record Centers

As was discussed in Chapter 2, the Record Center site template creates sites designed to store and manage records (see Figure 10-8). These sites contain many items we have previously discussed, such as content organizer, preconfigured within the site. Additional menu options and management pages to help you manage these resources are also made available. Use Record Centers when you want to create a site that can collect and manage company records.

Figure 10-8. *Record Center site*

Configuring Record Center Sites

Sites created from the Record Center site template need to be configured to support the types of documents to be managed within them. The configuration activities that need to be performed within this type of site include creating and adding content types representing documents supported by the record center to the Drop Off library. (Creating and managing content types are discussed in detail in Chapter 9.) For example, if you intend to use the record center site to manage contracts, you must create one or more content types with the proper column details to support the contract documents that are to be managed in the site and then associate the content types with the Drop Off library so that this type of file can be uploaded to the site.

Another part of configuring a record center site is creating record repository libraries. These libraries act as the final storage locations for content routed to the site. You will need to create one or more of these libraries depending on your document storage and organization requirements. To continue with the contracts example, you might decide to add only a single record repository, called Contracts, in which to store all contract documents routed to the site. Alternatively you might create a second record repository library, called Classified Contracts, with restricted security for storing employment agreements and other types of highly confidential contracts. Any record repository libraries must be configured with the content types representing the materials they will be used to manage.

■ **Note** The same content types used in the repository libraries to store documents should also be used in the Drop Off library to support uploading of the documents. The Drop Off library ought to contain the content types used in all of the record repository libraries in the site.

With the libraries where content is to be managed configured, you will need to create content organizer rules to route documents from the Drop Off library to the appropriate record repository libraries (how to create and manage these rules is discussed earlier in this chapter). Create the rules in record center sites to control routing of documents to the appropriate repository libraries. Within the Settings menu, these sites have an additional option (see Figure 10-9) that navigates you to the Record Center Management page.

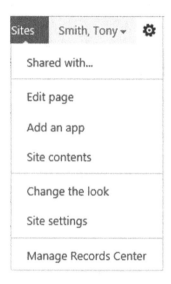

Figure 10-9. Settings menu in a record center site

The Record Center Management page is provided to list the steps necessary to configure the site. The page provides instructions on how to manage the details discussed so far, as well as to provide access to the Create and Manage Content Organizer Rules options. You can initiate the creation of a new content organizer rule or select an existing rule to be edited within the provided Content Organizer Rules view in the same way as you can access and manage these rules by selecting the Content Organizer options from the Site Settings page (discussed in the "Content Organizer" section, above).

To configure record center sites, you will also need to create record retention policies that will determine documents' life cycles and manage any record declaration requirements needed for the items routed to the library.

Managing Documents in Record Center Sites

Once record center sites are configured, you can manage the collection and retention of documents in these sites. Documents can be uploaded to record center sites using any of the standard document upload options discussed in Chapter 7, such as navigating to the Drop Off library and choosing the New Document option or selecting the Upload Document option from the Files menu. A record center, however, also includes a Submit a Record button on its home page. The button can be clicked to initiate the upload of a new document.

A new document uploaded to a record center site is listed in the My Records Pending Submission section until routed to its final retention library. Items listed in this section (as well as how long they are listed there) depend on defined content organizer rules and on whether any manual steps have to be performed on them before they can be routed to their final storage libraries.

Site administrators of record center sites can tailor these sites' layout as needed to reflect their purposes and objectives.

Document Centers

Document center sites (see Figure 10-10) are designed to store and manage corporate documents. Record center sites (discussed earlier) include the resources necessary to automatically route materials to document libraries based on the document properties using content organizer. Document center sites are the better choice when the goal is to have users upload documents directly into a document repository library, where it is expected to stay rather than be routed elsewhere.

Figure 10-10. Document Center sites

When created, a document center site includes a single document library, called Documents, where uploaded materials are expected to reside. The site also includes a task list. Its purpose is to track activities related to the stored documents that need to be performed. As items are added to the library, they appear in the two library views listed on the document center's home page.

- *Newest Documents*: This view lists those documents most recently added to the library, in descending order by the Created date.

- *Modified by Me*: This view lists the documents in the library most recently modified by the user viewing the site.

The document center site's home page also includes an Upload a Document button. It can be used to initiate the upload of a document into the site's Documents library.

Document center sites, like others in SharePoint, support records management policies allowing materials in them to be subject to structured management processes. Manual records declaration can also be configured in these sites to support content retention requirements.

Content Holds

A content hold is used to identify content and suspend its expiration or deletion by users or expiration policies. Holds can be created in sites where the Hold feature is active. Placing a hold in this way is called a local hold. By default record centers have the Hold feature enabled to support creation of local holds, whereas other sites need this feature activated to support local content holds. Holds can also be created within eDiscovery Center portals. These portals, created with the eDiscovery Center site collection template, are specifically designed to support the creation of cross-environment content holds that can be used to identify and hold content all across SharePoint, as well as from Microsoft Exchange mailboxes.

Local Holds

Local holds are used to create locally managed content holds in the site where the content resides. They are useful when all of the content needing to be held is located within a single site. Local holds can be created in any site where the Hold site feature is activated. To activate the Hold site feature, do the following:

1. Navigate to the site where you want to activate the Hold feature.

2. On the site's home page, select the Site Settings option from the Settings menu.

3. On the Site Settings page, select the Manage Site Features option from the Site Actions section.

4. On the Site Features page, select the Activate button for the Hold feature.

With the Hold feature activated, local hold functionality is available in the site.

Creating Local Holds

To create a hold in a site whose Hold feature is activated, do as follows:

1. Navigate to the site where you want to create the local hold.

2. On the site's home page, select the Site Settings option from the Settings menu.

3. On the Site Settings page, select the Holds option from the Hold section.

4. On the Holds page, select the New Item option from the Items ribbon tab.

5. On the Item Edit page, do the following:

   a. Enter a name for the hold.

   b. Enter an optional description for the hold.

   c. Enter the optional Managed By information used to identify the individual responsible for managing the hold.

   d. Click the Save button.

The new hold is created in the site.

Adding Items to Local Holds Individually

Once a local hold is created, you can identify items to be managed by the hold. Items added to the hold are restricted from being removed from the environment manually or with information management policies or workflows. To add an item to an existing hold do the following:

1. Navigate to the list or library containing the item to be added to the hold.

2. On the list or library view page, select the Compliance Details option from the list item's context menu or the document's hover panel menu.

3. In the Compliance Details window, select the Add/Remove from Hold option from the Hold Status section.

4. On the Item Hold Status screen, do the following:

   a. Click the Add to a Hold option, and select the hold to place the item in.

   b. Enter an optional comment for the hold of the item. The comment will be included in the audit log for the hold.

   c. Click the Save button to save the hold of the item.

   The item is added to the selected hold and locked so that it cannot be edited or deleted.

Adding Items to Local Holds through Search

Picking individual documents to add to holds assumes you know which documents contain the information that triggers placement of the item in the hold. Often, however, you will not know all of the documents to include in a hold, nor will you be able to select them individually without reading through each item to determine whether it should be placed in the hold. In such a case, you can use search to locate the items to be added to the hold. To use search to identify items to add to a hold, do the following:

1. Navigate to the site where content needs to be held.

2. On the site's home page, select the Site Settings option from the Settings menu.

3. On the Site Settings page, click the Discover and Hold Content option from the Hold section.

4. On the Search and Add to Hold page, do the following:

   a. In the Search Criteria section, enter terms to use to locate content through search and add it to the hold. Select the Preview Results option to view a list of items located by using the entered terms.

   b. In the Local Hold or Export section, identify how to handle items located. Selecting the "Keep in place and add to hold directly" option adds items located by the search to the specified hold. Selecting "Copy to another location and add the copy to a hold" creates copies of the identified items, places them in the hold, and leaves the original documents untouched. If you select this option, also select a destination location to which to copy the items.

   c. In the Relevant Hold section, identify the hold to place the located items in, or choose to create a new hold. Creating a new hold opens the New Hold window (discussed in the "Create Local Holds" section of this chapter).

   d. Click the Add Results to Hold button to add the located items to the selected hold.

5. On the confirmation screen for adding the request to the scheduled process, click the OK button.

The hold request is submitted to the scheduled process tasked with adding the items to the hold. The process searches for and locates the items and adds them to the hold.

Removing Items from a Local Hold

Items added to a local hold can later be removed from the hold and returned to their previous state, where they can be managed by information management policies, by workflows, and manually. To remove an item from a local hold, do the following:

1. Navigate to the list or library containing the item to be removed from the hold.

2. On the list or library view page, select the Compliance Details option from the list item's context menu or the document's hover panel menu.

3. In the Compliance Details window, select the Add/Remove from Hold option from the Hold Status section.

4. On the Item Hold Status screen, do the following:

    a. Select the Remove from Hold option, and choose the hold from which the item is to be removed.

    b. Optionally enter a comment for the item's removal from the hold. The comment is included in the audit log for the hold.

    c. Click the Save button to save the removal of the item from the hold.

Once the item is removed from the hold, the restrictions placed on it are released.

Viewing All Items in a Hold

To view the list of items placed in a local hold, do the following:

1. Navigate to the site where you want to view the details of a local hold.

2. On the site's home page, select the Site Settings option from the Settings menu.

3. On the Site Settings page, select the Hold Reports option from the Hold section.

4. On the Hold Reports page, click the name of the hold report to view.

The selected hold report is opened and can be reviewed.

Viewing All Holds Associated with an Item

We have discussed how to view all the items associated with a specific hold. To view all the holds associated with a specific item, do as follows:

1. Navigate to the list or library containing the item whose hold you want to view.

2. On the list or library view page, select the Compliance Details option from the list item's context menu or the document's hover panel menu.

3. In the Compliance Details window, select the Add/Remove from Hold option from the Hold Status section.

4. Select the Remove from Hold drop-down list to see all of the holds associated with the item.

You can view the holds associated with the item and, if necessary, remove the item from a listed hold, as described in the "Remove an Item from a Local Hold" section, above.

eDiscovery Center Holds

In addition to the local holds discussed so far in this chapter, SharePoint 2013 includes an eDiscovery Center portal template that can be used to create eDiscovery Center sites (see Figure 10-11). (The elements included in the eDiscovery Center sites are discussed in Chapter 2.)

Figure 10-11. *eDiscovery Center site*

eDiscovery Centers are site collections that include capabilities to create and manage content holds spanning the entire SharePoint environment and Microsoft Exchange mailboxes. eDiscovery centers are organized with the following structure to create and manage holds:

*   *Cases*: Are sites used to create and organize holds associated with a specific event.

*   *eDiscovery Sets*: Specify the content sources from which the hold will locate content to be included and filters to be applied to identify the content.

- *Queries*: Identify the search criteria used to select hold content to be reviewed and exported.

- *Exports*: Identify extracts of the held content to be used to provide materials to appropriate parties.

Creating Cases

A case, used to identify and organize content holds, is a site created to store holds associated with a specific event, typically a litigation event. Cases are created from the eDiscovery center home page as follows:

1. Navigate to the home of the eDiscovery Center site.

2. On the site home page, select the Create New Case option.

3. On the New SharePoint Site page, do the following:

   a. In the Title and Description section, enter the title for the new case site and an optional description.

   b. In the Web Site Address section, enter the URL for the new site.

   c. In the Template section, leave the eDiscovery Case site selected.

   d. In the Permissions section, identify whether the case site is to inherit permissions from the parent site or use unique permissions.

   e. In the Navigation section, select whether the site is to be listed in the Quick Launch of the eDiscovery Center root site.

   f. In the Navigation Inheritance section, specify whether to inherit the navigation bar from the parent site or create one unique to the case site.

   g. Click the Create button.

The new case site is created, and you are taken to the home page of the new site (see Figure 10-12).

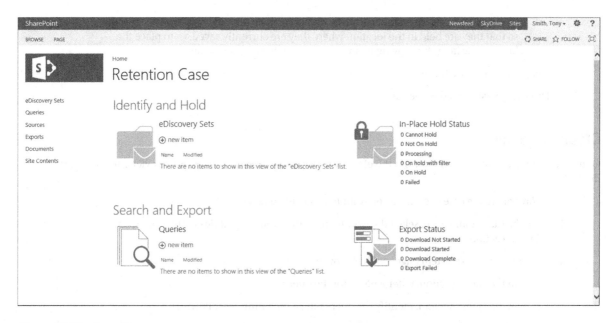

Figure 10-12. *Case site*

Creating eDiscovery Sets

Once a case is created, you can store holds in the case site by creating eDiscovery Sets that define the characteristics of content to be included in the hold. To create an eDiscovery Set, do the following:

1. Navigate to the case site where the eDiscovery set is to be created.

2. On the case home page in the Identify and Hold section, select the New Item in the eDiscovery Sets.

3. On the eDiscovery Sets home page, do the following:

    a. In the eDiscovery Set Name section, enter a name for the new eDiscovery set.

    b. In the Sources section, click Add & Manage Sources, and on the Sources page, select the mailboxes and sites to use as sources for the content search. Then click the OK button. Continue to add sources until all sources of content are identified.

    c. In the Filter section, specify the criteria for identifying content to contain within the hold. Criteria should include some combination of the following elements. Then click the Apply Filter option.

        • *Filter*: Identifies text to be used to perform the search.

        • *Start Date*: Limits the items returned to those dated on or after the entered date.

        • *End Date*: Limits the items returned to those dated on or before the entered date.

        • *Author/Sender*: Limits content to items created by or mail messages sent by the selected person.

        • *Domain*: Limits content returned to include only items from a specific domain.

    d.   In the In-Place Hold section, identify whether to place the hold on the items in place, so that they are held in the location where they are currently saved, or to place the hold on the items by copying them to a different destination location.

    c.   Click the Save button.

The eDiscovery Set is added to the case.

Creating Queries

Queries are created to locate content from the eDiscovery set to be included in an export or view. To create a query, do the following:

1. Navigate to the case site where you want to create the query.

2. On the Case home page, select the New Item option from the Queries in the Search and Export section.

3. On the Query: New Item page, do the following:

    a.   In the Name section, enter a name for the query.

    b.   In the Query section, identify the query filters, including the following:

        i.   Query terms: Identifying search terms to be used to locate content.

        ii.   Start Date: Limiting items returned to those dated on or after the entered date.

        iii.   End Date: Limiting items returned to those dated on or before the entered date.

        iv.   Author/Sender: Limits content to items created by or mail messages sent by the selected person.

        v.   Select the Advanced Query option to show the Advanced Query window, where advanced query properties can be entered. Then click the OK button to save the entered options.

    c.   In the Sources section, select Modify Query Source to change the source details to include all case content identified, only content in specific eDiscovery sets, or content only in specific sources.

    d.   On the Exchange tab, identify whether to limit items only to specific types of Exchange messages.

    e.   On the SharePoint tab, identify whether to limit the query only to files of certain types and limit items by any additional properties.

    f.   Click the Save button to save the query details.

The query is created and saved to the case.

Exports

After queries are created, you can export query items to copy needed held items for reference or to share them with other parties. To export the content referenced by a query, do the following:

1. Navigate to the case home page containing the query to export content from.

2. In the Queries list of the Search and Export section, click the name of the query to export content from.

3. In the Query window, click the Export button.

4. In the Export window, do the following:

    a. In the Options section, identify whether to remove duplicate content when querying content in Exchange and whether to include versions of a document and encrypted content or content with unknown formats.

    b. Click the OK button.

5. On the Export: Download page, select whether to download the resulting items or download a report of the items by clicking the Download Results or Download Report option.

6. If prompted to do so with the Application Run Security Warning window, click the Run button.

7. In the eDiscovery Download Manager app window (see Figure 10-13), specify where to save the downloaded files to or where to create the report file. Then click the OK button.

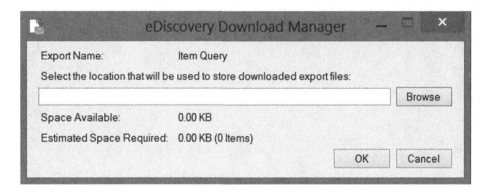

Figure 10-13. eDiscovery Download Manager app window

8. Once the file download is completed, click the Close button on the eDiscovery Download Manager app window.

The eDiscovery Download Manager app closes, and the files or reports become available in the selected download location.

CHAPTER 11

Search

SharePoint 2013 includes a new search platform that can be used to locate information across SharePoint and the rest of your enterprise. The SharePoint 2013 enterprise search is based on the FAST Search platform, which was available in conjunction with the SharePoint 2010 platform. SharePoint 2010 had included both an enterprise search and the separate FAST Search for SharePoint product. As these were two separate services, organizations needed to decide whether they wanted to use the provided enterprise search or introduce FAST Search to support their search needs.

SharePoint 2013 incorporates a single consolidated search platform that includes not only those capabilities available in both the SharePoint 2010 enterprise search and the FAST Search for SharePoint but an entirely new set of services that provide a complete and comprehensive enterprise search experience. This platform allows searching a variety of sources, including SharePoint, Exchange, file shares, web content, and database content, and provides intelligent query management and robust result views.

Using SharePoint Search

SharePoint search offers a rich interface that allows you to search for and locate information, based on its content and associated properties, relevant to work you are performing. Results can then be refined and reviewed to isolate the desired materials. SharePoint combines several features to create this robust search experience, including the following:

- *Content Crawling*: This feature scans content to be included in a search. It identifies properties and security attributes used by query services to determine when to display crawled items to users as part of search results.

- *Query Services*: This feature allows specification of information to be used by the SharePoint search to find content to display in search results.

- *Query Results*: This feature organizes and displays results of executed queries.

- *Refiners*: These features let you identify details to be used to further filter listed results based on defined properties related to the results.

All of these capabilities come together to provide the SharePoint 2013 search experience.

Performing a Search

SharePoint offers several interfaces to help you take full advantage of its search services to locate relevant information. These interfaces support searches in the overall environment or specific sites, lists, and libraries.

Searches can be initiated from any site page within SharePoint. Whether a page is a web part, a wiki, or a publishing page, the search box is at the top of the page to give you easy access to search services. The search interface either provides a standard search box, as shown in Figure 11-1, or a search box with integrated options, which allow selection of verticals to use in targeting the search (see Figure 11-2). When you execute a search from the site's search box, the scope will initially default to the current site, but you can expand it to search across the entire environment instead.

Figure 11-1. *Standard search box*

Figure 11-2. *Search box with sources*

You can also initiate a search in list and library views. A search box is part of list and library view headers (see Figure 11-3), next to the views list. Searches performed in a list or library view are scoped to return results just from the associated list or library.

Documents

Figure 11-3. *List or library view search*

Finally, you can initiate a search in search pages. Whether your environment uses the standard search page or a search center, the search page includes a search box similar to the one found on a normal site page. A search page search is initially scoped to search all available crawled content.

To perform a search in SharePoint, navigate to any of the search boxes described, and enter the search text you want to use. When the search box allows the selection of verticals, you can also identify the desired vertical to run the search against. The executed search will then scope to the appropriate content set and navigate you to the search results page.

Working with Search Results

Once a search is performed, search results are presented. The results returned for a search include items that meet query conditions contained in the identified scope and that the user performing the search has rights to access. That is, search results will not include content that the searcher does not have rights to access. The order of the results returned is determined by the items' relevance, which is based on a variety of factors, including how closely the result meets the query, how active or current the item is, and how relevant the item is to the searcher. Presentation of results returned is further defined by additional factors, including whether result blocks are defined and result type definitions are in use.

Result Blocks

Query rules can be created within SharePoint search to define rules to extend search queries beyond standard search text queries. These rules are made up of a set of conditions and actions that are executed when search text meets identified conditions. Result blocks, defined as part of query rules, group sets of highly relevant content. For example, a search for "sales videos" would typically search crawled content for items containing those words or that phrase and return those items. However, when a search for "sales videos" is run, it is more likely the searcher is looking for video files related to sales than for content containing those two words. A query rule in SharePoint can specify that when the word "video" is used in a search, the query should look for video files. The query can be extended so that when "sales videos" is the query text, the most relevant content would be video files in the Sales site. Such highly relevant content can be presented in a result block (see Figure 11-4), which groups these items and so elevates their importance above the other returned results.

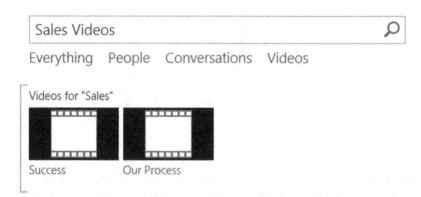

Figure 11-4. *Result block*

Promoted Results

Much as query rule actions are used to create result blocks, query rule actions can be used to define promoted results, which are result items defined by a rule to always appear at the top of the search result set when searches meeting the query rule conditions are executed. For example, if you have a specific approved company logo file that should be used whenever the logo is needed, you may create a query rule that returns the logo file as the most relevant result when a search is performed for "company logo". Promoted results replace the best bet capabilities available in previous versions of SharePoint for defining specific elevated results for queries. They also replace visual best bets available in FAST Search.

Standard Search Results

Beyond specialized result blocks and promoted results, a search yields a set of standard search results that list materials matching the executed search. The layout of listed search results is based on the type of items listed, called result types. For example, documents and discussion items have different search result layouts. The layout of the items in the results is defined for each result type based on the display template associated with that result type. The display templates define the item details to list in the results and how these details are organized.

The standard search results view also includes a hover panel for each listed result. This panel lists additional details about the item in a format also determined by the display template for the associated result type. The hover panel, which appears when the mouse is allowed to hover over the item, can provide in-depth information about the item and organize actions available to be performed against it. To continue the example of the discussion item and the document, hovering over a discussion item shows a listing of the details for the item, including the discussion text and the original post the item is associated with (see Figure 11-5). The hover panel also includes options to navigate to the item and to the associated discussion.

Figure 11-5. *Discussion item hover panel*

A Word document's hover panel (see Figure 11-6) incorporates a preview along with general details about the document. With this hover panel you can also open the document, follow it, send it, navigate to the associated library, and if you have the rights, edit it.

Figure 11-6. *Word document hover panel*

■ **Note**   Office Web Apps must be installed and configured in your SharePoint environment for document previews to appear in the hover panel.

Items listed as search results are organized by relevance, which is a ranking given based on how well items seem to meet the query. Relevance rankings are based on a complex formula that includes factors such as property weighting, query authority, and freshness.

Refiners

Refiners are sets of filters found to the left of the search results. They can be used to further filter those results. Refiners are a set of defined attributes whose values typically are based on those found in the returned content. By default, the refinement panel allows filtering by result type, author, and date modified. This list, however, can be expanded or otherwise changed by having a SharePoint technical administrator configure additional refiners. Refiners can be text options that, when clicked, filter results, or they can be graphical tools that allow more advanced filtering. For example, the Modified Date refiner appears as a slider that lets you adjust the time frame by sliding a ruler within the graphic (see Figure 11-7).

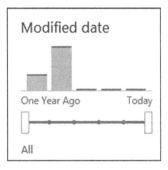

Figure 11-7. *Modified Date refiner*

Working with Search Centers

A standard search initiated in SharePoint from the standard search box (see Figure 11-1) is executed through the default search page, the OSSSearchResults.aspx page, or a search center. These search pages allow results to be displayed, refiners to be leveraged, and additional searches to be performed.

The standard SharePoint search results page provides a rich search query and results management interface incorporating the various search capabilities of SharePoint. However, should you want to extend these capabilities, you can access more advanced filtering or introduce a customizable search page to meet specific organizational needs. Search centers allow this sort of advanced search management. Two search center templates can be leveraged in SharePoint Server Standard and SharePoint Server Enterprise to create search center sites, which you can use as locations for routing and execution of searches.

Standard SharePoint Search Centers

By default, two search center templates are available in SharePoint Server Standard and SharePoint Server Enterprise: the Basic Search Center and the Enterprise Search Center. These templates are used to create search center sites configurable as primary search pages in a SharePoint environment.

Basic Search Centers

Basic search center sites provide an interface that lets standard searches be performed against the SharePoint search service, as shown in Figure 11-8.

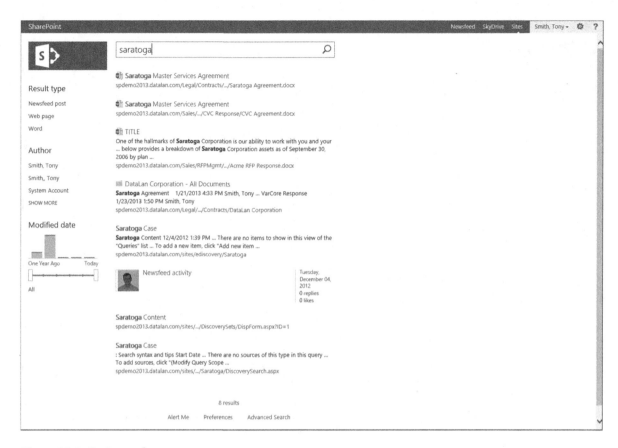

***Figure 11-8.** Basic search center*

A basic search center presents all of the search results and refiner details discussed earlier in this chapter and allows you to perform additional searches from the search center home page. Basic search center sites, however, do not include the ability to select different verticals over which to execute a search. They are designed to allow standard search execution and results management without advanced source filtering.

Enterprise Search Centers

Enterprise search center sites (see Figure 11-9) provide all of the capabilities of the basic search centers and also allow selection of available verticals that you can use for targeted searches.

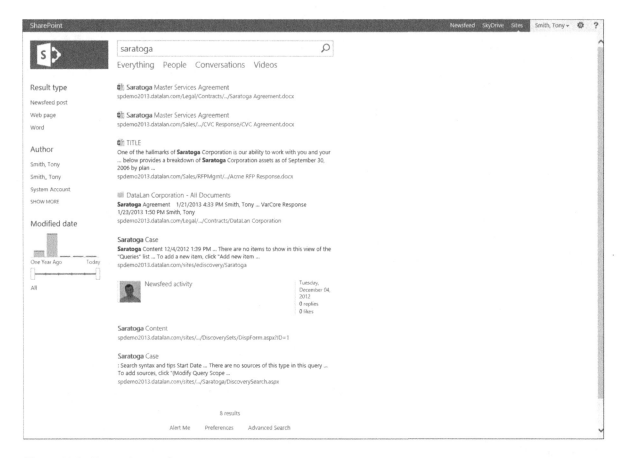

Figure 11-9. *Enterprise search center*

By default the enterprise search center lets you perform searches over the following sources of content:

- *Everything*: All content crawled by SharePoint

- *People*: SharePoint users

- *Conversations*: SharePoint social discussions

- *Videos*: Video files

- *Reports*: Report files; this option is not available by default but can be added by activating the necessary features.

Use of a listed vertical limits the executed query to the selected content and brings you to a site's search page used to perform queries and display results for the selected vertical.

Executing Advanced Searches

One benefit of using a search center instead of the default search page is that you can perform advanced searches. In a standard search in SharePoint, the text you enter is used to locate matching material based on the items' content and associated properties. These searches look across all crawled elements to identify whether there is a match to the query details entered. Advanced searches allow you to more granularly specify search terms. You can locate entered text in specific columns, locate exact phrases, exclude items containing identified content, and limit results based on language.

To access the Advanced Search page in a search center site, select the Advanced link located at the bottom of the search center page. The Advanced Search page (see Figure 11-10) allows entry of specific search criteria to granularly target the search.

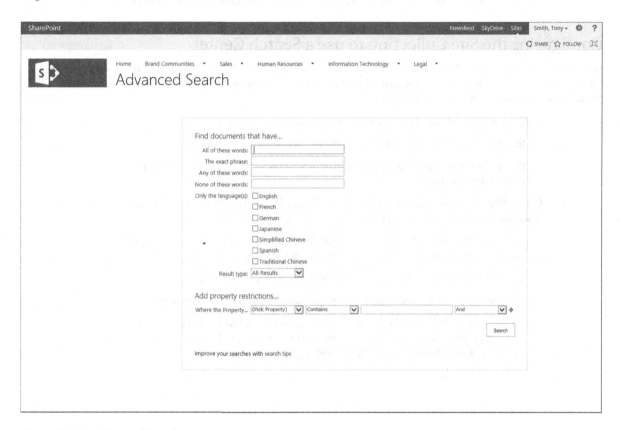

Figure 11-10. *Advanced Search page*

On an advanced search page, you can specify any combination of the following details to perform targeted searches against the content in your SharePoint environment:

- *All of these words*: Specifies that items are returned only if they contain all words entered in the field.

- *The exact phrase*: Specifies that items are returned only if they contain the exact phrase entered, not just the words included in the phrase.

- *Any of these words*: Specifies that results are returned if they contain any items entered in this field.

- *None of these words*: Specifies words that, when found, exclude an item from returned results.

- *Only the language(s)*: Limits returned items to those containing content only in the selected language or languages.

- *Result type*: Limits returned items to a specifically selected type, such as a Word document or PowerPoint presentation.

- *Add property restrictions*: Allows selection of specific item attributes on which to search for details. You can identify multiple properties and specify conditions for each property where results are to be returned. For example, select a Date field from the list of properties to specify that you want to locate items whose column value falls on or before an entered date.

Configuring the Site Collection to use a Search Center

When you configure a site collection to use a search center, you specify that searches performed in the site will be routed to the search center for execution instead of to the standard SharePoint search results page. To configure a site collection to use a search center, do the following:

1. Navigate to the root site in the site collection.

2. On the site's home page, select the Site Settings option from the Settings menu.

3. On the Site Settings page, select the Search Settings option from the Site Collection Administration section.

4. On the Site Collection Administration Search Settings page (see Figure 11-11), do the following:

   a. In the Enter a Search Center URL section, enter the URL to the basic or enterprise search center to be used in performing searches in the site collection.

   b. In the "Which search results page should queries be sent to" section,

      i. Specify whether the page is to use the same results page as the parent.

      ii. If you are not using the same results page, select whether to specify a results page. If you do, either select the page to use, or turn on the drop-down menu in the search box and use the first node as the results page.

   c. Click the OK button.

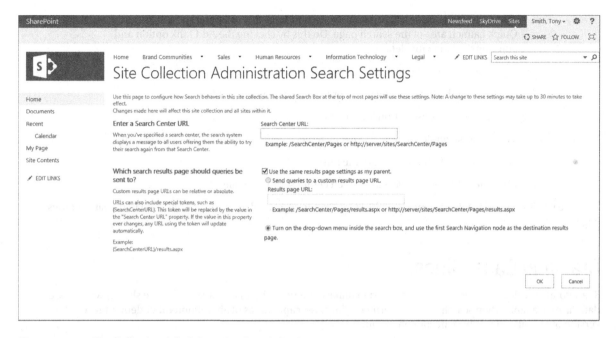

Figure 11-11. *Site Collection Administration Search Settings page*

The site collection is updated to use the search center specified, and you are returned to the Site Settings page.

Configuring a Site to use a Search Center

At times you might want to override the site collection search center settings for a specific site within the collection. This may happen if you are interested in leveraging a different view of the search page or a different search results layout when performing a search in a specific site. To update the search center settings for a specific site, do the following:

1. Navigate to the site where you want to configure the search center.

2. On the site's home page, select the Site Settings option from the Settings menu.

3. On the Site Settings page, select the Search Settings option from the Search section.

4. On the Search Settings page, do the following:

    a. In the Enter a Search Center URL section, enter the URL to the basic or enterprise search center to be used when searching in the site collection.

    b. In the "Which search results page should queries be sent to" section,

        i. Specify whether the page is to use the same results page as the parent.

        ii. If you are not using the same results page, select whether to specify a results page. If you do, either select the page to use, or turn on the drop-down menu in the search box and use the first node as the results page.

    c.   In the Configure Search Navigation section, identify any links you want to list in the Quick Launch area of the search page. Do this by clicking the Add Link option and entering the following details:

        i.   Title for the link.

        ii.   URL for the link. Specify whether to open it in a new window.

        iii.   An optional description for the link.

        iv.   Optional audience details. Specify target groups to make the link available to.

        v.   Click the OK button to save the link.

    d.   Click the OK button to save the search center settings details.

The site is updated to take advantage of the search center specified, and you are returned to the Site Settings page.

Crawling Capabilities

SharePoint crawling services can be configured to make content in SharePoint, Exchange, file shares, web sites, and databases available when searches are performed. The crawl capabilities of SharePoint differ depending on the version of SharePoint you have in your environment.

- *SharePoint Foundation Search*: Search as part of SharePoint Foundation provides the most basic set of search services of the three SharePoint 2013 versions. SharePoint Foundation crawling is limited to crawling content within the local SharePoint environment.

- *SharePoint Server Standard Search*: SharePoint Server Standard provides enterprise content crawling capabilities that allow crawling of content in a variety of sources, including SharePoint, Exchange, file shares, and web sites. SharePoint Standard Search, however, cannot crawl database content.

- *SharePoint Server Enterprise Search*: The search services of SharePoint Server Enterprise crawls the types of content SharePoint Server Standard search crawls as well as database content by means of Business Connectivity Services connections.

Defining content to be crawled and configuring the crawls' properties, including their frequency, are managed by SharePoint technical administrators through the SharePoint Central Administration site. Some configurations however, can be made in site collections to identify elements to be included or excluded by the search services.

Managing Managed Properties

Crawled properties identify list and library properties to be crawled for inclusion in search. Executing a query searches for the query text across all of the crawled properties and in the content of crawled documents. When columns are added to lists and libraries, they become, by default, crawled properties. Crawled properties can be extended by making them managed properties. Managed properties are list and library properties that can be specifically referenced by search queries when performing searches. They specify that entered query text is to be located only in a specific column.

For example, you would use managed properties if you manage documents related to a specific product. These documents may have a property, called Product, that identifies the product the document is associated with. Performing a general search across these product documents for those related to a specific product would return all documents that reference that product name in any way that does not limit the search to only the items specifically identified as related to the product. For instance, several documents that contain footnotes may reference the product but in no other way relate to it. Since these footnote references exist, a search for the product name returns these items. If you specify that the Product property be configured as a managed property. The crawling service will know not only to index the fact that the product name was referenced as part of the document details but to maintain the property and property value relationship. Specific searches can then be performed using the Product property identifying the documents, where the Product column contains the desired product name. The results you get are then limited to just those items specifically identified as related to the desired product.

Managed properties can be defined by IT technical administrators in the SharePoint Central Administration site to make them available in all site collections in a SharePoint environment. However, managed properties can also be created in a specific site collection for use only within that context.

Creating Site Collection Managed Properties

Creating site collection managed properties defines directly searchable properties in the site collection. Managed properties created at this level have some limitations compared to those created by SharePoint technical administrators in Central Administration. Limitations include the following:

- Site collection level managed properties support only the creation of Text and Yes/No typed valued properties. Other formats, including Integer, Decimal, Date and Time, Double Precision Float, and Binary, are not supported at this level.

- Managed properties created at the site collection level cannot be made sortable or refinable.

- Site collection level managed properties can be used only in the site collection they are created in.

To create a new site collection managed property, do the following:

1. Navigate to the root site in the site collection.

2. On the site's home page, select the Site Settings option from the Settings menu.

3. On the Site Settings page, select the Search Schema option from the Site Collection Administration section.

4. On the Managed Properties page (see Figure 11-12), select the New Managed Property option.

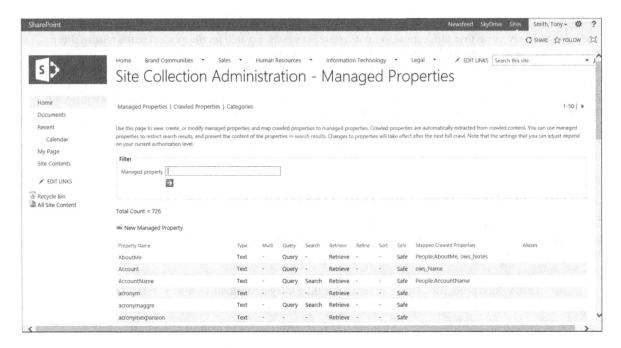

Figure 11-12. *Managed Properties page*

5. In the New Managed Property window, do the following:

    a. In the Name and Description section, enter a name for the new managed property and an optional description.

    b. In the Type section, select the type of information to be stored in this property, with options limited to Text and Yes/No.

    c. In the Main Characteristics section, click the Searchable option to ensure the managed property can be used for searches.

    d. In the Advanced Searchable Settings section, click the Advanced Searchable Settings button to open the Choose Advanced Searchable settings window.

        i. In the Full-Text Index section, you can change the full-text index in which the column data are to be placed when crawled.

        ii. In the Weight Group section, you can identify the weight grouping in which the crawled details are to be placed.

        iii. Click the OK button to save the advanced searchable settings.

    e. In the Queryable section, click the Queryable check box to allow search queries to run directly against this managed property.

    f. In the Retrievable section, click the Retrievable check box to allow content return in search results.

    g. In the Save for Anonymous section, identify whether this managed property can be used when performing anonymous searches. This option is relevant only when anonymous access is configured in your site collection.

h.   In the Alias section, enter an alias name to use when referencing the managed property if you want to manage the property by a name other than the defined managed property name itself.

i.   In the Token Normalization section, leave the Token Normalization option checked.

j.   In the Complete Matching section, check the Complete Matching option only if you want queries executed against the property to find the value if only the full value of the field is used. For example, if the property value is "butterfly" and the search is for "butter", when the Complete Matching option is checked, the item is not returned.

k.   In the Mappings to Crawled Properties section, click the Add a Mapping option. Then in the Crawled Property Selection window, search for and select the crawled property to connect to the managed property. Then click OK to save the association.

l.   In the Company Name Extraction section, check the Company Extraction option if you want to scan the managed property for company names when it is crawled. If a company name is part of the value, search results can be filtered through refiners by this value.

m.   In the Custom Entity Extraction section, specify whether to scan the managed property for any custom word or word part extractions to allow filtering through refiners by a custom refiner set. Select these options only if the custom extraction dictionaries are in use. Custom extraction dictionaries must be configured by a SharePoint technical administrator.

n.   Click the OK button.

The new managed property is added. It becomes available upon performance of a full crawl of the content where the managed property is used.

Editing the Details of an Existing Managed Property

You can update the properties of an existing managed property in order to change the configuration of the item to meet the search needs of information contained within the corresponding crawled properties. To edit the details of an existing managed property, do the following:

1.   Navigate to the root site in the site collection.

2.   On the site's home page, select the Site Settings option from the Settings menu.

3.   On the Site Settings page, select the Search Schema option from the Site Collection Administration section.

4.   On the Managed Properties page (see Figure 11-12), do the following:

a.   Enter the name of the managed property to be edited, and select the search icon.

b.   In the Properties list, select the managed property to be edited.

5.   On the Edit Managed Property page, do any of the following as necessary:

a.   In the Alias section, edit or add an alias for the managed property.

b.   In the Mappings to Crawled Properties section, add or remove associations with crawled properties.

   c.   In the Company Name Extract section, update the company extraction option.

   d.   In the Custom Entity Extraction section, update the custom extraction option.

   e.   Click the OK button.

Changes made to the managed property are saved. The updates appear after the next full crawl of the lists and libraries using columns associated with this managed property.

Deleting Managed Properties

To remove managed properties from SharePoint, do the following:

1.   Navigate to the root site in the site collection.

2.   On the site's home page, select the Site Settings option from the Settings menu.

3.   On the Site Settings page, select the Search Schema option from the Site Collection Administration section.

4.   On the Managed Properties page, do the following:

   a.   Enter the name of the managed property to be deleted, and select the search icon.

   b.   In the Properties list select the Delete option from the item's context menu.

5.   In the deletion confirmation window, click the OK button.

The managed property is removed from the site collection.

Reindexing a List or Library

At times you might want to have the SharePoint crawling services recrawl the content throughout the environment or in a specific list or library—for example, when you remove a large number of documents from a library or move a large number of documents to a new location. You need to reindex the content for such changes to be reflected.

Reindexing of your entire environment must be done by a SharePoint technical administrator. However, a specific list or library can be flagged for reindexing when the next scheduled crawl is run in the list or library itself. To flag a list or library for reindexing during the next scheduled crawl, do the following:

1.   Navigate to the list or library you want reindexed.

2.   On the list or library view page, select the List or Library Settings option from the List or Library ribbon tab.

3.   On the Settings page, select the Advanced Settings option from the General Settings section.

4.   On the Advanced Settings page in the Reindex List or Reindex Document Library section, click the Reindex List or Document Library button.

5.   In the Reindex List or Reindex Document Library window, click the Reindex List or Reindex Document Library button.

The list or library is flagged to be reindexed, and you are returned to the Advanced Settings page.

Excluding Sites from Search

If you specify that sites are not be included in search results, content in the identified site will be excluded from the content crawl, and this content will not appear in search results. This is done as follows:

1. Navigate to the site you want to exclude from the search.

2. On the site's home page, select the Site Settings option from the Settings menu.

3. On the Site Settings menu, select the Search and Offline Availability option from the Search section.

4. On the Search and Offline Availability page, select No for the "Allow this site to appear in search results?" option, and click the OK button.

The site is excluded from search, and its contained content is not listed in search results.

Excluding a List or Library from Search

You can configure a specific list or library to be excluded from search. You would do this to limit the exposure of the content in the list or library by making it available only to users browsing to it directly. When you exclude a list or library from search, the rest of the site's content continues to participate in search results. Only the selected list or library is excluded. To exclude a list or library from search, do the following:

1. Navigate to the list or library that you want to exclude from search.

2. On the list or library view page, select the List or Library Settings option from the List or Library ribbon tab.

3. On the Settings page, select the Advanced Settings option from the General Settings section.

4. On the Advanced Settings page in the Search section, select No for the "Allow items from this list or document library to appear is search results?" option, and click the OK button.

The list or library is excluded from search. You are returned to the Settings page.

Excluding List or Library Columns from Search

At times you will want to keep content of a list or library available through search but not want it to crawl all of the list or library columns. You might, for example, have a Notes column where general comments about an item are placed. If crawled, the column's contents would dilute a search's effectiveness. You want Notes left uncrawled so its content does not influence search results. To exclude a column from search, do the following:

1. Navigate to the site where the column is to be excluded from search.

2. On the site's home page, select the Site Settings option from the Settings menu.

3. On the Site Settings page, click the Searchable Columns link in the Search section.

4. On the Searchable Columns page, check the check box for the column to be excluded from search, and click the OK button.

The selected column is excluded from search, and you are returned to the Site Settings page.

SharePoint Query Capabilities

The query capabilities of SharePoint define services and features related to performing search requests. Search requests identify criteria used to locate content crawled by the SharePoint search services. SharePoint 2013 provides several configurable options that can be tailored to align the environment's query capabilities with your information searching needs.

Managing Query Rules

One of the most powerful tools available for configuring search queries are query rules. Query rules allow you to define conditions that, when met as part of entered search criteria, make a corresponding action occur. Query rule actions are designed to help improve searches' relevance by refining details returned in specific scenarios. For example, if you expect people in the organization to search for videos, and you want to ensure that a search performed with the word "video" returns video files, a query rule can be used to specify that the use of the word "video" indicates that specific types of files, such as wmv or mp4 files, are to be searched for instead of simply any items that contain the word "video".

Adding Query Rules

When a SharePoint technical administrator creates query rules in SharePoint Central Administration, you can use them across your SharePoint environment. Creating a query rule in a site collection or site limits the rule's impact to the specific site collection or site. To create a site collection query rule, do the following:

1. Navigate to the root site in the site collection where you want to create a new query rule.

2. On the site's home page, select the Site Settings option from the Settings menu.

3. On the Site Settings page, select the Search Query Rules option from the Site Collection Administration section.

4. On the Manage Query Rules page, do the following:

   a. In the "For what context do you want to configure rules?" section, identify the context in which to apply the new query rule. The context information that can be selected includes the following:

      - *Result Sources*: Identifies the type of result the query rule is based upon.

      - *User Segment*: Defaulted to All User Segment. This option lets you limit the query rule's application to a specific user segment.

      - *Topic Categories*: Defaulted to All Topic Categories. Lets you select specific topic categories to limit the rule to.

   b. In the New Query Rule section, click the New Query Rule link to open the Add Query Rule page.

5. On the Add Query Rule page, do the following:

   a. In the General Information section, enter a name for the new query rule.

   b. Optionally expand the Context section, and do the following:

      i. For Sources, specify whether to expand the query rule to include all sources, or click the Add Sources link and pick an additional source for the rule to act upon. Save this source to add it to the sources list.

ii. For Categories, choose whether to use the query rule on all categories or on select categories. If you click Add Categories to open the Categories Search, you can search for and select term store categories and save these to the list of categories that the query rule is to be associated with.

iii. For User Segments, decide whether to use all user segments, or select the Add User Segment option to add user segments and user segment terms to be leveraged as part of the query rule.

c. In the Query Conditions section, identify the condition in which to invoke the query rule and the condition values. Add more conditions by selecting the Add Alternate Condition link, and then enter the additional conditions and condition values.

d. In the Actions section, do the following:

i. To add a Promoted Result, click the Add Promoted Result link. On the Add Promoted Result page, specify the title and URL for the promoted result and whether it is to appear as a banner or hyperlink. Optionally add a description for the items.

ii. To add Result Blocks, click the Add Result Blocks link. In the Add Result Block window, do the following:

1. In the Block Title section, enter a value for the title of the result block.

2. In the query section, identify the query and source details on which to base the result block.

3. Optionally expand the Settings section, and specify whether to list a More link and, if you do, what URL the link is to navigate to. Also in this section, you can update whether to show the result block above other core results or rank it within the results. Finally, you can identify templates for display of the group and items within the group.

4. Optionally expand the Routing section to specify a URL to use for routing to a Content Search web part.

5. Click the OK button.

iii. Select the "Change ranked results by changing the query" option to build a query, and specify a sort order to use to locate items for the result block.

e. Optionally expand the Publishing section to specify whether the rule is active and has a start and end date when it is active. Also, identify whether the rule needs to be reviewed and, if it does, by whom.

f. Click the Save button to save the new rule.

The query rule is saved, and you are returned to the Manage Query Rules page. This query rule will influence searches performed throughout your site collection.

As mentioned earlier, you can create query rules that impact only a specific site. Do this when you want to create a specialized rule, one relevant only within a specific location in your site collection. To create a query rule scoped to a specific site, do the following:

1. Navigate to the site in which the query rule is to be created.

2. On the site's home page, select the Site Settings option from the Settings menu.

3. On the Site Settings page, select the Query Rules option from the Search section.

4. On the Manage Query Rules page, do the following:

   a. Identify the context in which you want to configure rules by selecting a Result Source and, optionally, a specific user segment and topic category. Doing this will show a list of query rules filtered by the selected items.

   b. Click the New Query Rule link to open the Add Query Rule page.

5. On the Add Query Rule page, do the following:

   a. In the General Information section, enter a name for the new query rule.

   b. Optionally expand the Context section, and do the following:

      i. For Sources, identify whether to expand the query rule to include all sources, or click the Add Sources link and then pick an additional source for the rule to act upon. Save this source to add it to the sources list.

      ii. For Categories, decide whether to use the query rule on all categories or on select categories. If you click Add Categories to open the Categories Search, you can search for and select term store categories and save these to the list of categories that the query rule is to be associated with.

      iii. For User Segments, decide whether to use all user segments, or select the Add User Segment option to add user segments and user segment terms to be leveraged as part of the query rule.

   c. In the Query Conditions section, identify the condition in which to invoke the query rule and the condition values. Add more conditions by selecting the Add Alternate Condition link, and then enter the additional conditions and condition values.

   d. In the Actions section, do the following:

      i. To add a Promoted Result, click the Add Promoted Result link. On the Add Promoted Result page, specify the title and URL for the promoted result and whether it is to appear as a banner or hyperlink. Optionally add a description for the items.

      ii. To add Result Blocks, click the Add Result Block link. In the Add Result Block window, do the following:

         1. In the Block Title section, enter a value for the title of the result block.

         2. In the query section, identify the query and source details on which to base the result block.

         3. Optionally expand the Settings section, and specify whether to list a More link and, if you do, what URL the link is to navigate to. Also in this section, you can update whether to show the result block above other core results or rank it within the results. Finally, you can identify templates for display of the group and items within the group.

         4. Optionally expand the Routing section to identify a URL to use for routing to a Content Search web part.

         5. Click the OK button.

      iii. Select the "Change ranked results by changing the query" option to build a query, and specify a sort order to use to locate items for the result block.

e.   Optionally expand the Publishing section to specify whether the rule is active and has a start and end date within which it will be active. Also, identify whether the rule needs to be reviewed and, if it does, by whom.

f.   Click the Save button to save the new rule.

The rule is saved and is ready to be used in queries performed in the site.

Editing Query Rules

You can edit query rules created at the site collection and site levels to tailor their impact on searches. To edit an existing query rule, do the following:

1.   Navigate to the site collection's root site to edit a site collection query rule or to the associated site to edit a site query rule.

2.   On the site's home page, select the Site Settings option on the Settings menu.

3.   On the Site Settings page, select the Search Query Rules option from the Site Collection Administration section to edit a site collection query rule, or select the Query Rules option from the Search section to edit a site-level query rule.

4.   On the Manage Query Rules page, do the following:

a.   Select the Result Source for which to show query rules, and optionally identify a User Segment and Type Category by which to filter the rule context to be displayed.

b.   Select the Edit option from the query rule's context menu.

5.   On the Edit Query Rules page, update any of the listed query rule details. Once complete, click the Save Button.

The updates to the query rule are applied, and you are returned to the Manage Query Rules page.

Deleting Query Rules

To delete an existing query rule, do the following:

1.   Navigate to the site collection's root site to edit a site collection query rule or to the associated site to edit a site query rule.

2.   On the site's home page, select the Site Settings option on the Settings menu.

3.   On the Site Settings page, select the Search Query Rules option from the Site Collection Administration section to edit a site collection query rule, or select the Query Rules option from the Search section to edit a site-level query rule.

4.   On the Manage Query Rules page, do the following:

a.   Select the Result Source for which to show query rules, and optionally identify a User Segment and Type Category by which to filter the rule context to be displayed.

b.   Select the Delete option from the Query rules context menu.

c.   In the deletion confirmation window, click the OK button.

The query rule is removed. It will no longer influence search queries.

Search Result Capabilities

Search results in SharePoint 2013 are designed to provide highly relevant details for search queries. Search results are configured to be easy to work with and to let you easily identify materials meeting your specific needs. SharePoint has several capabilities for organizing search results and presenting them to users. This section discusses those capabilities and how to manage them.

Managing Result Sources

Result sources identify the set of materials a search query will run through to locate content. Your SharePoint environment can include multiple result sources, some within SharePoint and others outside it. Result sources replace scopes, the concept available in previous versions of SharePoint, and specify the following details for queries using them:

- The source location for the materials to be searched.

- The protocol, such as OpenSearch, to be used to retrieve results.

- Any narrowing conditions, such as limiting items to a specific type of file or content type.

There are several default result sources available in SharePoint 2013, including the items listed in Table 11-1.

Table 11-1. *Result Sources*

Result Source	Description
Conversations	Content in microblogs, newsfeeds, and community sites
Documents	Microsoft Office and PDF documents
Items Matching a Content Type	Items of the same content type as that specified in the performed query
Items Matching a Tag	Items that match a term specified by the incoming query
Items Related to Current User	Items related to the user performing the query
Items with Same Keyword as this Item	Items having the same keyword details as those specified by the query
Local People Results	People included in the profile database for the local profile service
Local Reports and Data Results	Excel documents, Office Data Connections, Report Definition Language items, and Items in Report libraries
Local SharePoint Results	All items in the local SharePoint search index with the exception of people
Local Video Results	Video files, including wmv, avi, mpg, asf, mp4, ogg, ogv, and webm files
Pages	SharePoint web pages
Pictures	Image files
Popular	Documents and list items sorted with the most viewed items at the top
Recently Changed Items	Documents and list items sorted with the most current items at the top
Recommended Items	Documents and list items that were recommended for the query performed
Wiki	SharePoint wiki pages

Result sources, like query rules, can be created at three levels in SharePoint:

- Centrally, for use in the entire SharePoint environment by SharePoint technical administrators using the SharePoint Central Administration site.

- Within a site collection, for use in an entire site collection.

- Within a specific site, for use only in that site.

Creating a Site Collection Result Source

Site collection administrators can create result sources in their site collections. You might do this if you have searches you want to perform only for audio files or a specific type of Microsoft Office document. To create a result source for a site collection, do the following:

1. Navigate to the root site in the site collection.

2. On the site's home page, select the Site Settings option from the Settings menu.

3. On the Site Settings Page, select the Search Result Sources option from the Site Collection Administration section.

4. On the Manage Result Sources page, select the New Result Source option.

5. On the Add Result Source page, do the following:

   a. In the General Information section, enter a name for the new result source and an optional description.

   b. In the Protocol section, identify the protocol to use to connect to the result source. There are several options.

      - *Local SharePoint*: Indexed items managed by the local SharePoint environment.

      - *Remote SharePoint*: Indexed items managed by a different SharePoint environment.

      - *OpenSearch 1.0/1.1*: Non-SharePoint items indexed by a system or service supporting the OpenSearch protocol.

      - *Exchange*: Exchange server-based content.

   c. In the Type section, decide whether to run the search across the entire SharePoint index or only across people profiles.

   d. In the Query Transform section, identify the search terms used to limit results for the result source.

   e. In the Credentials Information section, specify whether the result source is to use default SharePoint authentication credentials or a specified user name and password.

   f. Click the Save button to save the new result source.

The result source is saved, and you are returned to the Manage Result Sources page. When creating result sources there are times when the new source you want to create is very similar to an existing result source. When this is the case, you can start creating a new result source by copying an existing one. This is done as follows:

1. Navigate to the root site in the site collection.

2. On the site's home page, select the Site Settings option from the Settings menu.

3. On the Site Settings Page, select the Search Result Sources option from the Site Collection Administration section.

4. On the Manage Result Sources page, select the Copy option from the result source to copy's context menu (see Figure 11-13).

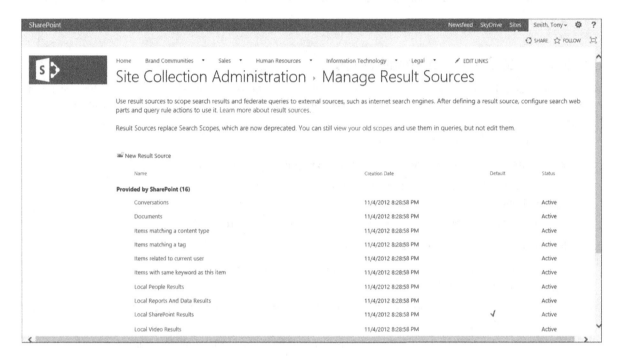

Figure 11-13. *Result source context menu*

5. On the Add Result Source page, do the following:

   a. Change the name for the new result source, and add an optional description.

   b. Update the details as appropriate in the Protocol, Type, Query Transform, and Credentials sections.

   c. Click the Save button.

   The new result source is created. You are returned to the Manage Result Sources page.

Creating Site Result Sources

You can create result sources that are available only in a specific site in your site collection. You would create a site-level result source when you need a tailored source within a site, one that will not be used elsewhere. To create a new site-level result source, do the following:

1. Navigate to the site where you want to create the new result source.

2. On the site's home page, select the Site Settings option from the Settings menu.

3. On the Site Settings page, select the Result Sources option from the Search section.

4. On the Manage Result Sources page, select the New Result Source option.

5. On the Add Result Source page, do the following:

    a. In the General Information section, enter the name for the new result source and an optional description.

    b. In the Protocol section, identify the protocol to use to connect to the result source. There are several options.

        • *Local SharePoint*: Indexed items managed by the local SharePoint environment.

        • *Remote SharePoint*: Indexed items managed by a different SharePoint environment.

        • *OpenSearch 1.0/1.1*: Non-SharePoint items indexed by a system or service supporting the OpenSearch protocol.

        • *Exchange*: Exchange server-based content.

    c. In the Type section, decide whether to run the search across the entire SharePoint index or only across people profiles.

    d. In the Query Transform section, identify the search terms used to limit results for the result source.

    e. In the Credentials Information section, specify whether the result source is to use default SharePoint authentication credentials or a specified user name and password.

    f. Click the Save button to save the new result source.

The new result source is created within the site, and you are returned to the Manage Result Sources page.

As with site collection result sources, you can create site result sources as copies of existing result sources. This is done as follows:

1. Navigate to the site where you want to create the new result source.

2. On the site's home page, select the Site Settings option from the Settings menu.

3. On the Site Settings Page, select the Result Sources option from the Search section.

4. On the Manage Result Sources page, select the Copy option from the result source to copy's context menu.

5. On the Add Result Source page, do the following:

    a. Change the name for the new result source, and add an optional description.

    b. Update the details as appropriate in the Protocol, Type, Query Transform, and Credentials sections.

    c. Click the Save button.

The new result source is created in the site. You are returned to the Manage Result Sources page.

Editing Existing Result Sources

You can edit site collection and site-level result sources as needed to update their details. You can edit only the custom result sources that were created within your site collection or sites, not the default ones. To edit an existing site collection or site level result source, do the following:

1. Navigate to the site collection's root site to edit a site collection result source or to the site containing the site-level result source you wish to edit.

2. On the site's home page, select the Site Settings option from the Settings menu.

3. On the Site Settings page, select the Search Result Sources option from the Site Collection Administration section to edit a site collection result source, or select the Result Sources link from the Search section to edit a site-level result source.

4. On the Manage Result Sources page, select the Edit option from the result source item's context menu.

5. On the Edit Result Source page, update the details for the result source as necessary, and click the Save button.

Updates to the result source are saved, and you are returned to the Manage Result Sources page.

Deleting Result Sources

If necessary, you can delete a result source created in your site collection or in a site within your site collection. To delete a site collection or site-level result source, do the following:

1. Navigate to the site collection's root site to edit a site collection result source or to the site containing the site-level result source you wish to edit.

2. On the site's home page, select the Site Settings option from the Settings menu.

3. On the Site Settings page, select the Search Result Sources option from the Site Collection Administration section to edit a site collection result source, or select the Result Sources link from the Search section to edit a site-level result source.

4. On the Manage Result Sources page, select the Delete option from the context menu of the result source to remove.

5. In the deletion confirmation window, click the OK button.

The result source is deleted, and you are returned to the Manage Result Sources page.

Managing Result Types

Result types are rule sets that identify which display template to use when search results are presented. Each type of item returned in a search result (such as Word Documents, PDF files, videos, and so on) has its own display template, used to identify the layout of the item's details when they appear in search results This includes the hover panel details displayed when a mouse hovers over an item in the search results page. As with result sources, result types can be created in any of the following levels in SharePoint:

- Within the SharePoint Central Administration environment, by a SharePoint technical administrator for use across the entire SharePoint environment.

- Within a site collection, making it available in searches performed across the site collection.

- Within a site, making it available only in the specific site.

Creating Site Collection Result Types

To create a result type available in your entire site collection, do the following:

1. Navigate to the root site in your site collection.

2. On the site's home page, select the Site Settings option from the Settings menu.

3. On the Site Settings page, select the Search Result Types option from the Site Collection Administration section.

4. On the Manage Result Types page, click the New Result Type option.

5. On the Add Result Type page, do the following:

    a. In the General Information section, enter a name for the result type.

    b. In the Conditions section, identify the result source to use as the base of the result type and the type of files to apply the result type to.

    c. In the Actions section, select the display template to use for the presentation of the result type, and specify whether to optimize the template for frequent use.

    d. Click the Save button.

The new result type is created and made available in the site collection. You are returned to the Manage Result Types page.

To create a new result type by copying an existing result type, do as follows:

1. Navigate to the root site in your site collection.

2. On the site's home page, select the Site Settings option from the Settings menu.

3. On the Site Settings page, select the Search Result Types option from the Site Collection Administration section.

4. On the Manage Result Types page, select the copy option from the context menu of the result type to copy.

5. On the Add Result Type page, do the following:

    a. In the General Information section, update the name for the result type.

    b. In the Conditions and Actions sections, update details as necessary.

    c. Click the Save button to save the new result type.

The result type is saved for use in the site collection, and you are returned to the Manage Result Types page.

Creating Site-Level Result Types

Creating result types at the site level confines their impact to the results display for the site where you create them. Doing this allows you to tailor result displays to specific site needs. To create a site-level result type, do as follows:

1. Navigate to the site where you want to create the result type.

2. On the site's home page, select the Site Settings option from the Settings menu.

3. On the Site Settings page, select the Result Types option from the Search section.

4. On the Manage Result Types page, select the copy option from the context menu of the result type to copy.

5. On the Add Result Type page, do the following:

   a. In the General Information section, update the name for the result type.

   b. In the Conditions and Actions sections, update details as necessary.

   c. Click the Save button to save the new result type.

The result type is created, and you are returned to the Manage Result Types page.

As with site collection result types, you can create a site-level result type as a copy of an existing result type. This is done as follows:

1. Navigate to the site where you want to create the result type.

2. On the site's home page, select the Site Settings option from the Settings menu.

3. On the Site Settings page, select the Result Types option from the Search section.

4. On the Manage Result Types page, select the copy option from the context menu of the result type to copy.

5. On the Add Result Type, page do the following:

   a. In the General Information section, update the name for the result type.

   b. In the Conditions and Actions sections, update details as necessary.

   c. Click the Save button to save the new result type.

The result type is created, and you are returned to the Manage Result Types page.

Editing Result Types

Result types created in a site collection or site can be edited as needed to adjust the result type. To edit an existing result type, do as follows:

1. Navigate to the site collection's root site to edit a site collection result type or to the site containing the site-level result type you wish to edit.

2. On the site's home page, select the Site Settings option from the Settings menu.

3. On the Site Settings page, select the Search Result Types option from the Site Collection Administration section to edit a site collection result source, or select the Result Types link from the Search section to edit a site-level result source.

4. On the Manage Result Types page, select the Edit option from the context menu of the result type to be edited.

5. On the Edit Result Type page, update the details as needed, and click the Save button to save the changes.

The changes to the result type are saved, and you are returned to the Manage Result Types page.

Deleting Result Types

If you need to, you can delete a result type created in a site collection or a specific site. To delete a result type from a site collection or site, do the following:

1. Navigate to the site collection's root site to edit a site collection result type or to the site containing the site-level result type you wish to edit.

2. On the site's home page, select the Site Settings option from the Settings menu.

3. On the Site Settings page, select the Search Result Types option from the Site Collection Administration section to edit a site collection result source, or select the Result Types link from the Search section to edit a site-level result source.

4. On the Manage Result Types page, select the Delete option from the context menu of the result type to delete it.

5. In the delete confirmation window, click the OK button.

The result type is deleted, and you are returned to the Manage Result Types page.

Exporting and Importing Search Configurations

You have seen how to manage the various aspects of search at a site collection level as well as at a site level. Once you have configured search the way that you want, you may decide that the configuration is appropriate for another site collection or site in your environment. In SharePoint 2013 you can export customized search configurations and then import them into other site collections and sites to replicate a search configuration you created. The export and import process includes all of the settings configured for query rules, result sources, result types, ranking models, and general site search settings.

Exporting and Importing Site Collection Search Configurations

To export the search configuration of a site collection, do the following:

1. Navigate to the root site of the site collection containing the configuration to be exported.

2. On the site's home page, select the Site Settings option from the Settings menu.

3. On the Site Settings page, select the Search Configuration Export option from the Site Collection Administration section.

4. In the "Do you want to save the SearchConfiguration.xml file" message, select the Save option, and identify the save location.

The site collection search configuration is saved to the SearchConfiguration.xml file, which can then be used to import the saved search configuration into another site collection. This is done as follows:

1. Navigate to the root site of the site collection containing the configuration to be imported.

2. On the site's home page, select the Site Settings option from the Settings menu.

3. On the Site Settings page, select the Search Configuration Import option from the Site Collection Administration section.

4. On the Import Search Configuration page, select the SearchConfiguration.xml file to import, and click the Import button.

The search configuration is imported into the site collection, and you are taken to the Search Config List page showing the status of the import.

Exporting and Importing Site Search Configurations

As with site collection search configurations, site-level search configurations can also be exported and then imported into another site to replicate a created search configuration elsewhere in the environment. To export a site-level search configuration, do the following:

1. Navigate to the site containing the search configuration to export.

2. On the site's home page, select the Site Settings option from the Settings menu.

3. On the Site Settings page, select the Configuration Export option from the Search section.

4. In the "Do you want to save the SearchConfiguration.xml file" message, select the Save option, and identify the save location.

The SearchConfiguration.xml export file is saved to the identified location. You can then use this file to import the search configuration into another site by doing the following:

1. Navigate to the site containing the search configuration to import.

2. On the site's home page, select the Site Settings option from the Settings menu.

3. On the Site Settings page, select the Configuration Import option from the Search section.

4. On the Import Search Configuration page, select the SearchConfiguration.xml file to import, and click the Import button.

The search configuration is imported into the site, and you are taken to the Search Config List page showing the status of the import.

Using Search with Web Parts

SharePoint has several web parts that leverage search services to present information in site pages. These web parts offer an alternative approach to use crawled content. They also provide ways to show content roll-ups collecting details throughout the environment, using a method that has no negative impact on the performance of the environment.

Content Search Web Part

The most versatile web part with which to present information in SharePoint pages sourced from the search index is the Content Search web part. It can be configured to present a variety of content types.

The content and layout of the information presented in the content search web part is dictated by the web part's configuration, which is made through its properties. To configure a content search web part, add it to the appropriate page using the Add Web Parts options (the web part is located in the Content Roll-up category). Then edit the web part properties (adding web parts to pages and configuring them is discussed in Chapter 4). On the web part properties page, do the following:

1. In the Search Criteria Section,

   a. Click the Change Query button to define the query on which the search results presented is to be based. Do so as follows:

      i. On the Basics tab,

         1. In the Select a Query section, identify the result source to use as the basis for the query.

         2. In the Restrict by App section, specify whether to scope the search to include only items in a certain location.

         3. In the Restrict by Tag section, specify whether to restrict results by tags associated with the content.

         4. In the Restrict by Content Type section, specify whether to restrict returned results to content of a specific content type.

         5. In the Add Additional Filters section, identify whether to use additional search text to filter returned results.

      ii. On the Refiners tab, select refiner values to further limit search results presented, and select the Add button to add any refiners to the Selected Refiners list.

      iii. On the Settings tab,

         1. In the Query Rules section, identify whether to make results listed in the search web part subject to any defined query rules.

         2. In the URL Rewriting section, identify whether items returned from a catalog are to use the catalog's URL settings.

         3. In the Loading Behavior section, specify whether to execute the query synchronously, from the server, or asynchronously, from the client. Running the query synchronously prevents the page from loading until the query is executed and results can be listed in the page. Running the query asynchronously allows the page itself to load more quickly as it loads separately from the query being executed and the results presented in the web part.

         4. In the Priority section, identify the priority level of the query's execution within the search service. This establishes an order of execution in the event that the search service is overloaded and multiple queries are queued for execution.

      iv. On the Test tab, run the defined query to view the results that will be returned.

      v. Click the OK button.

   b. Identify the maximum number of results to show in the web part.

2. In the Display Templates section,

    a. Identify the layout for the web part. Choose whether to show items as a list, as a list that allows paging, or in a slideshow format.

    b. Select the item display format identifying the layout of individual items in the web part. There are several display format options.

    - *Diagnostics*: This option shows the link and managed property details for the listed items.

    - *Large Picture*: This option represents each item using a single preview image associated with the item.

    - *Picture on Left, 3 Lines on Right*: This option lists a preview image with the item's details to the right of the image.

    - *Picture on Top, 3 Lines on Bottom*: Here the preview image appears with the item's details below the image.

    - *Recommended Items: Picture on Left, 3 Lines on Right*: This option has the same layout as the Picture on Left, 3 Lines on Right format but shows the recommended items from the query.

    - *Two Lines*: This selection lists each item's properties.

    - *Video*: This selection provides a video player thumbnail for each item. If it is a video, details are shown below the player.

    c. Specify whether to display anything in the web part if no results are returned.

3. In the Property Mappings section, identify whether to map the properties used in the display template to the default item properties for those elements or to other item properties. You can remap the Picture URL, Line 1, Link URL, File Extension, View Count, and Video File URL properties.

4. In the Settings section,

    a. Identify whether displayed query results are to be provided by the web part itself or by some other web part on the page.

    b. Identify the results table to be used when identifying results, with options including PersonalFavoriteResults, RefinementResults, RelevantResults, and SpecialTermResults.

    c. Identify the first result to display from the results list.

    d. Optionally identify an alternative error message to be displayed if the web part generates an error.

5. Click the OK button in the web part properties.

The web part properties are saved, and the web part is updated to reflect the new configuration.

Other Search Web Parts

Besides the Content Search web part, there are several other standard SharePoint web parts that take advantage of the search service to display content. Because the components that make up the standard search pages are web parts that are also available within the web part listing and that can be added to and configured in other pages, you can create your own specialized search pages. You can find these web parts in the Search category when you add web parts to a page (adding web parts to pages is discussed in detail in Chapter 4). These web parts include the following:

- *Search Box*: Shows a standard SharePoint search box, such as may be seen in the standard SharePoint search page.

- *Search Results*: Lists search results based on an executed search query.

- *Refinement*: Lists the refinement panel, which allows filtering of listed search results.

- *Search Navigation*: Lists search verticals, which can be used to scope the search query being performed.

- *Taxonomy Refinement Panel*: Lists refiners based on term set data. Refiners can be used to filter listed search results.

- *Find by Document ID*: Adds the Document ID search, used by default in Record Center sites, to locate items by their associated document IDs.

Along with the standard search component web parts that you can use to construct your own search pages, there is a second set of web parts that take advantage of the search services to display specific content within SharePoint pages. These web parts, available in the Search-Driven Content category, include the following:

- *Catalog-Item Reuse*: Displays items contained in a catalog.

- *Items Matching a Tag*: Lists items tagged with a specific term.

- *Pages*: Lists items based on the Pages content type.

- *Pictures*: Lists items based on the Picture or Image content types.

- *Popular Items*: Displays items identified as most popular—that is, those defined as items viewed by the most people.

- *Recently Changed Items*: Lists items most recently modified.

- *Recommended Items*: Lists recommended content based on content recommendation rules.

- *Videos*: Lists items based on the Video content type.

- *Web Pages*: Displays items based on the Pages content type.

- *Wiki Pages*: Lists items based on the Wiki Page content type.

CHAPTER 12

■ ■ ■

Personalization and Social Features

SharePoint 2013 contains a comprehensive set of personalization features that enhance personal productivity and social features that facilitate team development, communication, and collaboration. The personalization features streamline personal productivity and enhance awareness of relevant activities. The social features then allow individuals to come together into teams that focus on similar activities, which enable peer knowledge sharing, support, and idea capture and development.

In this chapter we review the personal productivity and social capabilities that make up SharePoint 2013 and discuss how to take advantage of these resources. These capabilities, which are available in both SharePoint Server 2013 Standard and SharePoint Server 2013 Enterprise, and do the following:

- *Enhance Personal Productivity*: By providing capabilities that help individuals keep current on information important to them, easily manage activities and tasks related to them, and find information and people they need based on skill sets and knowledge.

- *Share and Extend Content*: By allowing information to be shared and commented on and tracking its value and use.

- *Building Communities*: By facilitating the development of communities that bring people together around common topics of interest, promote discussions, and foster collaboration.

Enhancing Personal Productivity

SharePoint includes several capabilities designed to help make individuals more productive by reducing the amount of time needed to locate information and complete tasks and by allowing them to be kept aware of changes to relevant information and activities. Previous chapters discussed how processes can be automated through workflow to enhance efficiencies and how searches can be used to locate needed materials. Personal productivity tools in SharePoint augment these other capabilities and enable the following:

- Identifying materials relevant to you and allowing you to stay aware of changes to this information.

- Tracking and managing work efforts assigned to you.

- Monitoring activities performed by individuals involved in related tasks and keeping you aware of any impactful events.

- Locating people you need based on their skills, relationships, or knowledge.

In this section the personalization and social features that enhance personal productivity in SharePoint are discussed.

About Me and the Profile

SharePoint users' profiles are used as the foundation on which the SharePoint personal productivity and social capabilities are based. The profiles contain details about users that support communicating relevant information and representing users in the environment. Details include contact information, profile pictures, notification preferences, and more.

Many details included in the profile are centrally managed and typically populated from Active Directory and other sources. Examples are e-mail addresses, names, and titles. Other details are available for users to edit themselves in the profile management tools, including the profile picture and About Me details. Information available in the profile and edit settings are configured and managed by SharePoint technical administrators in the SharePoint Central Administration tools.

About Me Page Shared View

The About Me page in SharePoint has a dual purpose. When other people access someone's About Me page, they see its public view. This view (see Figure 12-1) lists key details about the person, including the following:

- *Ask Me About*: Lists topics the person is knowledgeable about. A visitor can click on a topic and create a post for the person related to the topic.

- *About Me*: Lists the self-descriptive About Me text created by the individual.

- *Activities*: Summarizes the individual's recent activities in the environment.

- *Contact Information*: Lists basic contact details for the person including title, e-mail, phone, office location, and the like.

- *In Common*: Identifies people the viewer has in common with the individual, such as shared managers, people both users follow, and so on.

- *Org Chart*: Displays where the individual fits in to the organization's structure.

Figure 12-1. About Me Shared View page

About Me Private View

The second About Me page view is the private view, displayed when you view your own About Me page (see Figure 12-2). To navigate to this page, select the About Me option from the user menu at the top of the SharePoint pages.

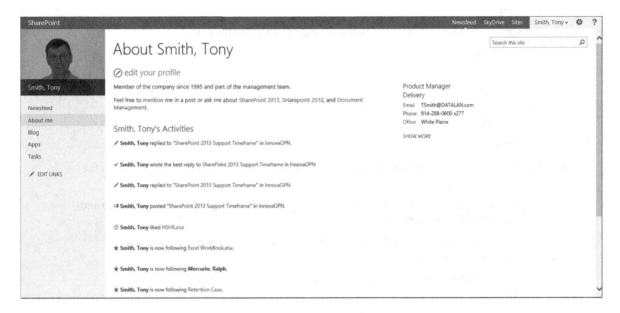

Figure 12-2. *About Me Private View page*

This view provides some of the same details as the public view of the page including the Ask Me About details and the user's activities and contact information. However, your private view also has a link to the Edit Your Profile page. It brings you to the Edit Details page, where you can update your profile. The Edit Details page has five separate tabs to organize and manage profile information:

- *Basic Information*: This tab lists general contact details that are typically read-only and pulled from the Active Directory. Initially included are details the user can manage about themselves, such as:

    - About Me: Text describing the person and display on the About Me page.

    - Picture: An image that can be uploaded and used to represent the person profiled both here and in other areas of SharePoint, such as newsfeeds and search results, containing references to the person.

    - Ask Me About: Identifies topics in which the user has expertise. Viewers can request assistance from the person on these topics.

- *Contact Information*: The Contact Information tab lists details typically pulled from Active Directory and some editable details that can be populated to assist others when they communicate with the individual, including these:

    - Work E-mail

    - Mobile Phone

    - Fax

- Home Phone

- Office

- Office Location

- Assistant

- *Details*: The Details tab lists these general demographics about the person:

  - Past Projects

  - Skills

  - Schools

  - Birthday

  - Interests

- *Newsfeed Settings*: This tab lists information notifications and shares detail preferences for the individual, including these:

  - Followed #Tags: Identifies hash tags the person currently follows and allows addition and removal of followed items.

  - Email Notifications: Identifies activities in the environment that cause an e-mail notification to be sent.

  - People I Follow: Specifies whether to let other users see the people the individual is following.

  - Activities I Want to Share in My Newsfeed: Identifies the types of activities to be listed in the person's newsfeed when they occur.

- *Language and Region*: Allows management of language, time zone, and region preferences. By default, all details are inherited from the server, but they can be overridden as needed. Options managed in this section include these:

  - Language Preferences: Identifies the individual's language choices in order of preference. Display language preferences and content and search language preferences can be configured.

  - Time Zone: Identifies the individual's default time zone.

  - Region: Lists regional settings for the person, including local time and calendar format and workweek.

My Tasks

Another personal productivity tool in the SharePoint My Site area is My Tasks. It includes an aggregated view of tasks that exist anywhere in the SharePoint environment, Exchange, and Project Server. You can view and manage tasks listed on this page regardless of where they were created.

To get to the My Tasks page (see Figure 12-3), navigate to your About Me page, and select the Tasks option from the left-hand navigation area.

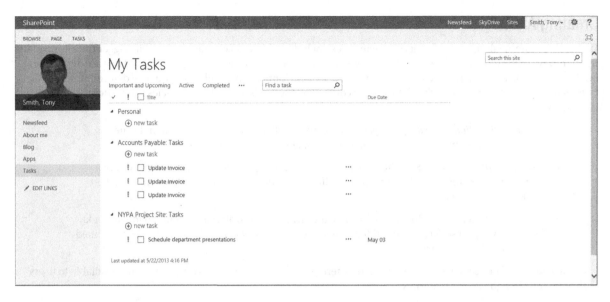

Figure 12-3. *My Tasks page*

Once you are there, clicking on a listed task brings you to the Edit Item page for that task. There you can manage the task's details. Check the check box next to a listed task on the My Tasks page to mark it as complete.

The My Tasks page initially includes four views you can use to review tasks assigned to you in SharePoint. In these views you can see the following:

- *Important and Upcoming*: Tasks coming due, past due, or of high priority.

- *Active*: All tasks not yet marked as completed.

- *Completed*: All tasks marked as completed.

- *Recently Added*: Tasks that were most recently added to SharePoint.

Alerts

Previous chapters discuss how SharePoint is used to store and manage documents and lists of information and how workflows and content organizer can act on this information to route content to other locations. You have seen how search is used to locate content stored throughout the environment. All these capabilities enable SharePoint to host a wide variety of business resources. As the amount of information in the environment grows, it can become difficult to keep track of relevant information as it matures.

Alerts in SharePoint let you identify content that you want to be made aware of when it is changed. Alerts are used to create e-mail or text message notifications for users when such identified actions occur. You can specify the type of changes an alert is to track and the frequency of notifications. You can create alerts for the following items in SharePoint:

- *List Items or Documents*: Enables notifications to be sent to identified individuals when changes are made to a specific document or list item.

- *Lists or Libraries*: Used to notify identified individuals of relevant changes to content in a specific list or library.

- *Pages*: Notifications are sent when the page content is changed.

- *Search*: Notifications are sent when items that satisfy a defined search query are changed.

Creating Alerts

When you create an alert, you define its characteristics, including the types of changes that will trigger the alert and its frequency of notification. Several types of changes can be identified that cause alerts to be sent. They are dependent on the type of object the alert is created for. The several existing options for an alert's frequency determine when notifications are sent to the individuals the alert is configured for. The following frequencies can be defined for the various alerts.

- *Send Notification Immediately*: Specifies that the notification is to be sent when the alert is triggered. This option is available for all types of alerts except search alerts.

- *Send a Daily Summary*: Specifies that all activities that trigger the alert are compiled into a daily summary report and sent to the identified individuals once a day at the time specified when the alert was created.

- *Send Weekly Summary*: Identifies that activities triggering the alert are compiled into a weekly summary report sent to the identified individuals once a week on a day and at a time specified when the alert was created.

You can create alerts anywhere in SharePoint where you have the Create Alerts right, which is available to users with at least Read rights to the materials.

■ **Note**   Alerts can be created only in environments where a SharePoint technical administrator has configured outbound e-mail settings.

Creating List Item and Document Alerts

Alerts created for a specific list item or document send notifications for changes to that item. To create an alert for a specific list item or document, do the following:

1. Navigate to the list or library containing the item for which you want to create the alert.

2. On the list or library view page, check the check box next to the list item or document where you want to create the alert, and choose the Set Alert on This Item/Document option from the Alert Me drop-down menu on the Items/Files ribbon tab (see Figure 12-4).

Figure 12-4. *Files Ribbon tab*

3. In the New Alert window, do the following:

    a. In the Alert Title section, optionally change the default title given to the new alert. The default title is listed as a colon-separated combination of the list or library name followed by the item name.

    b.   In the Send Alert To section, site managers can update the list of individuals to be alerted allowing them to include others. Other individuals can create alerts only for themselves in the site.

    c.   In the Delivery Method section, specify whether to send the alert via e-mail or text message. The text message option is present only if a SharePoint technical administrator configures the environment for SMS (text messages). To send an alert via text message, specify the SMS number and whether to send the item's URL as part of the message.

    d.   In the Send Alerts for These Changes section, identify what changes to the item will trigger the alert. Options are as follows:

- *Anything Changes*: Triggers the alert when any change is made to the item.

- *Someone Else Changes a Document*: Triggers the alert when someone other than the alerted user makes a change to the item.

- *Someone Else Changes a Document Created by Me*: Triggers the alert only if the item was created by the alerted user and only when someone other than that user changes it.

- *Someone Else Changes a Document Last Modified by Me*: Triggers the alert only if the item was last modified by the alerted user and only when someone other than that user changes the item.

    e.   In the When to Send Alerts section, identify how frequently to send the alert notifications. Select from these options (discussed earlier in this section):

- Send Notification Immediately

- Send a Daily Summary

- Send a Weekly Summary

    f.   Click the OK button.

The alert is created, and you are returned to the list or library view. You can also create list item and document alerts when viewing the item's properties. Select the Alert Me option from the list item or document properties view page, and follow the steps listed here.

Creating List and Library Alerts

There are many times when you might want to be alerted to changes to content in a specific list or library. For example, if you are working on a project and all of the documents related to the project are in a single library, you will want to stay aware of items added to the library and changes made to the existing materials. To do this, use the list and library alerts, which can notify you of changes to the content in an identified list or library. To create a list or library alert, do the following:

1.   Navigate to the list or library where you want to create the alert.

2.   On the list or library view page, select the Set Alert on This List or Library option from the Alert Me drop-down menu on the List or Library ribbon tab.

3.   On the New Alert page, do the following:

    a.   In the Alert Title section, optionally change the default title, initially set to the name of the list or library, given to the new alert.

b. In the Send Alert To section, site managers can update the list of individuals to be alerted. Other individuals can create alerts only for themselves in the site.

c. In the Delivery Method section, specify whether to send the alert via e-mail or text message. The text message option is available only if a SharePoint technical administrator configures the environment for SMS (text messages). To send an alert via text message, specify the SMS number and whether to send the item's URL as part of the message.

d. In the Change Type section, identify what changes to content in the list or library will trigger the alert. Options are as follows:

- *All Changes*: Triggers the alert in the list or library when any types of updates are made to content, when new items are added, and when items are deleted.

- *New Items are Added*: Triggers the alert only when a new item is added to the list or library.

- *Existing Items are Modified*: Triggers the alert when an existing item in the list or library is edited.

- *Items are Deleted*: Triggers the alert when an item in the list or library is deleted.

e. In the Send Alerts for These Changes section, identify what types of changes to the item will trigger the alert. Options are as follows:

- *Anything Changes*: Triggers the alert when any change is made to an item.

- *Someone Else Changes an Item*: Triggers the alert when someone other than the alerted user makes any change to an item.

- *Someone Else Changes an Item Created by Me*: Triggers the alert only for an item created by the alerted user and only when someone other than the creator makes a change to the item.

- *Someone Else Changes an Item Last Modified by Me*: Triggers the alert only for an item last modified by the alerted user and only when someone other than that user makes a change to the item.

f. In the When to Send Alerts section, specify how frequently to send the alert notifications. Select from these options (discussed earlier in this section):

- Send Notification Immediately

- Send a Daily Summary

- Send a Weekly Summary

g. Click the OK button.

The new alert is created, and you are returned to the list or library view page.

Creating Page Alerts

To create a page alert in SharePoint to notify users of changes made to wiki, web part and publishing page content, do the following:

1. Navigate to the page in which you want to create the alert.

2. On the page, select the Set an Alert on this Page option from the Alert Me drop-down menu on the Page ribbon tab (see Figure 12-5).

Figure 12-5. *Page ribbon tab*

3. In the New Alert window, do the following:

   a. In the Alert Title section, optionally change the default title, initially set to a combination of the colon-separated library name followed by the page name, given to the new alert.

   b. In the Send Alerts To section, site managers can update the default set of individuals to be alerted. Other individuals can create alerts only for themselves in the site.

   c. In the Delivery Method section, specify whether to send the alert via e-mail or text message. The text message option is present only if a SharePoint technical administrator configures the environment for SMS (text messages). To send an alert via text message, specify the SMS number and whether to send the item's URL as part of the message.

   d. In the Send Alerts for These Changes section, identify what types of changes to the item will trigger the alert. Options are as follows:

      • *Anything Changes*: Triggers the alert when any change is made to the page.

      • *Someone Else Changes a Wiki Page*: Triggers the alert when someone other than the alerted user makes a change to the page.

      • *Someone Else Changes a Wiki Page Created by Me*: Triggers the alert only for a wiki page created by the alerted user and only when someone other than the creator makes a change to the page.

      • *Someone Else Changes a Wiki Page Last Modified by Me*: Triggers the alert only for a page last modified by the alerted user and only when someone other than that user makes a change to it.

      • *Someone Else Changes an Item that Appears in the Following View*: Triggers the alert when a change is made to an item included in a specifically identified view.

   e. In the When to Send Alerts section, specify how frequently to send the alert notifications. Select from these options (discussed earlier in this section):

      • Send Notification Immediately

      • Send a Daily Summary

      • Send a Weekly Summary

   f. Click the OK button.

The alert is created for the page, and you are returned to the page.

Creating Search Alerts

The discussion so far assumes you know the location of the content for which you want to configure alerts. Use a search alert when you are interested in creating an alert that spans several locations. You configure a search alert with a search query, so that you learn of changes to any content meeting the query, regardless of the content's location. For example, if you are responsible for a certain client and need to learn of any activity related to materials referencing that client, create a search alert for a query of the client's name. To create a new search alert, do the following:

1. Perform a search from the SharePoint search box or within a search page (searches are discussed in Chapter 11).

2. On the search results page, select the Alert Me option at the bottom of the search results.

3. On the New Alert page, do the following:

    a. In the Alert Title section, optionally update the default title (initially set to Search: followed by the query text entered) given to the new alert.

    b. In the Delivery Method section, the e-mail option is selected. You cannot choose to send text message notifications for search alerts.

    c. In the Change Type section, specify what type of change will trigger the alert. Options are as follows:

       • *New Items in Search Result*: Triggers the alert when an item not previously included in the result set for the query is added.

       • *Existing Items are Changed*: Triggers the alert when an item already part of the result set for the query is edited.

       • *All Changes*: Triggers the alert when a new item is added to the result set for the query or when items already part of the result set are edited.

    d. In the When to Send Alerts section, schedule when alert notifications are to be sent. Schedule options for search alerts include:

       • Send a Daily Summary

       • Send a Weekly Summary

    e. Click the OK button.

The search alert is created, and you are returned to the search results page.

Working with Alerts

After you configure an alert or a site owner configures one for you, the changes associated with the alert will trigger it. Alert e-mails reference to the changes to content that caused the alert notification to be sent (see Figure 12-6).

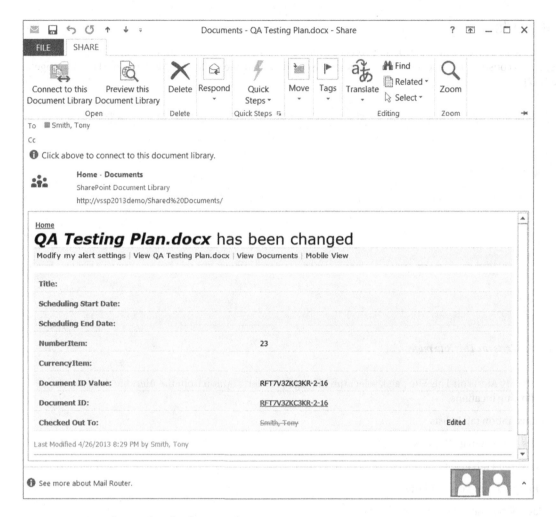

Figure 12-6. *Send Immediately Alert e-mail*

Alert notifications include the following details:

- Title identifying the item and type of change causing the alert.

- A link to navigate to the My Alert Settings page to manage alerts.

- A link to navigate to the item the alert was sent about.

- A link to navigate to the list or library containing the item.

- A link to the mobile view of the list or library containing the item.

- The list of the item's properties, with changes to the properties indicated.

Managing Alerts

Alerts you create in a site (regardless of whether you create them for list items, documents, lists, libraries, pages, or searches) are all consolidated into a single management screen for that site, called the My Alerts on This Site page (see Figure 12-7).

Figure 12-7. *My Alerts on This Site page*

To access the My Alerts on This Site page, select the Manage My Alerts option from the Alert Me drop-down menu in the following locations:

- Items ribbon tab in lists

- Files ribbon tab in libraries

- List ribbon tab in lists

- Library ribbon tab in libraries

- Page ribbon tab on site pages

The My Alerts on This Site page lists alerts created in the current site. This page lets you add, edit, and delete alerts in the site. Search alerts are listed in the site collection's root site when the default search results page is in use and in the search center site when a search center is in use.

Editing Existing Alerts

To edit an alert on the My Alerts on This Site page, do the following:

1. On the My Alerts on This Site page, click on the name of the alert to edit.

2. On the Edit Alert page, update the details about the alert, and click the OK button to save the changes.

Deleting Existing Alerts

To delete an alert on the My Alerts on This Site page, do the following:

1. On the My Alerts on This Site page. click the check box next to the alert to be deleted, and click the Delete Selected Alerts link.

2. In the deletion confirmation window, click the OK button.

The alert is deleted, and you are returned to the My Alerts on This Site page.

Adding Alerts from the My Alerts on This Site Page

While viewing the My Alerts on This Site page, you can create new list and library alerts. To create an alert from this page, identify the list or library for which to create the alert, then configure the alert itself. To create a new alert from the My Alerts on This Site page, do the following:

1. On the My Alerts on This Site page, click the Add Alert Link.

2. On the New Alert: Choose a List or Document Library page, select the list or library for which to create the new alert. Then click the Next button.

3. On the New Alert page, do the following:

    a. In the Alert Title section, optionally change the default title which is defaulted to the name of the list or library.

    b. In the Send Alerts To section, site managers can update the default set of individuals to be alerted. Other individuals can create alerts only for themselves in the site.

    c. In the Delivery Method section, specify whether to send the alert via e-mail or text message. The text message option is available only if a SharePoint technical administrator configures the environment for SMS (text messages). To send an alert via text message, specify the SMS number and whether to send the item's URL as part of the message.

    d. In the Change Type section, specify what type of change to content in the list or library will trigger the alert. Options are as follows:

        • *All Changes*: Triggers the alert when existing content is updated in any way and when new items are added to the list or library.

        • *New Items are Added*: Triggers the alert only when a new item is added to the list or library.

        • *Existing Items are Modified*: Triggers the alert when an existing item in the list or library is edited.

        • *Items are Deleted*: Triggers the alert when an item in the list or library is deleted.

    e. In the Send Alerts for These Changes section, identify what types of changes to the item will trigger the alert. Options are as follows:

        • *Anything Changes*: Triggers the alert when any change is made to an item.

        • *Someone Else Changes an Item*: Triggers the alert when someone other than the alerted user makes a change to an item.

- *Someone Else Changes an Item Created by Me*: Triggers the alert only for an item created by the alerted user and only when someone other than the alerted user makes a change to the item.

- *Someone Else Changes an Item Last Modified by Me*: Triggers the alert only for an item last modified by the alerted user and only when someone other than that user makes a change to the item.

f. In the When to Send Alerts section, identify how frequently to send the alert notifications. Select from these options (discussed earlier in this section):

- Send Notification Immediately

- Send a Daily Summary

- Send a Weekly Summary

g. Click the OK button.

The new alert is created, and you are returned to the My Alerts on This Site page.

Following and the Newsfeed

You have seen how to use alerts to be notified via e-mail to changes made to items in lists and libraries. An alert works well when you want e-mail notifications for changes to content. However, as the volume of content requiring alerts grows, e-mail notifications can become difficult to track. Another way to stay abreast of activities is to follow resources in the environment. When you follow resources, changes to them and to activities related to them are posted to your newsfeed, where they are listed for review in chronological order. You can follow these items in SharePoint:

- *People*: When you follow people in SharePoint, activities related to them are listed in your newsfeed.

- *Documents*: Changes to documents you follow are listed.

- *Sites*: When you follow a site, activity in its conversations is listed.

- *Tags*: Conversation items that reference followed tags are listed.

Following People

You can track the activities of people you follow, such as those you work with, in your newsfeed. Here is how to start following someone:

1. Click on the name of the person you want to follow from any reference to the person in the site, such as from a list view of a document he or she created or last modified, from a discussion post, or from a reference in search results.

2. On the About page for the person, click the Follow This Person link.

Your profile is updated to let you follow the person. If later you want to stop following the person,

1. Navigate to the person's About page through any reference in a site.

2. On the About page, select the Stop Following This Person link.

Your profile is updated so that you no longer follow the person.

You can also view and manage items you follow from your newsfeed (newsfeeds are discussed in detail in a later section).

Following Documents

You can choose to follow a document in your SharePoint environment and track changes made to it in your newsfeed. To follow a document, do the following:

1. Navigate to the library containing the document to be followed.

2. On the library view page, click the check box next to the document to be followed, and select the Follow option from the Files ribbon tab.

The document is added to your followed content, and changes to it are tracked in your newsfeed. You can also follow a document in a library by selecting the Follow option from the document's hover panel in either library view or a search results list (see Figure 12-8).

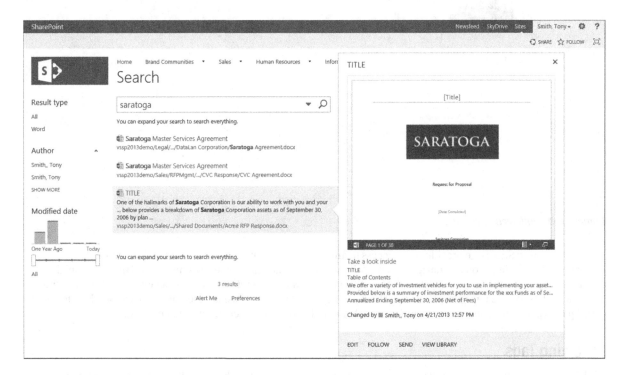

Figure 12-8. *Document hover panel*

As a later section explains, you can also stop following a document in the newsfeed.

Following Sites

In your environment you can follow sites and conversations taking place within them. When you follow a site, its newsfeed is rolled into your newsfeed for review. By default, sites you create are automatically added to the sites you follow. To follow other sites in SharePoint, click the Follow option at the top of the site's page.

Followed Sites Page

SharePoint includes a page that lists all the sites you are following and provides suggestions for other sites to follow, as Figure 12-9 shows.

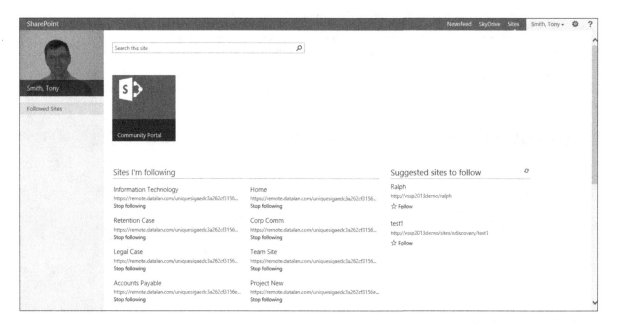

Figure 12-9. *Followed Sites page*

The Followed Sites page provides easy access to any sites you are following throughout your SharePoint environment. From here you can navigate to any followed site by clicking on the site name or its URL. You can also stop following sites from the Followed Sites page. Just click the Stop Following option associated with the listed site.

The Followed Sites page also recommends sites for you to follow. This list is based on details about the site and its active participants. To follow a site in the Suggested Sites to Follow list, select the site's Follow option.

Following Tags

Hash Tags are used to categorize related content (overall management of hash tags is discussed in a later section). Here is how to follow a hash tag:

1. Click on a reference to the hash tag from a newsfeed.

2. On the About page for the hash tag, click the Follow This #Tag link.

The hash tag is added to the items you are following. If later you want to stop following a tag, choose the Stop Following This #Tag link from the hash tag's About page.

Newsfeed

So far our discussion has concerned how to follow people, documents, sites, and hash tags to track activities related to them. Once you have selected items to follow in your environment, you can use the Newsfeed page to view tracked activities. Navigate to the Newsfeed page (see Figure 12-10) by clicking the Newsfeed link located at the top of all of your SharePoint pages.

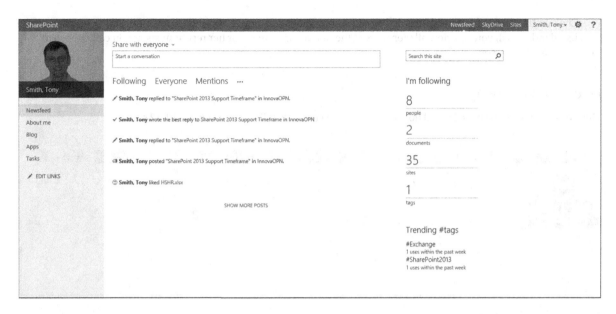

Figure 12-10. Newsfeed page

The Newsfeed page initially lists all activities for followed items, with the most recent activities at the top. Each activity has a link to the items and people the activity is associated with. This page also summarizes the number of people, documents, sites, and tags you are following in the environment. Click on any of the listed totals to see items of that type you follow. From this details view page, you can navigate to any listed item.

People I'm Following

Available from the Newsfeed page by clicking on the count of people you follow, the People I'm Following page (see Figure 12-11) lists all of them.

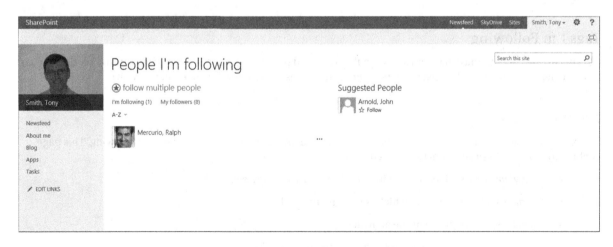

Figure 12-11. People I'm Following page

Click on the name of anyone listed on the page to navigate to his or her About page. If you open the hover menu for a listed individual, you can view all mentions of the person or all of his or her recent posts or you can choose to stop following the person.

Docs I'm Following

The Docs I'm Following page lists all documents you are currently following, as Figure 12-12 shows.

Figure 12-12. *Docs I'm Following page*

Click on the name of any listed item to open the associated file. You can also choose to stop following the item by clicking the Stop Following link listed with the item. The Docs I'm Following page also provides a list of suggestions for other documents you might want to follow. This list is based on your activities and how they relate to the materials in the environment. You can navigate to or follow any of these listed suggestions.

Sites I'm Following

Clicking on the followed sites count in the Newsfeed page takes you to the Followed Sites page. You can also get there by clicking on the Sites link at the top of any SharePoint page. (The Followed Sites page is discussed earlier in this chapter.)

Tags I'm Following

Clicking on the count for hash tags you follow on the Newsfeed page takes you to the Newsfeed settings section of your profile where the Followed #Tags list appears (User Profile pages are discussed in an earlier section).

Newsfeed Search

The Newsfeed page also includes a search that lets you view activities other than those you are following. This page enables you to view these additional sets of activities:

- *Everyone*: Shows all recent activities available for you to review.

- *Mentions*: Lists activities in which you are mentioned.

- *Activities*: Shows all recent site activities.

- *Likes*: Shows recent activities related to items you have liked.

This page also allows you to create new posts to be listed in your activities.

Targeting

SharePoint includes a mechanism, called targeting, used to restrict display of certain items, such as web parts and navigation links, to identified users or groups. Targeting, which is not the same as setting permissions, does not make content or pages unavailable. It simply hides web parts in pages and links within the navigation. When you target an element, you identify the users or groups to make the item visible for and thus surface details to specific users. For example, if you have a web part that lists sales by region, you may decide to list it on the home page of your portal but display it only to your sales teams. To do this, target the web part to the team so that it appears only when the group's members visit the page.

To target a web part or navigation item, do the following:

1. Navigate to the Web Part Properties window to target the web part or to the item's Edit window to target a navigation item. (Managing navigation and the properties of web parts are discussed in Chapters 3 and 4, respectively.)

2. On the Properties or Edit page, update details for the Audience option. Enter the targeted user or group, and then click the OK button.

Other items in SharePoint support audience targeting beyond web parts and navigation links, such as links in the Summary Links web part. Managing targeting for these other items is handled in the same way as managing targeting for web parts and navigation links in that you add the targeted users or groups in an Audience selection area.

Sharing and Extending Content

SharePoint 2013 has several capabilities that provide the ability to easily share relevant information with others and add context to content in the environment by tagging, rating, and liking materials.

E-mail a Link

One of the most basic ways to share information is to e-mail references to the information. Sending a reference to a list or library instead of attaching a copy of an item helps ensure that when the referenced materials are opened, the most recent version is viewed and edited. E-mailing someone a link instead of the file itself also helps protect documents from being accidentally shared with others if the e-mail is forwarded. You have the ability to e-mail a link to a list or library to reference details you want to share. To e-mail a link to a list or library, do the following:

1. Navigate to the list or library that you wish to e-mail a link for.

2. On the list or library view page, select the E-mail a Link option from the List or Library ribbon tab.

3. In the opened e-mail message, identify the desired recipient and subject details, and then send the e-mail.

■ **Note**   The option in previous versions of SharePoint to e-mail a link to a document or list item is not available in SharePoint 2013. This option is available only to e-mail references to lists and libraries.

RSS Feeds

Another way people can share and consume content in SharePoint is through list and library RSS feeds. An RSS (Real Simple Syndication) feed enables access to a list's or library's contents from any RSS-enabled application, such as Outlook, . Each list and library has an RSS feed that can be accessed by doing the following:

1. Navigate to the list or library.

2. On the list or library view page, select the RSS Feed option from the List or Library ribbon tab.

3. On the RSS Feed page, click the "Subscribe to this RSS Feed" link to subscribe to the feed using your default RSS Feed application. *

The RSS feed is connected to your RSS feed reader application.

SkyDrive Pro

In SharePoint, SkyDrive Pro refers, not to the Microsoft cloud storage solution called SkyDrive, but instead to a personal document library for storing private files in SharePoint. SkyDrive Pro lets you not only store files but also select people you want to share them with. To access SkyDrive Pro, click the SkyDrive link at the top of SharePoint site pages. This link takes you to the SkyDrive Pro Documents library (see Figure 12-13).

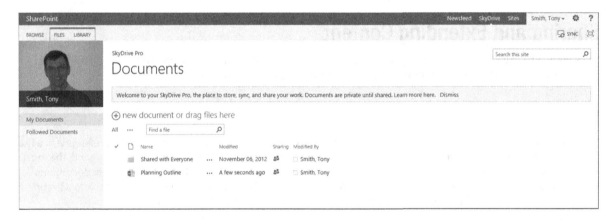

Figure 12-13. *SkyDrive Pro Documents page*

The SkyDrive Pro Documents library offers the same capabilities of other document libraries (described in Chapters 5 and 7), as well as some additional ones to make sharing files with others easier. The library has an integrated Sharing option listed next to each file. This option allows you to select individuals to share the file with and identify the level of access they have to the item. To share a listed file or folder, do the following:

1. From any page in the site, navigate to the SkyDrive Pro Documents library by clicking the SkyDrive option at the top of the page.

2. On the SkyDrive Pro Documents page, click the Sharing icon for the item to be shared.

3. In the Shared With window, click the Invite People option.

4. In the Share window, do the following:

   a. Select the individuals to share the item with.

   b. Select whether to give identified individuals Edit or View rights.

    c.   Optionally include a message in the invitation going to the person.

    d.   Optionally click the Show Options link to show the Send an Email Invitation option. Uncheck the option if you do not want to send an e-mail notification to individuals being given rights to the item.

    e.   Click the Share button.

The item's security is updated to add the identified rights to the selected user. If you left the invitation option checked, an e-mail message is sent to the individual notifying him or her of the resource's availability. You are then returned to the Documents list view.

To manage permissions for items in the Documents library more granularly, select the Advanced option in the Shared With window. You are taken to the standard Permissions page for the library, where you can manage the item's permissions (discussed in detail in Chapter 7).

■ **Note**   Consider instituting a governance plan for use of the SkyDrive Pro Documents libraries to keep these locations from becoming an overly used general storage tool. Your plan should address storage limits, usage guidelines, and retention management.

Enterprise Wikis

An Enterprise Wiki is a knowledge repository designed to let large audiences collectively mature information related to a topic. Its pages support the inclusion of references to other wiki pages to allow easy navigation between related pages. An Enterprise Wiki site is configured to categorize pages into logical groupings and rate a page while it is being viewed (see Figure 12-14). A wiki site is used to collect team or community knowledge and make it more broadly available to those who need it. Collecting this knowledge captures information that typically resides only in people's heads or in scattered notes and e-mails.

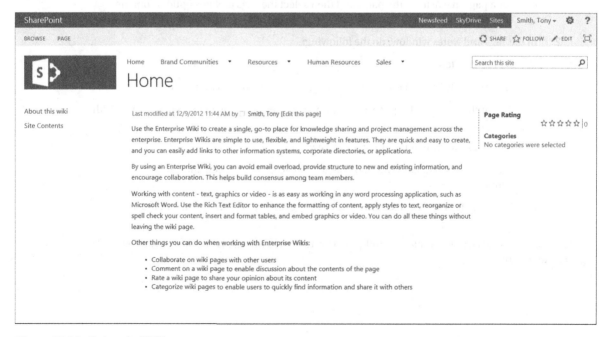

Figure 12-14. *Enterprise Wiki*

As wiki pages support entry of full rich text, you can develop pages containing text, images, and videos. You can also enter references to other pages directly into the page text by entering two pairs of brackets ([[). When this is done, a list of available wiki pages appears in a context menu for the selection. You can reference a page in the listed context menu or make a reference to a page that has not yet been created. Do this by entering a title for a new page within double brackets; for example, [[My Page]]. After a page is saved that contains a reference to a page that does not exist, the first person to click on the page reference link is prompted to create a new page. If he or she accepts the prompt, the page is created, and the person is taken to it, where he or she can enter appropriate content.

Tags and Notes

Tags and notes provide context to content within SharePoint. Unlike hash tags, content tags allow categorization of content, and notes allow creation of commentary related to the content. Together they are used to add context to materials to support business efforts.

Creating Tags and Notes

Tags and notes can be created for lists, libraries, pages, list items, and documents. To create one or more tags or notes, do the following;

1. Navigate to the item for which you want to create tags and notes. Then do one of the following:

    a. For a list or library, navigate to the list or library, and then select the Tags & Notes option from the List or Library ribbon tab.

    b. For a list item or document, navigate to the list or library containing the item, click the check box next to the item, and then select the Tags & Notes option from the Items/Files ribbon tab.

    c. For a page, navigate to the page, and then select the Tags & Notes option from the Page ribbon tab.

2. In the Tags and Notes window, do the following:

    a. On the Tags tab,

        i. In the My Tags section, enter the tag name to be created for the item.

        ii. In the Suggested Tags section, optionally select any existing tags to associate with the item.

        iii. Click the Save button to save the new tags.

    b. On the Note Board tab, enter the note to be placed on the item, and click the Post button.

    c. Close the Tags and Notes window once all tags and notes have been entered and saved.

The Tags and Notes window is closed, and you are returned to the page from which you selected the Tags & Notes option.

Viewing Tags through Tag Clouds

You can use the Tag Cloud web part to view tags associated with items in SharePoint. The listed tags are sized based on the number of items associated with the tag. The more items associated with the tag, the larger the tag text in the tag cloud will be. Click on any tag to get to the Tag Profile page, where all its associated items are listed (see Figure 12-15).

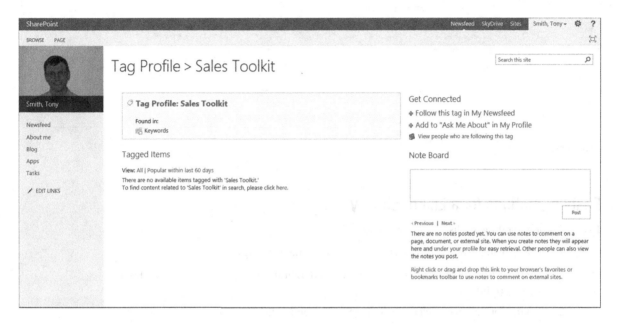

Figure 12-15. *Tag Profile page*

The Tag Profile page lists items associated with the tag, along with a note board that can be used to create additional notes to be associated with the tag.

Rating Content

Content can be rated in SharePoint to allow users to identify the value or effectiveness of listed items. For an item SharePoint presents the average rating and the number of ratings made (see Figure 12-16).

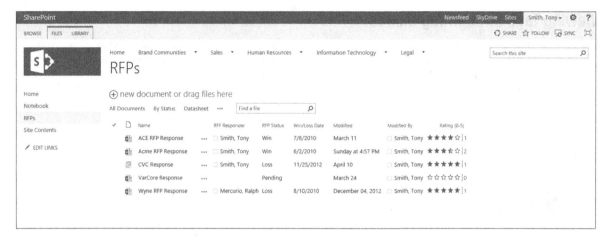

Figure 12-16. *Ratings*

Enabling Ratings for a List or Library

To enable content rating in a list or library, do the following:

1. Navigate to the list or library where you want to enable ratings.

2. On the list or library view page, select the List or Library Settings option from the List or Library ribbon tab.

3. On the Settings page, select the Rating Settings option from the General Settings section.

4. On the Rating Settings page, do the following:

   a. Select Yes for the "Allow items in this list to be rated" option.

   b. Select Star Ratings for the "Which voting/rating experience you would like to enable for this list?" option.

   c. Click the OK button.

   Ratings are added to the list or library.

Rating Content in a List or Library

To add a rating to an item in a list or library where ratings are enabled, click on the star representing the rating you want to apply to the item. This updates listed ratings by adding yours to the average and raises the number of ratings applied by one. If you rate an item a second time, the previous rating you gave it is updated instead of a new rating being added.

Liking Content

"Liking" content is another way to rate it. You can indicate that you like list items, documents, comments, and posts. Liking content is an activity that is listed in newsfeeds for persons indicating they like the item, as well as in newsfeeds of those who follow the persons doing the liking.

Enabling Like for a List or Library

Liking is available by default for newsfeeds, but you must activate it for lists and libraries. To enable liking in a list or library, do as follows:

1. Navigate to the list or library where you want to enable liking.

2. On the list or library view page, select the List or Library Settings option from the List or Library ribbon tab.

3. On the Settings page, select the Rating Settings option from the General Settings section.

4. On the Rating Settings page, do the following:

   a. Select Yes for the "Allow items in this list to be rated" option.

   b. Select Likes for the "Which voting/rating experience you would like to enable for this list?" option.

   c. Click the OK button.

The ability to like content is added to the list or library.

Liking/Unliking Content

When the ability to like content is available, you can like an item by clicking the Like link associated with it. This increases the item's number of likes and adds the activity to your newsfeed. To unlike a previously liked item, click the item's Unlike option.

Building Communities

Communities are built by people who come together to address topics of common interest. Communities allow sharing and development of ideas and promote common objectives. SharePoint Server 2013 has many capabilities that support and foster community building. This section discusses these capabilities and how they are applied.

Site Newsfeeds

Newsfeeds in SharePoint sites give users a simple way to share information. Site newsfeeds are available by default in team sites with SharePoint Server Standard and SharePoint Server Enterprise in place. Site newsfeeds can be added to any other site by enabling the Site Feed site feature in that site. Site newsfeeds support many features found within standard microblogs.

- The ability to share informational posts with other site users.

- The ability to reply to posts.

- The ability to target posts to individuals using @ references. To create an @ reference, enter an @ and then the user you want to target. Targeting a post to a specific individual adds the post to the person's newsfeed.

- The hash tagging option, to make topics followable and shareable throughout the environment. Hash tags are discussed in detail in the next section.

- The inclusion of pictures that can be made part of the post.

- The ability to like posts.

- Following items so that activities in the site newsfeed can be surfaced within your personal newsfeed.

To add a post to a site newsfeed, entering its details into the Start a Conversation box creates a new main post in the newsfeed. To reply to an existing post, reply in the Add a Reply box corresponding to the desired post. Finally, to add a picture to a post, click the camera icon displayed in a conversation or reply box, then select the image to be inserted.

Hash Tags

SharePoint 2013 supports the use of hash tags in newsfeeds and discussions. Hash tags, used to reference topics posts or discussions, are objects that can be followed to track the topic's activity. A hash tag also has its own About page (see Figure 12-17) that lists conversations where the tag is referenced and allows identification of related tags.

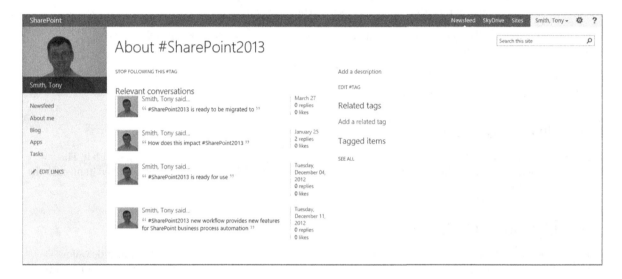

Figure 12-17. *Hash Tag About page*

To create a hash tag reference in a conversation or discussion in SharePoint 2013, enter the hash (#), and start typing. A context menu listing tags matching the entered text appears. Either select one of the listed tags or continue typing to create a new one.

■ **Note**   A hash tag does not have spaces in its name. If you enter a space when referencing a hash tag in a post or discussion, the remaining text typed will not be part of the tag.

Blogs

SharePoint blogs allow topic details to be posted and posts to be commented on. A blog is best described as a virtual press conference where a presenter publishes news, a discussion, or an article that can be reviewed. Consumers of the blog post can enter comments or questions, which in turn prompt additional comments or questions. Because blogs allow interaction on topics, many organizations use them as a tool to share news and announcements.

You can start blogs in SharePoint 2013 by using the Blog site template when creating a new site. The template creates a new SharePoint 2013 blog site (see Figure 12-18).

Figure 12-18. *Blog site*

Blogs consist of posts and comments. Unlike newsfeeds, which are designed for short comments and statements, blogs support full enhanced rich text, allowing inclusion of videos, images, and links. Blog posts can be short statements, like simple announcements, or lengthy articles full of details on an important topic.

Blog comments are short statements entered to provide context or clarity on the details in the blog or to question blog content. While blog comments cannot be replied to, follow-ups can be posted to listed comments and questions as new blog comments. Blog comments are organized chronologically and therefore appear in a discussion-like layout.

Blog posts can be organized into categories that structure and filter the posts in order to establish interrelationships and make locating relevant items easy.

Managing Blog Posts

A Blog Tools web part, listed on a blog's home page, provides references to manage the main blog site capabilities. To create a blog post on a blog site, do the following:

1. Navigate to the blog site, where you want to create a post.

2. On the blog site home page, select the Create a Post option from the Blog Tools.

3. On the New Post page, do the following:

    a. Enter a title for the new post.

    b. Optionally enter body text for the post. The body of the blog can be enhanced with rich text details, including images and videos.

    c. Optionally identify categories the blog is to be associated with. Use of categories allows grouping of related posts.

    d.   Identify the published date. The default is the current date and time, but this can be updated as necessary.

    e.   Select the Publish button to publish the blog.

The new blog post is added to the blog. When a blog post is added to a blog site, the post includes options to do the following:

- Like the post.

- E-mail a link to the post to others.

- Edit the post—that is, alter any of the details of the post you created.

Commenting on Posts

Comments can be added to published blog posts by navigating to the blog post page. Click on the title of the post in the blog site, and then enter a comment in the Add a Comment box. Once a comment is posted, it becomes associated with the blog and listed below the post. You can later edit your comment by clicking on the Edit link next to the comment and then editing the details presented on the Comment Edit page.

Managing Categories

Blog post categories are used to organize posts into related groupings. A single blog post can be associated with multiple categories. Blog posts are assigned to categories when the posts are added or edited. To manage blog categories, select the Manage Categories option from the Blog Tools. You are taken to the Categories list, where you can add, edit, and delete items (this is a standard SharePoint list; manage it as you would any other). Managing lists and list items is discussed in detail in Chapters 5 and 6.

Using the Blogging App

The blog site lets you link it with Microsoft Word's blog post capabilities to allow creation of posts in Word. Clicking the Launch Blogging App link in the blog site's Blog Tools opens Word and prompts you to configure the connection to the blog site (you must confirm the URL and verify your credentials). As Figure 12-19 shows, Word's blog posting tools are opened.

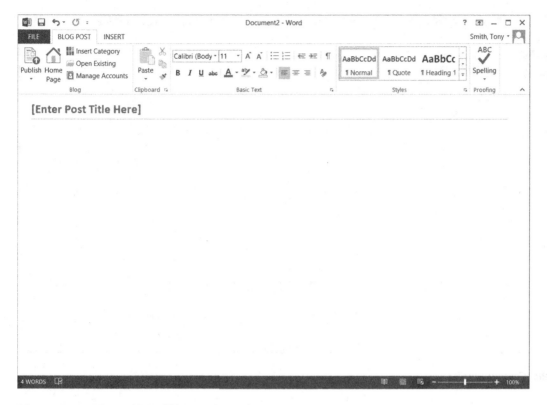

Figure 12-19. *Microsoft Word blog posting tools*

These tools allow you to create blog posts in Word and then publish the posts on the blog site. You can connect to multiple blog sites from the Word blog posting tool and so can manage content on all of your blog sites.

Community Sites

Community sites let you organize discussions and other materials on specific topics. These sites are designed to consolidate knowledge and foster communication. To create a community site (see Figure 12-20), select the Community Site template when you create a new site.

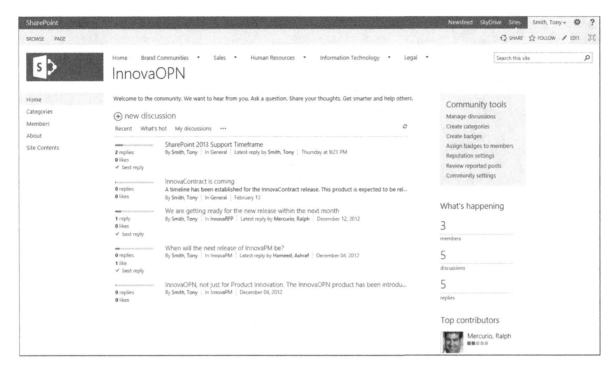

Figure 12-20. *Community Site*

Community sites combine several SharePoint social capabilities designed to support and manage collaborative efforts.

Discussions

Community sites include a discussion list used to store and manage discussions in the community. Discussions are similar to newsfeeds in that items posted can be replied to and can be liked. Discussions are also similar to blog posts in that the body of a discussion post can utilize full rich text, including images and videos. However, unlike both newsfeeds and blog posts, discussions have additional capabilities to facilitate the development of a dialogue, including the following:

- *Identifying Best Replies*: Specific replies can be recognized as being the best answers or comments related to the discussion.

- *Questions*: Discussion posts can be flagged as questions. Items identified as questions do not simply comment or provide details on a topic but indicate to the community that an answer is being sought.

- *Marked as Featured*: A discussion marked featured is elevated in the community to a key position.

While discussion lists are by default found only in community sites, they can be accessed in any other SharePoint site by adding a discussion list to the site and configuring it for use there. (Working with lists is discussed in detail in Chapters 5 and 6.)

The discussion list in the community site includes several views to help organize community discussions. These views include the following:

- *Recent*: Discussions having the most recent activity are placed at the top.

- *What's Hot*: The discussion order is based on popularity.

- *My Discussions*: Shows discussions started by the person viewing the list.

- *Unanswered Questions*: Lists discussions marked as questions but with no best reply selected.

- *Answered Questions*: Lists discussions marked as questions with a best reply selected.

- *Featured*: Identifies items or discussions flagged as featured.

Creating New Discussions

To create a new discussion in a discussion list, do the following:

1. Navigate to the discussion list. For community sites, navigate to the community site's home page, where the discussion is displayed.

2. At the top of the discussion's list view, click the New Discussion option.

3. On the New Discussion page, do the following:

   a. Enter a subject for the new discussion.

   b. Optionally enter the blog details for the new discussion. The discussion body can include rich text, images, and videos.

   c. Identify whether the new discussion is a question.

   d. Identify the categories to associate with the new discussion.

   e. Click the Save button.

The new discussion is added to the discussion list.

Editing Discussions

To edit existing discussions to change their details, do as follows:

1. Navigate to the discussion list.

2. In the discussion's list view, select the discussion to be edited.

3. In the discussion view, choose the Edit option in the item's context menu.

4. On the Edit Item page, make any necessary updates to the discussion, and click the Save button.

The discussion is updated, and you are returned to the discussion list view.

Replying in a Discussion

By replying to discussions and to existing discussion replies, you create a hierarchy of communication. To reply to a post or an existing reply, click the Reply link for the item you want to reply to, enter the reply's details, and click the Reply button. The reply is added to the discussion thread.

Marking a Best Reply

Identifying a reply in a discussion thread as the best reply not only flags the item as the best answer or comment but also lists it, together with the original post, at the top of the discussion and labels it best. There can be only one best reply for a discussion, so if you have already identified a best reply and then identify another, the new item will override the previous selection. You identify a best reply by selecting the Best Reply option from the associated reply's context menu.

Deleting Posts and Replies

You can delete posts and replies from a discussion list. Deleting an item deletes all items associated with that item. If you delete the discussion's main post, that post and all of its associated replies are deleted. If you delete a reply, the selected reply and any replies to it are deleted. To delete a post or a reply from a discussion list, select the Delete option in the item's context menu, and then confirm that the item is to be deleted.

Managing Discussion Categories

If discussions are grouped into categories, they can be organized by topic. You create and manage categories through the Categories list in the community site. To access this list, select the Create Categories option from the Community Tools.

Reputation

Community sites let you manage reputations of community members. Reputation is calculated based on individuals' activities in the site. Different activities (such as creating posts, replying to posts, having post or replies liked, having a reply marked the best) generate reputation points used to calculate reputations in the community site.

Managing Reputation Settings

Reputation is configured in the Reputation Settings page in a community site. These settings allow management of points received for various community activities and of thresholds and levels of reputation available. Reputation is managed as follows:

1. Navigate to the community site where you want to manage reputation.

2. On the community site home page, select the Reputation Settings option from the Community Tools.

3. On the Community Reputation Settings page, do the following:

    a. In the Rating Settings section, identify whether items in the community discussion are to be rated and, if they are, whether to use likes or star ratings.

    b. In the Member Achievements Point System section, identify whether achievement points are to be managed and, if they are, how many points to grant for each of the following activities:

        •   Creating a new post

        •   Replying to a post

        •   Member's post or reply gets liked or receives a rating of 4 or 5 stars

        •   Member's reply gets marked as "Best Reply"

    c.   In the Achievement Level Points section, identify the number of points needed to reach each of the listed five achievement levels.

    d.   In the Achievement Level Representation section, identify whether achievement levels are to be represented by a level image or by text-based titles. If by titles, then identify the titles for the levels.

    e.   Click the OK button.

Once reputation settings are configured, site members' reputations are subject to the thresholds.

Badges

Badges, like reputation, can be used to identify experts in a community. However, where reputation is calculated, community members are awarded badges by community managers. Before you award badges, you must create them. To create a badge in a community site, do the following:

1.   Navigate to the community site.

2.   On the community site home page, select the Create Badges option.

3.   On the Badges list page, add, edit, or delete badges as appropriate by direct list management (editing lists and list items is discussed in Chapters 5 and 6).

The badges are created for users. Once the badges are available, they can be assigned to community members by doing as follows:

1.   Navigate to the community site where you want to assign badges.

2.   On the site's home page, select the Assign Badges to Members option from the Community Tools.

3.   On the Community Members page, click the check box next to the item, and then select the Give Badge option from the Moderation ribbon tab.

4.   On the Gifted Badges page, select the badge to give the user, and click the Save button.

The badge is assigned and is listed in the site with the person's name.

Top Contributors

Community sites track activities in them and track the top contributors. A listing as a top contributor is based on the reputation a user has developed in the community.

Managing Offensive Content

SharePoint community sites can be configured to allow site members to identify whether there is content that can be considered offensive in the site. To turn on offensive content monitoring, do as follows:

1.   Navigate to the community site.

2.   On the community site home page, select the Community Settings option from the Community Tools.

3.   On the Community Settings page, check the "Enable reporting of offensive content" option from the Reporting of Offensive Content section, and click the OK button.

The ability to report offensive content is added to the site. To identify a post or reply as offensive, select the Report to Moderator option from the items context menu. Then identify what the problem is with the item. Site managers can then view the items identified as offensive by selecting the Review Reported Posts option from the Community Tools.

Community Portals

The community portal is a site collection that lists all community sites in your SharePoint farm to which you have rights (see Figure 12-21).

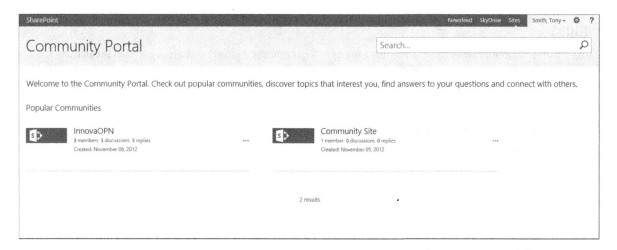

Figure 12-21. Community Portal

The community portal helps people identify communities that they would like to join. In a community portal you can view the list of communities organized by their popularity and search for communities to locate those of interest to you. Communities are listed in the portal with these details, which help you identify whether you want to join the community:

- Member, discussion, and reply counts
- The most popular discussions in the list

When you identify a community you want to join, click on its name to navigate directly to it. The community portal also enables you to follow listed communities by selecting the Follow option from the hover panel for the communities.

CHAPTER 13

■ ■ ■

Metrics and Reporting

As your SharePoint environment matures and your use of it grows, the ability to understand how it is being used can give you valuable insight needed to enhance and extend the services SharePoint provides. In this chapter the various types of metrics and reports in SharePoint are discussed. You can use them to understand resource usage and trends in your site collection. Within SharePoint are both broad, system-level metrics available only to SharePoint technical administrators and specific, site and site collection metrics that your site collection and content administrators can view. This discussion focuses on the metrics and reports available to site collection and content administrators.

The analytical and reporting capabilities of SharePoint Foundation and SharePoint Server differ greatly. SharePoint Foundation leverages site usage reporting services that provide basic content volume and usage statistics. These services process usage logs that collect data necessary to support usage reporting. SharePoint Server Standard and Enterprise use a new set of services that leverage the new Analytics Processing Component. They use the SharePoint 2013 search services to support compilation and surfacing of managed metrics.

The metrics that are part of SharePoint can be organized into three categories:

- *Storage Metrics*: Provide details of storage space usage in the environment.

- *Usage Metrics*: Present information on usage trends and volumes across content.

- *Search Metrics*: List search query statistics and analytics.

Storage Metrics

As the content managed in SharePoint increases, you should stay aware of the volume of information maintained and how it is distributed so you can identify sites requiring reorganization or lists and libraries whose content volumes call for enhancement through metadata-driven navigation or search tool configurations. Reviewing this information over time can help you understand content growth trends needed for capacity planning.

SharePoint 2013's storage metrics offer your site collection detailed content volume metrics for review and analysis, and they are available in all versions of SharePoint Foundation and Server (see Figure 13-1).

Figure 13-1. *Storage Metrics*

The storage metrics report lists all objects in the site collection, including sites, lists, libraries, and documents. Click into any site, list, or library to view storage statistics for specific items and their content. To access storage metrics details, do the following:

1. Navigate to the root site in the site collection where you want to view storage statistics.

2. On the site's home page, select the Site Settings option from the Settings menu.

3. On the Site Settings page, select the Storage Metrics option from the Site Collection Administration section.

The Storage Metrics page that appears shows overall storage usage details for the sites, lists, and libraries located in the site collection's root. From here, click on the name of any listed item to show its details. Among the statistics presented as part of the storage metrics details are the following:

- *Total Size*: Provides the sum, in megabytes (MB), for the listed object. When shown for a site, Total Size details reflect the total amount of space used by all list and library content stored in the site. When Total Size details refer to a list or library, they show the total amount of space used by the content stored in that list or library.

- *% of Parent*: Lists the percentage of the overall content used by the listed element in the level displayed. When you first access the Storage Metrics page, the figure shown reflects the overall percentage of space used by the site collection. As you navigate through the listed items, the figure will reflect the percent of space the elements use in the selected site, list, or library. For example, if you click on a site in the Storage Metrics page to see the storage details for items in that site, the figures you see will show the percent of storage used by each subsite, list, and library in the selected site. These details help identify the locations and items that use the most storage space in the environment.

- *Last Modified*: Identifies the date and time an item was last modified. This lets you see how recently information has been managed and helps identify sites, lists, and libraries whose lack of activity indicates they may no longer be needed.

SharePoint Foundation Reports

SharePoint Foundation offers two sets of reports. You can use them to understand how site users interact with the environment's resources. Among the reports in SharePoint Foundation are the Site Collection Web Analytics Reports. They provide statistics about the overall site collection. The Site Web Analytics Reports provide site-level usage statistics.

Site Collection Web Analytics Reports

The Site Collection Web Analytics Reports page provides high-level site collection statistics for the current collection (see Figure 13-2).

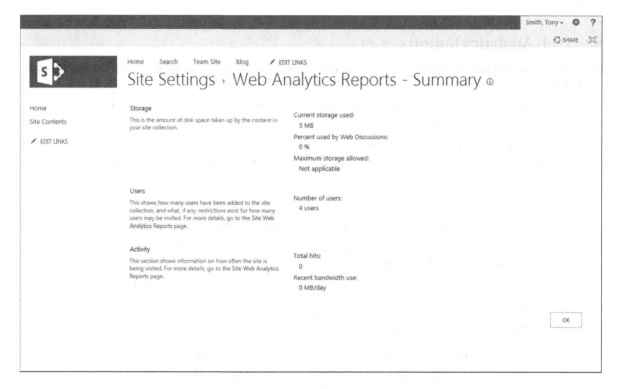

Figure 13-2. Site Collection Web Analytics Reports

To access Site Collection Web Analytics, do the following:

1. Navigate to the root site in your site collection.

2. On the site's home page, select the Site Settings option from the Settings menu.

3. On the Site Settings page, select the Site Collection Web Analytics Reports option from the Site Actions section.

The Web Analytics Reports - Summary page that appears lists the summary details for the site collection, including the following information:

- *Current Storage Used*: Lists the total volume of content stored in the site collection.

- *Percent used by Web Discussions*: Identifies the overall percentage of the total storage used by discussion data.

- *Maximum Storage Allowed*: If storage limits are in place in the site collection, the storage limit details are listed here. If there are no storage limits, "not applicable" appears.

- *Number of Users*: Lists the number of users added to the site.

- *Total Hits*: Lists the number of times the site collection has been accessed.

- *Recent Bandwidth Use*: Identifies daily bandwidth usage for the overall site collection.

The Site Collection Web Analytics Report page provides overall statistics that can be used to view storage used by the site collection and user access volumes. These details can be reviewed from time to time to help track and manage environment growth.

Site Web Analytics Reports

SharePoint Foundation includes a set of reports that provide access statistics for sites in a site collection. The seven reports available provide a variety of user access statistics for a site, including the following:

- *Number of Page Views*: Includes details about how many times pages and documents within your site have been accessed.

- *Number of Unique Visitors*: Includes information about how many individuals access your site.

- *Number of Referrers*: Identifies the number of URLs from which users who access the site have navigated.

- *Top Pages*: Lists the pages accessed in the site, with access counts and percentages.

- *Top Visitors*: Lists the visitors accessing the site, with access counts and percentages.

- *Top Referrers*: Lists the URLs that users who access the site have navigated from and includes both access counts and percentages.

- *Top Browsers*: Lists the browsers used to access the site, with access counts and percentages.

To view Site Web Analytics Reports for a site, do the following:

1. Navigate to the site whose statistics you wish to view.

2. On the site's home page, select the Site Settings option from the Settings menu.

3. On the Site Settings page, select the Site Web Analytics Reports option from the Site Actions section.

4. On the Site Web Analytics Report page, click the name of the report to be viewed from the list of reports in the Quick Launch area.

The selected statistics are displayed.

SharePoint Server Reports

SharePoint 2013 server reports include access and usage statistics collected and organized using SharePoint search services. These reports show general usage statistics as well as access trends over time. There is also a set of audit log reports, which report activities tracked through information management audit policies (information management policies are discussed in detail in Chapter 9).

Site Collection Audit Reporting

You will recall that Chapter 9 discusses how to configure auditing for site collection resources and for specific lists, libraries, and content types in SharePoint. You can audit a variety of performable activities. Once auditing details are configured, related activities are tracked. A set of reports allows you to review these activities (see Figure 13-3).

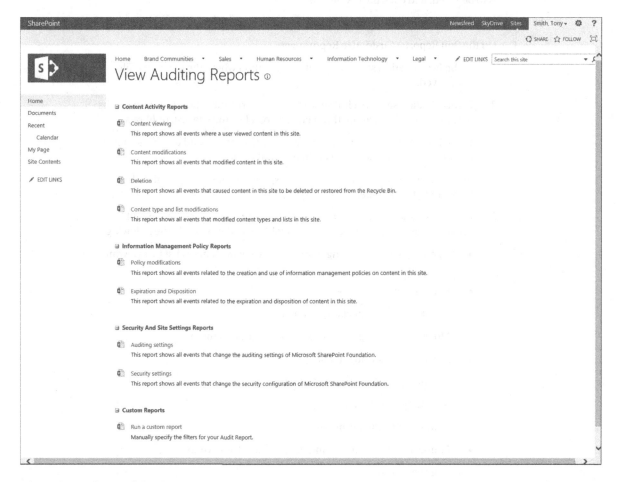

Figure 13-3. *View Auditing Reports*

To access these audit reports, do the following:

1. Navigate to the root site in the site collection.

2. In the root site, select the Site Settings option from the Settings menu.

3. On the Site Settings page, select the Audit Log Reports option from the Site Collection Administration section.

4. On the View Auditing Reports page, do the following:

    a. For all reports but the Custom Reports,

        i. Click the name of the auditing report to be accessed.

        ii. On the Run Reports: Customize Report page, select the location where the report is to be saved, and click the OK button.

    b. For the Custom Reports, do the following:

        i. On the Run Reports: Customize Report page,

            1. In the File Location section, specify the location where the generated file is to be saved.

            2. In the Location section, choose whether to restrict the report to return results only for a specific location. If you choose to, select the site, list, or library.

            3. In the Date Range section, optionally identify start and end dates and times to which to restrict the report audit details displayed.

            4. In the Users section, optionally select a specific user that report details are to be restricted to include.

            5. In the Events section, optionally specify whether to restrict the types of activities the report is to include. Selectable activities include the following:

                - Opening or downloading documents, viewing items in lists, or viewing item properties

                - Editing items

                - Checking out or checking in items

                - Moving or copying items to another location in the site

                - Deleting or restoring items

                - Editing content types and columns

                - Searching site content

                - Editing users and permissions

                - Editing auditing settings and deleting audit log events

                - Workflow events

                - Custom events

            6. Click the OK button.

The report is generated and placed in the identified save location. Reports available from the View Auditing Reports page include the following:

- Content Activity Reports

  - *Content Viewing*: Lists logged events for viewing content in the site.

  - *Content Modifications*: Lists logged events for changes to site content, including documents, list items, and pages.

  - *Deletion*: Lists logged events for content deletions and restorations.

  - *Content Type and List Modifications*: Lists logged events for modifications to content types, lists, and libraries.

- Information Management Policy Reports

  - *Policy Modifications*: Lists logged events related to creation and use of content information management policies.

  - *Expiration and Disposition*: Lists logged events related to expiration and disposition of content.

- Security and Site Settings Reports

  - *Auditing Settings*: Lists logged events related to changes made to auditing settings.

  - *Security Settings*: Lists logged events related to SharePoint security configuration settings.

- Custom Reports

  - *Run a Custom Report*: Lets you create a custom report to retrieve logged events for specific actions.

Popularity and Search Reports

You can run popularity and search reports for a site collection. These reports give general site usage and search usage details needed to understand usage trends in the environment. The reports open in Microsoft Excel. To run usage and search reports, do the following:

1. Navigate to the root site in the site collection where you want to run the reports.

2. On the root site's home page, select the Site Settings option from the Settings menu.

3. On the Site Settings page, select the Popularity and Search Reports link in the Site Collection Administration section.

4. On the View Usage Reports page (see Figure 13-4), click the name of the report to run.

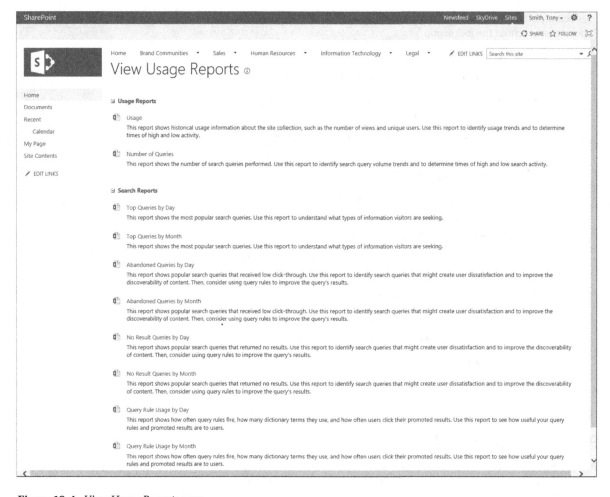

Figure 13-4. *View Usage Reports page*

5. In the Open or Save browser message window, click the Open button.

The selected report opens in Excel.

Usage Reports

Reports that can be run from the Usage Reports page fall into several categories. The first includes Usage Reports, which provide general environment usage details. They are as follows:

- *Usage*: A Usage report lists general site collection usage statistics (see Figure 13-5), including details of daily and monthly usage traffic volume. Both of these report types list and graphically represent hit and unique user access totals. Hits are accesses made, regardless of who made them. Unique users are distinct individuals who accessed the resources.

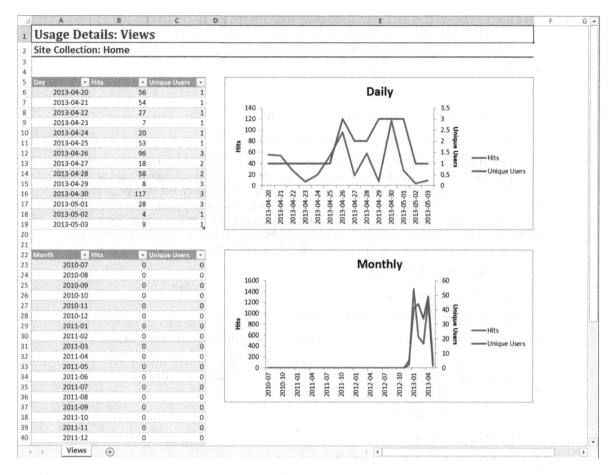

Figure 13-5. *Usage Report*

- *Number of Queries*: A Number of Queries report counts the search queries executed in the site collection by day and by month. Information appears in both tabular and chart format, in a layout similar to a Usage report's.

Search Reports

The second report category on the View Usage Reports page is the Search Reports category. It includes statistics related to search queries executed in the site collection.

- *Top Queries by Day*: Lists the most common search queries executed per day. The report file is organized as multiple Excel tabs, each tab listing the top query details for the day. This report shows the following details:

    - The result source of the query

    - The actual query executed

    - The total times the query was run within the day

    - The percent of query executions the query represents

- *Top Queries by Month*: Lists the most common search queries run per month. Like the Top Queries by Day report, the Top Queries by Month report is organized into multiple Excel tabs, each tab representing a single month. This report lists the following details for each listed query:

  - The result source of the query

  - The actual query executed

  - The total times the query was run within the month

  - The percent of query executions the query represents

- *Abandoned Queries by Day*: Lists the most frequently executed queries where a result was not selected. With this report's details you can identify queries that might require query rules or other search adjustments to help users locate desired results for the query. For example, if you notice people are running queries to find "tax bundles" and not getting appropriate results, you might create a query rule identifying a file type for tax bundles or a result source identifying where tax bundle materials are located. This report includes a tab for each day that lists queries run but for which no result was selected. Details listed for the queries include the following:

  - The result source of the query

  - The actual query executed

  - The total times the query was run within the day

  - The percentage of times the query was run in the week without a result being clicked

- *Abandoned Queries by Month*: Provides the same details the Abandoned Queries by Day report does but has a tab per month with abandoned queries totals for the given month. Details listed in the report include the following:

  - The result source of the query

  - The actual query executed

  - The total times the query was run within the month

  - The percentage of times the query was run in the month without a result being clicked

- *No Result Queries by Day*: Lists queries executed for which no results were returned. Like the Abandoned Queries reports, this report can be used to identify queries that may need query rules or result sources defined. The No Result Queries by Day report lists the following details:

  - The result source of the query

  - The actual query executed

  - The total times the query was run within the day

  - The percentage of times the query was run in the week with no results returned

- *No Result Queries by Month*: Lists queries executed each month for which no results were returned. This report, organized into a tab per month, lists the following details for the queries performed in the corresponding month for which no results were returned:

  - The result source of the query

  - The actual query executed

  - The total times the query was run within the month

  - The percentage of times the query was run in the month with no results returned

- *Query Rule Usage by Day*: Lists query rules configured in the environment in order to show how many times rules were triggered by search queries each day. The statistics for each day appear on separate tabs in the report. The details for the query rules included in the report are the following:

  - The result source of the query

  - The query rule

  - The container (owner) in which the query rule is configured

  - The type of object in which the query rule is configured

  - The number of dictionary terms included

  - The number of times the query rule was executed during the listed day

  - The promoted result details configured as part of the query

  - The number of times the promoted result item was clicked in the search results during the day

  - The percentage of times the promoted result was clicked based on the number of times the query rule was executed during the day

- *Query Rule Usage by Month*: Gives details broken down by month of how many times executed search queries triggered rules configured in the environment. Monthly statistics, organized on separate Excel tabs, include the following:

  - The result source of the query

  - The query rule

  - The container (owner) in which the query rule is configured

  - The type of object in which the query rule is configured

  - The number of dictionary terms included

  - The number of times the query rule was executed during the listed month

  - The promoted result details configured as part of the query

  - The number of times the promoted result item was clicked on the search results during the month

  - The percentage of times the promoted result was clicked based on the number of times the query rule was executed during the month

Site Popularity Trends

Each site in a SharePoint Server environment is able to run a Popularity Trends report. This report summarizes access statistics, or popularity, for the site. The report contains details similar to those in a usage report for the site collection (discussed in an earlier section). As Figure 13-6 shows, the site usage report lists details, in both tabular and graphical format, of hits and unique user access by day and by month for a given site.

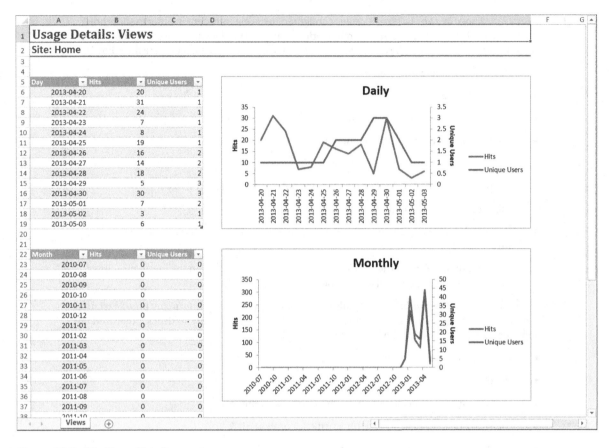

Figure 13-6. *Site Usage Details report*

To access the site usage details report for a desired site, do the following:

1. Navigate to the site where you want to run the report.

2. On the site's home page, select the Site Settings option from the Settings menu.

3. On the Site Settings page, select the Popularity Trends option from the Site Administration section.

4. On the View Usage Reports page click the Usage report form the Usage Reports section.

5. In the web browser Open or Save message box, click the Open button

The Usage Details report for the site appears. It lists overall site access details broken down by day and by month. For each of the days and months listed, hit and unique user summary details are provided.

Library Most Popular Items

Since SharePoint tracks usage of items in libraries, it gives you the ability to understand which resources are most accessed. To view usage details for a library, do the following:

1. Navigate to the library where you want to view usage details.

2. On the library view page, select the Most Popular Items option from the Library ribbon tab.

You are brought to the Most Popular Items page for the selected library (see Figure 13-7).

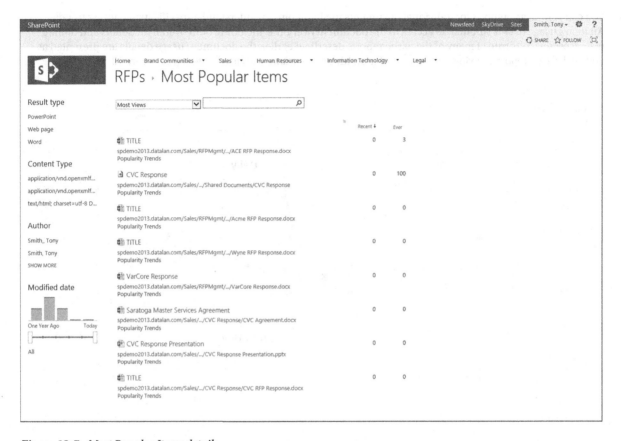

Figure 13-7. *Most Popular Items details*

This page lists the items contained in the library and sorts them by placing the most recently accessed materials at the top of the list. You can organize the information for viewing in any of three different content access groupings:

- *Most Views*: The default option; items are ordered by most to least viewed. This view has two separate groupings. The first grouping lists items by recent views, and the second lists items by overall view details.

- *Most Viewed by Unique Users*: Lists recent and overall view counts based on access to the item by unique individuals.

- *Most Recommendation Clicks*: Lists items with both recent and overall access based on the items' usage patterns.

You can filter information displayed in the Most Popular Items views based on search criteria entered in the page's search box. You can also directly open a listed item's usage report by clicking on the Popularity Trends link accompanying the item.

Document Popularity Trends

You can view usage reports for individual documents in SharePoint to understand a specific item's access trends. An item's usage details summarize access to the document over time, including both overall hit details and unique user accesses. As is true of many of the usage reports described earlier, the document usage details are presented as an Excel-based report showing both daily and monthly access summaries for the item (see Figure 13-8).

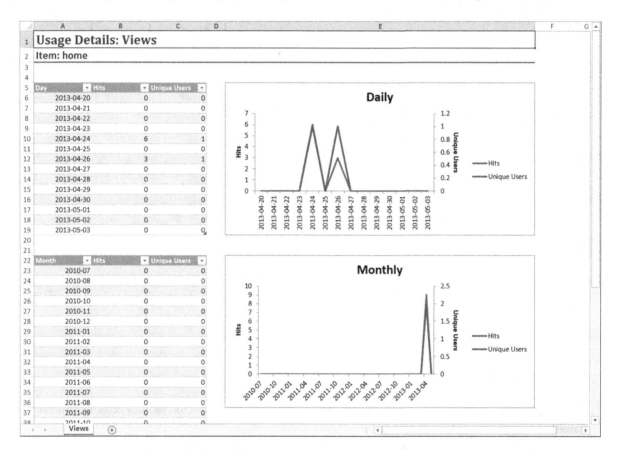

Figure 13-8. Document Usage Details report

To access the usage details report for a document, do the following:

1. Navigate to the library containing the item whose usage details you want to view.

2. On the library view page, click the check box next to the document to be viewed, and select the Popularity Trends option from the Files ribbon tab.

3. On the Open or Save message box of the web browser, select the Open option.

The Usage Details report for the item is opened in Excel.

CHAPTER 14

Enterprise Office Services

SharePoint has a set of services that expand the capabilities of Microsoft Office and extend these personal productivity tools to enhance team productivity and functionality. The following enterprise office services in SharePoint enhance Word, Excel, PowerPoint, OneNote, InfoPath, and Visio.

- *Office Web Apps*: Web-based version of Word, Excel, PowerPoint, and OneNote allowing for web-based management of Office files providing document view and edit capabilities without the need for Office to be locally installed.

- *Excel Services*: Allows for the publishing of all or part of an Excel file for sharing with others.

- *Form Services*: Publishes InfoPath forms rendering them as web forms that can be populated without the need for InfoPath to be installed.

- *Visio Services*: Allows Visio diagrams to be accessed via the browser for viewing and commenting without Visio being installed.

All of these enterprise office services are designed to expand the capabilities of Microsoft Office. Making Office resources available through the web browser extends their reach and availability without the need to manage the programs. In this chapter each of these services is discussed, and how they are configured and used is described.

Office Web Apps

Microsoft Office Web Apps are web-based versions of Microsoft Word, Excel, PowerPoint, and OneNote. Office Web Apps are installed separately from core SharePoint services but are then leveraged by SharePoint to allow web-based editing and viewing of Office files. There are two common scenarios in which Office Web Apps provide significant value.

- When you need to work with Microsoft Office documents on a device that does not have Microsoft Office installed. While this may be uncommon on standard workstations, it is often the case on alternative devices, such as tablets.

- When you need to take advantage of Office 2013 features, like simultaneous document editing, but the version of Microsoft Office installed on your computer does not support these capabilities.

Note To take advantage of Microsoft Office Web Apps, the services must be deployed and configured by a SharePoint technical administrator.

While the Office Web Apps version of Office applications allows editing of Office documents, its functionality has limitations, the most notable of which are the following:

- Word

    - Encrypted documents cannot be opened.

    - No auto save feature.

    - Document styles cannot be modified.

    - No find and replace functionality.

    - No zoom in Edit view.

    - Page layout, margins, and orientation cannot be changed.

    - Themes and backgrounds cannot be edited.

    - Grammar check is not available.

    - Track changes cannot be turned on or off.

    - Table styling is not available.

    - Picture cropping is not available.

    - WordArt cannot be edited.

- Excel

    - Cannot edit workbooks that use data validation.

    - Protected workbooks cannot be opened.

    - Some functions work differently, including

        - Info: returns an error.

        - Now: returns date and time on the server.

        - Today: returns date and time on the server.

    - Changes made to the file are saved automatically.

- PowerPoint

    - Cannot open password protected files.

    - Changes are saved automatically.

    - No find and replace functionality.

    - Cannot change slide master or modify slide layouts.

    - Cannot edit tables.

    - Cannot insert charts, equations, WordArt, or symbols.

    - Cannot manage headers or footers.

- OneNote

    - Command for creating empty space on a page is not available.

    - Rule lines are not displayed.

- Cannot mark notes as read or unread.

- No command to insert current date and time.

- Cannot link notes.

Opening Files in Office Web Apps

When Office Web Apps is available in SharePoint you can choose whether to open a Word, Excel, PowerPoint, or OneNote file in the associated Microsoft Office program or in Office Web Apps. To open a document in Office Web Apps do the following:

1. Navigate to the library containing the document to be opened.

2. Select the Edit in Browser option from the hover panel menu (see Figure 14-1).

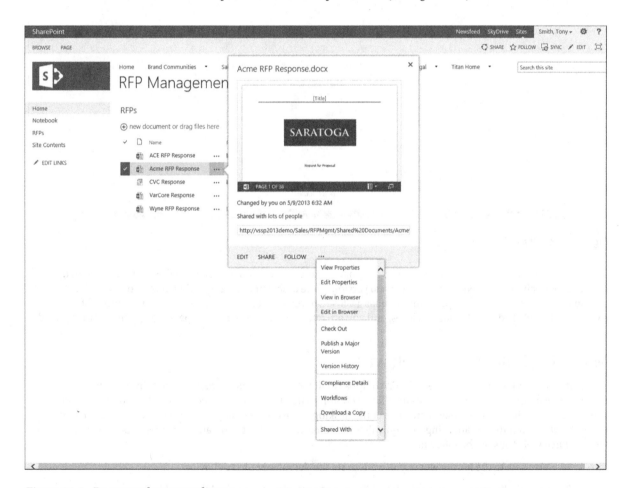

Figure 14-1. Document hover panel menu

The document opens in the web app version of the Office program. Web-based versions of Word, Excel, PowerPoint, and OneNote look much like the full versions (see Figure 14-2).

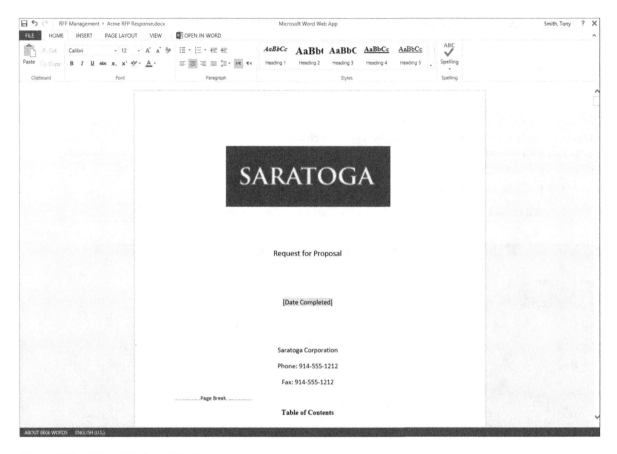

Figure 14-2. *Office Web Apps: Word*

Inside Office Web Apps you can work with and make changes to documents as needed. Select the Open In option on the ribbon tab row to open the file in the local version of the associated program when it is loaded on a local computer. The Office Web Apps program includes a Close option, located in the upper-right-hand corner of the window. When clicked, the document closes, and you are returned to the SharePoint page from which it was opened.

Managing Default Open Behavior

While site users can open a file in the Office Web Apps version of the program, a manager of a library can set the default behavior of a library to open files in Office Web Apps when the file is selected or the Edit option is clicked. You might do this if you do not have control over the desktops of users accessing the files but want to ensure that people working with the file are using the equivalent of Office 2013. To set the default document opening behavior for files in Office Web Apps do the following:

1. Navigate to the library where you want to set the default opening behavior.

2. On the library view page, select the Library Settings option from the Library ribbon tab.

3. On the Settings page, select the Advanced Settings option from the General Settings section.

4. On the Advanced Settings page in the Opening Documents in Browser section, set the "Default open behavior for browser-enabled documents" to "Open in the browser."

The document library is now configured so that when the Edit option is selected for Office documents, the file opens in Office Web Apps instead of the client program.

Excel Services

Excel Services is a SharePoint Server Enterprise service that allows you to publish all or part of Excel documents to view and interact with through the web browser. Excel Services and the Excel program in Office Web Apps are not the same thing. The Excel part of Office Web Apps provides an interface for editing Excel diagrams, just as you would with the full program. Excel Services allow you to publish Excel resources for reporting and analysis.

Excel Services can be used to publish all or part of a document. Published information can be viewed when browsing the files and through web parts that place resources on SharePoint pages where online report views, analysis dashboards, and scorecards are created.

Publishing Elements to Excel Services

As mentioned above, Excel documents can be published in whole or in part through Excel Services for sharing within SharePoint. You can publish the following elements of an Excel document through Excel Services:

- An entire Excel workbook

- A sheet within an Excel workbook

- A specific object within a sheet, such as a PivotTable or pie chart

- A named range of cells in a sheet

While Excel Services does not allow editing of cells in published views, you can configure named cells to be updated through parameters added to the Excel Services view or passed into the Excel Services views.

Creating Named Cells for Parameters

When Excel Services is used with charts or calculations that require input from the user viewing the item or input passed in via a filter or connected web part, the Excel document must be configured to allow parameter management. To add named cells to support parameters in either Excel 2013 and Excel 2010, do as follows:

1. Open the document in Microsoft Excel.

2. In Excel, highlight the cell to be updated by the parameter.

3. Type a name for the cell in the Name box to the left of the formula bar.

With the cell named, it can be configured to have values passed in via a parameter.

Creating a Named Range

As just mentioned, named ranges in Excel can be published in Excel Services. You can publish a select group of cells in a sheet without having to show the entire sheet or workbook. Create a named range by highlighting the cells to be included, and then type a name for the range in the Name box.

Publishing an Excel Sheet to Excel Services

Once the content to be published is configured and parameter names and named ranges are added, you can publish it to Excel Services. The approach for publishing content differs depending on the version of Excel you are using.

To publish resources from Excel 2013, do the following:

1. In Excel, select the File ribbon tab.

2. On the File menu, select the Save As option.

3. In the Save As section, select SharePoint.

4. In the SharePoint section, select or browse to the library where the file is to be saved.

5. In the Save As window, select the Browser View Options button (see Figure 14-3).

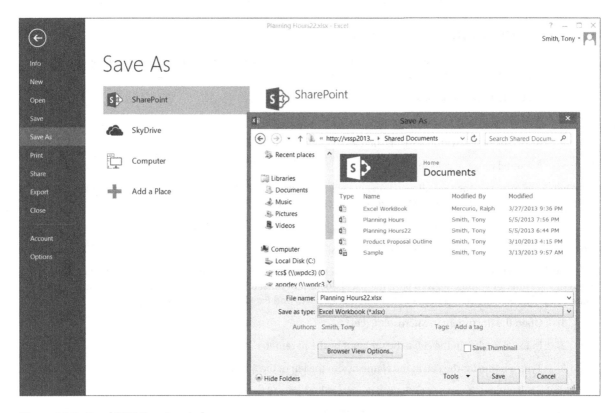

Figure 14-3. *Excel 2013 Save As window*

6. In the Browser View Options window, do the following:

   a. On the Show tab select the item to publish. Options include:

   - An Entire Workbook

   - Sheets (requires selection of the sheets to be published)

   - Items in the Workbook (requires selection of PivotTables, charts, and named ranges to be published)

    b.   On the Parameters tab, add any parameters identifying editable cells. This is done as follows:

        i.   Click the Add button.

        ii.   In the Add Parameters window, click the box next to the parameter cells to be included, and click the OK button.

    c.   Click the OK button.

7.   Click the Save button in the Save As window to save the file to SharePoint.

The file is saved to SharePoint, and the identified resources are published.

When working in Excel 2010, the publishing process is slightly different from the process just described. To publish resources from Excel 2010, do the following:

1.   In Excel, select the File ribbon tab.

2.   On the File menu, select the Save & Send option.

3.   In the Save & Send section, select the Save to SharePoint option.

4.   In the Save to SharePoint section, select the Publish Options button (see Figure 14-4).

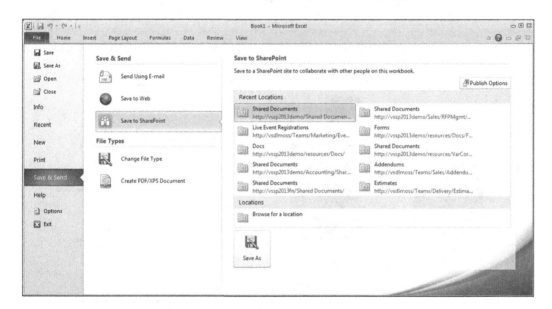

Figure 14-4. *Excel 2010 Save to SharePoint screen*

5.   In the Publish Options window, do the following:

    a.   On the Show tab, select the item to be published. Options include:

- An Entire Workbook

- Sheets (requires selection of the sheets to be published)

- Items in the Workbook (requires selection of PivotTables, charts, and named ranges to be published)

      b.   On the Parameters tab, add any parameters identifying editable cells. This is done as follows:

          i.   Click the Add button.

          ii.   In the Add Parameters window, click the box next to the parameter cells to be included, and click the OK button.

      c.   Click the OK button.

6.   In the Save to SharePoint section, click the Save As button.

7.   In the Save As window, enter a name for the file, and click the Save button.

The document is saved. The published items can be accessed through Excel Services.

Viewing Excel Services Published Content

Once items are published through Excel Services, they can be viewed in the library where the file is saved and through web parts added to SharePoint pages. To view Excel Services published content in the library containing the file, select the View in Browser option from the document's hover panel menu. Selecting this option opens the published content and gives access to all of the published views that were created, as Figure 14-5 shows.

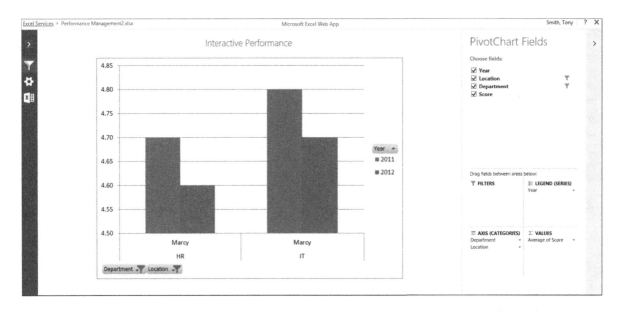

Figure 14-5. *Excel Services published content*

The view of the Excel Services published file includes the following options:

- *Filters*: Lists filters configured for the published content that can be used to filter the information presented.

- *Options*: Provides management options available when viewing a file published with Excel Services. The options available, which depend on the rights of the individual viewing the information, include the following:

    - *Save a Copy*: Lets you save a copy of the workbook under a different name.

    - *Download*: Initiates download of a copy of the file to be saved locally.

    - *Print*: Lets you print the full workbook or the item being viewed.

    - *Share with People*: Brings you to the Sharing window for the document in the library.

    - *Find*: Allows content searching in the current view.

    - *Refresh All Data*: Reloads the information in the Excel Services sheet.

    - *Calculate Workbook*: Reruns the calculations used in the document.

- *Do More*: Provides additional management options available to you in the workbook. Options provided in this section, which depend on the rights of the user viewing the item, may include:

    - *Edit in Excel*: Opens the item in the locally installed copy of Excel.

    - *Edit in Excel Web App*: Opens the document in the Excel Office Web Apps application.

The view of the Excel Services published content also includes a listing of all of the published components in the file. This information is listed in the View section, and items can be selected to update the display that shows the selected published component.

Using the Excel Web Access Web Part

Content published through Excel Services can be displayed on SharePoint pages with the Excel Web Access web part, which can be configured to display a specific published item in an Excel document that has been published to Excel Services. To use the Excel Web Access web part, add it to a web part, wiki, or publishing page, and configure it to display the appropriate published item (working with pages and web parts is discussed in Chapter 4).

When configuring the Excel web access web part, the following options are available:

- Workbook Display

    - *Workbook*: Identifies the Excel document that is the source for the content to be displayed in the web part. Browse to the item by clicking the ellipse button, or enter the path directly into the box.

    - *Named Item*: Identifies the element to be displayed. If this option is left blank, the web part shows the workbook. You can enter a sheet or object name that has been published.

- Toolbar and Title Bar

    - *Autogenerate Web Part Title*: Identifies whether to automatically generate the web part title or manually type it in the Title field of the web part.

    - *Autogenerate Web Part Title URL*: Identifies whether to automatically configure the URL used when clicking on the title of the web part.

- - *Type of Toolbar*: Determines the configuration of the toolbar appearing at the top of the web part.

  - *Toolbar Menu Commands*: Allows identification of the commands to make available in the Toolbar menu of the web part.

- Navigation and Interactivity

  - *Navigation*: Identifies whether to include hyperlinks for navigation.

  - *Interactivity*: Identifies the types of activities to allow with the published item being displayed.

Once the Excel Web Access web part is added to a page and configured, it shows the identified Excel Services published content, which can be combined with other Excel Web Access web parts, reporting web parts, images, and the like to create a dashboard or scorecard page used to relay important analytics.

Form ServicesOne of the tools available in the Microsoft Office suite is InfoPath, which is used to create forms to collect information. You can create InfoPath forms that contain information for managing such processes as employee time-off requests or sales staff expense management. The forms can contain logic needed to ensure that information collected is accurate and complete. When InfoPath forms are used independent of SharePoint, people that need to fill out the form must have InfoPath installed on a local computer and must also have the most current copy of the form template used when the instances of the form are created. These requirements add management overhead and can result in use of the wrong templates or keep people from participating in the process if they do not have the appropriate version of InfoPath.

SharePoint's Form Services, available in SharePoint Server Enterprise, is used in conjunction with Form libraries, which let you publish InfoPath form templates to SharePoint and render them as web forms. Since the form templates are managed in SharePoint, you can be certain that newly generated forms are based on the correct and most current template. Since the forms are rendered in the web browser, you ensure that all users that need access to the form get it, regardless of whether they have InfoPath on their local computer.

Creating Forms and Form Libraries

To create a new InfoPath form and publish the form to a form library for use with Form Services, do the following:

1. Create an InfoPath form containing the desired layout fields and business logic.

2. On the InfoPath File tab, select the Publish option.

3. On the Publish page click, the SharePoint Server option.

4. If the form is not yet saved locally, save it when prompted, and identify a save location. (Any accessible location will do. It has no direct relationship with the form library or template where the item is published.)

5. In the first Publishing Wizard window, enter the URL for the SharePoint site where the form is to be created, and click the Next button.

6. In the second Publishing Wizard window, do the following:

   a. Verify that the "Enable this form to be filled out by using a browser" option is clicked.

   b. Select the Form Library option.

   c. Click the Next button to continue the publishing process.

7. In the third Publishing Wizard window, either create a new form library in the specified site, or select an existing form library to update the form template within. Then click the Next button.

8. If you chose to create a new form library, in the fourth Publishing Wizard window, enter a name for the new form library and an optional description, and click the Next button.

9. On the fifth Publishing Wizard screen, identify fields from the form to include as columns in the library and to use as parameters for creating connections with other web parts for filtering purposes. Then click the Next button.

10. On the sixth Publishing Wizard page, click the Publish button. This will perform the publishing of the form.

11. In the Publish Confirmation window, click the Close button.

A new form library is created. It uses the created InfoPath form as the template when new items are created in the library. The form will be rendered through the web browser.

Populating Forms

Once a form is published as the template for a form library, site users can create new instances of the form, populate the details, and submit the completed form to the library. This completed form can be reviewed or can initiate a workflow process to further mature the collected information or pass it through an approval process. (Creating and managing workflows is discussed in Chapter 9.)

To create a new instance of a form managed through a form library, do the following:

1. Navigate to the form library.

2. In the library view, click the New Document option, or select the New Document option from the Files ribbon tab.

3. Fill out the presented form. Once you are done, click the Submit button, if it is available, or the Save option (see Figure 14-6).

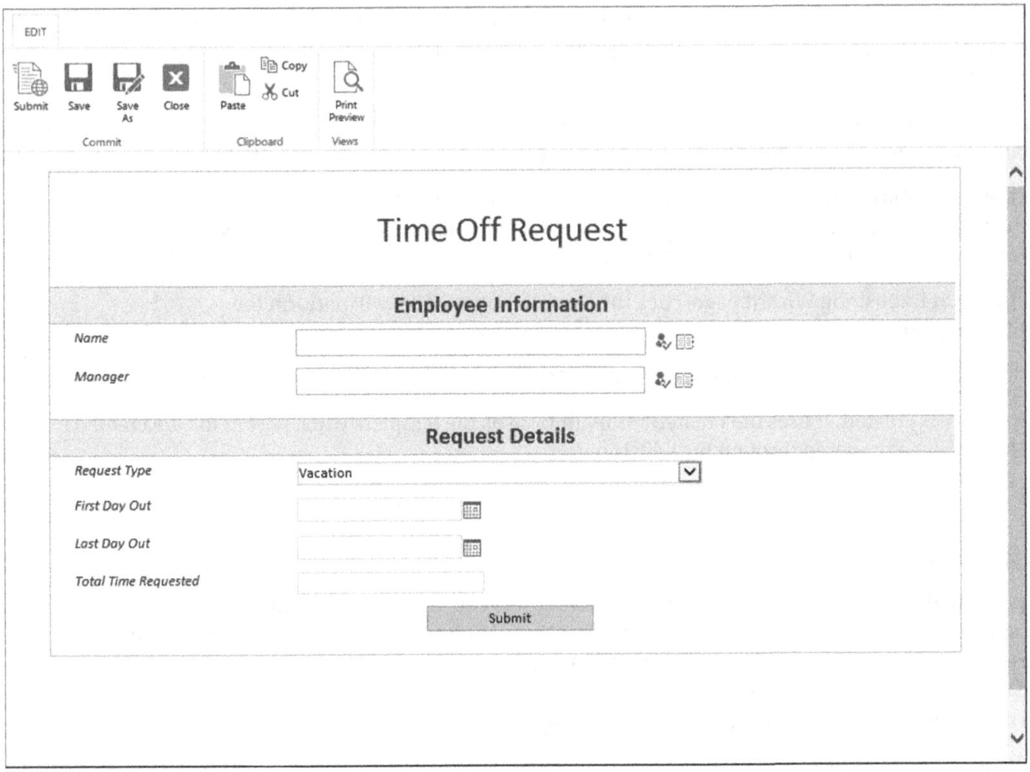

Figure 14-6. InfoPath Form in Form Services

When populating a form through Form Services, the following form management options are available:

- *Submit*: Only available if the form was configured with a Submit option. If available and selected, the Submit option saves the form in the library and runs any workflows associated with the form.

- *Save*: Saves the form to the form library. This option differs from Submit in that here you can save a partly completed form and submit it when you have finished populating it.

- *Save As*: Saves the opened form under a new name in the form library.

- *Close*: Closes the form without saving any changes made.

- *Paste*: Pastes the clipboard content into the currently selected field.

- *Copy*: Copies highlighted content to the clipboard.

- *Cut*: Copies highlighted content to the clipboard and removes it from the field.

- *Print Preview*: Opens a printable view of the form.

Using the InfoPath Form Web Part

Published forms can be presented in a web part and added to pages in SharePoint. That is, you can place the entry form on the same page as other resources(for example, when using a form to collect survey-like information related to page content). To use the InfoPath Form web part, add it to the appropriate page, and configure it to render the desired form in SharePoint. The configuration options in the InfoPath Form web part are as follows:

- *List or Library*: Selects the form library with the form template to be used.

- *Content Type*: Selects the content type used for display in the form library.

- *Show InfoPath Ribbon on Toolbar*: Identifies whether to display the InfoPath ribbon option when the page is viewed.

- *Send Data to Connected Web Parts when Page Loads*: Specifies whether to send form information to a connected web part when the SharePoint page loads.

- *Views*: Selects the default form view to be displayed on the page.

- *Submit Behavior*: Specifies form behavior when the Submit option is selected.

Visio Services

Visio Services renders Visio files stored in SharePoint Server Enterprise through the web browser. Thus, you can view those diagrams without having Visio on a local computer. This is useful when people without access to Visio need to view Visio diagrams or when the Visio diagram needs to be placed on a page with related components and information.

To publish a Visio diagram through Visio Services, save the file to a SharePoint document library as a Visio Web Drawing (vdw) file, if you use Visio 2010, or as a Visio 2013 (vsdx) file. Once saved to one of these formats in a document library, you can view the file in the web browser through Visio Services by selecting the View in Web Browser option from the document's hover panel menu. This opens the document in the browser (see Figure 14-7).

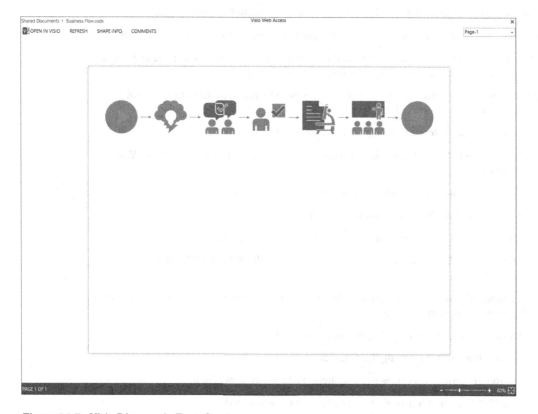

Figure 14-7. *Visio Diagram in Form Services*

When you view a Visio diagram through Visio Services, the following options are available to support users accessing the file:

- *Open in Visio*: An option present when Visio is available to open the file. Selecting it opens the file in the locally installed Visio program.

- *Refresh*: Reloads the diagram in the view.

- *Shape Info*: Allows you to view the details of the listed shape.

- *Comments*: Available only when viewing a VSDX file, this option lets you create and place comments on objects in the diagram. To create a comment, select the object. Then click the Comments option to enter the comment.

As discussed with Excel Services and Form Services, Visio Services also includes a web part that allows display of Visio Services published files in SharePoint pages. The Visio Web Access web part allows identification of a displayed Visio diagram on a page. When added to a page, this web part is configured through management of the following options:

- *Web Drawing URL*: Allows for selection of the Visio diagram file, either a vdw or vsdx file, to be displayed. Browse to a file by selecting the ellipse button and choosing the file from the Select an Asset window.

- *Force Raster Rendering*: Applying only to vdw files, identifies whether to use raster rendering with the file.

- *Automatic Refresh Interval*: Defines the schedule in which to refresh the web part data.

- *Fit All Shapes in View*: Identifies whether to size the diagram to fit into the view.

- *Index of the Initial Page to Show*: Identifies the page in the diagram to be presented initially.

- *Expose the Following Shape Data Items to Web Part Connections*: Specifies the shapes in the diagram whose data can be used in connections to other web parts.

- *Toolbar and User Interface*: Identifies the toolbars to be included in the diagram view. The following options are available for selection:

  - Show Refresh: Reloads the diagram in the web part.

  - Show Open in Visio: When selected, opens the diagram in the locally installed Visio program.

  - Show Page Navigation: Lists selectable pages in the diagram.

  - Show Status Bar: Presents the diagram status bar.

  - Show Shape Information Pane: Allows viewing of selected shape details.

  - Show Default Background: Identifies whether to use the default background when presenting the diagram.

- *Web Drawing Interactivity*: Lets you disable interactivity capabilities available to users viewing the diagram. The options include

  - Disable Zoom: Allows zooming in and out of the diagram.

  - Disable Pan: Allows panning the diagram.

  - Disable Hyperlink: Identifies whether hyperlinks are to be available.

  - Disable Selection: Identifies whether objects can be selected.

Index